Cub Scout Leader How-To Book

Successful Ideas to Add Sparkle To Den and Pack Activities

BOY SCOUTS OF AMERICA

1985 Printing
Copyright 1985
Boy Scouts of America
Irving, Texas
No. 3831 • Printed in U.S.A.
ISBN 0-8395-3831-6

Contents

1 Introduction

This book includes a broad assortment of time-tested activities for Cub Scout dens and packs. It should be used with *Cub Scout Program Helps* to plan den and pack programs. As a resource for program ideas, it is a companion book to the *Cub Scout Leader Book,* No. 3221.

Many of the program activities in this book call for family participation. Many offer opportunities for Cub Scout advancement. By using these activities, leaders not only help strengthen family relationships but provide opportunities for boys to have fun while they are advancing in rank.

An effort has been made in selecting activities for this book to keep them within the capabilities and interests of Cub Scout-age boys. Cub Scouting has a special word that expresses this idea very well—"KISMIF," which means Keep It Simple, Make It Fun. That should be your guide as you plan year-round fun for the den and pack.

Purposes of Cub Scouting

But Cub Scouting has serious purposes, too, and all den and pack activities should reflect one or more of them. The program's statement of purpose follows.

The Cub Scout program of the Boy Scouts of America is designed for families, leaders, and organizations to use with boys who are 7 and have completed the second grade, or are 8, 9, and 10 years of age for the purpose of:

• Influencing the development of character and encouraging spiritual growth.

• Developing habits and attitudes of good citizenship.

• Encouraging good sportsmanship and pride in growing strong in mind and body.

• Improving understanding within the family.

• Strengthening the ability to get along with other boys and respect other people.

• Fostering a sense of personal achievement by developing new interests and skills.

• Showing how to be helpful and do one's best.

• Providing fun and exciting new things to do.

• Preparing them to become Boy Scouts.

2 Games

Why We Use Games

Games are the sunny side of Cub Scouting. Skills and interests developed in childhood teach self-confidence, independence, and the ability to get along with others. Children learn through play.

For these reasons, games are an important part of Cub Scouting. Games not only help to accomplish Cub Scouting's overall objectives of citizenship training, physical fitness, and character development, they have educational benefits, too.

Games teach a Cub Scout to follow rules, to take turns, to respect the rights of others, to give and take, and to play fair. Some games help to develop skills, body control, and coordination. Some teach self-confidence and consideration for others.

How To Select Games

Consider first the physical aspect, the release of surplus energy. An active game should be satisfying to the strongest boy and yet not overtax the weakest. It should stimulate the growth and development of muscles. Most outdoor games meet this test.

Boys of Cub Scout age are growing rapidly. They like to run, jump, climb, lift, balance, crawl, bend, yell, chase, and hide. But long walks or runs and other exercise involving great endurance are not suitable for boys of this age. The danger signals are breathlessness, quick and shallow breathing, pain in the region of the heart, spots before the eyes, and throbbing of eyeballs. Boys who have had recent severe illness should not take part in active games.

Some games are selected for their mental values because they have an element of excitement or accomplishment. Games can help develop quick thinking, alertness, and sometimes even strategy. Many games offer opportunities for feelings to be expressed and emotions to be released, which is healthy. Boys need to learn to play fair and to follow the rules. They also need to learn they can't always be winners. Many boys of Cub Scout age have not yet learned to lose gracefully. The leader's task is to make it clear that losing a game is not the end of the world, and that a loss should be an incentive for the boy to try to improve his skills.

Some games are selected for their educational value. Boys' minds are more receptive to learning when there is fun involved. Their interest and concentration are probably never higher than in play. Games are a way to help boys learn that rules and self-discipline are necessary and that doing one's best is important. Most Cub Scout games help in character development because they require teamwork, fair play, and consideration for others.

Consider these factors when selecting games:

- Purpose (physical, mental, educational)
- Space available
- Number of players
- Equipment available
- Skills and abilities of players

Whether the game involves group competition with team winners, individual competition, or is just for fun, the results should be positive and result in character building and the growth and development of boys.

Fitting Games to Themes

It is not essential for games played at den and pack meetings to fit the monthly theme, but theme games help tie the whole month's program together. Many of the games included here fit monthly themes; others can be easily adapted to themes.

Sometimes all that is necessary to fit a game to a particular theme is to change the name of the game. For example, The Cowboy Relay could become Bareback Rider Relay to fit a circus theme.

Games can also be altered to fit themes by making minor changes. In the game, Toys for Sale, the storekeeper could become Santa Claus for a Christmas theme. Or in the game Travelers, players can travel to different planets to fit a space adventure theme.

Leading Games

Boys will like most games if leaders have fun leading them. Anyone can be a successful games leader by following these simple suggestions:

- Know the rules of the game and have the necessary equipment on hand. Plan not only what you are going to do, but how you are going to do it.

- Start with your best game, one that is easy to explain and enjoyable to play. In addition to bolstering your own confidence, a successful game will enhance the morale of the players.

- Make sure the space available is large enough so everyone can play.

- Remove potential hazards from the play area. Follow health and safety rules.

- Get the full attention of the group, then explain the rules of the game simply, briefly, and in proper order. Be enthusiastic.

- For team games and relay races, you must have equal numbers on each team. If the teams are unequal, one or more boys on the smaller team must compete or race twice.

- As a rule, Webelos Scouts are larger and stronger than the 8- and 9-year-old Cub Scouts. For some pack competitions, it may be wise to give Webelos dens a handicap of some type to equalize the contest.

- Teach the game by steps or demonstration.

- Ask questions to make sure everyone understands.

- Be sure the rules are followed. Insist on good sportsmanship and fair play.

- If the game is not going right, stop it and explain the rules again.

- Don't wear a game out. Quit while the boys are still having fun.

- Have enough leaders to handle the group.

- Keep it simple, make it fun (KISMIF).

Selecting Boys to Lead Games

There are many ways to select the Cub Scout who will be "It" for any game. Here are some suggestions, but make up others that work with your group.

- By birthdays, starting with January 1st.
- By alphabet, using first or last names.
- By drawing a name out of a box. After a name is drawn, it goes into a second box marked "It." When all names are in the "It" box, put them back in the first box to begin all over again.

When selecting teams, try one of these ideas:

- Even-numbered birthdays against odd-numbered birthdays.
- First half of the alphabet against the last half.
- Select names from a box. Have each Cub Scout decorate a craft stick with his name and any other creative artwork he wishes. When you need teams for a game, pull out two sticks and put them in separate piles. Continue to pull out pairs of sticks, separating into two piles. When all the sticks are used, the boys whose sticks are in one pile are on one team and the others are on the second team. When you are finished, replace all the sticks so they will be ready for the next team game.
- Make a game of choosing sides. Have the Cub Scouts sit in a circle. Whisper in each Cub Scout's ear the word "Wolf" or "Bear." Then the Cub Scouts must make the appropriate animal sound to find the other members of their team.

Resources for Games

Your public library, school libraries, and book stores have a wide variety of game books. Games can also be found in children's magazines and on children's television programs.

However, in addition to this book, the best resources for Cub Scout games are *Cub Scout* and *Webelos Scout Program Helps, Boy's Life* magazine, the *Den Chief Handbook,* the monthly district roundtable, and the annual Cub Scout leaders' pow wow.

Here are a few games resources which may be found at your public library:

- *More New Games & Playful Ideas,* by Andrew Fluegelman

- *Outdoor Games,* by David Buskin
- *The New Fun Encyclopedia,* by E. O. Harbin
- *The New Games Book,* Andrew Fluegelman, ed.

Games Equipment

The games included in this book require inexpensive equipment or no equipment at all. Most of the needed materials can be found around the house or made by the boys during a den meeting. Equipment can be stored in a den game chest such as the one shown on page 46 of the *Cub Scout Leader Book.* Listed below are a few items which may be used in games.

Small Balls. Try softballs, tennis balls, table tennis balls, sponge balls, or beanbags. They can be pitched, tossed, passed, batted, kicked, bounced, dribbled, carried, or rolled.

Large Balls. These can be kicked, bounced, thrown, carried, or batted.

Sticks. Broom handles are ideal. They can be used to jump over, for pushing other objects, or for batting. (Be sure sticks won't give boys splinters.)

Tin Cans. These can be rolled or kicked along a course or between obstacles, set up as targets or markers, or used to roll objects into. (Make sure edges are clean and smooth)

Rings. Rubber, metal, or rope rings can be used for tossing over nails, pegs, hooks, or stakes. Use them to play shuffleboard or throw them into tin cans, boxes, or other containers.

Paper Bags. Bags can be used for masks or blindfolds, to blow up and burst, or to wear as hats.

Ropes. Clothesline or sash cord can be used to jump over, spin as a lariat, or thrown as a lasso. Try rope as a marker for start and finish lines or to tie knots. For tug-of-war, use ¾-inch or larger diameter rope.

Newspapers. Can be used as stepping stones, markers, or obstacles; rolled for swatters, or rolled into balls.

Bottle Caps. Can be used as markers or obstacles, checkers, small objects to hide, or objects to throw for accuracy.

Den Games

Den games are designed for a small group of boys. Quiet games are helpful when weather prohibits outdoor activities. Active games help boys release excess energy and will help prepare them for quieter den activities. Most of the games in this book are suitable for dens.

Den games may be competitive or non-competitive. Remember, some games are played just for fun. It isn't always necessary to have a winner. Choosing up sides can be done by drawing straws, going in alphabetical order, numbering off, or selecting two captains to choose alternately. Use the method that works best for you.

Pack Games

Pack games are played with larger groups of boys and adults at pack meetings and activities. Relay games are a great favorite. Shuttle relays require less space.

Pack games should include as many boys as possible, preferably all boys in the pack. If all cannot participate, select representatives from each den. Involve parents and leaders whenever possible. Boys love to see parents or guardians participating in a game.

If prizes are awarded, keep them simple and inexpensive. Suckers, bubble gum, balloons, etc., are appropriate.

And remember, above all, pack games should be fun for everyone—those who play and those who watch.

Ball Games

BASEBALL CATAPULT

Place the center of a 4-foot, 1- by 4-inch board over a wooden block like a seesaw. Attach a jar ring or jar lid to one end of the board and rest a softball on it. Cub Scouts stamp sharply on the high end of the board, making the softball soar into the air. Give points to players who catch their own flies.

TETHER BALL

Erect a 10-foot pole on a standard or embed a longer pole in the ground so it is 10 feet high. Mark a line around

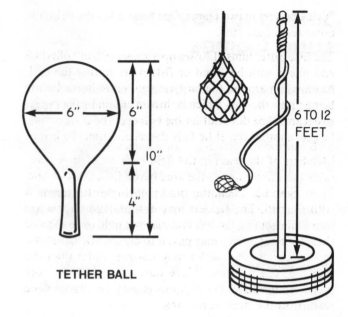

TETHER BALL

the pole 6 feet from the ground. Draw a circle with a 6-foot radius on the ground around the pole. Then divide the circle with a straight line 15 feet long. The tetherball is either a tennis ball encased in a net or a ball with a soft padded center with a tape sewn on to attach it to a 7½-foot rope which hangs from the top of the pole.

Regular tetherball paddles may be used, but almost any kind of paddle or racket will do; or the ball may be batted by hand. The object of the game is to wind the cord around the pole above the 6-foot marked line. The two players must stay in their own court marked by the straight line on the ground. Both hit the ball with their hands or paddles, trying to wind the rope in opposite directions. Neither player may step into the circle.

BUCKETBALL

This is a kind of basketball that can be played with any type of ball that bounces and a couple of large containers such as laundry baskets, bushel baskets, or large wastepaper baskets. Place the baskets (goals) about 60 feet apart—less if necessary because of space. Divide Cub Scouts into two teams and play, using basketball rules. No points are scored if the ball does not remain in the basket or if the basket turns over.

BAT BALL

Any outdoor area or gym will do. Mark a home base in the middle of a 40-to 50-foot end line and draw a line 20 feet away and parallel to the end line. Then mark a far base about 80 feet from home base.

Divide players in two teams. One team takes the field; the other team bats first.

The first batter himself tosses up a soccer ball or volleyball and hits it with his hand or fist. After hitting the ball, he must run around the far base and return home before being hit by the ball, which is thrown at him by the defensive team. If he does not hit the ball over the 20-foot line, he gets another try. If he fails the second time, he is out.

Members of the team in the field have no definite positions but scatter about the area beyond the 20-foot line. They try to put the batter out by hitting or tagging him with the ball. The fielders may not take more than one step while holding the ball and may not hold the ball more than 3 seconds. They may pass it to another fielder closer to the runner. The batter may not run wider than the extent of the end line. Three outs retire the side. Any predetermined number of innings may be played. The team with the most runs wins.

KICK BALL

The play area is similar to a baseball field with 45 feet between bases and 30 feet from the pitcher's box to home plate.

The pitcher rolls a soccer or volleyball to the batter, who kicks it. Outs are made when a batter kicks three fouls, a fielder catches a fly ball, or the runner fails to circle the bases ahead of the ball. The runner must try for a home run.

On a fair ball not caught on the fly, the fielder throws the ball to the pitcher who throws to either the first or third baseman, who then relays it around the bases. Each baseman must be standing on his base before he can pass the ball to the next base.

If the batter succeeds in beating the ball around the bases, he scores a run for his team. Three outs make an inning and nine innings are a game.

LINE-UP BALL

Divide the players into two teams. One team takes the field. The pitcher rolls a soccer ball or volleyball to the first batter who kicks the ball into the field and runs to the far base 80 to 90 feet from home base and back home. The fielder who retrieves the ball holds it over his head and all other fielders line up behind him in single file. If the runner gets back home before the line is formed, he scores a run for his team. If the line forms before he reaches home base, he is out. Three outs for a team make an inning.

NEWSPAPER SOFTBALL

Divide players into two teams. Place two tin cans on either side of home plate and a rolled newspaper across the tops of the cans. The first batter stands behind the newspaper

NEWSPAPER SOFTBALL

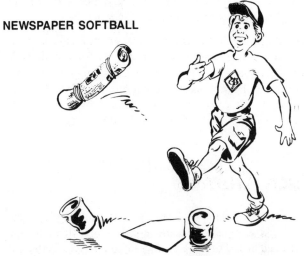

and kicks it with his instep, and the game is on. All the rules of softball are followed, except for the method of putting the ball into play.

SOAKOUT

This is another variation of kickball. The pitcher rolls a soccer ball or volleyball underhand to the batter, who kicks it and runs all four bases while members of the defensive team try to "soak" him by hitting him with a direct throw. The ball may not be relayed.

The batter is out after three strikes, when a fly ball or foul tip is caught, or when he is soaked or tagged by a member of the defensive team. When he kicks the ball, he must make a home run but may run the bases in any order. He may halt, dodge, or run any direction on the playing area, but must touch all bases before coming home. If he receives a base on balls, he is not permitted to leave first base until a succeeding batter hits the ball.

PASS BALL

Divide the Cub Scouts into two teams, which form two circles — one inside the other, both facing out. Give three balls to each circle. The object is to pass these balls around the circles, in opposite directions, and keep them going at a fast pace. If a player drops a ball, he is out of the game. The team with the most players at the end of an allotted time wins.

BOMBARDMENT

BOMBARDMENT

Place several inflated balls in the center of the play area. Divide the group into two teams and arrange them on goal lines at each end of the area. On signal, players from each side race to get as many balls as possible and throw them at their opponents. No member of either side may cross the center line. Any player hit by a ball drops out. If a player is successful in catching a thrown ball, he is not ruled out. The team with the most players left at the end of a designated time wins.

TIN-CAN BOWLING

Cut out the bottoms of six 1-quart cans and sink them in the ground at surface level. Have one in the center and the others in an 18-inch radius circle. Bowl from a line 20 feet away, using croquet balls. Each player bowls two balls each turn. The center can counts five points while the others count one point each. Twenty-one points make a game.

Variation. Use smaller cans sunk in ground; players hit golf balls or tennis balls with croquet mallets to play tin-can golf.

CHAIN DODGE BALL

Divide players into teams of five or six. Arrange one team in a file with each player grasping the player in front of him around the waist, forming a chain. The other team forms a circle around the chain and tries to hit the player at the end of the chain with a softball. The players forming the circle may pass the ball around in any manner while those in the chain try to keep the player on the end

from being hit. Only the first player in the chain may use his hands to bat the ball. When the end player is hit, he leaves the game. Continue until all players in the chain are eliminated, then change sides.

CHAIN SOCCER

Divide group into two teams and line them up in the center of a play area, facing each other about 2 feet apart. Have the players hook elbows with those on either side to form a chain. Establish a goal line for each team on opposite ends of the play area. Start the game by rolling a soccer ball between the two teams.

By using their feet, the teams try to advance the ball toward their goal line without breaking the chain. The first team to kick the ball over the goal line wins the game or earns one point, depending on the time allotted for play.

CHAIN SOCCER

CALL SOCCER

Divide the players into two teams and line them up facing each other about 30 feet apart. Number the players on each team from opposite ends of the line. Midway between the two lines, place a soccer ball or volleyball. The leader calls a number and the two players having that number run up to the ball, each trying to kick it back to his line. The player who kicks it to his line scores two points for his team. Then the leader calls another number and two more players begin. The first team with 10 points wins.

SOCCER BOWLING

Set up 10 Indian clubs, bowling pins, or blocks of wood in bowling pin order. Players kick a soccer ball or basketball at them from a line 25 to 35 feet away. Keep score as in bowling.

KEEP AWAY

Divide the group into two teams. Give one team a basketball or rubber ball, which they pass among themselves, counting one point for every completed pass. When the other team intercepts, its players do the same. The leader keeps track of the number of passes. Winner is the team with the most points after a set time.

FRISBEE FOOTBALL

Divide group into two teams, which begin play at opposite ends of a play area. Play begins with one team "kicking

FRISBEE FOOTBALL

off" (throwing the Frisbee). The receiving team then tries to score a touchdown by passing the Frisbee and advancing it downfield to the other team's goal line. The other team tries to intercept and score a touchdown. No player may run with the "ball" and no player may hold it more than 5 seconds. Play is continuous. There are no downs.

MONKEY IN THE MIDDLE

This game is played by three players. Choose one to be the Monkey. The other two players stand about 10 feet apart while the Monkey stands between them. The two end players toss a volleyball back and forth, trying to keep it high enough or fast enough so the Monkey can't catch it. If a player fails to catch the ball, the Monkey can scramble for it, or he can intercept when it is thrown back and forth. If the Monkey gets the ball, he changes places with the player who threw the ball.

SPUD

Choose one player to start the game. All players stand in a circle. The starter throws a soft ball high and yells his own name or the name of one of the other players. Everyone scatters quickly except the one whose name was called. He runs in to retrieve the ball and throw it at another player. When a player is hit, every other player must stand still as he tries to hit someone with the ball. If he misses, all may run again, until he recovers the ball. The ball must be thrown from where it fell. When a player is hit, he becomes "it" and the game starts over again.

3-PIN BOWLING

Set up three pins (plastic bottles, cardboard mail containers, tin cans, bowling pins) in a triangle with the two rear pins a little further apart than the width of the ball to be used. Draw a foul line with a stick or chalk 20–30 feet from the head pin. It helps to mark the spots where the pins are placed.

In scoring, credit the player with four points for knocking down the head pin and three for either of the back pins. Strikes, spares, and number of frames played are as in regular 10-pin bowling. All other bowling rules apply. To speed the game along, it helps for one of the players to act as pinsetter.

Bean bags, rather than balls, may be used when playing indoors. Beanbags don't bounce and don't need to be chased.

ANTE OVER

Divide group into two teams, with one team on each side of a house or building with a sloping roof. A rubber ball is given to a player on one team. He shouts "Ante over!" and throws the ball over the building so that it hits the roof at least once before falling to the other side. If a player on the other team can catch the ball in the air, he may run around ether side of the building and attempt to hit any member of the throwing team with the ball. If he is successful, the person hit becomes a member of his team. When the ball is thrown over the building and no one catches it before it hits the ground, the player who retrieves it must shout "Ante over!" and throw it back over the roof in the same manner. Continue until all players are on one team.

FIVE HUNDRED

A batter tosses up a softball and bats it to the other players, who attempt to catch it. A fielder scores 100 points for catching a flyball, 75 points for catching the ball on one bounce, 50 for two bounces, and 25 for fielding a grounder cleanly. When a fielder reaches a score of 500, he exchanges places with the batter. With each new batter, the scoring starts over.

BALLOON VOLLEYBALL

Stretch a string across the room to represent the net. Divide players into two groups—one on either side of the string. Throw an inflated balloon into play. Each side bats the ball in the air, trying to keep the balloon from touching the floor on their side. They bat it back and forth over the string with their hands. Each time the balloon hits the floor, the opposing team scores one point. The game is 10 points.

ONE O'CAT

Homeplate and first base are set up. One player is batter; the others are catcher, pitcher, and fielders. The batter is out when he makes three strikes or when a fly or foul ball is caught. When he makes a hit, he must run to first base and return home before the ball is returned to the catcher, who must touch homeplate to put him out. When the batter is out, all players move up in rotation. The batter moves out to right field. If a player catches a fly, he replaces the batter.

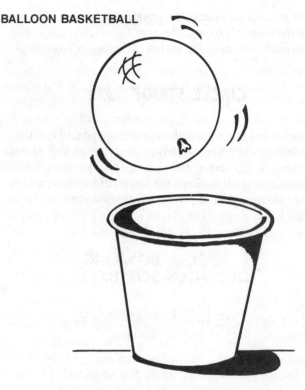

BALLOON BASKETBALL

Use an inflated balloon for the ball and boxes or wastepaper baskets for the goals. Score as in basketball, except that a broken balloon counts five points off for the offending side.

DODGE BALL

Divide the Cub Scouts into two groups. Have one side form a large circle and the other scatter inside it. The circle players throw a volleyball or playground ball at the Cub Scouts inside, who try to avoid being hit without leaving the circle. Those hit are out and leave the circle. The last player in the circle is the winner. When all have been eliminated, have the sides change places.

Variation: Have those Cub Scouts who have been hit by the ball join the circle players.

BALL OVER

Draw a line to divide the area. Divide the group into two teams—one on each side of the line. Players must not cross the line. Blindfold one Cub Scout and provide him with a whistle. When he blows the whistle, the ball is put into play by throwing it from side to side. The object of the game is to keep the ball on the opposing team's side. One point is counted against the team that has the ball each time the whistle is blown. The blindfolded player can blow the whistle whenever he wishes. The lowest score wins.

CIRCLE STRIDE BALL

Players stand in a circle with their feet spread and touching the foot of the player on either side. The player who is It stands in the center with a volleyball. He tries to roll it out of the circle between the feet of any of the players. If he is successful, the person who allowed the ball to go through becomes It. The players may use only their hands to stop the ball and may not move their feet.

ONE PITCH SOFTBALL

This is a very fast game with the following rules. It is played on a regular softball diamond.

- Any number of Cub Scouts can play. The team in the field has a catcher, four or five infielders, and any number of outfielders. The pitcher is a member of the team at bat. He tries to let his teammates hit and does not field a batted ball.

- Each team establishes its own batting order.

- Each batter gets only one pitch. The batter runs on a fair ball; anything else is an out (foul ball, strike, ball, or whatever).

- As soon as the third out is made, the batting team runs to its fielding positions. As soon as the pitcher and bat-

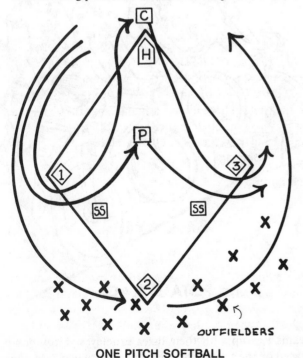

ONE PITCH SOFTBALL

ter are in position, they may start play whether or not the fielders are ready.

- All players must observe counter-clockwise rotation plan to get from "Up to Bat" position to "In the Field" position. If any player fails to run on the outside of first or third base, all players must go back and run around the base.

Bicycle Games

SNAIL RACE

The object of this race is to see which rider can travel slowest, and that's quite a feat in cycling. The last rider to cross the finish line wins.

OBSTACLE SPEED RACE

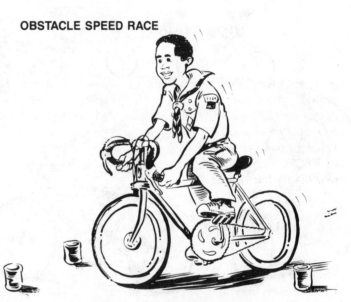

OBSTACLE SPEED RACE

Set up empty coffee cans slalom style, with the first can 20 yards from the starting line and three additional cans about 10 feet apart. Rider must follow a course that zigzags from the right of one can to the left of the next, and so on. Rider completing the course in the least time wins.

COASTING RACE

The object of this race is to see which rider can coast the longest distance. Each rider pedals as hard as possible for a set distance (at least 15 feet) to a starting line and then must stop pedalling. Mark the spot where a rider's foot touches the ground. The next rider tries to beat the mark.

NEWSPAPER RACE

On a 100-yard race course, place six or eight large boxes or baskets about 15 feet apart. Put the first basket about 10 feet from the starting line. Each player rides along on a line about 8 feet away from the baskets. As he passes each one, he tosses in a folded newspaper. The player who gets the most newspapers in the baskets wins.

PURSUIT RACE

This is a speed race. All riders line up around a circular course about 3 yards apart. At a signal, they all ride in the same direction around the circle. The idea is for a rider

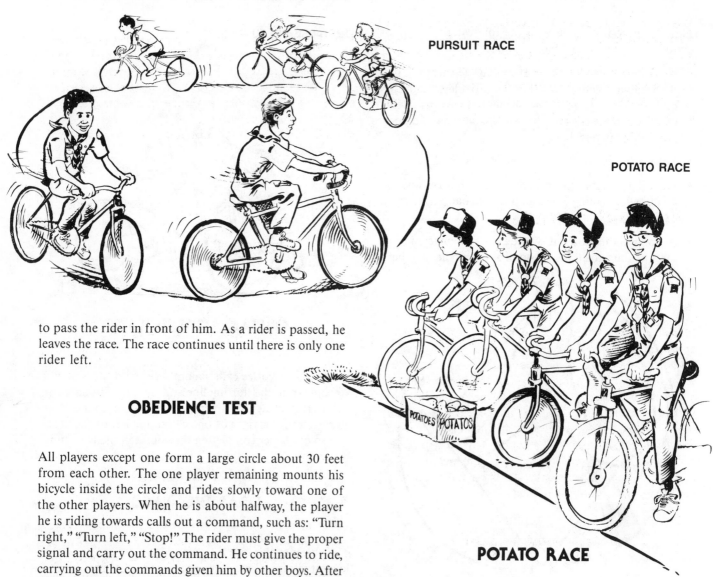

PURSUIT RACE

POTATO RACE

to pass the rider in front of him. As a rider is passed, he leaves the race. The race continues until there is only one rider left.

OBEDIENCE TEST

All players except one form a large circle about 30 feet from each other. The one player remaining mounts his bicycle inside the circle and rides slowly toward one of the other players. When he is about halfway, the player he is riding towards calls out a command, such as: "Turn right," "Turn left," "Stop!" The rider must give the proper signal and carry out the command. He continues to ride, carrying out the commands given him by other boys. After five commands, he takes a place in the circle and another player rides the course. Score one point against a player who fails to signal, gives the wrong signal, or does the

wrong action. When all players have had a chance to ride, total scores. The winner is the one with the fewest penalty points.

BIKE RELAY

Establish a starting line and mark off turning lines about 50 feet away in opposite directions. Divide group into two teams. The teams will ride in opposite directions. The teams should be about 20 feet apart to avoid collisions as the riders return to the start-finish line. On signal, the first rider on each team races to his turning line and back. The next rider may not start until the first rider's front wheel has crossed the line. Continue until all have raced.

POTATO RACE

Teams line up with their bikes in relay style. A box is placed on the starting line in front of each team. At intervals of 5 yards or more in front of each team, mark four circles into which a potato or beanbag is placed before the game begins. On signal, the first player on each team rides out and picks up the potato in the first circle, returns to the starting line and places it in the box. He then rides for the second, third, and fourth potatoes, returning each time to put it into the box. When he has finished, he touches off the second player, who rides out carrying one of the potatoes to place in the first circle. He returns for the second, third, and fourth in similar fashion, replacing them one at a time. Continue in this way, with one teammate removing the potatoes and another replacing them, until all have taken part.

HITTING THE TARGET

This game requires skill, coordination, timing, and marksmanship. Four to six coffee cans or other containers are set up about 15 feet apart in a straight line along a 100-foot course. Each rider is given a small object (marble, stone, bottle cap) for each of the cans. Riders follow each other down the course at average speed, dropping one object into each can. The winning team is the one with the most hits.

Blindfold Games

BLIND TRAIN

Mark two curving "train tracks" on the ground or floor, approximately 4 feet apart. Divide group into two teams. Each team lines up single file at the start of one track, with each player grasping the belt of the one in front of him. All players except the last in each line are blindfolded. Place various obstacles, such as tin cans, on either side of the twisting lines. The player at the end of the line must direct his team through the hazards. Score 5 points for completing the course; subtract one point each time the train touches an obstacle or crosses the opposing team's line. Team with the most points wins.

GHOSTS AND WITCHES

Divide group into two teams — the Ghosts and Witches. Place a grinning jack-o-lantern with a glowing candle inside in the center of a table. Lead each Cub Scout to

the table, one at a time. Blindfold him, turn him around three times, and ask him to blow out the candle. He may blow three times. If the candle goes out, he wins a point for his team.

BLIND BELL

In this game there is one Runner and all other players are Chasers. The Chasers are all blindfolded, but the Runner is not. He carries a bell that he must keep ringing continuously. The blindfolded Chasers try to tag the Runner. The one who succeeds trades places with him.

SWAT THE MOSQUITO

Blindfold one Cub Scout, give him a rolled newspaper, and seat him in the center of the room on a stool or box. The other Cub Scouts are Mosquitoes. They tiptoe up to him and buzz in his ear, quickly withdrawing as he strikes at them with the newspaper. Anyone hit becomes the swatter. The swatter is permitted to swing only when he hears a buzz. Cub Scouts may buzz only when they are very near the swatter.

WALK THE PLANK

WALK THE PLANK

Lay a long board flat on the ground (a 2 x 4 is best). One by one, blindfold each Pirate and have him try to walk the length of the plank. If he steps off at any point, he has fallen into shark-infested waters and is out of the game. If the Cub Scouts find this too easy, turn the board on edge. For variation, use two or more boards, side by side and form teams for a relay race.

RATTLESNAKE TAG

Arrange Cub Scouts in a circle 20 feet in diameter. Blindfold two players, giving one a rolled newspaper and the other a tin can containing some pebbles. Stand these two players on opposite sides of the circle. When the first player says, Rattle, the other must shake his tin can and then try to avoid the swatter. The first player continues to command the other to rattle until he succeeds in swatting him squarely. Then the two change places. The one who "kills the rattler" in the shortest time is the winner.

SLEEPING GUARD

Choose one Cub Scout to be the Sleeping Guard. The others are Stalkers. The Guard sits blindfolded on the ground, guarding a precious object. (This could be a rock, flag, neckerchief, etc.) The Stalkers form a ring around the guard about 20 feet away. On signal, they begin to advance as quietly as possible, trying to get close enough to steal the object without waking up the Guard. When the Guard hears an approaching stalker, he points a finger in that direction. If his finger points at the Stalker, the Stalker is out. If a Stalker succeeds in getting the object without being caught, he is the Guard for the next game. No running or diving for the object is permitted.

Circle Games

ABOVE AND BELOW

Arrange the Cub Scouts in a circle. One at a time, call out the names of things that are found either above the ground or below. For example:

Strawberries grow above ground, potatoes grow below. When you call something that is found above the ground, the players stand; if below, they sit down. Failure to respond correctly eliminates a player. The last player to remain in the game is the winner.

Variation: Call out names of things that fly and crawl.

AMIMAL TRAINER

Arrange Cub Scouts in a circle. Stand in the center and name a stunt or movement to be performed by everyone.

For example: "Bark like a dog; walk like an elephant; hop like a kangaroo . . ."

AUTO RACE

Arrange Cub Scouts in a circle, with the den chief in the center. He gives each player the name of an automobile, being sure to use the same name more than once so that several players have the same car. To start play, the den chief then calls out the name of an auto. The first player with that car name to touch him and return to his place wins the race. The game continues as the den chief calls out another auto.

DEADLY CIRCLE

Tie the ends of a long rope together to form a large circle. Mark off another circle on the floor or ground, about one-third the size of the rope circle. All Cub Scouts take hold of the rope with both hands, forming a ring around the marked circle. On signal, all try to pull as many of the other players as possible into the circle while keeping out of it themselves. As soon as a player steps into the middle circle, he is out of the game. The game continues until only one player remains.

COVER THE CHAIR

The Cub Scouts are seated in a circle. One player is It and stands in the circle, leaving his chair empty. When he commands, "Move to the right," all players try to get into the chair to their right. While this is going on, It tries to get a seat. If he succeeds, the person who should have gotten that seat becomes It. To confuse the players, It may suddenly call, "Move to the left," and he stands a good chance of finding a place.

BEAR IN THE PIT

Cub Scouts form a circle. One player inside the circle is the Bear. While the others hold hands tightly, the Bear tries to get through the ring by force or by dodging under their arms. He may not use his hands to break the grip of the players in the ring. When he does break through, the others try to catch him. The first one to tag him is the next Bear.

FISH AND NET

Three to five Cub Scouts join hands to catch Fish by surrounding individual players. Those who are caught become a part of the "net." The last five Fish caught make up the net for the new game.

GRAB BAG

GRAB BAG

Fill a laundry bag with an assortment of old clothing (hats, shirts, shoes, stockings, suspenders, belts, etc.). The Cub Scouts stand in a circle. Give the bag to one of them. On signal, he passes the bag to the player on his left, and he to the next, and so on around the circle. As the bag is being passed around, the den chief blows a whistle. Whoever has the bag in his hand when the whistle sounds must reach inside, take out an article of clothing and put it on. Play continues until all clothing is being worn.

HA, HA, HA

Arrange Cub Scouts in a circle. Ask the first to say, "Ha," the second, "Ha, ha," the third, "Ha, ha, ha," and so on around the circle. The "Ha-ha's" must be said without laughing. Those laughing while saying their parts are eliminated. The one staying in the longest wins.

HOPTOAD

Cub Scouts form a circle, standing about 3 feet apart. On signal, they place their hands on their hips and stoop down until they are almost sitting on their heels. Then they start hopping around the circle clockwise, clapping their hands first in front of them and then behind them. The Cub Scouts continue to stoop while they hop. Anyone who tips over must leave the circle. The last one to continue hopping without falling over is the winner.

HOT POTATO

Cub Scouts form a circle, with It in the center. One of the players is given an object for passing. When It calls, "Pass the potato," the player with the object starts passing it around the circle. When It calls, "Hot potato," whoever has the object at that moment becomes It.

NAME AND TELL

Cub Scouts sit in a circle. The first player names an object beginning with the letter A and tells something about it, and so on, around the circle and through the alphabet. Examples: "A is for air—we breathe it." "B is for birds—they fly."

TOYS FOR SALE

Each Cub Scout is given the name of a toy—soldier, trumpet, clown, jumping jack, top, kite, etc. The Toys sit in a circle with the Storekeeper outside the ring. The Storekeeper walks around the circle and calls out the names of the Toys in any order. As they are named, the Toys leave the circle and follow him, imitating the toy they represent until there is a long line walking around the circle. When the Storekeeper shouts, "Sold!" the Toys rush back to their places and sit down. At the same time, the Storekeeper tries to find a seat. The one left standing is the next Storekeeper.

Variation: Give Cub Scouts names of pets and have a pet store owner.

BALLOON BATTLE ROYAL

Arrange Cub Scouts in a large circle, each with an inflated balloon hanging from a string tied to his ankle. On signal,

BALLOON BATTLE ROYAL

have each player try to break all other balloons by stamping on them. When a balloon is broken, its owner leaves the circle, and the game continues until only one player is left.

BAT AND MOTH

Cub Scouts form a circle 10 to 15 feet across. One Cub Scout, the Bat, is blindfolded and stands in the center. Three other players are Moths and also stand in the circle. The Bat tries to catch the Moths. When the bat calls, "Bat!" the moths call back, "Moth!" Their voices help identify their location in the circle so the blindfolded Bat can tag them. Each Moth tagged take his place in the circle until all Moths are tagged. Then other players are chosen to be the Bat and Moths. Explain to the boys that when the Bat calls out, he is sending out his radar signal to see if anything is there. His cry bounces off the Moths and returns to him. The return signal is the word, "Moth," and tells him that Moths are near.

PASS THE RING

Cub Scouts sit in a circle, each holding onto a rope with both hands. The rope has a ring or washer on it. One Cub Scout is It and stands in the center. On the "go" signal, the Cub Scouts start to move the ring around the rope, trying to conceal its location from It. It tries to guess the position of the ring. The Cub Scout who holds the ring when It guesses correctly is It for the next game.

FIND THE LEADER

The Cub Scouts sit in a circle. Select one to be It and have him leave the room. The remaining Cub Scouts select a leader. It is then called back into the center of the circle and the leader slyly starts some motion, such as waving his hands, clapping, making a face, etc. The others in the circle immediately imitate the leader. It keeps watchful eyes on everyone to find out who is starting the motions. The leader should change motions frequently. When It discovers who the leader is, the leader becomes It and a new leader is chosen.

IN THE POND

Arrange the Cub Scouts in a circle around you just outside a chalkline. If you order, "In the pond!" all are to jump forward. When you call, "On the bank!" all should jump back. If the order, "In the pond!" is given when all are in, no one should move. Such orders as, "On the pond!" or "In the bank!" should be ignored. Anyone making a mistake is out of the game. The last remaining player wins.

Hiding, Chasing, Hunting Games

AIRLIFT

Divide the group into two equal teams. Mark out a large rectangular area. One end of the area is home base, the other is the outpost, and in between is enemy territory. The job of the airlift team is to carry supplies (apples) from home base to the outpost without getting "shot down" (tagged three times) by the enemy team. The airlift team may carry one apple each or may let one or two Cub Scouts carry several while the others protect them as they race from home base to the outpost. Boys who are tagged three times while carrying apples are out, and the enemy gets their apples. Those of the airlift team who are not carrying apples may run freely without fear of being tagged. The team that has the most apples at the end of the game wins.

CAT'S TAIL

Divide the group into two teams. Hide several pieces of cloth or yarn—a different color for each team. One Cub Scout on each team is a Cat Without a Tail. At the signal, all players search for tails of their color. As each piece is found, it is tied to the belt of their Cat. The winner is the team whose Cat has the longest tail at the end of 5 minutes.

CROWS AND CRANES

Divide Cub Scouts into two teams. Teams line up facing each other about a yard apart. One team is the Crows and the other the Cranes. Mark off a baseline 30 to 50 feet behind each team or line them up in the center of a room and use the walls for bases. When the leader calls, "Crows," the Crows must race to their base without being tagged by the Cranes. When the leader calls, "Cranes," they try to get back safely. The leader can add suspense by prolonging the commands, "Cr-r-r-rows" or "Cr-r-ranes."

EAT THE FISHTAIL

EAT THE FISHTAIL

Cub Scouts line up in single file, holding each other around the waist. The first Cub Scout is the fish Head; the last one is the Tail. On signal, the Head tries to catch the Tail while the Tail tries to avoid being caught. All must continue to hold onto each other. The longer the fish, the better.

Variation: Put a neckerchief or bandana in the belt of the Tail. The Head must snatch the neckerchief from the Tail.

FOLLOW THE LEADER

Have the Cub Scouts form single file behind the den chief and imitate anything he does. The den chief keeps the line moving and performs stunts for the others to copy. He gradually does more difficult tasks, such as climbing or vaulting over obstacles; jumping certain distances; taking a hop, skip, and jump; walking backward; turning around while walking, etc. Anyone failing to perform the required feat drops out of the game. The last Cub Scout following the leader is the winner.

KICK, HIDE, AND SEEK

Mark a circle on the ground 3 feet in diameter and place a soccer ball in it. One of the Cub Scouts is It and kicks the ball as far as possible. While the others run and hide, It runs to recover the ball and place it in the circle before going in search of the players. When he sees someone, he calls, "I spy (name)," and both run for the ball. The one who reaches it first kicks it and runs for a hiding place. The other player is It and must return the ball to the circle, then search for the others.

RED LIGHT

Play this game outdoors or in a large room. It turns his back on the rest of the Cub Scouts, who are lined up 30 to 50 feet away from him. The object is for the Cub Scouts to walk or run toward It while his back is turned as he counts to 10. At "10," he shouts, "Red light!" and turns quickly. Any player who is moving when It turns must go back to the starting line. The first to get to It and touch him wins the game.

TAILS

Divide the Cub Scouts into two teams. All players tuck their neckerchiefs loosely into their belts in back as tails. On signal, each team rushes toward the other, trying to get their tails. Once a tail is taken, the Cub Scout who loses it, is out of the game. The capturer ties the tail around his waist. The team that captures the most tails wins. This is a good stalking game in a place where brush or shrubbery provides cover.

PIONEERS AND INDIANS

Divide the Cub Scouts into two groups—the Pioneers and the Indians. One Pioneer is the Starving Captain, who sits in a blockhouse. Give each of the other Pioneers a slip of paper with the name of a food and its allotted playing value: flour, 25; baking powder, 20; dried beef, 15; hardtack, 10; jam, 10; fruit, 5; sugar, 5; and corn, 5. A Chief chosen by the Indians places his braves in the Indian territory which surrounds the Pioneers' blockhouse. The Pioneers surround the Indians and look for ways to break through the Indian lines to take supplies to their Starving Captain in the blockhouse. The Indians try to capture the Pioneers by tagging them. They search their captives and confiscate any "food" found on them. After about 15 minutes of play, tally the score. The Indians add up the value of the captured supplies. The Starving Captain figures the value of the supplies that have been delivered to him. The side with the highest value of supplies wins.

BACK TO BACK

Arrange all Cub Scouts except one in pairs, standing back to back with their elbows locked. They are scattered at random over the play area. When It calls, "All change!" each Cub Scout must find a new partner and hook elbows

HANG TAG

with him. At the same time, It tries to find a partner. The Cub Scout left without a partner becomes the next It.

GIVEAWAY TAG

One Cub Scout is It. The others are scattered around the play area. One of them holds an object such as a ball, rolled newspaper, or hat. It tries to tag the Cub Scout holding the object. The boy with the object may run with it or pass it to another Cub Scout. The player tagged becomes It.

HOT POTATO TAG

Play this tag game with a ball or potato. The Cub Scouts form a circle with one in the center. The potato is passed or thrown around the circle, while the Cub Scout in the center tries to tag the one who has it.

SHERE KHAN

(The Tiger Game; it is also known as Pom-Pom-Pullaway.) One Cub Scout is Shere Khan, the tiger. All others line up against a wall. Shere Khan stands in the center of the play area. The object of the game is to cross to the opposite goal without being tagged. To start the game, Shere Khan says, "Who's afraid of Shere Khan?" The others answer, "No one," and immediately run across the open space towards the opposite side. All Cub Scouts tagged help Shere Khan tag the remaining players. The last one caught becomes Shere Khan the next time.

Variation: With a big field and a large number of players, half can be Shere Khans and half men.

HANG TAG

This excellent fitness game requires arm strength and agility. It is played like regular tag except that to escape being tagged, Cub Scouts must support their weight by hanging from something so that their feet are off the ground (tree branch, horizontal bar, etc.). So that It cannot simply wait until a Cub Scout falls from exhaustion, he must count off for 10 seconds (1,001, 1,002, 1,003, etc.) when he is trying to tag someone. If the Cub Scout does not touch the ground by the time It reaches 1,010, he must leave and try to tag someone else.

BRONCO TAG

Pair off all Cub Scouts except two. The pairs stand 8 to 10 feet apart. In each pair, one stands in front and the other behind clasping his partner around the waist. The Cub Scouts who are not joined are the Chaser and the Runner. The Runner tries to get in front of one of the pairs so that the front player can grab him around the waist. If the Runner succeeds, the rear player becomes the Runner and tries to join another pair. Meanwhile, the Chaser is trying to tag the Runner.

The front player in a pair always tries to help the Runner join on, while the rear player tries to prevent this by swinging his partner out of the way. If the Chaser catches the Runner, they change places.

CHAIN TAG

The Cub Scouts are scattered over the play area. One player is It and tries to tag any another player. The first Cub Scout he tags joins hands with him and helps in tagging others. Both may use only their free hands to tag. Each player tagged joins hands with the one tagging him. The line grows longer as more players are tagged, but only the players at the two ends of the chain may do the tagging. Tagging is not fair if the chain is broken. The game continues until all Cub Scouts have been tagged.

TURTLE TAG

TURTLE TAG

One Cub Scout is It and the others are Turtles. It may not tag a Turtle who is on his back with all four feet in the air. But turtles must hop up and run at least 10 steps by the time It counts to 10. They can then again assume the safe position or keep moving.

DUCK ON THE ROCK

DUCK ON THE ROCK

Each Cub Scout has a rock or stone. A large rock is used as a stand. The player who is It places his rock (the Duck) on the stand and stays close by as guard. The other players stand at a throwing line, 15 to 20 feet away, and toss their stones at the "Duck on the rock." They then take a position where their stones come to a stop. When the Duck is knocked off, the guard immediately replaces it, then tries to tag the others, while they pick up their stones and run back to the throwing line. If anyone is tagged, he becomes It. The players may pretend to pick up their rocks without penalty, but if they touch their stone, they can be tagged. It may not touch anyone while his Duck is off the stand. If a player tosses his rock and it hits another player's, both of them are allowed home without danger of being tagged.

BLOB

It joins hands with the Cub Scouts he tags and together they chase the others. Everyone tagged by the Blob joins in, but only the first and last in line may tag others. The Blob may split into two parts and the first and last in line in the new part may also tag others.

SQUAT TAG

One Cub Scout is It. He tries to tag anyone who is standing up. No one may be tagged while in the squat position. If a Cub Scout is tagged, he becomes It.

JAPANESE TAG

Any player who is tagged must place his right hand on the spot where he has been touched (arm, chest, back, ankle, etc.) and in this position he must chase the other Cub Scouts until he has tagged one of them.

SARDINES

Select one Cub Scout to be It. He hides while the other players count to 100. Then they all search for him. When someone finds It, he hides with him. Continue until the last Cub Scout has located It. The first Cub Scout to find It becomes It for the next game.

SQUIRREL GAME

Have all except two Cub Scouts form circles of three or four boys each. Each circle counts off, and the No. 1's go into the circles and become Squirrels. The others then form "hollow trees" by holding hands. The other two Cub Scouts are the Fox and the Homeless Squirrel. The Fox tries to catch the Homeless Squirrel and, when the chase becomes too hot, the Homeless Squirrel takes refuge in any tree, thereby forcing the Squirrel inside to leave. The Fox now tries to catch this one. If caught, the Squirrel becomes a Fox, and the chase continues. After a few minutes, have the No. 2s in each circle become Squirrels.

ALPHABET SCAVENGER HUNT

Give each Cub Scout a pencil and paper which has the alphabet listed vertically. Ask them to look in a designated area for nature items which begin with each letter of the alphabet and write the names of the items they see, but they must leave the items where they are. Examples: A—acorn, B—bark, C—cone, D—dandelion, etc.

LITTER SCAVENGER HUNT

Make a list of common litter items in the area, such as three pop-top rings, one gum wrapper, two candy wrappers, etc. Give each Cub Scout a copy of the list. Set a time limit and a specific area for searching. Have a signal for boys to return.

DUPLICATION

This is a good game for getting boys interested in nature. In advance, gather from the area about 10 common nature objects, such as rocks, seeds, pine cones, leaves, etc. Lay the objects out on a neckerchief and cover them with another neckerchief. Tell the Cub Scouts that under the neckerchief are 10 natural objects that can be found nearby. Lift the neckerchief and let them look for about 30 seconds. Tell them to try to remember what they see. Then ask the players to hunt for identical items. Allow 10 to 15 minutes for the search. Then hold up each object one at a time, telling something about it, and ask if anyone found one like it. Be careful not to use scarce items. Conserve nature!

ANIMAL GUESSING GAME

Divide the group into two equal teams. Each team chooses an animal and thinks up six riddle clues for that animal. When both teams are ready, have them face each other across a line. Draw a line for each team's home base about 15 feet behind the teams. The teams take turns giving one clue at a time. When one of the teams guesses correctly, they begin to chase the other team towards their home base line. Players who are caught switch teams. Examples of clues: "I eat flying insects"; "My front teeth are large and I gnaw a lot"; "My eyes are very large."

OWLS AND CROWS

Divide group into two equal teams—one are the Owls and the other the Crows. The teams line up, facing each other, about two feet apart. About 15 feet behind each team is their home base line. The leader makes a statement. (This could be related to the monthly theme or nature items.) If the statement is true, the Owls chase the Crows toward their base line. If it is false, the Crows chase the Owls. Anyone caught must join the other team.

GRAB IT

Divide group into two teams. Call one the Defenders and the other the Destroyers. Toss an inflated balloon between them. The Destroyers try to break the balloon by grabbing it, clapping their hands on it, or stepping on it. The Defenders try to protect it by batting it out of reach. Keep track of the time required by the Destroyers to break the balloon. When it is broken, the Defenders become the Destroyers. Give each team three turns as Destroyers, then add their times. Team with the least total time wins.

Homemade Games

PUTTING GAME

Make a putting "green" from heavy cardboard or plywood. The putter is made from a piece of 2-by-2 and a dowel. Cut a hole for the cup and insert a tin can.

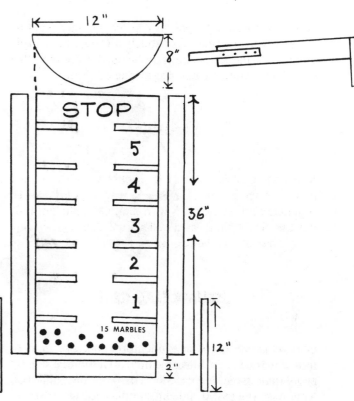

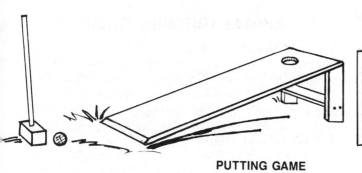

PUTTING GAME

MARBLE ROLL GAME

TEETERBOARD JOUSTING

Make two teeterboards as shown (24 inches in diameter with 4-inch high rockers). Make the jousting poles from plumber's suction cups, soft rubber balls, and squares of cloth, or stuffed socks. Place the boards so that the players are just within reach of each other.

Build a rocker box as shown (12-by-36-by-4 inches) from wood or a cardboard carton. Place a rocker on one end and handles on the other end. Divide the box into compartments by using strips of 1-by-1. The object of the game is to get the highest score possible with 15 marbles. The minute you get even one marble in the stop section, your turn is over. Total the score by multiplying the number of the section by the number of marbles in it.

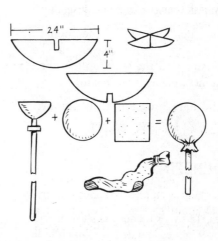

TEETERBOARD JOUSTING

TURTLE RACE

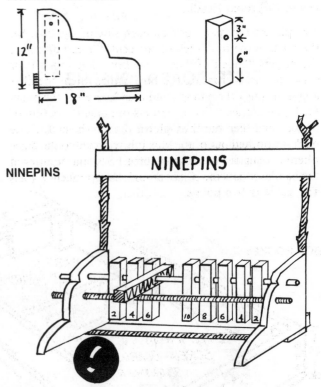

TURTLE RACE

Cut animals from ¼- or ⅜-inch plywood. Use 15 to 30 feet of twisted cord. Make the hole in the animal slightly larger than the cord. Let the boys decorate and paint their names on their own animals. If the race is to be run indoors, it will help to add rubber bumpers to the rear feet to give traction on smooth floors and to lessen the sound. Attach one end of the cords to a peg driven in the ground or a chair indoors. The cord should be the same height from the floor as the hole in the animal.

Start the animals leaning or flat on the ground with their heads toward the Cub Scouts. The animals are made to walk toward the Cub Scouts by pulling gently on the cord, lifting the head and body, which drags the feet forward. Relaxing the line lets the cord slip through the hole. By alternately tightening and relaxing the cord, the players make their animals move toward the finish line. Jerking the cord or excited play will make the animal flip in the wrong direction, slowing down its progress.

This race can be run as a den relay. When the animal's nose has crossed the finish line, the first player runs the animal back along the string to the starting line, then hands the string to the next player, who begins racing.

Variations: Tortoise and hare, frog, crow, locomotive, cars, etc.

NINEPINS

Cut the two end pieces, 12-by-18 inches, as shown. Cut nine pieces of 2-by-2-by-9 inches and drill a ⅝-inch hole 3 inches from the top of each. Slide these pins on a ½-inch

dowel rod 30 inches long. Insert the dowel rods into the end pieces as shown and fasten in place. Brace the end pieces in the lower back corner with 1-by-2s. Be sure the pins swing freely. To play the game, roll a croquet or hard ball at the base of the pins. The object is to flip them onto the front dowel bar. Count the numbers turned up to determine the score.

NINEPINS

MOOSE TOSS

Cut the moose head from plywood, sand, and paint with contrasting colors. Use rubber or plastic rings for tossing.

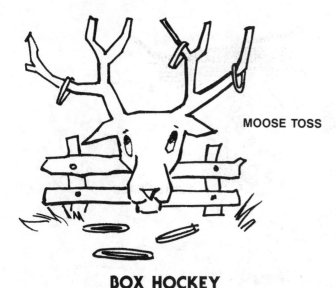

MOOSE TOSS

FISHPOND GAMES

BOX HOCKEY

This is an all-time Cub Scout favorite. For a good backyard box hockey game, build a box 3 feet wide and 6 feet long. Use 1-by-6-inch lumber for the frame and plywood for the base. Reinforce the corners with 2-by-2-inch blocks glued and fastened with screws. The center board takes a terrific pounding and should be fastened securely and braced on both sides. Follow the illustrations shown. The puck is cut from a piece of 1-by-2-inch wood. For hockey or shinny sticks, use a 30-inch length of broom handle.

Two players take part, one on each side of the box. Set the puck in the top notch of the center board and have the players "knock off" as in hockey. They touch their sticks to the bottom of the box, knock them together above the puck three times, and then knock off the puck. Each player tries to bat it into his opponent's section of the box and then out through the hole in the end. If the puck is knocked out of the box, it is returned to the place where it went out and play resumes. Score a point each time a player gets the puck through his opponent's goal. The game is five points.

FISHPOND GAMES

An infinite variety of games is possible with a "hook," a line, and a pole. Make hooks from coat-hanger wire, paper clips or open safety pins. Cut the fish from felt, cardboard, or wood. Use a cardboard carton or a piece of corrugated cardboard for the ocean bottom or trout stream.

The players can catch the fish by hooking them and lifting them out of the ocean or stream. Fish can be marked with different point values or different colors can be worth different points.

BOX HOCKEY

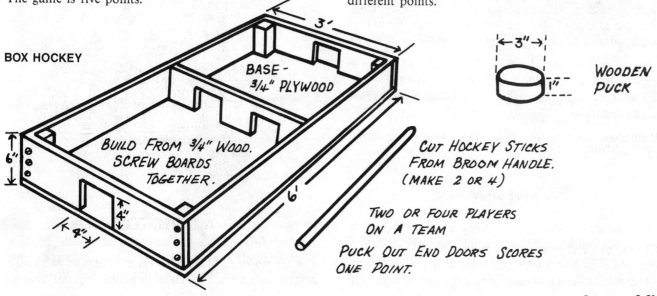

BASE - 3/4" PLYWOOD

BUILD FROM 3/4" WOOD. SCREW BOARDS TOGETHER.

WOODEN PUCK

CUT HOCKEY STICKS FROM BROOM HANDLE. (MAKE 2 OR 4)

TWO OR FOUR PLAYERS ON A TEAM

PUCK OUT END DOORS SCORES ONE POINT.

RING TOSS

Invert a shallow cardboard box and stick clothespins through. Mark each pin with a number of points. Cub Scouts toss rubber, metal, or plastic rings from a distance away.

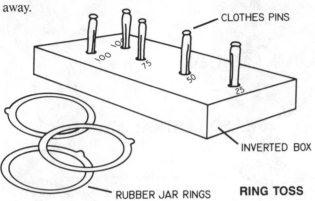

CLOTHES PINS

INVERTED BOX

RUBBER JAR RINGS

RING TOSS

HAND BADMINTON

Make "poputs" as shown in illustration, using feathers, a cardboard circle, and a stuffed sock. Use a cord stretched across the room for net. Play as in regular badminton, batting the poputs with the palm of the hand.

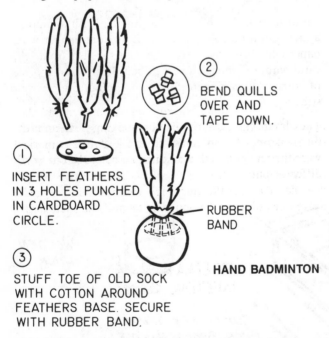

② BEND QUILLS OVER AND TAPE DOWN.

① INSERT FEATHERS IN 3 HOLES PUNCHED IN CARDBOARD CIRCLE.

RUBBER BAND

③ STUFF TOE OF OLD SOCK WITH COTTON AROUND FEATHERS BASE. SECURE WITH RUBBER BAND.

HAND BADMINTON

TOSSING BOARDS

Draw design on corrugated cardboard or plywood, such as face or animal head, with mouth cut out. Paint or decorate with colored markers. Toss beanbags into hole for score.

DRAW ON LARGE PLYWOOD. CUT OUT SHADED AREAS AND PAINT.

TOSSING BOARDS

PROP BOARD AGAINST WALL. STAND BACK AND TOSS.

COUNTER TOSS

Make the game board from ¼-inch plywood as shown. Attach hooks and paint scores. Cut out six wooden or cardboard counters and paint two colors. Each Cub Scout in turn tosses one of his three counters. Score is total of figure on board and upper figure on the counter. High score wins.

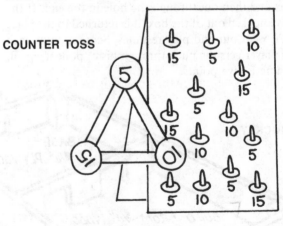

COUNTER TOSS

PIG, PIG

Get your pigs in their pen first and win. Make two sets of five pigs from ¼-inch plywood and decorate. Make the pen from plywood with 1-by-4-inch rails. Make it approximately 2 feet by 6 inches and decorate as desired. Cub Scouts take turns, snapping pigs with finger.

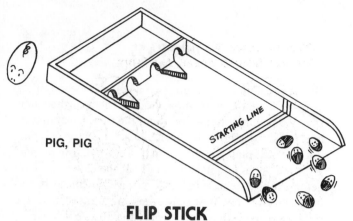

PIG, PIG

FLIP STICK

Drill a hole 5 inch from the end of a wooden paint stirrer. Glue a long wedge of wood ¾-inch wide to the stirrer, ½-inch from the hole. Glue a tongue depressor or popsicle stick to top of the long wedge. Insert a 9-inch string into hole and knot on bottom side of stirrer 2 inches from string end. Make a knot on the other side of the stirrer, too. Then knot string 4 inches from its top end. Drill a

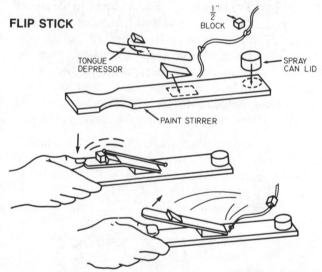

FLIP STICK

hole through center of a ½-inch square block to pull the string through. Knot string again to lock block in position. Stretch string on tongue depressor to find correct place for the short wedge. Glue the short wedge (¾-inch wide) in place. Tack plastic spray can cap in position.

To play, place block on tongue depressor behind short wedge. Depress stick and try to flip block into cap. Practice will make you a champ.

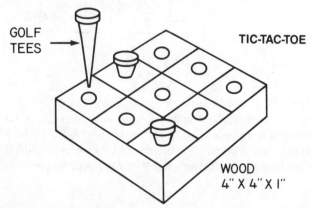

TIC-TAC-TOE

Cut block of wood 4-by-4-by-1-inch. Mark evenly spaced holes and drill. Paint golf tees — 5 of one color for "X" and 5 of another color for "O." Play as in pencil and paper tick-tack-toe.

Line Games

GRAND CENTRAL STATION

Line up two rows of chairs or benches facing each other about 30 inches apart. Some Cub Scouts sit on benches and others stand between them. When you shout, "Change for (name of city)," everyone must change seats. Those standing try to get a seat. When you shout, "Grand Central Station — everybody transfer!" the Cub Scouts must go out the front end of the benches, run around to the back, and then try to get a seat.

CLUB SNATCH
(Or Steal the Bacon)

Form two lines facing each other about 25 feet apart. Place an Indian club, bowling pin, or bean bag in the center. Count off the Cub Scouts in each line from opposite directions. The leader calls out a number and the opponents with that number run to the center. The object of the game is for a Cub Scout to snatch the club and get back to his side without being tagged by the one with the same number from the other side. Score two points if a player brings the club back without being tagged. Score one point for the opposing team if the snatcher is tagged.

FIREMAN PACK
MEETING GAME

Choose one Cub Scout to be the Fire Chief. Line up the dens on a starting line 30 feet from the goal line. Have the Fire Chief stand in the middle and call, "Fire, fire, Station No._____!" The den with that number runs to the opposite goal line and back. The first player to touch the Fire Chief's hand trades places with him for the next game. On the call, "Fire, fire, general alarm!" everyone runs.

GHOST TRAIN

Divide the group into equal teams and line them up single file. (Several teams can play). Place a chair approximately 15 feet in front of each group. The first Cub Scout in each team is the Ghost and wears a sheet over his head. Other members of the team hook on by grasping the waist of the person in front of them. On signal, all start walking quickly straight ahead, around the chair and back. The second person in each line guides his Ghost, who can't see. The first group to return to its original position wins. If a team breaks into a run, it is disqualified.

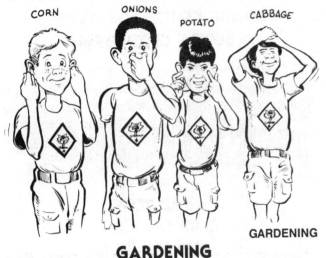

GARDENING

Divide the group into two parallel lines about 10 feet apart. A leader stands at the head to call out the names of vegetables. When "corn" is called, the Cub Scouts are to grasp their ears. For "onions" they hold their noses; for "potatoes" they point to their eyes; for "cabbage" they hold their heads. Another leader referees to see which line responds first with the desired action. The first line to have all its members perform the correct action scores a point. The winner is the line that scores 10 points first.

FOX AND CHICKENS

Line up the group in single file. Each Cub Scout holds the waist of the player in front of him. The boy at the head of the line is called the Mother Hen and the others are Chicks. Another Cub Scout — the Fox — stands in front of the line. On signal, the Fox starts around the line, trying to catch the last Chick. The Mother Hen flaps her wings and follows the Fox to prevent him from catching the Chick. The others turn away from the Fox as they keep in line with their leader. If the last Chick is caught, he falls in behind the Fox, and the game continues until all Chicks are caught.

LINK PASS

Divide the Cub Scouts into two lines facing each other. They lock elbows with those next to them in their line. Place 10 pebbles on the floor near the first player in each line. On signal, those two each pick up a pebble and pass it to the next player in line, who passes it on. The players' arms must remain linked throughout the game. If a Cub Scout drops a pebble, he must retrieve it without breaking the chain. The first player may start another pebble right away. The first line to pass the 10 pebbles wins.

I.D. GAME

This game will help Cub Scouts learn the names of trees and shrubs. In advance, collect seven to 10 small samples of leaves, flowers, or seeds from trees and bushes. Form two equal teams and line them up facing each other about 30 feet apart. Put the plant samples in a row on the ground between the two teams. The teams count off separately so each player has a number. The leader calls out the name of a tree or shrub and then calls a number. The player on each team whose number is called races to the samples and tries to find the correct one. Each player who is successful earns two points for his team. Choosing the wrong sample deducts two points from the team's score.

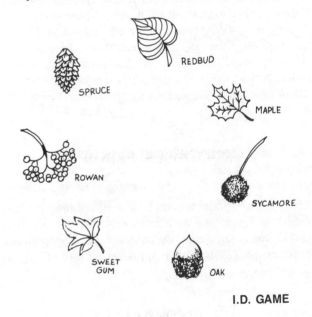

I.D. GAME

SMILE

Two teams line up facing each other about 10 feet apart. One team is Heads, the other is Tails. Flip a coin and call it. If "heads" comes up, that team laughs and smiles while the other team keeps a sober face. Any players who laugh at the wrong time switch teams. Then flip the coin again.

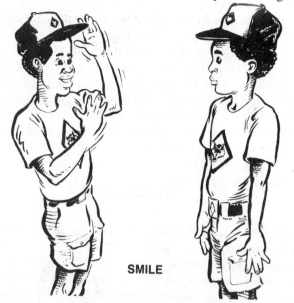

SMILE

Quiet Den Games

ART CONSEQUENCES

Give each boy a pencil and paper and have him draw the head of a man, woman, or child. After he draws the head, he folds the paper so that only the neck shows. Each paper is passed on to the next player, who draws the shoulders, folds the paper, and passes it on. This continues, with others adding the waist, hips, legs, and feet. When the drawings are finished, they are opened and passed around so all can see.

TOOTHPICK PICKUP

Arrange Cub Scouts around a table or kneeling in a circle on the floor. Give each a saucer with two toothpicks and 12 beans. On signal, the contest is on to see who can be the first to lift out five beans using the toothpicks like chopsticks.

BLOWBALL

Seat the Cub Scouts at a table small enough so they are close together. Put a table tennis ball in the center of the table. On signal, the players, with their chins on the table and their hands behind them, try to blow the ball away from their side of the table. If the ball falls on the floor, return it to the center of the table and continue.

CHANGE CARS

Prepare for the game by fastening a picture of different types of automobiles to the back of each chair. Have each Cub Scout check the name on his chair and sit down. One player is It and stands in the center of the circle of chairs. When the names of two cars are called, the boys in these chairs try to exchange seats while It tries to get a chair for himself. The boy left without a chair becomes It.

Variation: Use different types of transportation, such as car, plane, boat, train, or names of animals.

BOTTLE CLOTHESPIN

Place a narrow-mouth jar upright on the floor. Give each Cub Scout in turn 10 clothespins and have him stand over the bottle. He holds the pins at eye level and tries to drop them one at a time into the bottle. Keep score on the number of pins each boy drops into the bottle.

CARD TOSS

Place a hat on the floor about 6 feet from a chair. Have each Cub Scout in turn sit in the chair, take a deck of playing cards, and toss them one at a time into the hat. It looks easy, but if a beginner gets more than five cards in the hat on his first try, he is doing well.

ELECTRIC SQUEEZE

Cub Scouts hold hands in a circle, with It in the center. One player starts the "shock" by squeezing the hand of one of the Cub Scouts next to him. That player passes it on. The shock may move in either direction. It watches the faces and hands of the players, trying to spot the location of the shock. When he guesses correctly, the player caught becomes It.

COOTIE

Cover a small cube with plain paper and write one of the following letters on each side: A for antenna, B for body, T for tail, L for leg, H for head, E for eye. Give each player a pencil and paper. Everyone gets a turn at shaking the cube. If a Cub Scout shakes a B he draws a body on his paper. He may continue as long as he can add to the "cootie" he is drawing. If he shakes a letter for a part that cannot be added yet or one he has already completed, he loses the cube to the next player. No one may begin drawing until he shakes a B. The first player to draw a complete cootie (one body, one head, one tail, two antennae, two eyes and six legs) wins.

CRAZY ARTIST

Divide the den into two teams for a relay drawing contest. Provide each team with a piece of crayon or a marking pen. Place two large pieces of paper or poster board on a wall or table across the room. The object of the game is for each team to draw a house, with each Cub Scout drawing no more than two straight lines. A player from each team runs to the paper, draws his two lines, then returns and hands the chalk to the next player in line. The team with the best looking house wins.

FIVE DOTS

Give each Cub Scout a paper and pencil and ask them to place five dots on the paper wherever he wishes. Players exchange papers and try to fit a drawing of a person into the dots, with the head at one dot, the hands at two, and the feet at the other two dots.

WIGGLES

Give each Cub Scout a piece of paper and pencil and ask him to draw a wavy or zigzag line. They exchange papers and make the line into a picture. The one with the funniest or best picture is the winner.

INITIALS

The den chief or den leader is the questioner and asks a question of each Cub Scout in turn. The player must answer in two words that begin with his initials. For example: "What is your favorite snack?" Chuck Parker might answer "Cherry pie"; Jimmy Davis might answer "Juicy donuts." A player who answers incorrectly or not at all is out of the game. The funnier the answers the better. To make the game easier, ask for one-word answers, using the initial of the first name.

GRAB IT

Arrange the den in a circle on the floor. In the center, place one less clothespin than the number of boys. One of the boys is selected as storyteller. He starts a story and whenever he says the word "and," all the players grab for a clothespin. Everyone except the boy who was too late gets a point. Change storytellers so all have a chance.

LOG CABIN ON A POP BOTTLE

Divide Cub Scouts into two groups. Give each Cub Scout 10 flat toothpicks. Alternating between teams, players place a toothpick, one at a time, across the top of the bottle until the stack falls. That player's team must take the toothpicks which were knocked off. The first team to get rid of all its toothpicks wins.

LOG CABIN ON
A POP BOTTLE

BIRD, BEAST, OR FISH

Cub Scouts are arranged in a circle with a leader in the center. The leader calls a category bird, beast, or fish to anyone in the circle. That player must give a specific species of that category before the leader counts to 10. When one of the players fails to name the required bird, beast or fish, he becomes the leader. A player may not use a name of bird, beast, or fish that has been used by any other person until a new leader begins a new game. For variety, you may call, "Fin, Fur, or Feathers." It is great fun to stretch out the words, "F-f-f — f-f-in," etc.

DETECTIVES

Two Cub Scouts are chosen to be Detectives and are sent out of the room. The others select an object which the Detectives will try to discover. This may be a piece of furniture, a book, a button on someone's clothing, or anything else. The Detectives are called back in and try to solve the mystery by asking questions. They can ask each of the other players three questions only. Suggest that they try to find the location first, then identify the object.

INDOOR SKI RACE

TRAVELERS

The leader tells the Cub Scouts that they're going on an imaginary trip. Each player can go anywhere he wishes, but he must use only words beginning with the first letter of the name of the place he is going. The leader starts the game by asking one of the players where he is going. The reply might be "San Francisco." What are you going to do there?" asks the leader. "Sing silly songs" or "Slurp sundaes" would be correct answers. A player going to Paris might paint palaces, or one going to Chicago could chase cars. Answers may be two or three words and players should be given a reasonable time to think of them.

REVERSE

The leader calls out instructions to the group, such as "Hold your left ear with your right hand." All do this. The leader calls out another instruction such as "Rub your stomach with your left hand and pat the top of your head with your right hand." In the midst of the instructions, the leader calls out, "Reverse," and the Cub Scouts must switch hands and reverse their actions.

INDOOR SKI RACE

Line up the den along a starting line and give each boy one sheet of newspaper. On signal, each tears his sheet in half, places one piece under each foot, and "skis" to a goal line. This game must be played on a smooth floor so the "skis" will not tear.

RHYMING WORDS

Cub Scouts sit in a circle. The first player says a one- or two-syllable word. The next boy must say a word that rhymes, and so on around the group. Example: Pan, can, tan, man, fan. When a Cub Scout cannot think of a rhyming word, one point is scored against him, but he starts the game over with a new word. When any player has three points scored again him, he is out of the game.

ALPHABET GAME

Give each Cub Scout seated at a table a sheet of colored paper, a toothpick, and 2 tablespoons of alphabet macaroni. The toothpicks are used to push the macaroni letters quickly into place on the colored paper. On signal, the players are to begin making three letter words. The one who makes the most words in a given time is the winner. (Sort the letters in advance so that all players have the same chance.)

ZOO

In advance, hide several peanuts in the room. Divide the den into groups of three or four and give each group the name of some animal. One member of each group is chosen to be the Keeper. The Cub Scouts start to hunt for the peanuts. When a player finds one he must not pick it up. Instead he stands still and makes a noise like the animal his group represents. He keeps on barking or growling until the Keeper for his group comes and picks up the peanut. The team with the most peanuts at the end of a designated time wins.

BUZZ-FIZZ

In turn, Cub Scouts begin counting. When a player comes to five or any number with a five in it, he says, "Buzz." When a player comes to seven or a number with seven in it, he says, "Fizz." For example: 1, 2, 3, 4, buzz, 6, fizz, 8, and so on; 55 would be "buzz buzz"; 57 would be "buzz fizz." When a player misses, he drops out and the next player starts over at 1.

WHAT'S IN THE BAG?

On eight paper sacks print one letter of the words *Boys' Life*. Place an object that begins with that letter in the appropriate sack. String up the sacks so they spell out the words. Give each Cub Scout a card with the words *Boys' Life* printed vertically so he can write down what he thinks is in each bag after he feels the objects without looking at them. Give prizes to those who get the most correct answers.

CELEBRITIES

From newspapers or magazines cut pictures of famous athletes, statesmen, performers, etc. and paste them on numbered cards for the boys to guess their names. The player who identifies the largest number wins a prize. This game can be varied by using pictures of wildlife or any other category.

CRAZYBONE

The idea of this game is to discover how many objects each Cub Scout can identify by touching them with his elbow. Gather together in advance such things as an eraser, a ring, a penny, a pencil, a piece of sandpaper, a grape, a hairpin, etc. Let none of the players see them in advance. Have each player roll up his sleeve and place his arm on the back of his chair. Then move behind and hold one of the objects against their elbows, one at a time, and let them all write down what they think the object is. The Cub Scout with the most correct answer wins.

KIM'S GAME

Arrange 20 objects in an orderly fashion on a tray or table. Keep the objects covered until the game begins. Have the players study the objects silently for 60 seconds. Then the objects are again covered and the Cub Scouts move to another part of the room to write down the names of as many objects as they can remember. The one who has the longest correct list wins.

THINK FAST

Divide den into two groups. Ask the following questions and, after each, score a point for the side that gives the correct answer first.

What letter is a beverage? (T)

What letter is a bird? (J)

What letter is a vegetable? (P)

What letter is a question? (Y)

What letter is a body of water? (C)

What letter means a debt? (O)

CUB SCOUT UNIFORM GAME

When preparing for a den uniform inspection, have the denner slip in with his uniform rearranged in the following manner and ask the other Cub Scouts to tell what is wrong.

1. Cap on backwards.
2. Campaign button on cap.
3. Wearing den chief cord.
4. Service star on neckerchief.
5. Neckerchief twisted into a roll.
6. Neckerchief tied around the neck.
7. Belt buckle worn to one side.
8. One sleeve rolled up.
9. Button unbuttoned.
10. Pocket turned inside out.

CALENDAR PITCH

Place one page from a large calendar on the floor as the target. Each player tosses three checkers or bottle caps from a distance of 5 to 6 feet and totals his score according to the numbers on which his checkers land. Markers on a line don't count. Winning score may be 75 points or more. For added excitement, score double points for holidays, such as 50 points for December 25, or 28 points for February 14.

SENSORY TEST

Place eight numbered dishes around the room. Each dish is covered by a paper napkin in which several holes have been punched. In the dishes are things like cloves, grated orange rind, peppermint extract, cinnamon, pineapple, coffee, etc. Each Cub Scout is given a paper and pencil and tries to identify the contents of the covered dishes by smelling them.

CHECKER HOCKEY

CHECKER HOCKEY

Each Cub Scout's "hockey team" of four checkers is lined up horizontally on a checker board, facing the other team with an empty row between. One red checker carries the "puck" (a button or other small object that can sit on a checker). A goal is scored by advancing the puck to the opponent's back row. The puck carrier may go one square at a time in any direction, and it may jump any piece. The opponent tries to jump the checker carrying the puck. When he does, he takes over the puck and moves one more space in any direction, but he may not make a jump move. The puck carrier may not move into any of the four corner squares.

MARBLE CHOP SUEY

Put six marbles in a small dish. The Cub Scouts use two pencils as chopsticks, and using only one hand, try to move the marbles into a second dish. This is a little easier if they use pencils with eraser tips.

HANUKKAH PEANUT HUNT

Use 20 peanuts. On four of them mark "H"; on the others, four each of "A", "N", "U", and "K." Hide these peanuts, plus many other unmarked peanuts, around the play area. On signal, Cub Scouts start hunting. After about 10 minutes, stop the hunt and score as follows: 10 points for the most peanuts found; 5 points for each lettered peanut found; and 20 points for anyone who can spell out "Hanukkah" with his peanuts.

BLAST OFF

One Cub Scout is Mission Control. The others are given the names of planets and are seated around the room. Mission Control walks around the room, calling out the names of various planets. When his planet is named, a player gets up and follows Mission Control. When most of the boys are walking, Mission Control calls, "Blast off!" and all players, including those still sitting, must find a new seat. The player left standing is the new Mission Control.

JUGGLER TOSS

Pair off the Cub Scouts and divide them into two lines. Have pairs stand about 5 feet apart in two lines facing each other. Each player has a rubber ball or orange. They toss their balls simultaneously. Score one point for the two-boy team when both make the catch. After each catch, they step back one pace and repeat. Winning pair is the one with the most points after a set time limit.

RING TOSS

Clamp clothespins around the rim of a bucket or wastebasket. From 10 feet away, Cub Scouts try to toss jar rings over the clothespins.

DO THIS, DO THAT

Cub Scouts stand in a line several feet behind a goal line. The den chief or den leader stands in front of the den and performs certain movements, preceding each with "Do this" or "Do that." All movements following the order, "Do this," must immediately be copied by the players. They must not move when the leader says, "Do that." A player who makes a mistake moves backward one step. Continue for a predetermined length of time. The winner is the player nearest the goal line.

LOOK SHARP

Divide the group into two teams which stand in lines facing each other. Cub Scouts are given 1 minute to observe their partners on the opposite team. On signal, they turn their backs and each player marks three changes in his attire. He may undo a button, alter the position of a badge, change neckerchief slide with a neighbor, etc. At the next signal, all turn to face their partners again and try to determine what changes have been made. Each change correctly identified counts one point. Team with the most points wins.

NOAH'S ARK

Write the names of animals on cards—two cards for each animal. If there is an odd number of Cub Scouts, write one animal's name on three cards. There should be a card for every player. Shuffle the cards and hand them out. Each player reads his card to himself but keeps his identity a secret. Collect the cards. On signal, each player begins acting out the sounds, shape, and typical movements of his animal, trying to attract his partner. There could be baying, croaking, screeching, strutting, flapping, and leaping. Talking is prohibited. Game ends when each player finds his partner.

PRINCE OF PILSEN

Cub Scouts line up facing the leader. They count off and remember their numbers. The leader says, "The Prince of Pilsen lost his hat. No. 5 (or any number) has it." The player whose number has been called immediately responds, "No, sir, not I, sir," before the leader can say, "No. 5, to the foot." If the leader beats the player, the player must go to the foot of the line, and the leader calls out another number. If the player beats the leader, the leader says, "Who then, sir?" and the player questioned gives any other number, except the number of the boy at the foot of the line. The game continues as long as desired. If any player calls the number of the player at the foot of the line by mistake, he automatically goes to the foot himself.

Physical Fitness Activities

Because many of these contests are tests of strength, coordination, and agility, the older, stronger boys will have a distinct advantage. For this reason, it is a good idea to try to match contestants by size and age, especially for the two-person contests like the first few listed here.

INDIAN LEG WRESTLE

Two Cub Scouts lie side by side on their backs with their heads in opposite directions. They hook right elbows. When the leader counts, "One," they raise their right legs and touch them together. At count "two" this is repeated. At "three" they hook their right knees and try to turn each other over. The player who is completely turned over is the loser.

HAND PUSH

Two Cub Scouts stand facing each other with their toes touching and their palms together at shoulder height. In this position each tries to push the other's hands until one is forced to step back. The player who forces his opponent backward is the winner.

FINGER BEND

Two Cub Scouts stand facing each other. They extend their arms over their heads and clasp each other's hands, interweaving the fingers. On signal, they back apart and bring their hands down. The stronger player will force the other to a kneeling position. The one who has to kneel is the loser.

GAME ROOSTERS

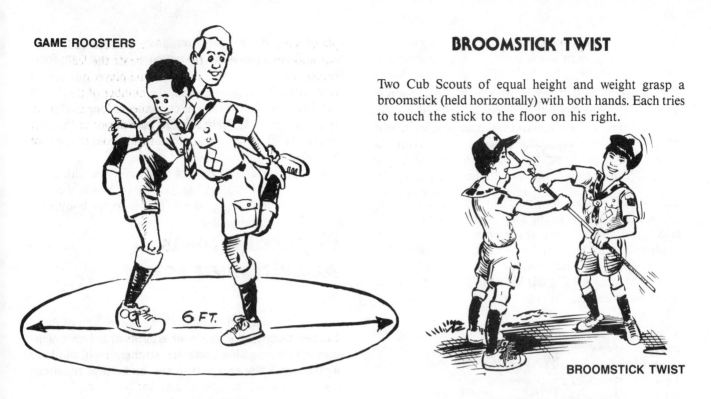

GAME ROOSTERS

Two Cub Scouts stand in a circle about 6 feet in diameter. Each holds his left foot with his right hand behind his back, and then grips his right arm with his left hand behind his back. On signal, they hop at each other, trying to force the other out of the circle or out of position. When a player lets go of his foot or arm or leaves the circle, he loses the contest.

ARM LOCK WRESTLE

Pair off the Cub Scouts according to height and weight. They sit on the floor, back to back, with their legs spread and arms locked at the elbows. On signal, each tries to pull his opponent over to the side so that his left arm or shoulder touches the floor.

COCKFIGHT

Two Cub Scouts hold their left ankle behind them with their left hand and keep their right arm close to their side. The arm must not be used to strike or shove. On signal, they try to upset each other by charging or shouldering, or try to force the other to drop his left foot. With a large number of players, a free-for-all may be held. The last player to remain standing wins.

BROOMSTICK TWIST

Two Cub Scouts of equal height and weight grasp a broomstick (held horizontally) with both hands. Each tries to touch the stick to the floor on his right.

BROOMSTICK TWIST

BROOMSTICK WRESTLE

Two Cub Scouts face each other, grasping a broomstick with their hands about 18 inches apart. On signal, each tries to cause the other to move his feet. The defeated player is the one who first takes a step or releases the stick.

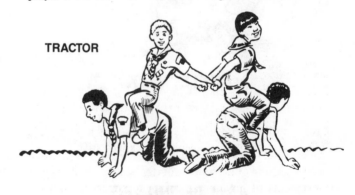

TRACTOR

TRACTOR

Two Cub Scouts, on their hands and knees and facing in opposite directions, are the "tractors." Other players straddle each tractor and, holding on with their legs, reach both hands back to grip the hands of their opponent. On signal, a tug-of-war begins.

CIRCLE HOP FIGHT

Draw a circle about 6 feet in diameter and stand two Cub Scouts inside. They face each other with their arms folded

Games   2-31

and one leg extended in front. On signal, they try to upset or force each other from the circle by using the extended leg. They may hook or lift with the leg, but must not touch their opponent with any other part of the body. Kicking or pushing with the uplifted leg is not permitted.

PILOT'S TEST

Use a stick about 3½ feet long. The Cub Scouts, one at a time, place one end of the stick on the ground and put both hands on top. Then the player puts his head on his hands and closes his eyes. Spin him around 10 times. He then tries to touch a target with the end of the stick. The target should be about 5 feet high and 10 to 15 feet from where he was spun.

ANKLE WALK

ANKLE WALK

Have each boy bend until he can grasp his ankles, then walk in a straight line, keeping his knees stiff.

ARM BEHIND LEG

Cub Scouts stand with their feet about 6 inches apart, bend their knees, swing their right forearm behind the right leg and then forward between their legs, then across in front of the right leg and touch the floor *outside* their right foot.

BALANCE WITH CLOSED EYES

Cub Scouts stand upright, placing their right foot in front of the left foot, and raise their arms sideward. With their eyes closed, they see how long they can maintain their balance in this position. Alternate the left and right foot forward.

CHINESE GETUP

Two Cub Scouts sit on the floor back to back with their arms locked. Without letting go, they try to stand erect. This is done by bringing the feet close to the body and pushing back against back.

DEEP BOW

Cub Scouts place both hands on the floor in front of their left foot and extend their right leg backward. They touch their head to the floor and then stand erect without losing balance. They reverse their feet and repeat the deep bow.

DIZZY

Cub Scouts hold their left ankle in back of their right leg with their right hand. Then they hop, making three turns in place without losing their balance. Then they reverse position and try hopping on the left leg.

CROSSING THE CHASM

Use a pipe or rope about 10 feet long, fastened high enough so that when players hang by their hands their feet will not touch the ground. Divide Cub Scouts into two teams, which start stand at opposite ends of the pipe or rope. On signal, the first player of each team starts "walking" across the pipe, hand over hand, passing the other player on route. When a player drops off at the other end, the next boy starts across. The first side to cross the chasm wins.

CUT THE CANE

A Cub Scout holds one end of a cane in his right hand, with the other end resting on the floor. He releases the cane, swings his right leg over the top of the cane, and grasps it again with his right hand without allowing the cane to fall. Repeat the stunt with left hand and left leg.

FROG HANDSTAND

Cub Scouts squat and place their hands flat on the ground between their legs. They lean forward slowly, shifting the weight of their bodies onto their hands and elbows until their feet swing free of the ground. They should keep their heads up and point their toes backward. (This is the first step in learning the handstand).

FROG HANDSTAND

FITNESS CIRCLE GAME

Form a circle as large as the room permits with all Cub Scouts facing the same direction. Give instructions for various activities as follows:

1. Start walking in a circle, and keep walking between these exercises.

2. Start hopping.

3. Make yourself as small as possible and continue walking.

4. Make yourself as tall as possible and continue walking. Now reach your hands high over your heads.

5. Bend your knees slightly, grasp your ankles, and continue walking.

6. Walk as if the heel of one foot and the toes of the other were sore.

7. Walk stiff-legged.

8. Squat down and jump forward from that position.

9. Walk on hands and one foot with the other leg held high, imitating a dog with a lame foot.

10. Walk forward at a rapid pace (don't run) while swinging the arms vigorously.

11. Take giant steps.

12. Walk forward, raising your knees as high as possible with each step.

13. Run, lifting your knees high.

14. Walk on your hands and feet.

ANKLE HOP

Tell Cub Scouts to stand erect and then take a squat position, grasp the ankles, and hop forward four times without breaking the ankle grip. They turn around and repeat, hopping back to their original places.

FROG HOP

Cub Scouts take a squat position, feet pointing slightly outward. They place their hands on the floor with the elbows slightly bent, arms between the knees. Then they take short hops by putting their hands just ahead of their feet and bringing their feet up to their hands.

HOOK ON

Send four Cub Scouts to the far side of the play area. The others line up along a wall or starting line. On signal, they rush at the four and try to hook onto one of them. Anyone who succeeds in grabbing the waist of one of the four tries to prevent anyone else from hooking on. But if someone does, then he is part of the chain. When all have finally hooked on, the line with the fewest boys wins. Four from that line become the next loose players.

HOP AND TURN

Cub Scouts hop in the air, make a half turn to the right, and land lightly on their starting place. They can vary the stunt by making a full turn. Repeat by turning the other direction.

HOPPING—CROSS FEET

Cub Scouts try to hop up on both feet, cross the right foot in front of the left, and land on their toes with heels together. Then they reverse feet.

HUMAN ROCKER

Cub Scouts lie face downward, grasp their ankles, and rock their bodies backward and forward on their thighs and chests.

INDIAN HAND WRESTLE

INDIAN HAND WRESTLE

Two Cub Scouts stand facing in opposite directions with the sides of their right feet touching each other. They clasp their right hands directly over the center of their feet. On signal, the wrestlers try to throw each other off balance by pushing, pulling, or swinging their hands. A player loses if either foot moves.

KNEE DIP

Cub Scouts stand on one foot and grasp the other foot behind their backs with the opposite hand. They try to touch the bent knee to the floor and return to a standing position without losing balance.

KNEEL

Cub Scouts try to kneel on both knees and return to standing position with arms folded behind their backs. They must not move their feet or lose balance.

NOVELTY WALK

Cub Scouts walk by swinging their right foot behind their left leg and then moving it as far forward as possible on the left side. Then they take the same type of step forward with the left foot and continue to walk in this manner.

PEPPER GRINDER

Have the Cub Scouts stretch out on the floor and then raise themselves on one hand. They try to walk in a complete circle around the supporting hand, keeping their bodies in a straight line.

PICKING UP A MATCHBOX

Each Cub Scout puts a broomstick behind his knees, brings his arms behind it, places his hands on the ground in front of him and then picks up a match box (standing on end) in his teeth from this position.

PULL-UP

Two opponents sit on the ground facing each other, with the soles of their feet touching. They both grasp a broom handle or bat with both hands. On signal, each tries to pull the other off the ground or make him break his hold.

PULL-UP

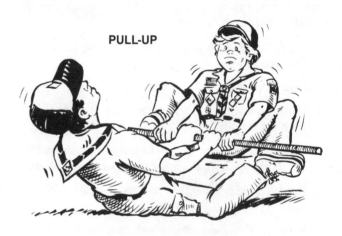

BICYCLE RIDE

Players lie flat on their backs and raise their feet as high as possible. Then, placing the hands under the hips, they support their body weight on the shoulders and elbows. From this position they pump feet as if pedalling a bicycle.

CRAB WALK

From a squat position the boys reach backward and put their hands on the floor without sitting down. They walk forward, keeping their heads and body in a straight line.

SKIN THE SNAKE

The Cub Scouts line up single file. Each stoops over and places his right hand between his legs and with his left hand grasps the right hand of the player in front of him. When all are ready, the last player in line lies on his back while the line moves back over him. The next player then lies down and so on until everyone is lying down. The last one to lie down rises to his feet and walks forward, each following in turn, until all are back in original place.

SIT AND TOUCH

Cub Scouts sit in chairs and bend sideways to the right and touch the floor with both hands. They return to an erect position and bend toward the left. They repeat up to eight times, making the action continuous.

STORK STAND

Everyone stands with hands on hips, placing one foot against the inside of the opposite knee while bending the raised knee outward. He then counts to 10 without moving from his place.

NO HANDS

Cub Scouts fold their arms, lie down on the floor, and try to get up without using their elbows or hands.

BALANCE

Cub Scouts try to walk on bricks, stones, or blocks of wood while balancing a staff horizontally on their heads. Add a simple act of dexterity such as throwing a ball into the air and catching it.

SQUAT JUMP

Cub Scout does a full squat with his weight on his toes and, from this position, jumps forward several times. Then stand and walk. Alternate these squatting, jumping, and walking actions.

SEAL WALK

Cub Scouts put their weight on their hands and toes, keeping backs flat, and move forward by walking with their hands.

MEASURING WORM

Each Cub Scout supports his body on his hands and feet with his legs extended backward. Keeping his hands in place and his knees stiff, he walks on his toes with short steps until his feet are near his hands. Then, without moving his feet, he walks forward on his hands with short steps until his original position is attained. He continues walking alternately with feet and hands.

HEEL CLICK

Cub Scouts line up and stand with their feet apart. They jump upward, strike their heels together, and land lightly with their feet apart.

SPARROW FIGHT

Establish a 6-foot circle. Standing in the circle, two Cub Scouts bend forward and grasp their ankles with their hands. Each then tries to upset his opponent or shoulder him from the circle.

STORK WRESTLING

Two Cub Scouts face each other standing on one foot and holding their left ankles with their left hands. They then clasp their right hands and try to push or pull their opponent off balance or cause him to let go of his ankle.

THREAD THE NEEDLE

Cub Scouts clasp their hands in front of their bodies. They bend forward and step through the loop formed by their arms with right foot, then left foot. They reverse the action by stepping backward with left foot, then right, keeping the hands clasped. If the hands are clasped near the floor, the action is easier to perform.

HAWK DIVE

In **shuttle relays,** each team is numbered off. The even numbers line up in file formation with Cub Scout No. 2 in front. The odd-numbered Cub Scouts do likewise, with No. 1 in front. Files are facing each other at opposite ends of the relay course. On the signal to begin, Cub Scout No. 1 runs and hands off the ball or beanbag or whatever game equipment is necessary to Cub Scout No. 2, then takes his place at the end of No. 2's line. Cub Scout No. 2 runs and gives No. 3 the ball or whatever and takes his place at the end of No. 3's line. This continues until all Cub Scouts are back at their original places.

HAWK DIVE

The Cub Scouts separate from each other to give themselves plenty of room. They kneel on one leg with the other leg stretched back, keeping the foot off the floor. They stretch both arms sideways, using them for balance. They bend forward slowly trying to touch their noses to the floor. Then they return to the starting position without letting any part of the body touch the floor except the leg they are kneeling on.

UNDER THE BROOM

Build two stacks of books about 3 feet high and 3 feet apart. Lay a broom across them. Each Cub Scout crawls under the broomstick and goes to the end of the line. When all have done that, remove two or three books to lower the broom and have the players try that. Keep removing more books each round.

See *Wolf Achievement 1* and *Bear Achievement 16* for additional fitness activities.

Relays and Races

Four types of relays are used in playing Cub Scout games.

In **file relays,** Cub Scouts on each team line up one behind the other. Cub Scout No. 1 goes forward to the goal line and returns to his team, tagging Cub Scout No. 2. This continues until all have had a turn. The team finishing first is the winner.

In **partner relays,** each Cub Scout has a partner. Teams consist of an equal number of partners. The partners stand side-by-side in file formation. In the relay the first set of partners in each team goes forward to the goal line in whatever manner prescribed by the game, returns to its team, and tags off the next set of partners.

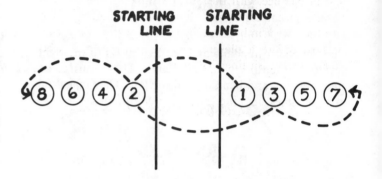

SHUTTLE RELAYS

Tagging off is a variation of the file relay. Instead of tagging the next teammate in line, a returning runner goes to the end of the line and "passes the tag" by touching the shoulder of the person in front of him, who in turn taps the next person. When the Cub Scout at the front of the line receives his tap on the shoulder, then he heads for the goal line.

ANTELOPE RACE

Line up the dens on a starting line. On signal, the boys run in single file, each with one hand holding the belt of the player ahead of him, to a point 50 yards away, make a left turn, and run back to the starting point. If anyone falls down or breaks apart from his group, he disqualifies his team.

BAGGAGE-CAR RELAY

Line up the dens for a relay. Each den has a suitcase filled with the following old clothing: a hat, a pair of adult trousers, a large shirt, and a man's jacket or overcoat. On signal, the first boy on each team races with the suitcase to the center of the floor, dons the clothing, and hurries back with the empty suitcase to the starting point. There he removes the clothing and repacks it in the suitcase. The second boy repeats these actions, and so on until all have finished. The first den through is the winner.

BALANCE RACE

Establish a starting line and a finishing line. Line up Cub Scouts on the starting line, each with a broomstick or long dowel balanced on his right forefinger. The stick may be held in balance with the other hand until the starting signal is given. On signal, all advance to the finish line with their stick in balance. If the stick drops, it must be replaced before a player can continue. The one who reaches the finish line first wins.

BALLOON-BATTING RELAY

This game may be played by two or more teams. Arrange teams in parallel lines with teammates spaced about 15 feet apart. On signal, the first player on each team bats the balloon with either hand toward his next teammate, who bats it to the next, and so on until the balloon reaches the finish line. If the balloon touches the ground, it must be brought back to the starting line and the team must begin again.

BEANBAG RELAY

Divide each team in half, putting one-half on opposite sides of the room. The first Cub Scout on the first side throws a beanbag to his first teammate on the other side, who holds the bag until the thrower has run up and tagged him. Then he in turn throws the bag to the second player on his team on the other side of the room, who holds the bag until he is tagged, etc., until all have had a turn. The thrower moves to the end of the line after he has tagged his man. The first team with players in reversed position wins.

BEAN AND STRAW RELAY

Line up the dens relay race fashion. Using a drinking straw, the first Cub Scout in each line picks up a bean by suction, carries it across the room, and deposits it in a bowl or cup. The first team to have all players succeed in carrying a bean wins.

BEAN AND KNIFE RELAY

Each relay team has a cup of dried beans and a table knife. In turn, each team member puts as many beans on the knife as he can and carries them to a given point and

BEAN AND KNIFE RELAY

deposits them in another cup. He then returns and hands the knife to the next Cub Scout in line. The team moving the largest number of beans wins the relay. *This is not a speed event.*

BIG BLOW

Prepare a paper cone for each den. Put a 30-foot string through the cone, tie each end to the back of a chair, and pull it tight. Line up the dens for a relay. On signal, the first boy in each den blows his cone along the string. (For best results, he should keep his head under the string.) When the cone reaches the end, he slides it back for the next teammate.

BUNDLE RELAY

The first Cub Scout on each relay team has a ball of twine or string. On signal, he passes it to his neighbor, but holds on to the end of the string. The ball is passed from player to player, unrolling as it goes. When it arrives at the back of the line, it is passed up the line behind the backs of the players until it reaches the first player again. The first team to "wrap itself into a bundle" is the winner. A sequel to the relay is unwrapping the bundle by passing the ball back and winding it up as it goes.

BUCKET BRIGADE RELAY

Line up two or more teams for a relay. Provide each team with two buckets—one empty and the other half full of water. Place the full buckets at the goal line. On signal, the first boy runs to the goal line, carrying the empty bucket, pours the water from the full bucket into the empty bucket, leaves the empty bucket there, and carries the full bucket back to his team. The next player carries the full bucket, transfers the water, and returns with the empty bucket. This continues until all team members have carried both an empty and full bucket. Team finishing first is the winner.

CASTING RELAY

Each Cub Scout in turn casts a fishing plug at a target. As soon as he scores a hit, he gives the rod to the player behind him and goes to the rear position on his team. The team back in its original order first wins.

Variation: Use boy/adult pairs on the teams, or have an adults-only relay.

CATERPILLAR RACE

Line up groups in single file. The first Cub Scout in each line places his hands on the ground. Each teammate behind him bends forward and grasps the ankles of the

player in front of him. On signal, the columns move forward in this position. When the last player in the column crosses the finish line the team has completed the race, provided that their line is still intact. The first team to complete the race wins.

CHARIOT RACE

Divide into teams of five. Designate a starting line and finish line 20 yards apart. Set a neckerchief up, tepee style, for each team halfway between the start and finish. Have each team form a chariot in this manner: The front pair of Horses clasp inside hands. The rear pair clasp inside hands and hold onto the belts of the front Horses with their outside hands. The Driver holds onto the belts of the rear Horses. On signal, they race towards the finish line. As they pass over their neckerchief, the Driver picks it up with his teeth without releasing his grip with either hand. The first team to cross the finish line without breaking any grips is the winner.

CHARIOT RACE

CENTIPEDE

Line up teams of 8, 12, or 16. Have the first four Cub Scouts on each team straddle a broomstick with their left hands grasping the stick. On signal, they run to a designated line, return, and give the stick to the next four players in their line. If any player releases his hold on the stick, he must regain it before his team may progress further. The first team through wins.

CLOTHESPIN RELAY

Give the first Cub Scout on each team five clothespins. On signal, the first player attaches a clothespin to the end of each finger on the second player's left hand. When all five pins are on, the second player takes the pins off one at a time and puts them on the fingers of the third player's left hand. This continues until the last player has the five pins on his hand. The team finishing first wins.

CRAB RELAY

Have the first Cub Scout in each line sit on the floor with his back to the finish line. On signal, he walks backward on his hands and feet with his body parallel to the floor. When he reaches the other end of the room he stands up, runs back, and touches off the next player, who repeats the action. The first team to finish wins.

BAREFOOT MARBLE RACE

The Cub Scouts remove their shoes and socks. Place two marbles on the starting line in front of each team. On signal, the first player on each team grasps a marble with the toes of each foot and walks to the finish line. When he reaches the other end of the room he picks up the marbles and runs back to give them to the next player in line, who repeats the action. The first team to finish wins.

DUTCH-SHOE RELAY

Provide each team with two shoeboxes. On signal, each Cub Scout in turn places his feet in the boxes and shuffles up to a goal line and back to the starting point where the next player repeats the action.

DUTCH-SHOE RELAY

GUM-GLOVE RELAY

Divide group into two teams and ask them to line up, facing each other. The first person on each team is given a paper bag which contains individual sticks of wrapped chewing gum and a pair of large work gloves. He must open the bag, put on the gloves, pull out a stick of gum, unwrap it, and put it in his mouth. As he starts chewing the gum, he removes the gloves, places them in the bag, closes the bag, and passes it to the next person, who repeats the action. The first team to finish wins.

SEED-PLANTING RELAY

In turn, each boy follows a line drawn on the floor by placing the heel of one foot against the toe of the other. About every 3 feet he must stop and place a seed in a small mouthed jar set about 1½ feet on each side of the line. When he reaches the end, he runs back and touches off the next person, who plants his seeds in the same manner.

THREE-LEGGED RACE

Run this contest on either an individual or team basis. Tie a boy's left leg to an adult's right leg. On signal, they make their way to the turning line and back again. The first team to complete the course wins.

WASH ON THE LINE

Stretch a clothesline 20 feet from the starting line. Divide into relay teams. Give the first Cub Scout on each team three or four garments or pieces of cloth and five or six clothespins in a large shopping bag. The first player on each team races to the clothesline, pins up the garments, and runs back to the starting line. The second player races up and takes down the clothes and brings them back to the third player, who pins them up again, and so on. The first team to finish wins.

PASS THE LIFESAVERS

For this relay race each Cub Scout holds a drinking straw in his mouth. On signal, a Lifesaver is passed from one straw to the next down the line until the last player has it.

LEG TUNNEL RELAY

Line up the dens single file and have the Cub Scouts stand with their feet apart. The last one in each line crawls through from one end to the other and stands up with his feet apart. The players follow in rapid succession, each standing up when he has crawled through. The first team to be back in its original order wins.

LEG TUNNEL RELAY

PEANUT RACE

Have the Cub Scouts roll a peanut with their noses on the floor for a short distance. They must not touch the peanut with their hands. The one who rolls his peanut across the finish line first is the winner.

Variation: A penny may be used instead of the peanut.

PILOT RELAY

Divide group into teams of three. In each team, two Cub Scouts stand with their backs to the starting line and the third is between them facing forward. The elbows of the three should be interlocked. The middle player runs forward while the other two run backward. They race to a turning point, where they start back, this time with the middle boy running backward and the other two players running forward. The team to finish first wins.

BALLOON ON A SPOON RELAY

The first Cub Scout on each team has an inflated balloon balanced on a teaspoon. The object of the game is for the boys to hurry to a goal line about 25 feet away and back, carrying the balloon on the spoon. If the balloon falls off, it must be replaced before he can continue.

BALLOON BURST RELAY

Give each boy a balloon. On signal, the first Cub Scout on each team runs to a chair about 20 feet away, blows up his balloon and ties it, sits on the balloon to burst it, then returns to the starting line. The other players follow until all balloons are burst. First team finished wins.

WAY DOWN YONDER RELAY

Cub Scouts sit on the floor in two lines which face each other. A dish containing kernels of corn is placed in front and to the right of the players at the head of each line, and an empty dish is at the end of each line. Each player is given a teaspoon. On signal, the first player takes a kernel in his spoon, transfers it to his neighbor's spoon, and so on down the line. The first player may start another kernel down the line right away. As the end player receives the kernel and drops it in an empty dish, he yells, "Way down yonder!" Any kernel that is dropped must be replaced on the spoon by the person who dropped it before it can be passed along. The team which succeeds in getting all the kernels in the second dish is the winner.

WHEELBARROW RELAY

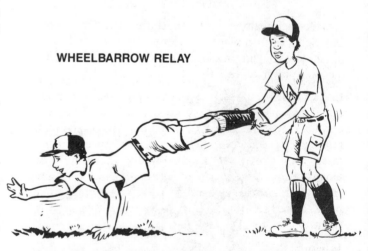

WHEELBARROW RELAY

Divide relay teams into pairs. One boy in each pair walks on his hands while the other holds his legs as they race to a turning line and back. The second pair repeats the action, and so on until all have raced.

WAGON TRAIN

WAGON TRAIN

Mark a circle 50 feet in diameter. Cub Scouts stand at intervals on the circle facing in a clockwise direction. They pretend to be pioneers racing for their lives from Indians. All run when the whistle blows. When one player is passed by another, he is captured and drops out. Sharp, unexpected blasts of a whistle signal an Indian attack, and all players reverse direction. Overly eager players may be caught unless they are really on their toes. Players pass on the outside and those captured sit in the center of the circle.

SNOW SHOVEL RELAY

A snow drift (pile of cotton balls or styrofoam packing "peanuts") is placed before each team, and a pie tin for each team is placed at a goal line about 20 feet away. The first Cub Scout on each team has a pancake turner. On signal, he scoops some of the "snow balls" on his "shovel" and hurries to the goal line, where he deposits the balls in the pie tin and races back to touch off his next teammate, who repeats the action. Players who drop snow along the route are not required to stop to pick it up. However, it must be gathered by the next players at some point, since the winning team must have all its snow in the tin.

Variation: Relay teams could carry a snowball (cotton ball) in a teaspoon to a goal line.

CRACKER EATING RELAY

Six to eight Cub Scouts line up on a line. Each is given six crackers. On a signal, they race to a mark about 20 yards away where they must eat the crackers, whistle a tune, and return to the starting line. Select a familiar tune to whistle so that competition will be fair. The first one back is the winner.

ROWING RELAY

Players on each team sit or kneel in a large cardboard box and propel themselves to the goal line and back by using two short broomsticks with rubber tips.

WITCH'S BREW RELAY

Teams line up 10 feet apart. Between the teams place a large ice-cream carton or box as a witch's caldron. Place two beanbags in the box, and give the first player on each team a beanbag. On signal, the first player in each team rushes to the caldron, exchanges his beanbag, places the new one on his head, and carries it back to the next player in line, who repeats the action. Hands may not be used while the beanbag is on the head. The first team to complete the exchange and line up in original positions yells, "Witch's brew!" and wins the relay.

RESCUE

Divide into teams. Each team picks one member as its "victim." The victim sits on a pile of newspapers about 12 feet from the team. On signal, the rescuers join 3-foot ropes with square knots to make a rope 15 to 20 feet long. One member casts the line to the victim and the team pulls him to safety. The victim rides on the newspapers, holding the rope with one hand, the newspaper with the other. Winner is the faster team.

EXPLOSION RELAY

At a goal line about 25 feet from each team is a stack of small paper sacks. Each Cub Scout in turn races to the stack, blows up a paper bag, bursts it with his hand, and races back to touch off the next player.

FUMBLE FINGERS RELAY

FUMBLE FINGERS RELAY

Each team has a pair of large canvas gloves or mittens. At a goal line is a fruit jar with a lid containing five toothpicks for each team. On signal, the first Cub Scout on each team races to the goal line, puts on the gloves, removes the lid, empties the jar, picks up the toothpicks and puts them back in the jar, and screws on the lid. He takes off the gloves and races back to hand them to the next player, who repeats the action.

BALLOON KICK RELAY

Give the first Cub Scout on each team an inflated balloon. On signal, the first boy kicks it across the room to a line and back to the second player, who repeats the action. The balloon may be touched only with the feet and legs. Continue until one team wins.

BALLOON KANGAROO JUMPING

Have Cub Scouts line up side by side, each with an inflated balloon between his knees. On signal, the boys hop to the other side of the room and back to the starting line. The

one finishing first wins. If anyone breaks his balloon, he is eliminated. If a balloon is dropped, it must be replaced between the knees before further progress can be made.

BALLOON SWEEPING RELAY

Arrange teams in parallel lines. Place an inflated balloon on the floor in front of each team. Give the first Cub Scout in each team a broom. On signal, they sweep the balloon to the turning line and back and hand the broom to the second player, who repeats this action.

BALLOON STEEPLECHASE

Lay out an obstacle course (indoors or outdoors)—the more obstacles the better. Use fences, trees, chairs, tables, etc. Give each Cub Scout an inflated balloon. On signal, the boys move to the first obstacle and begin to follow the course, bouncing their balloons in the air with their hands. If a balloon touches the ground, the player must repeat the previous obstacle. If a balloon breaks, the player gets a new one and continues.

IZZY DIZZY RELAY

Teams line up in relay formation. On signal, the first Cub Scout on each team runs forward to a line, puts one finger on the floor, and circles around the finger seven times. The finger must not leave the floor. When he has made seven turns, he staggers back and touches off the next player on his team. First team to finish wins. **Note:** Remove all hazards before starting.

BLIND HORSE RELAY

Each team lines up in double relay formation. Boys in one line are blindfolded as Blind Horses. The other line is the Drivers. Each team has a 4-foot rope with the ends tied together. On signal, the first Driver on each team slips the "reins" around the back of the neck and under the armpits of the first Horse and drives the Horse to a turning line and back to the starting line. He unbridles the Horse and hands the reins to the next Driver, who repeats the action with the next Horse. First team finished wins.

Tire Games

When selecting tires for these games as well as for use in obstacle courses, take time to examine the tires carefully. Some tires, especially steel-belted ones, may have sharp pieces of metal sticking up through the rubber. Don't use such tires because they may cause cuts and injuries.

TIRE SPRINT

Players line up at a starting line with tires ready to roll. On signal, they roll tires to the finish line by propelling them by hand.

ROLL FOR DISTANCE

Each Cub Scout rolls his tire as hard and fast as he can up to a stopping line where he must stop while the tire continues. Player whose tire rolls the farthest wins.

ROLL FOR DISTANCE

TIRE BOWLING

Milk cartons, tin cans, or plastic bottles are the pins, set up 20 to 30 feet from the "bowler." Roll a tire instead of a ball. Score as in bowling.

TIRE BOWLING

ROLL FOR ACCURACY

Same as roll for distance, except that tire is rolled at a target of two sticks set 3 to 4 feet apart about 20 feet from the stopping line.

MOVING TARGET

Cub Scouts take turns rolling a tire parallel to a line of other players 15 to 20 feet away who try to throw beanbags or balls through the rolling tire.

TIRE OBSTACLE RELAY

Place five tires on their sides in a row, all touching. Divide the Cub Scouts into two teams and station the teams in relay formation about 20 feet from each end of the row of tires. On signal, the first player for each team runs over the tires, stepping in each one. When they get past the last tire, they turn right and run back and touch the next player on their team. The first team finishing is the winner.

THROUGH THE TIRE RELAY

All Cub Scouts on two relay teams drop to hands and knees. The first player on each team sets up a tire. On signal, he goes through the tire head first, lets the tire fall to the ground and steps out of it. The next player sets up the tire and repeats. Continue until the last player on each team has finished.

BOA CONSTRICTOR

BOA CONSTRICTOR

Suspend four or five tires on ropes from a tree limb or horizontal bar about 3 feet off the ground and a foot apart. Cub Scouts must wiggle through the "boa constrictor." A race can be held by timing each boy. This is also a fine hazard for an obstacle race.

TIRE ROLLING RELAY

Form two teams and give the first Cub Scout of each team a tire. Place a stake or chair opposite each team on a turning line. On signal, the first player rolls the tire to the turning line, around the stake or chair, and back to his team.

TIRE TAG

Each Cub Scout, including It, has a tire that he must roll as he runs. A player is safe if he can balance astride his upright tire while resting both feet on it.

Water Games

Safety must be a primary concern when Cub Scouts are in and around water. Follow the Safe Swim Defense Plan described on pages 92–93 of the *Cub Scout Leader Book*.

PIRATE'S GOLD HUNT

This is a good game for non-swimmers. At least five pennies per boy (or ¾-inch iron washers painted gold) are scattered in shallow water. The Cub Scouts line up along the edge. On signal, players jump into water, duck under, and pick up one penny at a time. Each player (or den) has a home base to put the pennies. He brings one to his home base and then returns to find another one. The winning player (or den) is the one with the most "gold pieces."

ROPE THROW RESCUE

ROPE THROW RESCUE

Each den has a coil of rope or clothesline. Adults representing drowning persons are in the water. Each Cub Scout in turn throws the rope to a "drowning person," who grabs it and then lets go. The player recoils the rope and hands it to the next player. Repeat until all den members have cast successfully.

Variation: May be played on land, too.

EGG AND SPOON RACE

(For swimmers only) Cub Scouts line up in chest-deep water. Each has a spoon and a boiled egg. The egg is placed on this spoon, which is held between the teeth. On signal, players swim a short distance (about 15 feet) and return, keeping the egg on the spoon. If it falls off, the swimmer must stop and replace the egg before going on. This can also be a den relay race.

NAIL-DRIVING CONTEST

Each player has a hammer, five nails, and a piece of 2-by-4. Winner is the one who can drive the most nails underwater. Make sure nails will not go all the way through the wood.

UP AND UNDER

Dens line up in relay formation in waist-deep water. The first Cub Scout on each team is given a large ball. On signal, he passes the ball overhead to the second player, who passes it between his legs to the third, who passes it overhead, and so on to the end of the line. The last player runs to the head of the line and passes it as before. The first team back in its original order wins.

LEAPFROG
(For Swimmers)

Play in waist deep water. Divide den into two teams. Teams line up single file, with about 4 feet between members. On signal, the last player on each team leapfrogs over the boy ahead, then dives down and swims between the legs of the next. He continues leaping and diving until he reaches the head of the line and raises his hand. This is the signal for the last one in line to begin leaping and diving. First team through wins.

LIVE LOG

Establish a goal at one end of the pool. One Cub Scout is the "log." He floats on his back in the center of the pool. The others swim around him. At any time the "log" may roll over and begin chasing the others, who race for their goal. Any player who is tagged becomes another "log" and the game resumes. Continue until there is only one player left who has not been tagged.

BALLOON RACE

BALLOON RACE

Line up the Cub Scouts in chest-deep water. On signal, they propel inflated balloons to shore without using their hands. They can use their heads or blow the balloons. The first one to touch shore wins.

CORK RETRIEVE
(For Swimmers)

Scatter a dozen or more corks or blocks of wood on the far side of the pool. On signal, the Cub Scouts jump in and try to retrieve corks, bringing them back to the starting point one at a time. Winner is player with the most corks.

KEEPAWAY
(For Swimmers)

Divide den into two teams. Teams line up in straight lines parallel to each other and about 10 feet apart. The leader tosses a large ball in the center. The team which gets it tries to keep it by tossing it back and forth. No player may walk or swim with the ball, and he must not hold it more than 5 seconds. Count one point for each successful pass.

WATER BASKETBALL
(For Swimmers)

Play in waist-to-chest deep water. Use a beach ball of basketball size. Place two inner tubes or swimming rings at opposite ends or sides of the pool to serve as baskets. Divide den into two teams. Use usual basketball rules, except that a player dribbles by batting the ball ahead of him in the water.

WATER BASKETBALL

MINNOW AND CATFISH

One Cub Scout is the Minnow and tries to keep away from another, the Catfish. The rest of the den forms a circle, holding hands. The game begins with the Minnow inside the circle and the Catfish outside. The Catfish tries to break through the circle to tag the Minnow while its members try to keep him out. The Minnow may dodge in and out of the circle. When the Catfish finally tags him, two others take their places and the game continues.

FROG IN THE SEA

This is a good pack game which can be played in shallow water. Players form a circle around five "frogs." The players walk close to the frogs and try to tap them on the head as they repeat these words: "Frog in the sea, can't catch me." The frogs try to tag the players. Any tagged player changes places with the frog.

TURTLE FLOAT

The Cub Scouts pretend to be turtles. They start by standing in a circle of waist-deep water. On signal, they take a deep breath, grasp their ankles, and pull their knees

against their chests so that they float with their backs out of water.

CANDY HUNT

Wrap hard candies in aluminum foil and scatter a handfull along the bottom in shallow water. Players duck under water to retrieve the candy, which is their prize.

LIGHTHOUSE LIGHT

Players line up in waist-deep water facing the shore. On the shore, opposite each player, are candles and matches. On signal, the players race to shore, light their candles, walk back to the starting line carrying the lighted candles, turn around three times, then walk back to shore.

WATER WHEELBARROW RACE

Run this race in knee-deep water parallel to the shore. It is a good race for non-swimmers. Divide Cub Scouts into pairs. One walks on his hands in the water while the other grasps his legs and helps to propel him. On signal, pairs race to goal line.

WATER WHEELBARROW RACE

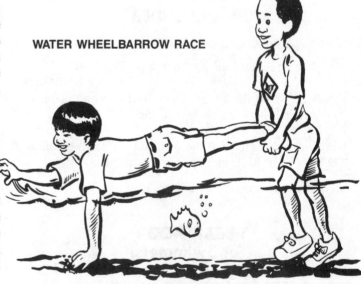

TOUCH-BOTTOM TAG

A regular tag game played in knee-deep water, with one Cub Scout chosen as It. As long as a player is touching the bottom of the pool with his hands, he's safe from being tagged.

WATER DODGE BALL

Divide into two teams. One team forms a circle around the other and throws a soft beach ball at those inside until they're all eliminated by being hit. Then the groups switch places.

PING-PONG RACE

Cub Scouts line up at a starting line in waist-deep water, each with a table tennis ball on the water in front of him. On signal, each blows his ball to shore. Players should not touch the ball or move it by making waves.

SHARKS' TEETH

Teams line up on opposite sides of the pool. Corks (at least five for each player) are thrown into water. On signal, players jump into the water, recover the corks by getting them between their teeth without using hands, carry them to a collecting spot, and return for more. Team with most corks after a designated time is the winner.

PEARL DIVERS

Play in waist-to-chest deep waters. One Cub Scout, the Oyster, is blindfolded. A table tennis ball, the pearl, is placed directly in front of the Oyster. One by one, the other players, who are Divers, advance to see who can get the pearl from the Oyster. The Oyster must keep his hands at least 6 inches above the pearl, but if he hears any noise or feels the water ripple, he may strike out where he thinks the Diver is. If a Diver is touched by the Oyster, he must return and give the other players a chance. The Diver who succeeds changes places with the Oyster.

WATER SPUD

A starter throws a soft rubber ball high into the air and calls out a player's name. That player recovers the ball while the others scatter about the pool. He tries to hit one of the other players with the ball. A player must stay in the same spot, but he may duck under to keep from being hit. If a player is hit, he picks up the ball and tries to hit someone else. If the ball goes wild, the thrower has one spud counted against him. When he gets three spuds against him, he must stand up, remain still with hands at sides, and let the other players give him a good splashing.

WATERMELON SCRAMBLE

Place a watermelon in a plastic bag and put it in the water, midway between two teams. On signal, both teams dive in and swim for the melon. From then on, it's one slippery scramble after another. Each team tries to get the watermelon out of the water to its home base. After two or three goals have been made, it's all legal and proper for the winners to cut the melon open for a summer-day feast, with the losers sharing in the spoils.

MARCO POLO

Have all Cub Scouts stand in shallow water. One is selected to be It, and he closes his eyes and keeps them shut (honor system). He calls out, "Marco!" All other Cub Scouts respond with "Polo!" It then tries to tag one of the responders while they duck under water and change locations to avoid being tagged. It should call out "Marco!" very frequently. When a Cub Scout is tagged, he becomes the next It.

Winter Games

SNOWBALL SPUD

Cub Scouts form a small circle in the snow. One player stands in the center, armed with a snowball. (Be sure the snowball is not icy.) He drops the snowball and calls the name of another player. All the other players scatter as far and as fast as they can while the one whose name was called runs to pick up the snowball. When he has picked it up he calls, "Stand," and all players must stop where they are. He throws the snowball at one of them. If he hits that player, the one hit picks up the snowball and tries to hit someone else. This goes on until someone misses. The player who misses scores one spud. The play is repeated with everyone forming a circle again and continues until one player has three spuds. Then he must stand with his back to the others about 15 to 20 feet away and everyone is allowed one shot with a snowball at the loser.

SNOWBALL SHARPSHOOTING

SNOW EXERCISES

Try cartwheels, skipping, leapfrog, hopping, headstand, forward roll, and racing in the snow. It's much different than on dry ground.

SNOWBALL CONTEST

Snow should not be too dry or powdery. On signal, boys compete to see who can make biggest snowball in 1 minute; the most snowballs in 3 minutes; and the tallest snowball tower in 5 minutes. Use a stopwatch to time them.

SNOWBALL SHARPSHOOTING

Hang an old sheet or blanket on a clothesline with plenty of clothespins. Cut three or four holes, 8 to 12 inches across, in the sheet. A large cardboard box can also be used. Boys stand 12 to 15 feet away and try to throw the snowballs through the holes. Each snowball that goes through a hole is worth one point. If boys are real sharpshooters, have them move further away to throw.

SNOW TUG OF WAR

Pile up a big mound of snow. Put the tug-of-war rope over this mound. Half the boys grab the rope on one side of the mound and the other half on the other side. Everyone pulls. Guess what happens to the boys on the losing team?

HOP ABOARD

One Cub Scout rides a toboggan down a hill. Three or four other players wait at strategic spots on the slope. The tobogganer tries to avoid the other players who try to hop on his toboggan as he passes. Players take turns as rider.

SNOW TUG OF WAR

SNOWMAN BUILDING CONTEST

On those days when snow can be packed easily, have a snowman building contest. Have available some props for the Cub Scouts to use: hats, scarves, etc. Have each Cub Scout make his own snowman (encourage small-sized snowpeople). Award prizes for biggest, smallest, most lopsided, funniest, and the like. Have a prize, possibly a home-made neckerchief slide, for each builder. Treat all the snow sculptors to a special snack.

FOX HUNTING

This game is played where there is plenty of untrodden snow. Two Cub Scouts are Foxes and start from the middle of an open area. Five minutes later the others follow their trail in the snow. The Foxes are not allowed to follow any human tracks, but they may walk along walls or tread in each other's tracks. Boundary limits should be set, with the Foxes trying to avoid capture for a certain period of time.

FOX AND GEESE

In a large flat area make a circle in the snow about 30 yards in diameter. Inside, make criss-crossing paths in any direction. Some may be dead-end. One player (the Fox) chases the others (the Geese), but all must stay on the paths. As players are caught, they become Foxes and help catch the other geese.

Games For The Handicapped

Many of the games included in this section are suitable for both mentally retarded and physically limited boys. However, there are a few things which leaders should keep in mind.

Games for mentally retarded boys should be kept simple with little organization. These boys cannot follow complicated verbal directions. A leader should show how the game is played, demonstrating the directions as he talks. For example: "I'll roll the ball to Pete" as he rolls the ball to Pete. At first a boy may understand only part of the

directions and therefore lose interest in the game; however, that doesn't mean he can't learn it. Once the routine is learned, he will feel comfortable and safe playing within the rules.

ADJUSTMENTS FOR THE HANDICAPPED

Physically limited boys can play many active games with a few adjustments in rules and equipment. Let boys who cannot stand up take part in games and activities while sitting or holding some support. The following suggestions will help leaders of physically limited boys:

Bowling. Let the boys bowl from wheelchairs, from a chair, or sitting or kneeling on the floor. Use lightweight balls and plastic pins, or substitute empty bleach bottles or milk cartons for pins.

Running Relays. The physically limited boy can be the one the runners tag or get objects from at a goal line.

Volleyball. Let the boy throw or serve closer to the net. He may play in a wheelchair or on crutches with little, if any, other modification or adaptation. Or allow the boys to catch and throw the ball rather than hitting it. Use a lightweight, easy to control ball or balloon.

Batting. Use a bat with the ball tied to it on a long string so that players can retrieve their own balls. Or set ball on a tee so both hands are free to bat.

Kickball. Modify the game so that a physically limited boy kicks but does not run, or runs only to first base where he is replaced by a courtesy runner.

Croquet Golf. Substitute stakes for wire wickets so boys simply hit stakes. Make large wickets from automobile tires or coat hangers.

ANIMAL BLIND MAN'S BLUFF

This game may be played with visually limited boys competing on an equal basis with other boys. One Cub Scout is blindfolded and takes his position in the center of a circle. The players in the circle clasp hands and dance around the Blind Man until he taps the floor with a staff. He then points the staff at one of the players and commands him to make an animal noise (a cat, duck, horse, etc.). When the noise is made, the Blind Man tries to guess the name of the player making the noise. If he is successful, they change places.

BALL WRESTLE

Two to six Cub Scouts (may be either sighted or visually limited) take a kneeling position in a circle around a basketball or soccer ball. Each boy puts one hand on the ball and the other hand on his hip. On signal, each player attempts to wrestle the ball from his opponents and stand up with it a full arm's length over his head. If the contest is not won in 2 or 3 minutes, it should be called a draw.

TIN CAN BOWLING

Place empty 48-ounce juice cans against a wall — one per team — about 6 feet apart and with open end facing team. Teams stand 12 to 15 feet from cans and take turns trying to bowl a rubber ball into their can without the ball bouncing out again. First team to have all its Cub Scouts do this is the winner.

FROG IN THE POND

Tie one end of a 2-foot length of string to a small paper cup and the other to an unshelled peanut. Toss the peanut in the air and catch it in the cup. Each Cub Scout completing this stunt passes it on to the next person.

PASS IT

Balance a lemon in a small paper cup and pass it to the next Cub Scout by transferring it to an empty cup held by that player.

PAPER CLIP BINGO

Teams are lined up at one end of room. An empty egg carton is placed opposite each team at the other end of the room. Each compartment in the carton is numbered with a point value. Each Cub Scout has a paper clip. In turn, players run to the carton and drop the paper clip in, at nose level, trying to get it into the hole with the highest number. If a player misses, he picks the paper clip up and tries again until it stays in the egg carton. Then he runs back to tag the next player on his team. When the last team finishes, points are added and team with most points wins.

BLOW ALLEY

Play this game on a table or on the floor. Set up golf tees like bowling pins. Cub Scouts propel an inflated balloon by blowing through a straw and try to knock down the pins. Pins may be given point values by numbering them or using various colors of tees.

3 Crafts

Why We Use Crafts

This section is filled with dozens of suggestions, patterns, ideas, plans, resources, and information on how to use crafts in den and pack meetings. Numerous crafts techniques are included, as well as lists of crafts which relate to monthly themes, achievements, and electives. These crafts are boy-tested and have been used successfully by dens and packs across the country.

As Cub Scouts work on craft projects, they not only learn to make useful items but also get valuable experience in using and caring for basic tools and materials, learning to follow directions, using their imaginations, and developing coordination and dexterity.

Crafts can help leaders to develop the monthly theme in den and pack meetings and tie the whole month's activities together. Some projects are for advancement requirements. Others are done just for fun.

Making his own craft project calls for creativity in each boy. He must plan the project and put it together. As he learns new techniques, he may need to measure, trace a pattern, cut or saw, sand, and assemble a project with nails, screws, or glue. Then he may need to paint or decorate it. For each of these steps he may require help from his leader and family.

As boys work with crafts, they learn to shape materials into useful articles. While decorating them, they learn that art is making useful things beautiful. They gain confidence to experiment with materials and tools and new ways to do things. Who can measure the satisfaction that comes to a boy when he produces with his own hands the exact item he has planned in his mind?

Crafts are a natural means of expression for most boys. Crafts develop their ability to understand and satisfy their urge to experiment. Physical development and mental growth are by-products of the craft program. Muscle coordination comes from lifting, moving, sawing, drilling, hammering, and pounding. Painting helps improve arm and hand control. Folding, cutting, shaping, filing, and sanding help to develop eye and hand coordination.

Handicraft improves a boy's alertness and mental skills through designing, planning, and making decisions and choices. He learns to choose materials, colors, tools, sizes, shapes, and weights, and figures out ways to hold work steady while sawing, drilling, or nailing.

The job of the leader is to stimulate each boy's interest and curiosity and to encourage him to try more difficult projects. The boy who is building a boat, rocket, or spaceship has an answer to the question: "What'll we do?" He is making more than just things. He is building dreams.

Teaching Crafts

All Cub Scout leaders have different backgrounds and experience, so their knowledge of craft techniques and tools will vary. Those with limited experience may enlist parents and other adults to teach specific techniques or to provide materials and tools.

The *Cub Scout Leader Book* provides some excellent tips for leaders working with boys on craft projects. In addition, the following steps will help leaders in teaching crafts:

1. Select a project with the help of the boys. Be sure it is something that has a purpose and that they will enjoy making.

2. Make a pattern, if needed. Have enough pattern pieces available so boys don't have to wait to trace them.

3. Make a sample to show the boys.

4. Gather materials and tools

5. Teach the craft step by step:
   - Cut out parts, as required
   - Put them together
   - Finish it (sand, polish, paint, etc.)
   - Clean up

6. If possible, start a craft in a den meeting that boys can finish at home with family help.

7. Display the craft projects at a pack meeting.

Materials for crafts should be simple and inexpensive. In most cases, they can be made from scrap materials found around the home. Some may be purchased at craft or hobby stores.

Leaders should guard against using crafts that are simply "busywork" or the "cut-and-paste" type which are below the boys' abilities and interests. All too often we find parents at a pack meeting looking skeptically at row after row of painted pop bottles, cloth-covered bricks, or plaster "whatsits." Some leaders think of crafts as mere handiwork and fail to use craftwork as a creative outlet, a form of expression, as well as a way to learn skills. By relating crafts to the monthly theme, we give each boy a chance to live a new dream each month and to make the costumes, props, and other items to help make that dream a reality.

Some leaders have the mistaken idea that it is necessary to have a craft project at every den meeting. That just isn't so. Crafts are only one of many activities used to accomplish the purposes of Cub Scouting. Overemphasis on crafts may discourage boys whose interests and abilities lean in another direction.

Measuring Results

Adults judge their own projects on the excellence of the workmanship and the quality of the product. This is because the adult who makes the project is working and doing a job. Since the boy does handicraft for fun, his effort should be measured by other standards. Leaders and parents need to see the boys' efforts through the eyes of a Cub Scout-age boy. This requires understanding, patience, and a willingness to invest time in working with boys. Each boy is expected to do his best, and each boy's best is different. His work should not be judged by adult standards.

The following is a good measuring stick to determine the value and success of den and pack craft projects.

- Are the boys learning things that will be helpful to them later?

- Are the craft projects within the interests and abilities of Cub Scout-age boys?

- Do the den and pack craft projects help bring about more family activity?

- Do the boys have fun working on crafts?

- Do they have adequate working space, tools, and materials?

- Are the boys given an opportunity to use their own initiative and imagination in planning and making the projects?

It is not what the boy does to the board that counts, it is what the board does for the boy.

Craft Tips For Leaders

USING SALVAGE

Many items that are destined for the trash can may be used for Cub Scout craft projects. Ask families to be on the lookout for scrap material. If you live in a manufacturing community, you may be surprised at the scrap wood, plywood cutoffs, odd pieces of metal, cardboard, leather, and plastics that you can get just for the asking.

Ask families to save such things as tin cans, boxes, tree branches, plastic bottles, buttons, cloth, linoleum, pine cones, spools, wire hangers, and paint.

Here is a partial list of useful scrap materials:

Bottle caps — for Christmas tree ornaments, foot scrapers, wheels, construction projects, markers for games.

Bottles — for musical instruments, containers.

Bowling pins — for human figures, games.

Broken baseball bats — for hardwood for various projects, lamps, den furniture.

Broom handles — for dowels for projects.

Cardboard cartons — for construction projects, stage props, puppet stages, storage.

Catalogues — for decorations, designs, cutouts.

Clothespins — for human figures, fastening items together, games.

Coathangers — for wires for mobiles and other constructions, skeletons for papier mâché work.

Coffee cans — for storage, planters, games.

Coloring books — for patterns for name tags, etc. Patterns can be enlarged for craft projects.

Cork stoppers — for fishing bobbers, printing tools, mobiles.

Corrugated cardboard — for stage props and scenery, bulletin board, shields, swords.

Cotton swabs — for paint brushes.

Ice cream spoons — for mixing paint, spreading paste, figures.

Ice cream cartons (3-gal.) — for helmets for astronauts or knights, Indian drums, masks.

Jars — for containers for paint, paste, and brushes; decorate for gifts.

Leather or vinyl scraps — for key chains, book marks, neckerchief slides, coin purses.

Linoleum scraps — for block printing.

Macaroni — for stringing for jewelry; pictures.

Men's shirts, pajama tops — for paint smock (cut off sleeves); costumes.

Paper plates — for plaques, masks, games.

Paper towels — for papier mâché, cleanup.

Pipe cleaners — for simple sculptures.

Shelf paper — for finger painting.

Soap bar — for carving.

Sponges — for painting, printing, cleanup.

Spools — for wheels, totem poles, toys, various construction projects.

Stockings and socks — for hand puppets, poputs.

Straws — for Christmas decorations, party favors, games.

Tin cans — for metal work, storage containers, planters.

Tongue depressors — for mixing paint, modeling tools.

Wallpaper — for book covers, paper for painting.

Wrapping paper — for murals, paintings.

Yarn — for hair for wigs, puppets, Christmas ornaments.

TIPS ON PAINTING

Tempera. Water-based paints such as tempera are best for Cub Scouts. Mix powdered tempera with water and add a little liquid starch; the paint goes farther and doesn't run. Powdered paint is more economical.

Poster paint. Combine ½-cup of cornstarch with ¾-cup of cold water. Soak one envelope of unflavored gelatin in ¼-cup cold water. Stir 2 cups hot water into the cornstarch mixture. Cook over medium heat until mixture boils clear. Remove from heat and stir in gelatin mixture and ½-cup powdered detergent. Divide into jars. Add food coloring or tempera to color.

Acrylics. Available in tubes or jars. Jar acrylic is more economical. Can be thinned with water. Brushes clean with water. Non-toxic and good for painting almost anything.

Spray painting. A spray bottle (such as window cleaner) works well for spray-painting large items. Use diluted tempera or poster paints.

Paint brush substitutes. For large items like scenery, use a sponge dipped in tempera. For small objects, use cotton swabs.

Painting plastics. For painting milk cartons or plastic bottles, mix powdered tempera with liquid detergent instead of water or starch. The paint will adhere better.

Painting styrofoam. Some types of paint will dissolve plastic foam. Use a type recommended for this purpose. Test first on scrap.

Painting wood. It is best to give raw wood a coat of wood sealer or thin shellac before painting, so paint will not soak in.

Finishing coats. Objects painted with tempera or poster paint will have a dull finish and will not resist moisture. For a shiny finish and protection, spray with clear plastic or clear varnish, or give it a coat of diluted white glue. Acrylic paint does not need a finishing coat.

Cleaning brushes. Different paints need different cleaners. For tempera, poster paint, or acrylics, use water. For varnishes, oils, or enamels, use turpentine, mineral spirits, or kerosene. For shellac, use shellac thinner. For model dope, use dope thinner. For lacquer, use lacquer thinner. These solvents are flammable and should be used outside and well away from sparks and flames. Adults should supervise this cleanup.

More Crafts Tips

Stuffing for puppets. Lint from automatic clothes dryers makes good, clean stuffing; or use plastic laundry bags or old nylon stockings.

Elasticizing clay. A permanent plastic clay can be made by mixing regular clay with glycerine and adding petroleum jelly. The proportion of clay to jelly varies according to desired consistency, from 10 to 50 percent.

Cutting styrofoam. Some types can be cut with a serrated knife or an electric carving knife. Adults should closely supervise or perform this operation. On heavier types, use a coping saw or jigsaw.

Punching holes in plastic. Use a hot ice pick or nail. If using a nail, hold it with pliers. Adult supervision is a must.

Coloring macaroni or rice. Rinse in cold water, then soak in diluted food coloring until rice, beans, or macaroni is desired shade.

Dyeing feathers. Soak feathers in diluted ammonia solution for 20 minutes. Rinse in warm water and put in solution of 2 cups of vinegar and a gallon of water. Add dye, making sure all feathers come in contact. Simmer until desired color is reached. Rinse in cool water, holding base up. Spread on paper to dry. To fluff, place in tightly closed pillowcase and fluff in automatic clothes dryer on low setting.*

TIPS ON ADHESIVES

- To save money, buy white glue in quart sizes and pour into small glue containers for the boys.

- To make a heavy-duty glue, mix cornstarch with white glue until mixture is as thick as desired.

- For small glue jobs, put glue in bottle caps and let boys use toothpicks or cotton swabs.

- Clear silicone is the best glue for plastics such as bottles and milk cartons. Available at hardware stores.

- Egg white is a good adhesive for gluing kite paper. It is strong and weightless.

- Tacky white glue is the best adhesive for plastic foam. A little goes a long way.

- Wheat paste (wallpaper paste) is a good for papier mâché. Flour and water make a good paste, too.

ENLARGING PATTERNS

The patterns found in this book can be enlarged to the desired size by using a ruler, tracing paper, pencil, and these simple directions:

1. Place tracing paper over the design you want to enlarge. Mark the design's outer limits.

2. Using these limits as guides, draw parallel horizontal and vertical lines on the paper, to create a grid. With a ruler, make the lines the same distance apart (approximately ¼-inch, depending on the size and detail of the pattern).

3. Letter each top square. Number down the left side.

4. Tape the grid over the original design and trace pattern onto grid.

Only the feathers of gregarious birds (chickens, ducks, geese, and the like), the English sparrows, starlings, and pigeons may be in the possession of non-native Americans. All other birds are classified as migratory and protected and it is against Federal law to possess their feathers.

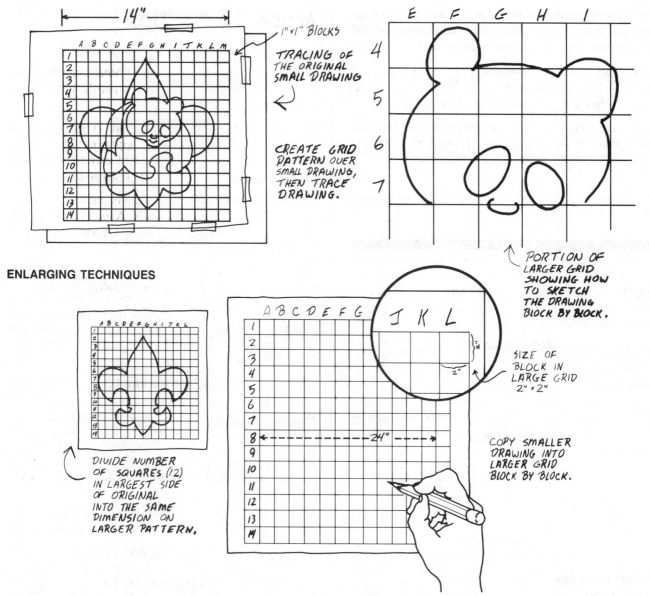

ENLARGING TECHNIQUES

1"×1" BLOCKS

TRACING OF THE ORIGINAL SMALL DRAWING

CREATE GRID PATTERN OVER SMALL DRAWING, THEN TRACE DRAWING.

PORTION OF LARGER GRID SHOWING HOW TO SKETCH THE DRAWING BLOCK BY BLOCK.

SIZE OF BLOCK IN LARGE GRID 2"×2"

COPY SMALLER DRAWING INTO LARGER GRID BLOCK BY BLOCK.

DIVIDE NUMBER OF SQUARES (12) IN LARGEST SIDE OF ORIGINAL INTO THE SAME DIMENSION ON LARGER PATTERN.

5. Decide how much of an enlargement is needed. Draw another grid with larger squares to the total width and length of the new pattern. Letter and number the new grid in the same manner.

6. Copy the pattern's lines into their exact position in each square of the large grid.

OTHER ENLARGING TECHINQUES

Several types of projectors will make enlargements. One of the easiest to use is an overhead projector. Trace over the design you wish enlarged, using thin plastic (such as notebook page protectors) and the special marking pens designed for use on plastic. Place the plastic sheet on the overhead projector "bed" and it can be enlarged to almost any size. This is especially helpful in making posters and other wall-hanging-size drawings.

An opaque projector can enlarge anything directly from the printed page. Most schools have opaque projectors which may be available for use by Cub Scouters.

Sometimes you may wish to make a poster and the best picture available is on a slide or even a negative. Use a slide projector to make these enlargements.

Using these techniques, anyone can become an artist!

Crafts For Advancement

The *Wolf Cub Scout Book* and *The Big Bear Cub Scout Book* are filled with craft ideas. Den leaders should help the boys pick out electives or achievements requiring crafts or get them started on a project that will help them meet the requirements. This will help hold the boys' interest and increase their desire to advance from one rank to the next.

Starting an advancement-related craft in a den meeting which the boys can take home to finish with the help of their families is a good way to get families involved.

Review the electives and achievements in the *Wolf* and *Bear* books. They offer many opportunities for interesting projects. The chart shows some possibilities.

Wolf	Bear

Achievement 1

Walking rail

Achievement 3

Display of State bird, flower, flag

Achievement 4

Chart of home jobs
Telephone list

Achievement 5

Poster of wild animal or bird
Bird feeders/birdhouses

Achievement 6

Collection   Chart/home water usage
Mounting boards
Storage cases
Scrapbooks

Achievement 7

Fingerprints
Plaster print of shoe

Achievement 8

Package wrapping   Scrapbook
   samples   Genealogical chart
Wrap ends of rope   Diary

Achievement 9

Bake cookies
Prepare part of meal
List of junk foods
Emergency road signal   Make snacks or dessert

Achievement 10

Homemade indoor   Family handicraft item
   games

Achievement 12

Trash bag poncho
Book cover   Tracks in aluminum foil

Achievement 13

Spending record

Achievement 14

Change a bicycle tire

Achievement 17

Letter to manufacturer

Achievement 18

Den doings
Things to do list
Letter
Invitation
Daily activities record

Achievement 19

Carving
Sharpening stick

Achievement 20

Tool box
Woodworking projects

Achievement 21

Model
Display for model
Floor plan

Achievement 22

Make a rope
Rope-throwing targets
Whipped ends of rope

Wolf   Bear

Elective 1

Invisible ink
Code messages

Pinhole planetarium
Model of rocket or
    satellite

Elective 2

Scenery for skit

Costume for skit
Sound effects
  equipment
Paper sack mask

Weather vane
Rain gauge

Simple barometer

Elective 3

Any useful craft project

Crystal radio set
Battery-powered radio

Elective 4

Homemade game

Electric buzzer game
Electric doorbell
Electric motor
Electromagnet

Elective 5

Rubber-band boat
Model boat

Elective 6

Model plane
Sketch/airplane

Elective 7

Stilts
Puddle jumpers
T-stick roller

Scooter
Cubmobile
Windmill
Water wheel

Elective 8

Lever
Pulley
Windlass

Musical instrument

Elective 9

Art project

Homemade toys
Pencil holder
Beanbag

Elective 10

Indian costume
Tomahawk, bow and ar-
row, spear, bell bands
Tom-tom, rattle, shield
Indian picture story

Papier mâché mask
Indian mask
Animal mask
Clown mask

Elective 11

Mount a picture
Picture story

Elective 12

Sketch
Cartoon story
Painted scenery

Stencil pattern
Poster

Shadow print of leaves.

Labeled leaf, insect,
seed, rock, and shell
collections
Eraser prints of animal
tracks
Spider web print

Elective 13

Birdhouse
Bird feeder
Bird bath

Magic trick
Puzzle

Elective 14

Landscape plan
Build a greenhouse

Elective 15

Box garden
Terrarium

Soil display

Elective 16

First aid kit
Poster/fire escape plan

Elective 17

Cook something

Refinish or repair an
item

Elective 18

Treasure hunt map
Adventure trail props
Obstacle race layout

Outdoor games
Outdoor gym equipment

Elective 19

Fishing rig

Elective 22

Trophy skin
Stamp collection

Elective 23

Map from home to
school or den meeting

Elective 24

Sand painting
Model/Indian house

Theme Crafts

Consider each monthly theme for its craft possibilities. If the projects are fun, the boys will want to do them. A wise leader will suggest wide project areas rather than require the same project of each boy. This gives the boys greater freedom of choice and an opportunity to use their imagination. For example, the theme, "Things That Fly," might produce kites, gliders, planes, boomerangs, or even flying insects.

During some months, all boys in the den and pack may be working on the same things, such as when the pack is preparing for a pinewood derby, raingutter regatta, or space derby. However, the cars, boats, and rockets for those events are son-parent projects, and no work is done on them in den meetings.

Ask a boy what Indians remind him of and you'll get every possible answer from tom-toms to tepees. Ask a boy what knights remind him of and you'll have everything from slaying dragons to building castles. Giving the boys an opportunity to talk about a theme and what they would like to make will provide an abundance of good ideas. They will have more fun making something they thought of than something the den leader decided on.

Theme crafts may include costumes, ceremony boards, game equipment, props for skits, gifts, decorations, toys, inventions, conservation and nature items, and more. The following list will give you some ideas on general theme topics:

Fitness

- Fitness equipment
- Beanbag toss
- Puddle jumpers
- Fitness chart
- Stilts
- Ring toss

Indians

- Costumes/headdresses
- Tepee
- Peace pipe
- Trophy skin
- Baskets
- Totem pole
- Shields
- Indian games
- Masks
- Rattles

Space/Future

- Rockets
- Helmet
- Space shuttle model
- Flying saucer
- Launching pad
- Costumes
- Robot
- Radarscope
- Space station model
- Star map

Health/Safety

- Posters
- Home fire escape plan
- Emergency road signal
- Traffic signs
- First aid kit
- Nutrition chart

Transportation

- Pinewood derby car
- Pushmobile
- Airport
- Glider
- Train model
- Cubmobile
- Model cars
- Model planes
- Helicopter

Knights

- Sword
- Shield
- Knight costume
- Banners/flags
- Castle model
- Cardboard castle
- Teeterboard
- Dragon

Water/Boats/Pirates

- Costumes
- Water pump
- Treasure chest
- Treasure map
- Pirate's sword
- Model boats
- Water wheel
- Waterscope
- Raft

Pioneers/Colonists

- Costumes
- Musket/powderhorn
- Homemade soap
- Homemade butter churn
- Puppets
- Quill pen and ink
- Model fort
- Old-time games

Fair/Circus

- Midway games
- Performer costumes
- Animal costumes
- Musical instruments
- Masks
- Puppets
- Peep show
- Noisemakers
- Prizes
- Banners/flags

Science

- Inventions
- Electric games
- Other games
- Barometer
- Rain gauge
- Science projects
- Telegraph key
- Electric buzzers
- Wind chimes
- Weather vane

Here are some additional resources for crafts ideas:

Cub Scout Fun Book

Golden Book of Crafts and Hobbies, by W. Ben Hunt

Indian Crafts and Lore, by Ben Hunt

Snips and Snails and Walnut Whales, by Phyllis Fiarotta

Easy To Make Contraptions, by Roland Berry

From Petals to Pinecones, by Katherine N. Cutler

Foxtails, Ferns and Fish Scales, by Ada Graham

The Beautiful Naturecraft Book, Search Press Limited

The Everything Book, by Eleanor G. Vance

Carpentry for Children, by Lester Walker

Nature

- Birdhouses
- Bird feeders
- Insect net
- Terrariums
- Bird treats
- Box garden
- Collection boxes
- Plaster casts
- Leaf prints
- Ant house

Communication

- Tin can telephone
- Codes
- Telephone directory cover
- Telegraph
- Telstar model

Resources For Craft Materials

There are many resources for craft materials in most communities. Collecting these materials requires legwork, headwork, and handwork. Most of the sources listed below have scrap that is available for the asking, or at minimum cost. Leaders should keep their eyes and ears open to the endless list of "beautiful junk" available for recycling into Cub Scout crafts.

Lumber Company. Wood scraps, sawdust, and curls of planed wood may be given away by the boxload. Make your contact and request, then leave a marked box to come back for later. Use for games and crafts of all kinds.

Grocery Store. Boxes of all sizes and shapes. Discarded soft drink cartons are excellent for holding paint cans.

Telephone Company. Empty cable spools make tables; old telephones can be used for skit props; colorful telephone wire can be made into many different projects.

Soft Drink Companies. Wooden soft drink crates may be available at minimal charge. They can be used for storage or for projects.

Ice Cream Stores. Empty 3-gallon cardboard containers. Use for wastebaskets, masks, storage.

Gas Stations and Garages. Tires and bike tubes for games and obstacle courses.

Wallpaper Stores. Wallpaper sample books of discontinued patterns.

Carpet Shops. Discontinued rug samples and soft foam underpadding.

Resources For Crafts Ideas

Ideas for crafts projects can be found in crafts books, children's magazines, crafts magazines, and on children's television programs. Public and school libraries have a wide variety of crafts books, and stores which carry teaching aids have even more. The best resources for Cub Scout craft ideas, in addition to this book, are *Cub Scout and Webelos Scout Program Helps, Wolf Cub Scout Book, Big Bear Cub Scout Book, Webelos Scout Book,* den leader workshops, the annual pow wow, and your district roundtable.

Tile Stores. Broken patterns of mosaic tile can be used for crafts projects.

Appliance Stores and Furniture Stores. Large packing crates are handy for skit props and puppet theaters.

Newspaper Companies. End rolls of paper.

Printing Companies. Scrap paper and card stock. Offset plates for tin crafts.

Pizza Restaurants. Cardboard circles are good for making shields and other crafts projects.

Travel Agencies. Discarded posters and maps.

Upholstery Shops and Drapery Shops. Fabric and vinyl scraps.

This is just a starter list of resources for craft materials. There may be places in your community to obtain aluminum foil, burlap, canvas, clay, cord, floor covering, leather and vinyl scraps, nails, paper bags, plastic rope, sandpaper, spools, etc. Check the yellow pages and begin looking.

Furnishing The Den

Cub Scout dens meet in many places—in basements, garages, backyards, apartments, small parks, and classrooms. Many dens meet in the den leader's home.

It's nice for the den to have a place the boys can fix up as their own. The Cub Scouts can make den furniture from boxes and scrap lumber. They can decorate the walls with pictures, charts, or other displays. They can make storage and game chests. Even if a den doesn't have this type of meeting place, it may have equipment that is stored between meetings. A fixing-up project will help bring the den members closer together. Projects should be simple, colorful, and easy to make.

On the following pages are ideas for den furniture and equipment. In addition, the Cub Scout Insignia Poster Set, No. 4648, could be mounted on the wall or a bulletin board, along with the Cub Scout Advancement Wall Chart, No. 4192. Use the den flag and a den doodle to help build den spirit. Use the Cub Scout Insignia Stickers, No. 4649 or 4650, to decorate storage boxes and benches.

MULTIPURPOSE SCREEN

This is a good project for dads or other adult family members. Make the frame from 1-by-2-inch pine, covered with masonite or heavy cardboard. Make the front about 3-by-5-feet; sides 2-by-5. Reinforce the corners with

plywood, as shown. Hinge front and sides for easy folding and storage. A free-sliding clothespole will help brace the screen. Let the boys decorate it.

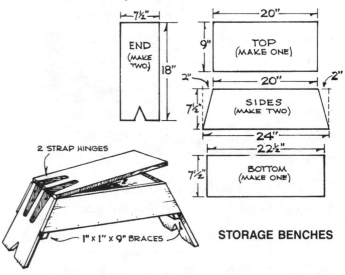

STORAGE BENCHES

STORAGE BENCHES

This type of bench will stack for easy storage. Make from 1-inch shelving as shown in illustration. Let each boy and an adult build and decorate one in their own style. This becomes the boy's seat at den meetings. It will also hold tools and materials.

MULTIPURPOSE SCREEN

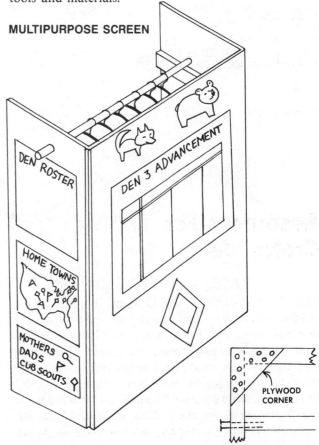

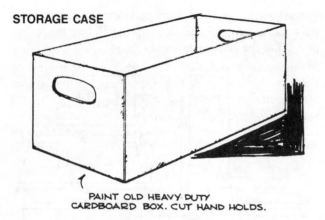

STORAGE CASE

PAINT OLD HEAVY-DUTY
CARDBOARD BOX. CUT HAND HOLDS.

STORAGE CASE

This can be made from an old heavy-duty cardboard box. The boxes that 10 reams of paper come in are excellent. Cut hand holds, then paint or cover with colorful adhesive-backed paper, if desired.

PENCIL CANS

These can be made from frozen orange juice or other similar size cans. Paint or cover with decorative adhesive-backed paper. Each boy could have his own for storage of pencils and crayons.

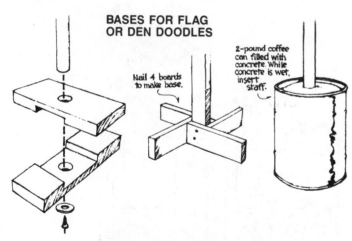

BASES FOR FLAG
OR DEN DOODLES

Nail 4 boards to make base.

2-pound coffee can filled with concrete. While concrete is wet, insert staff.

BASES FOR FLAG OR DEN DOODLE

Temporary bases can be made from wood as shown in the illustration or from a 2-pound coffee can filled with plaster. Cover the end of the flagpole with aluminum foil and grease heavily with petroleum jelly, so it will slip out easily after the plaster hardens. A permanent base can be made by inserting flagpole in a can filled with concrete and letting it harden.

DEN BULLETIN BOARD

Make an animal head pattern in desired size. Cut from ¼-inch plywood. Paint head and features. Cut the large mouth from sheet cork and glue to wood. Add a hanger so it can be hung on the wall.

ANIMAL HEAD CAP RACK

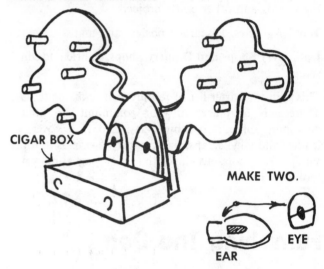

CIGAR BOX

MAKE TWO.

EAR

EYE

ANIMAL HEAD CAP RACK

Select an animal pattern with big ears. For a table model, use a heavy block of wood for nose and ¼-inch plywood for head, eyes, and ears. Attach dowels to ears. Paint as desired. For wall model, use lightweight wood.

DEN SILHOUETTES

DEN SILHOUETTES

Decorate the den meeting place with a silhouette of each den member. Trace each boy's shadow on plywood or thick cardboard, as shown. Cut out, paint black, and mount on colored or white background. Frame each picture and hang it in your "Hall of Fame."

DEN DOODLES

A den doodle is not only a clever way to record advancement progress of the boys, it is a colorful decoration for the den meeting place. With the boys' help, choose a design that fits the den. No two den doodles are alike. Each one is distinctive and has the den's number, a place for each boy's name, and a cord or thong for each boy's advancement record. Den doodles can be either table or floor models and be made from wood, cardboard, or other materials. Spools, bottle caps, colored beads, and shells are a few of the more common items used as symbols of progress. Each symbol is usually identified with an achievement or elective number or activity badge name.

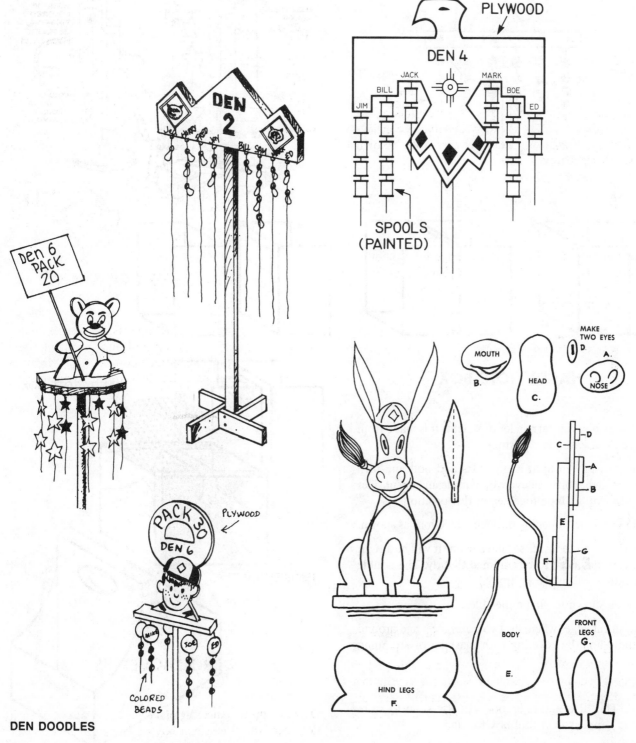

DEN DOODLES

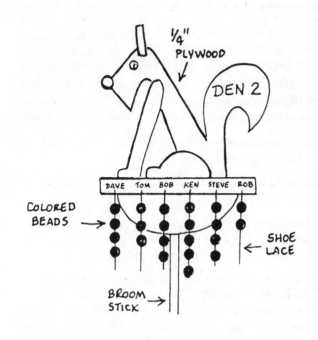

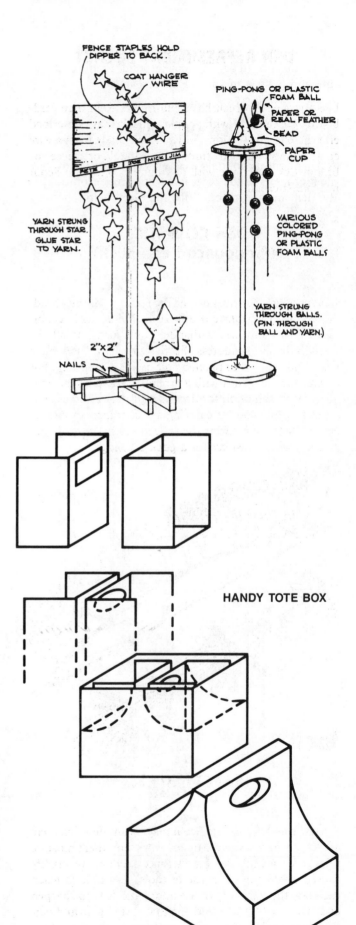

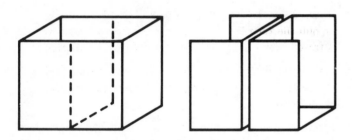

HANDY TOTE BOX

This sturdy box will carry a lot of weight. It is made from two identical cardboard cartons.

1. Cut one box in half, along sides and bottom. Turn pieces so that open sides are on outside and uncut sides are touching. Tape together in this position.

2. Cut out handle opening through all sections as shown.

3. Place this piece inside second carton. It will be a tight fit and may need to be trimmed slightly. The double thickness will make it strong.

4. Cut as shown to shape the sides.

5. Finish cut edges where the two boxes meet and around handle hole by covering with masking or strapping tape.

6. Paint if desired.

NOTE: This also makes a good gift for mom to store cleaning supplies or a tool box for dad.

HANDY TOTE BOX

DEN REFRESHMENT BUCKET

Use a large can which has a plastic lid. Reinforce cardboard containers with papier mâché as described elsewhere in this section. Add a handle made from a wire coat hanger slipped through a dowel or piece of broomstick. Decorate with den number and Cub Scout insignia stickers.

DEN COUPSTICK
(Pronounced coo-stick)

Indians of certain tribes earned the feathers for their headdresses by doing brave deeds. If an Indian had accomplished so many deeds that he could not put all the feathers in his headdress, he put the extra ones on a beautifully carved or painted pole called a coupstick. For a den coupstick, start with a broomstick and let the boys use their imagination for decorating it. It can be used as a den flagpole and for carrying any streamers or awards earned by the den during the year. It will make a colorful and interesting display for a pack meeting.

DEN COUPSTICK

Tools

SAFETY RULES

What is safe for one Cub Scout may be unsafe when there are two or more around. In any workshop there must be rules governing the use of tools. Since accidents are usually caused by the improper use of tools, take time to teach each boy the right way to use a tool and how to sharpen and take care of it. Remind him that cleaning up and putting away tools and materials are part of the job. Make sure tools and materials are easy to reach and replace.

- Use each tool for the job it is made for and the way it was intended to be used.

- Most accidents occur to the hands, face, or feet. Protect your eyes. Keep fingers and hands away from cutting edges of tools. Secure or clamp down wood which is being worked on.

- Be patient and never use force. Don't work with tools when you are tired. You need to be alert.

- Don't wear loose clothing or jewelry which can be caught in moving parts.

- Keep the work area clean, dry, and well-lighted. Never use electrical tools in damp or wet locations.

- If extension cords are used, be sure they are heavy duty. Don't use the type of extension cords which are intended for small appliances.

- If an electrical cord has a plug with three prongs, it should be plugged into a three-hole receptacle (outlet). If an adapter is used on a two-hole outlet, the adapter wire must be attached to a known ground (the screw in the middle of the outlet cover plate).

- Don't abuse the cord by carrying the tool by the cord or pull the plug by yanking on the cord. If the cord is frayed, don't use the tool until the cord is repaired.

- Unplug all electrical tools when you are finished and put them out of reach of children. Don't leave any tools unattended.

- Always unplug electrical tools when changing saw blades, drill bits, or other attachments.

- Keep tools sharp, clean, and oiled.

- An adult should be present when a Cub Scout uses a tool or until he has shown that he can handle it safely.

Remember, tools are replaceable; boys are not.

HAND TOOLS FOR WOODWORKING

Hammer. An 8- to 10-ounce hammer is the best size for a Cub Scout to grip and swing. If a nail bends, pull it out. Use a wooden block when pulling to prevent strain on the hammer handle.

Screwdriver. Use the longest one convenient to the job. Make sure the blade fits the screw slot. Keep the screwdriver and screw aligned.

Plane. Teach boys to use a block plane. It is the best type to use on their projects.

Brace and bit. Show boys how this drilling tool works. Explain that a brace holds bits, some braces have ratchets to permit partial turns of the handle, and auger bits are wood bits measured by 16ths of an inch. Show them how to start a bit by guiding it into place with one hand and how to secure a bit by holding the chuck and turning the handle of the brace clockwise. Have them learn to finish a hole from the underside to prevent splitting.

Handsaw. Teach Cub Scouts to use a 20-inch saw, recommended for boys their age. Show them that to start a saw, you first steady the blade with your thumb and then draw back on the mark on the board. Be sure to tilt the saw at approximately a 45 degree angle to the board when cutting across the grain of the wood. Explain that you straighten the saw handle to correct the direction of a cut.

Ripsaw. Use this saw to cut *with the grain* of the wood only. Show boys how to brace wood firmly on a sawhorse, bench, or vise. Start sawing gently, changing to light, steady strokes. Don't press. Take fairly long strokes and let the saw do the work.

Coping Saw. Teach boys to use this simple saw to cut curves and odd shapes from wood. Saw with the handle either above or below the wood, setting the blade to cut on the downstroke. Use a heavy blade and a long stroke. Clamp work securely in a vise or use a bench hook.

See Wolf Achievement 5 and Bear Achievement 20 for more information on hand tools.

POWER TOOLS

Power jigsaws can be used safely by boys of Cub Scout age. Den leaders have been using them in their dens for many years and have found they are safe and easy to use.

Both the vibrating saw and the rocket-action type are portable and can be plugged into any 110-volt AC outlet. These saws have an incredible capacity. They can cut a full 30-inch circle and will handle everything from light plywood shelf cutouts to den furniture. Most come equipped with a foolproof blade guard. They make an ideal tool for instructing the beginner in woodworking.

Follow these safety rules when using the jigsaw:

- If you are using a regular workbench, make a sturdy box or platform for the boys to stand on. Allow plenty of working room around the bench and the boys.

- Instruct the Cub Scouts to keep their eyes on the work and their fingers and hands away from the blade.

- An adult should be present at all times when boys use a power jigsaw. Do not lean over a boy's shoulder, but stand nearby where you can give guidance or assistance as needed.

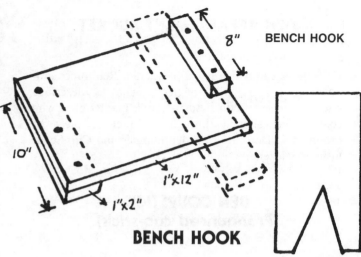

BENCH HOOK

Make this handy tool for your home workshop. Use 1-inch pine. Follow the plans and dimensions shown. To use, set the bench hook on your worktable or a chair. Butt the underside against the edge of a table or chair. Hold the piece of wood to be cut against the top block and saw with a level stroke as desired. The underboard protects the table or chair top. Countersink screws or use dowels to protect the table top.

Wood Craft

The wood craft projects in this section are suitable for Cub Scouts and leaders who have had little experience with wood. They require few tools. A few den rules about woodcraft projects will help the leader and the boys.

- Use only the tools provided. Some tools are off limits for boys.

- All tools must be clean and put away before the boys leave.

- All sawdust and sanding dust are to be swept up before the boys leave.

- All projects are to be marked on the underside with the owner's name or initials before the end of the den meeting.

- No one opens paint or stain until he can name the solvent in which the brush can be cleaned and has some of that solvent on hand.

- All solvents are used outdoors under the leader's supervision. Never use flammable solvents indoors.

Have on hand the materials and tools needed for the project. Find out what type of sandpaper is best for your project—what type of nails or brads. Use scrap wood which is free of knots. Knots can sometimes be dangerous.

Make a sample of the project to check out directions. Provide step-by-step instructions for the boys. Don't stifle creativity and imagination.

FINISHING WOOD PROJECTS

Wood craft projects should always be sanded before they are finished. Make a sander from a 2-by-2-by-3-inch wood block and wrap sandpaper around it. Always sand with the grain, never against it or in circles. To get the best results from sanding, use a filler for scratches and holes. When dry, sand again.

There are several finishes which can be used on wood projects—varnish, shellac, lacquer, enamel, latex paint, or even wood stains. A clear wax polish can be applied to raw wood to display the beauty of the wood grain.

Varnish. Prepare wood with one or two coats of thin shellac or wood sealer first, sandpapering between coats. This will fill the pores of the wood and prepare it for varnishing. Thin varnish with turpentine, if necessary. Clean shellac brush with shellac thinner or alcohol. Clean varnish brush with turpentine.

Enamel. Prepare wood in the same manner as for varnish. Enamel usually needs thinning with a small amount of turpentine. If it is too thick, it will leave ridges. Two thin coats of enamel produce a colorful finish. Clean brush with turpentine.

Wood Stain. To prepare the wood, moisten it with turpentine before applying the stain. Experiment on a scrap of wood to make sure the results please you. Clean brush with turpentine.

Varnish Stain. Prepare wood as for enamel or varnish. A shiny varnish may be dulled by rubbing it lightly with a mixture of oil and a small amount of powdered pumice stone. Rub gently, wipe off with a soft rag, and finish with wax.

Model Dope. Small objects can be painted with model dope. Clean brush with dope thinner.

Lacquer. This is used in the same way as enamel, except that the brush must be cleaned with lacquer thinner.

Tempera. Tempera and poster paint are not as good for painting wood projects as the other types listed above. The wood must be sealed so the paint will not soak in. Tempera will leave a dull finish, so you may want to give the project a top coat of clear varnish or shellac. Tempera brushes can be cleaned with water.

CAUTION: Many painting supplies are not only flammable, but explosive. Never use them near an open flame. Be sure windows are open for circulation. It is best to use them outdoors if possible.

WOOD PROJECTS

HUNT AND PECK

The boys will enjoy making this hungry chicken, watching him peck for food and eating as they hold the handle and swing the weight.

⅛-inch wood—base, head, tail, sides

¼-inch wood—leg, handle

Small cup or lid

Glue

12-inch string

Ball or small weight

Paint

1. Cut parts from wood as shown.

2. Drill small holes in the neck, tail, and sides.

3. Cut slits in the base and drill holes in the base and handle.

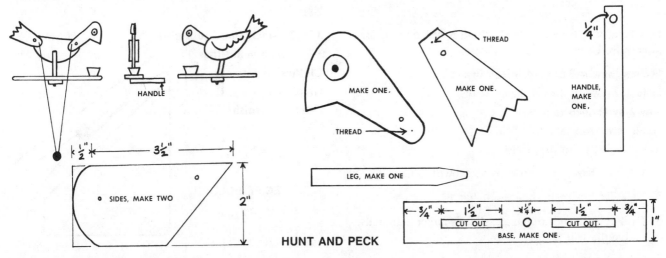

HUNT AND PECK

4. Glue the leg to one side of the body, insert leg in base, and place handle on leg at right angle to base. Glue in place. When glue has dried, place the head and tail in temporary position.

5. Tie a ball or small weight in the center of a 12-inch string, thread it through the slots in the base, and fasten to thread holes in head and tail. Keep the weight centered.

6. Glue the other side of the chicken to the leg. Allow glue to dry.

7. Put a small wire through the pivot holes in the body and neck and bend the ends to hold in place. Do the same with the tail.

8. Paint the chicken with bright colors. Glue a small cup or lid at the front of the base. Then have fun watching him eat.

ENLARGE TO DESIRED SIZE

KEY RINGS

KEY RINGS

Use one of the patterns shown or find your own in a coloring book. Enlarge to desired size. Cut from ⅛-inch plywood and drill hole for key chain. Paint as desired.

HANDYMAN'S HELPER

This helpful, but easy to make, item is welcome in any workshop. Use:

½-inch plywood 4-by-14 inches (base)
½-inch plywood 4-by-5 inches (ends)
2-by-2-by-13-inch (handle)
Small screw-top jars.
Nails, tacks, paint or varnish

1. Cut one base and two ends as shown. Sand.

2. Tack jar lids to both sides of handle.

3. Drill holes in ends of handle, slightly larger than nails, so handle will pivot.

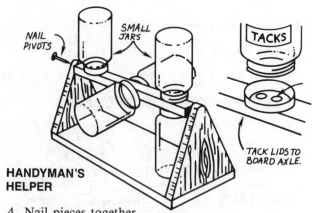

HANDYMAN'S HELPER

4. Nail pieces together.

5. Paint or varnish. Screw on jars.

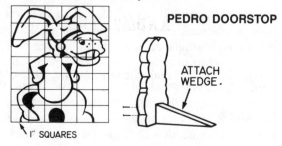

PEDRO DOORSTOP

1" SQUARES

ATTACH WEDGE.

PEDRO DOORSTOP

This handy item will be easy for the Cub Scout to make.

½-inch plywood
Nails, paint

1. Enlarge pattern.

2. Cut out Pedro and wedge as shown.

3. Nail pieces together.

4. Paint as desired.

RECIPE HOLDER

This usable kitchen gift can be made from scrap materials. Use:

3-by-2½-inch wood (upright)
3-by-3 inch wood (base)
Clothespin
Glue, nail
Paint or varnish

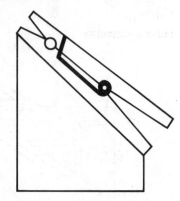

RECIPE HOLDER

1. Cut one upright and one base.

2. Saw off the top of the upright at an angle.

3. Glue and nail upright to base.

4. Glue clothespin in place as shown.

5. Paint or varnish as desired.

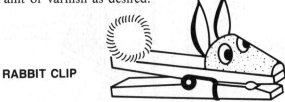

RABBIT CLIP

RABBIT CLIP

This makes a good mail clip or placecard holder. Use the following:

Clothespin
Cork
Glue
Felt
Map pins
Broom straws
Cotton ball

1. Cut a small cork in half and glue to clip end of a clothespin.

2. Make rabbit ears from felt and glue to cork.

3. Use map pins for eyes and nose, broom straws for whiskers, and cotton ball for tail.

BOOKENDS

These bookends are cut from one piece of wood, as follows:

½-by-8-by-18-inch board
Nail
Paint or varnish

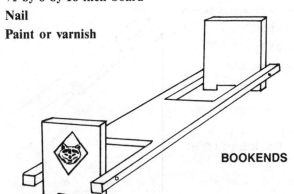

BOOKENDS

1. Cut pieces from each end of board.

2. Nail cutout pieces in upright position at ends of remaining piece of board.

3. Sand and finish as desired.

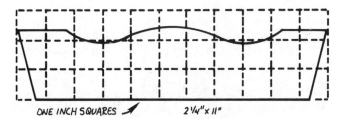

BREAD TRAY

GROOVE FOR BOTTOM BOARD

4" x 4½"

ONE INCH SQUARES

2¼" x 11"

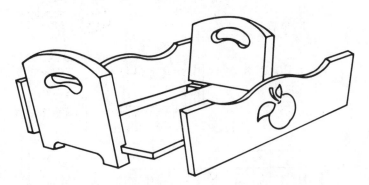

BREAD TRAY

This makes a nice gift for mom.

½-inch wood, 3-by-11 inches (sides)
½-inch wood, 4-by-4½ inches (ends)
½-inch wood, 4 ½-by-9½ inches (bottom)
Nails and glue
Paint or varnish
Decals if desired

1. Enlarge pattern.

2. Cut two ends, two sides, and one bottom from wood.

3. Mark handle openings on end pieces. Cut handles by boring two ½-inch holes and cutting out with coping saw.

4. Cut ¼-inch deep grooves ½-inch wide into ends, as shown, to fit bottom piece.

5. Nail pieces together.

6. Paint or varnish as desired.

KEY HOLDER

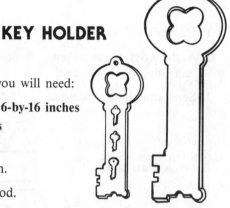

For this project, you will need:

¼-inch plywood, 6-by-16 inches
Brass screw hooks
Paint or varnish

1. Enlarge pattern.

2. Cut out plywood.

3. Drill hole in top, insert coping saw and cut out open section.

4. Drill hole for hanging holder on wall.

5. Sand. Paint or varnish as desired.

6. Insert screw hooks.

For key and calendar holder, glue calendar to back side of lower edge, using two strips of felt to secure it.

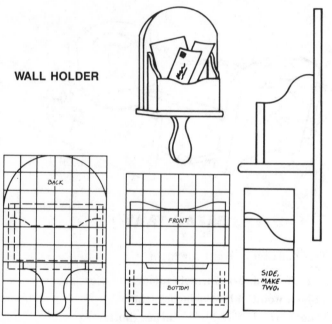

WALL HOLDER

WALL HOLDER

This attractive wall holder can hold mail, envelopes and notepaper, or a plant. Use:

½-inch wood
Nails, glue
Paint or varnish

1. Enlarge pattern to desired size.

2. Cut one back, two sides, one bottom, and one front.

3. Glue and nail pieces together.

4. Sand and paint or finish as desired.

DEN SCRAPBOOK

DEN SCRAPBOOK

This can be used to keep photos, certificates or awards, patches, advancement cards, etc. Materials include:

Two 9-by-12 inch pieces of light wood paneling
Two metal hinges
Leather thong

1. Cut front and back from paneling. Sand.

2. Drill holes for three-ring binder paper, large enough to hold leather thong.

3. Cut front about 2¼ inches from left edge as shown and hinge with metal hinges.

4. Paint or stain. Decorate as desired with decals or wood-burning set.

5. Insert 3-hole paper. Lace together with leather thong.

CUTTING BOARDS

Materials include:

¾-inch wood
Wood stain and paint
Paste wax

1. Enlarge pattern.

2. Cut out with coping saw or power jigsaw.

3. Drill hole for hanging.

4. Sand, then apply wood stain to one side. Wax that side.

5. Paint back side as desired so it can be hung as a decoration when not in use.

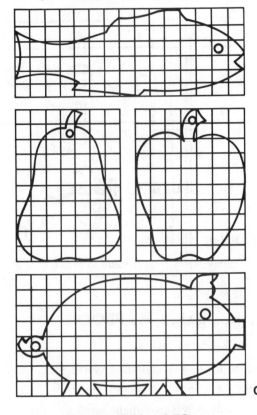

CUTTING BOARD IDEAS   1" SQUARES

CUTTING BOARDS

FOOT SCRAPER

This is a clever and inexpensive gift and will give Cub Scouts experience in hammering nails. Use:

¾-inch wood, 10-by-14 inches
Metal bottle caps
Hammer, nails

1. Cut wood approximately 10-by-14 inches or to desired size. (For example: make a large shoe sole.)
2. Nail bottle caps, upside down, to completely cover the wood.
3. Place scraper in front of door and scrape your feet.

JUMPING JACK

Can be made of wood, plywood, cardboard, or tin. You can also create other "jumpers" with slight variations on the pattern. Try an old man, a wolf, a bear, various clowns, Martians, and even people such as a den leader, soldier, or sailor.

Thin wood pieces or plywood, cardboard, or tin
Sandpaper, if using wood
Metal paper fasteners
String
Washer or bone ring
Paint

1. Trace the design on the construction material. Cut out the parts. Drill or punch holes in pieces as indicated on the patterns.
2. Insert metal paper fasteners in the large holes. Connect arms and legs with string as shown. Add ring to bottom of string.
3. Hold string by the ring and move your hand to make the puppet jump.

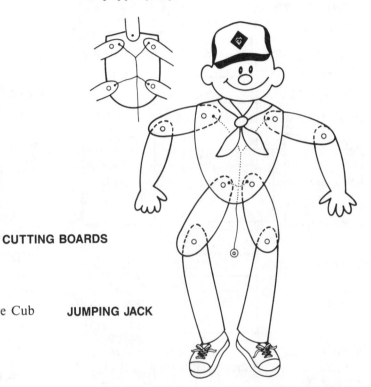

JUMPING JACK

BIRDHOUSES AND BIRD FEEDERS

Birdhouses provide nesting places where natural ones are lacking. In addition to those shown here, birdfeeders can be made from milk cartons, gourds, and other materials. For birdhouses, wood is the best building material. Avoid using metal, since it becomes unbearably hot if hung in the sun.

Your birdhouse construction will be successful if you remember these simple rules:

- Birdhouses should be durable, rainproof, cool, and easy to reach for cleaning.
- Make the roof slanted to shed water, with an overhang to protect the entrance hole from a driving rain.
- Make the house for specific birds, with the required specific measurements, entrance holes, height above ground, etc.
- Plan the house so water is kept from the nest. Drill a few small holes in the bottom of the box to drain off any water that may get in.

Crafts   3-21

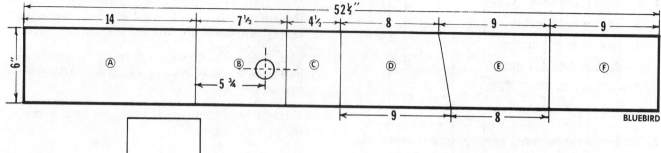

14 7½ 4½ 8 9 9

52½"

6"

Ⓐ Ⓑ Ⓒ Ⓓ Ⓔ Ⓕ

5¾

9 8

BLUEBIRD

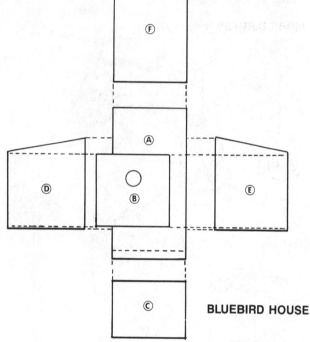

Ⓕ

Ⓓ Ⓐ Ⓔ

Ⓑ

Ⓒ

BLUEBIRD HOUSE

BLUEBIRD HOUSE

For this simple birdhouse, you'll need:

One 52½-by-6-by-¾-inch board
Nails, hinge
Paint

1. Cut board as shown.

   A — Back 6-by-14 inches
   B — Front 6-by-7½ inches
   C — Bottom 6-by-4½ inches
   D/E — Side 6-by-8-by-9 inches
   F — 6-by-9 inches

2. The entrance hole is 1½ inches.

3. No perch is necessary.

4. Nail together as shown. Paint. Place bluebird house on fence post, tree, or in an open area, 5 to 10 feet above ground. A bluebird trail can be laid out by placing one bluebird house every 500 feet for several miles.

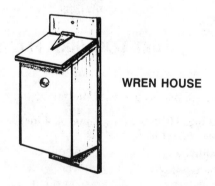

WREN HOUSE

• Build houses with ventilation slits under the roof overhang or two or three small holes near the top of the box.

Scrap lumber is good for building birdhouses. The plans shown here are for ¾-inch pine. Other materials needed are a hinge, nails, and paint. Modest tones such as brown, grey, or dull green blend best, except for houses placed in exposed areas (such as for purple martins), which should be painted white to reflect heat.

Birds won't like it if you:

• Make the opening too small.

• Put the house in a tree accessible to cats, squirrels, weasels, and small children.

• Hide the box in dense woods.

• Fail to protect birds nesting in the box.

Birds will like it if you:

• Place the house on a pole.

• Set the houses fairly low and space them far apart.

• Keep houses in partial sunlight.

• Set back side facing prevailing winds.

WREN HOUSE

Try this house and several variations for different birds. Use:

One 43-by-6-by-½-inch board
Nails, hinge
Paint

1. Cut board as shown.

   A — Back 6-by-12 inches

   B — Front 6-by-5½ inches

   C — Bottom 6-by-4½ inches

   D/E — Side 6-by-6-by-7 inches

   F — Top 6-by-7½ inches

2. This house can be used for several species and the size of entrance holes varies: For house wren — 1 inch; for nuthatch, titmouse, woodpecker — 1¼-inch.

3. No perch is necessary.

4. Assemble house with nails and paint.

5. Place house in backyard or open woodland on tree or post, 5 to 10 feet above ground.

6. The chickadee, nuthatch, woodpecker, and titmouse prefer bark-covered house.

7. Place wood chips in bottom for woodpecker.

SUET LOG BIRD FEEDER

This reliable feeder uses the following:

One log, 16 inches long, approx. 4 inches in diameter (or use 4-by-4-inch lumber)

Sandpaper

Spar varnish

Heavy screw eye

Suet

1. Drill six to ten 1-inch holes halfway through the log.

2. Taper top of log with an ax or knife (an adult should do this) and apply varnish to prevent checking of the wood.

3. Insert screw eye at the point and attach wire for hanging to a low branch.

4. Force suet into holes and hang feeder from a tree in the yard where it can be observed from the house. Hang it low enough for easy refilling, but out of reach of dogs and cats.

5. Suet-feeding birds are woodpeckers, nuthatches, chickadees, titmice, and brown creepers.

MORE BIRDFEEDERS

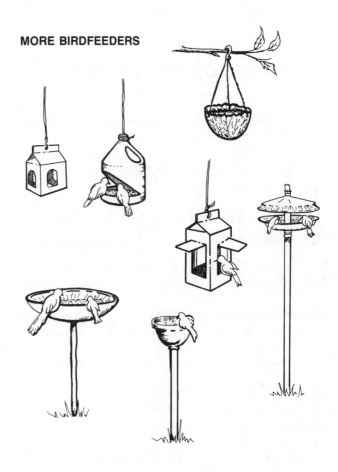

MORE BIRD FEEDERS

Try these different types of feeders.

- Half a coconut shell makes a good bird feeder. Tie it far enough out on the limb of a tree so that cats and squirrels can't reach it.

- Another good hanging feeder can be made from a coffee can. If you make one from a taller type of can, be sure to cut it in half so it isn't too deep.

- A plastic screen basket, such as a berry basket, makes a fine suet holder for meat-eating birds, such as chickadees and woodpeckers.

See the "Nature and Outdoor Activities" section of this book for more information on feeding birds.

Metal and Tin Craft

Metal, one of the basic craft materials, can be worked by Cub Scouts. Begin with aluminum foil to teach the skills of designing, measuring, cutting, modeling, nailing, polishing, and finishing. Then move on to tin or aluminum cans and other metals.

TOOLS FOR METAL WORK

Vise. To hold metal while working or to aid in bending material.

Tin shears. To cut cans and metal sheets and to cut designs or patterns.

Scratch awl. To mark lines or designs. (Nails can also be used for this.)

Center punch. To make dents in the design or to make holes. (Nails can also be used.)

Ball peen hammer. To pound nails, punches, chisels, or whatever you are using to impress design in metal.

Can opener. To open both ends of cans before cutting with tin shears.

Cold chisel. To cut slits in metal or tapped lightly to make designs.

HOW TO WORK WITH METAL

When working with tin, aluminum, or other metals, smooth sharp edges with a file and steel wool or emery cloth. Protect hands from steel wool by wearing gloves or holding it in a cloth.

TIN CANS

Tin cans are easy to accumulate. They come in a variety of sizes and shapes and can be used for many craft projects. They can be made into pencil holders, planters, bird feeders, storage containers, bracelets, napkin rings, bookmarks, airplanes, telegraph keys, and many other useful items.

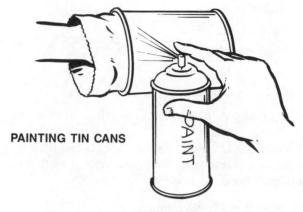

PAINTING TIN CANS

PAINTING

Remove any paper labels. Sand surface of tin can lightly with wet sandpaper to remove shine and make surface ready to paint. Wipe off with a wet sponge. Cans may be painted with enamel spray paint, latex paint, lacquer, or acrylic. When spray painting, insert small paper bag in opening to protect inside of can from paint, as shown in illustration. Spray three light coats, letting dry between coats.

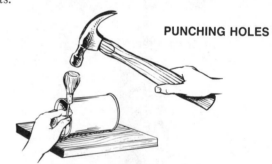

PUNCHING HOLES

PUNCHING HOLES

To make holes in cans, place can on top of a piece of scrap wood. Hold awl to inside of can and punch hole with hammer as shown.

JOINING CANS

To join cans, cut bottom out of one can and place on top of another. Secure with strong glue or strapping tape.

TAPE

JOINING CANS

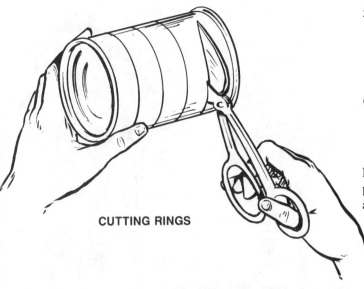

CUTTING RINGS

CUTTING RINGS

Use a pair of tin snips to cut metal rings from cans as shown.

DECORATING CANS

Painted cans can be decorated with plastic stick-on letters or dots, macaroni or seeds, tiny mosaic tiles, or scrap wallpaper. They can also be covered with jute twine or yarn.

ALUMINUM FOIL TOOLING

It is easy to tool designs in aluminum foil from frozen pies or dinners, or aluminum offset printing plates. The designs can be framed and hung on the wall. This method can also be used to tool book covers, belts, jewelry, and other items.

1. Select a design.

2. Sharpen a pencil-size dowel to a point for the basic tool (stylus). Sand the other end of the dowel to a flat slant. (A ball-point pen can also be used.)

3. Foil piece should be flat. It can be cut with kitchen shears.

4. Place foil on soft but firm surface, such as a stack of newspapers or a magazine. Tape it in place. Over this lay the pattern and trace around it with the stylus, including all details. Remove pattern and trace over the entire design again. This is the underside of the work.

5. Turn foil over to the front side and use the stylus just outside the ridges, pushing the background down and away from the design. Use the flat end of the stylus for working the background that isn't close to the design.

6. Turn the foil to the back side again and work the design out with the flat end of the dowel. Continue working both front and back to emphasize details and make the design stand out.

For variation, try hammering lightly on a heavy straight pin or nail over the background. Or use the coil end of a safety pin to provide a different texture.

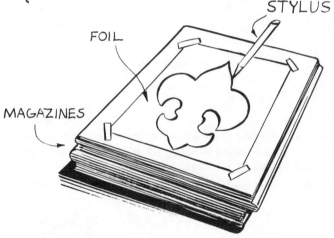

ALUMINUM FOIL TOOLING

TIN PIERCING

Tinsmiths in colonial America used tin piercing to make such items as lanterns, charcoal heaters, and cabinets.

Equipment needed for this activity:

Galvanized metal, sheet aluminum, or aluminum offset plates
Ball peen hammer
Small center punch or a 4-inch nail

For practice, cut the ends out of tin cans, flatten, and experiment with the tools.

1. Select a design to fit the piece of metal.

2. Transfer design to metal with a felt pen.

3. Place metal on a work surface such as a piece of scrap wood on a sturdy bench or table. Be sure that something is under the metal.

TIN CAN TELEPHONE

TIN PIERCING

4. Pierce the design with punch and hammer, using uniform hammer strokes and even spacing. Vary design by using different spacing and different-size holes on various parts. (If metal bends during piercing, wait until finished, then carefully bend back while wearing gloves.)

5. Clean the metal with a soft cloth dipped in rubbing alcohol.

6. Do not paint the metal, as this will plug the holes. If color is desired, paint the metal before piercing with a high quality metal paint.

7. The design can be framed or mounted on a piece of wood.

TIN CAN PROJECTS

TIN CAN TELEPHONE

Boys love to make and use these telephones to send important messages, discuss bright ideas and private plans, and tell deep, dark secrets.

Two small empty tin cans
20 feet sturdy cotton string

1. Cut out one end of the cans. Punch a small hole in the bottoms left intact.

2. Thread the string through the holes and tie knots in the ends to keep the string from pulling through.

3. Pull the string tight between the two "phones" and talk.

BUDDY BURNER

This is a fire starter which is used with a tin-can stove such as those shown here. They can also be used as emergency road flares (keep one or two in your car). You'll need:

One 6-ounce tuna or cat food can
Strip of corrugated cardboard
Paraffin
String

1. Cut a long strip of corrugated cardboard. The width should be slightly less than the height of the can. Remove the paper from one side. Roll the cardboard in a tight coil and place on edge in tuna can. The tighter the cardboard is rolled, the longer it will burn.

2. Insert a piece of string in the center for the wick.

3. Melt paraffin in a clean 1-pound coffee can set in a pan of water. Pour melted paraffin over cardboard in can until can is three-quarters full. Let wax harden.

BUDDY BURNER

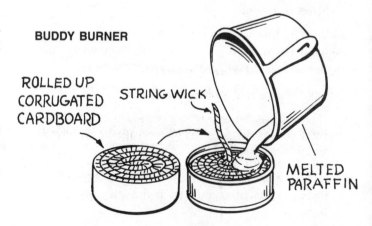

ROLLED UP CORRUGATED CARDBOARD

STRING WICK

MELTED PARAFFIN

TIN CAN STOVE

Cub Scouts will enjoy making this simple stove. Use:

No. 10 tin can
Beverage can opener
Tin shears

1. Cut one end out of the tin can.

2. Use tin shears to cut a hinged opening at bottom end of can. This door can be folded up or to one side. It allows a place to light the buddy burner. Smooth all sharp edges.

3. Use can opener to punch out triangular openings around side of can near closed end.

4. Set tin can stove over buddy burner, light wick, and you're in business.

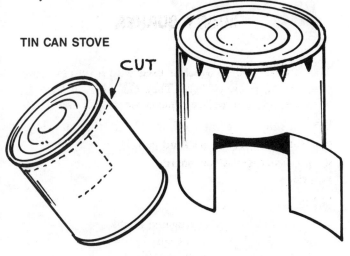

TIN CAN STOVE

CUT

CHARCOAL CHIMNEY

This handy tin can gadget is used in starting a charcoal fire, to help get all the pieces of charcoal equally hot at the same time. It's great for a backyard cookout. You'll need the following:

2-lb. coffee can
Beverage can opener
Screwdriver or other hard implement

1. Remove one end from coffee can.

2. Use beverage can opener to punch rows of triangular holes all around the sides of the can. Protect hands with heavy gloves.

3. Use screwdriver to flatten down metal inside can.

4. Cut out the other end of the can and the chimney is ready to use.

5. When filled with pieces of charcoal and lit at the bottom, the chimney helps the charcoal start with an even heat and more quickly than it would otherwise.

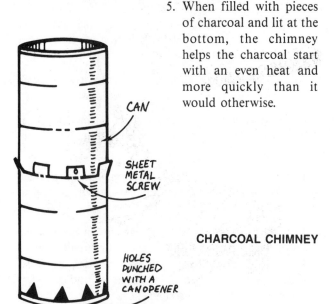

CAN

SHEET METAL SCREW

CHARCOAL CHIMNEY

HOLES PUNCHED WITH A CAN OPENER

INSECT CAGE (BUG JUG)

Cub Scouts can keep their insects alive in this easy-to-make cage. You'll need:

Two 6-ounce tuna or cat food cans
6-by-12-inch screen mesh
Pop bottle cap
Three round-head brass paper fasteners
Stick or branch
Plaster
Paint

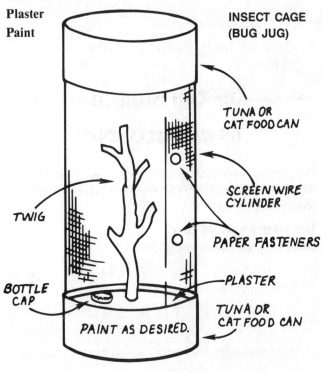

INSECT CAGE (BUG JUG)

TUNA OR CAT FOOD CAN

SCREEN WIRE CYLINDER

PAPER FASTENERS

PLASTER

TUNA OR CAT FOOD CAN

TWIG

BOTTLE CAP

PAINT AS DESIRED.

1. Remove one end from each can. Paint cans as desired.

2. Roll screen wire into a tube 12 inches long and as big around as the inside of the can. Fasten screen together with paper fasteners.

3. Mix enough plaster to fill the can to within ¼-inch from top. Set screen down into wet plaster.

4. While plaster is still wet, push in a small stick or branch (for the insect to climb on) and the bottle cap, open side up, as a "water hole."

5. If desired, a wire handle can be attached to the screen near the top for easy carrying. The lid sets on top so it is easily removed.

6. Remind boys that when they capture an insect alive and keep it for observation, they must remember to keep it alive by watering it. A few days later, the insect should be released. Encourage them to find out what types of food their insect prefers.

WATERSCOPE

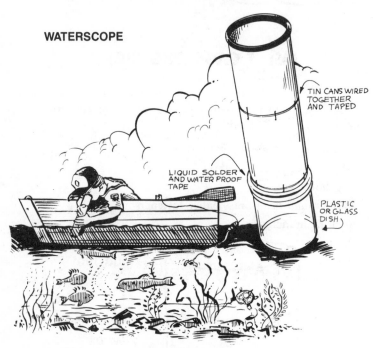

TIN CANS WIRED TOGETHER AND TAPED

LIQUID SOLDER AND WATER PROOF TAPE

PLASTIC OR GLASS DISH

WATERSCOPE

With this device, Cub Scouts can see the wonders of the underwater world. Use the following:

Three small fruit juice cans
Small dish or jar (plastic or glass)
1-inch wide waterproof adhesive tape
Wire

1. Remove both ends from cans. Punch holes near ends of cans so they can be wired together.

2. Align the seams of the cans, placing them end to end and fasten with wire and waterproof tape.

3. Insert this tin cylinder in a jar or glass and make the joint watertight by covering with waterproof tape.

4. Boys can watch the movements of fish or study underwater rocks or plants from the water's edge or a boat. The waterscope eliminates surface reflection and allows them to see directly under water.

SIMPLE TELEGRAPH

SIMPLE TELEGRAPH

Here's a simple telegraph key, made with the following:

6-volt battery with two terminals on top
Tin can
Two blocks of wood
Screws, nails, and wire

1. Cut and bend metal pieces as shown. Screw them to blocks of wood.

2. Hammer in nails for the receiver.

3. Wire as shown. In wrapping wire around the nails, start at the top of one nail and work down. Then go across to the other nail and work up. Have at least eight turns on each nail.

4. When the switch is closed, the receiver or sounder will be drawn down to the two nails and make a click. In Morse code, one click is a dot; two clicks, dash. (See *The Official Boy Scout Handbook* if boys want to learn the code.)

INDIAN DRUM

This authentic looking and sounding drum can be made from the following:

No. 10 tin can	**Leather or plastic lacing**
Rawhide or canvas	**Acrylic paint, brush**

1. Cut both ends from the tin can.

2. Cut two circles of rawhide or canvas, about 4 inches larger in diameter than the can. This will leave a 2-inch border for lacing.

3. Punch holes about ¾-inch from edge all around the rawhide circles, as shown.

4. Lace top and bottom to drum with leather or plastic lacing. Stretch tight.

5. Paint drum with Indian symbols.

6. Make a drumstick by covering a wad of cotton with a piece of rawhide and binding it to a stick or dowel with a sturdy string.

INDIAN DRUM

INDIAN ARM BANDS

Here's an easy-to-make arm band, using:

Two 6 ounce tuna or cat food cans
Brass paper fasteners
Turquoise enamel

1. Remove top and bottom of cans. Cut on the seam. Fold over the ends and hammer flat. File off any rough edges.

2. Decorate with turquoise stones (brass paper fasteners which have been dipped in enamel).

INDIAN ARM BANDS

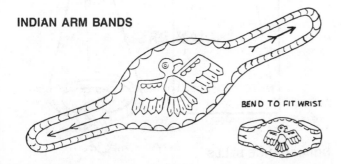

BEND TO FIT WRIST

INDIAN BRACELET

Use these materials to make this simple bracelet:

Foil pie pan
Knitting needle, blunt pencil, or dry ball point pen
Sandpaper

1. Cut bracelet shape from pie pan with scissors.

2. Use a knitting needle or blunt point of a pencil to trace over design, bearing down so it will be transferred to foil.

3. File rough edges with sandpaper.

4. Add a turquoise modeling dough stone in center of bracelet, if desired. (See index for modeling dough.)

5. Bend bracelet to fit wrist.

INDIAN BRACELET

NUT AND BOLT CHESS SET

Cub Scouts can learn to play chess on this unusual homemade set. Use:

Two small acorn nuts
Two ⅜-inch cap screws
Eight ⅜″ nuts
12 ⅜-inch flat-head socket cap screws
Four ⅜-inch thumb screws
Four ⅜-inch castle nuts or castellated nuts
Two external tooth lock washers
16 ¼-inch machine screws
16 ¼-inch nuts
Epoxy cement
Contrasting paint

Assemble and glue nuts and bolts together as illustrated. This makes enough for one chess game. Paint half of the

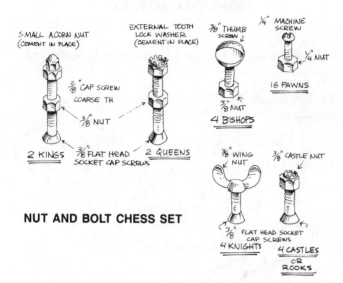

NUT AND BOLT CHESS SET

pieces one color and the other half a contrasting color. Or you might make one set of steel and one of brass nuts and bolts.

CONCHO BELT

Remove liners from bottle caps. Flatten caps on heavy piece of metal. Punch hole in center of cap, as shown, and insert turquoise gem (brass paper fastener dipped in turquoise enamel with colored strips of plastic attached). Push the conchos through holes in a leather or plastic belt, bend the ends over and cover with tape.

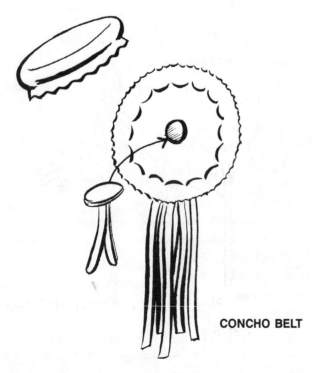

CONCHO BELT

MEXICAN TIN ORNAMENTS

You can make attractive Mexican ornaments from these everyday items.

Foil trays or aluminum offset plates
Orange stick or dry ball-point pen
Permanent markers

1. Cut desired shape from the foil tray or offset plate. (Use an emery board to file the edges smooth, if necessary.)

2. Place the ornament on a stack of newspaper. Use the orange stick or dry ball-point pen to draw in the details.

3. Color the ornament, using markers.

4. Punch small hole at the top for hanging. A few patterns are suggested here, but use your imagination to create others.

MEXICAN TIN ORNAMENTS

INDIAN DANCE BELLS

Make bells from pieces of tin rolled into a conical shape, as shown. Insert knotted cord and pull to top of cone. Tie bells in bunches of three or four and fasten to an ankle band.

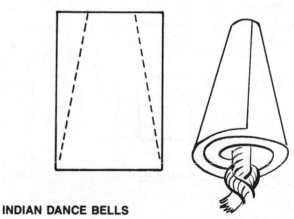

INDIAN DANCE BELLS

Wire Craft

Wire coat hangers are as helpful to a den leader as the hairpin was to the Model T Ford mechanic. Many simple and useful items can be made from this wire.

A few simple tools are helpful in working with wire coat hangers. A pair of wire cutters, pliers, and a bending board and/or a bending handle, as shown below, are useful.

BENDING HANDLE

Drill a ¼-inch hole through a 6-inch section of broomstick or dowel, as shown. Slip over coat hanger wire to bend or straighten it.

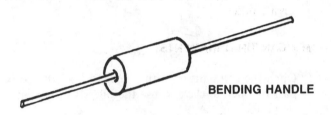

BENDING HANDLE

LITTER BAG

Here's a good way to keep your car free of litter. Use the following:

Wire coat hanger
No. 12 size paper bag
Paper clips or masking tape

1. Bend coat hanger as shown in illustration.

2. Fold the top of the bag over the holder and fasten with paper clips or masking tape.

3. Hang litter bag in car.

4. Bag may be decorated before assembling, if desired, with crayons or colored markers.

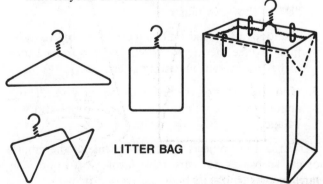

LITTER BAG

BENDING BOARD

Bend your wire in all shapes with this tool. You'll need the following:

12-by-1-by-4-inch piece of wood
Spools or sections of dowel
Wood blocks and circles
Nails

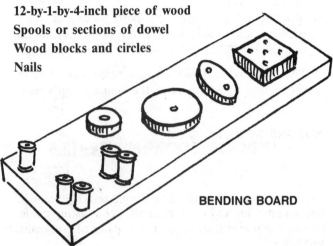

BENDING BOARD

Nail spools and blocks to wood as shown in illustration. Spools spaced at various distances will help in bending coat hanger wire in various shapes.

HUMMINGBIRD FEEDER

Take care of your hummingbirds with this simple feeder. Use these materials:

Wire coat hanger
Test tube
Foil pan
Sugar/water/red food coloring

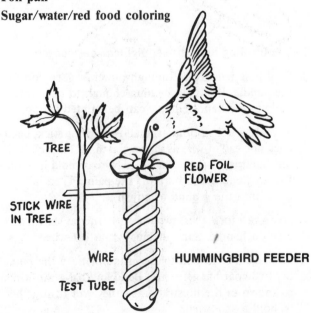

TREE

STICK WIRE IN TREE.

RED FOIL FLOWER

WIRE

TEST TUBE

HUMMINGBIRD FEEDER

1. Use one of the spools on the wire bending board to twist coat hanger into a coil to fit test tube, as shown. Leave one end of wire straight to stick in a tree.

2. Cut flower shape from foil pan, leaving an opening in center of flower. Glue to top of test tube.

3. Mix one part sugar and four parts water and add a small amount of red food coloring. Pour this solution into the test tube.

4. The feeder is ready to stick into a tree. Place it near the house so you can watch the hummingbirds feed.

OUTDOOR COOKING UTENSILS

Use coat hangers to make these simple cooking utensils. You'll need:

Coat hangers

1-by-4-inch dowel or corn cob

Bending handle

OUTDOOR COOKING UTENSILS

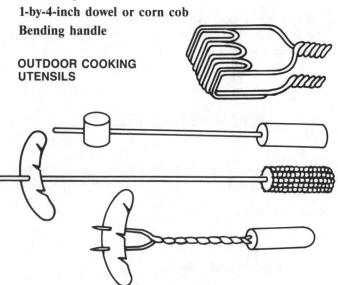

1. Use bending handle to straighten coat hangers.

2. Drill hole lengthwise through dowel or corn cob for the handle. It should be long enough to fit comfortably in the hand. Handle can be painted if desired.

3. To make a weiner or marshmallow roasting stick, bend back one end of wire as shown and insert through handle. Sandpaper the point of the wire or hold it in the fire long enough to burn off the paint. Then jab the point into the ground to polish it.

4. To make a fork, twist two wires together as shown and glue on handle. Sand or burn paint off wire.

5. To make a sandwich toaster, sand or burn the paint off two coat hanger wires. Bend and twist the wires as shown in the illustration so they will fit together to hold a sandwich.

MOBILES

A mobile is a sort of sculpture that moves. Mobiles are made by putting pieces together in a balanced design. They are often made of wires and cords connected so they move in the slightest breeze. Use the following materials:

Three wire coathangers

Cutouts (metal, cardboard, foil, wood) or other objects to be hung on mobile

Carpet thread, strong string, or fishing line

Pliers, yardstick

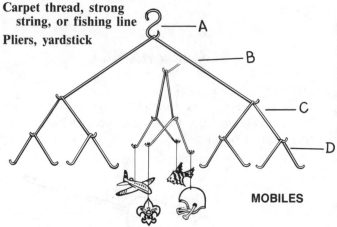

MOBILES

1. Open the coathangers with pliers. Cut off the hook part of one hanger and use the pliers to form an S shape hanger ("A").

2. Straighten all hangers and cut a 36-inch length of wire from each.

3. Make arm "B" from one 36-inch length. End it in the middle as shown in the illustration and curve the ends up. To get both sides even, draw an outline of one bent side on a sheet of paper and use it as a pattern for the other side.

4. Cut a second length of wire into equal pieces and make arms "C."

5. Cut the third length of wire into four equal parts and form arms "D."

6. To assemble the arms, hang the S-hook on the ceiling attachment from which the mobile will be hung. Hang arm "B" on S-hook. Then hang arms "C" on the ends of "B". Hold the "C" arms steady while hanging arms "D" as shown in illustration.

7. Tie loops of thread or fishline to the objects to be hung. Make the loops various lengths, from 2 to 6 inches to give an interesting effect.

8. Hook the loops on the arm ends, one at a time. Hang about the same weight on each end so the arm will balance.

NOTE: Cut-out objects can fit the theme of the month or use keepsakes, toy cars, table favors, driftwood, fish lures, sports emblems, badges, or other items.

RUBBER STAMP
(Branding Iron)

Make this stamp or branding iron from a piece of coat hanger wire and a gum eraser.

1. Carve design or brand on one side of eraser.

2. Punch hole lengthwise through eraser with coat hanger wire and twist to make handle.

3. Press stamp on an ink pad and you're ready to stamp a design on paper or brand a maverick.

Leather Craft

Leather, one of the basic crafts materials, has much to offer Cub Scouts, including learning new skills in creating useful and beautiful items.

Leather can be decorated by painting designs on it, dyeing it, tooling it, stamping patterns in it with punches, burning designs on it, or by weaving or braiding through it. Don't confine your work to simply lacing together precut kits. Tooling, embossing, and stamping are skills that can be learned by Cub Scout-age boys.

Leather can be expensive. Look for stores that will give away leather scraps or sell bags of scraps at a low price. Scrap leather is suitable for most Cub Scout leatherwork projects. Heavy scrap vinyl, such as upholstery vinyl, can be used as a substitute for leather in some projects.

Begin with leather tooling, one of the simplest types of leathercraft. This skill requires only one tool, a modeler or stylus, and a project can be completed in a short time.

LEATHER TOOLS

Although there are carving tools for many types of designs in leatherwork, Cub Scouts will need only a few, and they can be homemade. Make the modeling tools from hardwood dowels of different diameters and shapes, or check with your local Scout distributor or leather store.

Background Tools

These can be dowels shaped into dots or nails filed into many designs, such as flowers, stars, squares, circles, single lines, double lines, and cross-hatched lines. Use the edges of a square-headed nail to form lines into squares and triangles.

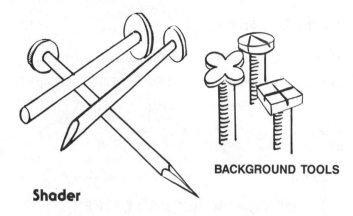

BACKGROUND TOOLS

Shader

Use this tool when depressed areas are needed. The angle at which you hold the tool determines the size and depth of the depression. Hold shader in left hand and strike it with a good firm blow of your striking stick.

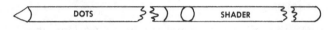

DOTS   SHADER

SHADER

Bevelers

Make these in two sizes. Use the large one for all long cuts and the small one on all sharp turns. To get a raised effect, depress the leather on the outside of the design, except on curves. Place the beveler on the cut lines and hold it in an upright position. Give the beveler light taps with a wooden mallet or striking stick as you move it forward with each stroke.

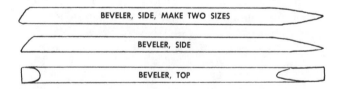

BEVELER, SIDE, MAKE TWO SIZES

BEVELER, SIDE

BEVELER, TOP

BEVELERS

Veiners

Make flowers, leaves, and ornamental designs with these tools. Hold the veiner in an upright position. Start at the base and work toward the point of the leaf. Lean veiner to the right or left depending on the design.

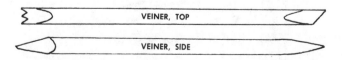

VEINER, TOP

VEINER, SIDE

VEINERS

Punch, Awl, Scriber

These tools can be made from spikes filed to desired point.

In addition to these tools, the following will be helpful:

Wooden Mallet. For striking stamping tools.

Leather Punch. Similar to a paper hole punch, to punch holes in leather for lacing, or punching belt holes.

TIPS FOR WORKING LEATHER

- Use a hard surface as a base when tooling leather. Marble is an excellent base since it doesn't absorb moisture. You can also use laminated counter-top scraps (from counter-top manufacturers and kitchen remodeling firms).

- Dampen all leather completely before working on it. Redampen from back side if it dries out before you are finished.

NOTE: Do not moisten leather which will have a burned design. Use regular wood-burning set.

LEATHER TOOLING

1. With a sponge or cloth, dampen the leather on the dough side with cold water. After a short while the dampness will reach the finished side of the leather. If it looks wet on the finished side, it is too damp to tool. Wait until it dries slightly and the natural leather color returns.

LEATHER TOOLING

2. Place pattern on front side of dampened leather. Fasten it in place with tape or a clamp. Trace the pattern with a stylus. Lift one end of the pattern to be sure all of the pattern has been transferred. Remove pattern.

3. Lay leather on a firm surface. Use the slanted end of the modeler or stylus to level around all the outside lines and around the inside of any other lines. Always draw the tool toward you. Keep an even pressure on the stylus to prevent making deep marks in the leather. This technique brings out a darker, waxed-like color in the leather, and the depression will produce an attractive design. If the design is not clear enough, go over it again. Redampen the leather if necessary.

4. When design is finished and leather is dry, apply final finish. Use wax, saddle soap, or leather dressing.

LEATHER STAMPING

1. Dampen leather on back side. Do not soak.

2. Place leather on hard surface.

3. Hold stamping tool in one hand and tap gently with a wooden mallet.

4. Strike tool carefully to prevent cutting through leather.

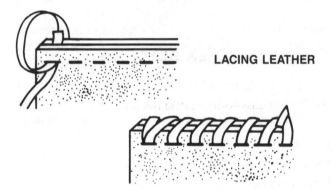

LACING LEATHER

LACING LEATHER

Leather or plastic lacing can be obtained at your local Scout distributor or at a craft or hobby store.

The spiral or whipstich, illustrated here, is the simplest lacing stitch. It consists of running a single lace, spiral fashion through successive holes. Always make the first and last lace a double one, to conceal the ends.

NOTE: If leather becomes soiled while working with it, it can be cleaned with saddle soap. Apply with an old sock to entire surface and allow to dry. Do this before applying wax.

——LEATHER PROJECTS——

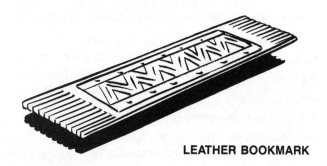

LEATHER BOOKMARK

LEATHER BOOKMARK

For this project, you will need the following:

2-by-8-inch leather

Leather tools

1. Select a design or monogram which will fit on the piece of leather.

2. Follow the instructions above for leather tooling to imprint design on leather.

3. Bottom of bookmark can be cut into a fringe, if desired.

LEATHER KEYCHAIN

This handy, easy-to-make item is a good gift for parents. The following are needed:

1 ¼-by-4-inch leather

Beaded key chain

Leather tools

1. Select a design or set of initials which will fit on the piece of leather.

2. Punch a hole near the top of the leather, large enough for the key chain to slip through easily.

3. Follow the instructions above for leather tooling to imprint your design on the leather.

A BELT WALLET

Your loose change, bills, and other odds and ends won't get lost if you use a belt wallet. These wallets fit securely on a belt and are easy to make from the following:

4-by-12-inch scrap of leather or vinyl

1 yard of ³⁄₃₂-inch leather or plastic lacing

Rotary leather punch

Awl

Knife or razor blade to cut leather

Leather tools as desired

Rubber cement

Cardboard or tracing paper pattern

1. Enlarge either of the patterns to the size indicated. (If you wish to make larger wallets, you will need a larger piece of leather and more lacing.) Be sure to space the holes evenly.

2. Cut the leather to size. Use paper clips to hold the pattern in position while cutting the leather and marking the hole centers with the awl.

3. Tool the leather in an original design or use initials.

4. Apply rubber cement along the edges where the holes will be placed. Lightly hammer the seams together, rough side inside. Punch holes with ³⁄₃₂-inch punch, going through all thicknesses.

5. Cut one end of the lacing to a sharp point. For pattern "A," use an in-and-out stitch, tucking the ends under. Add "Flap Strap" as shown in the pattern.

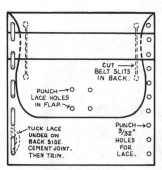

BELT WALLET

PATTERN A

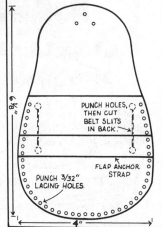

PATTERN B

For pattern "B," begin lacing at the top of either side, using the whip stitch described earlier in this chapter. Add the "Flap Strap" to the front over the sixth through eighth holes.

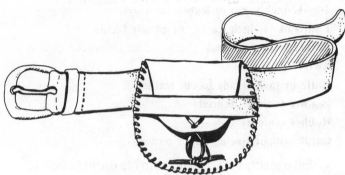

6. Use the rest of the lacing to make a decorative finish to the flap.

LEATHER NAME SIGN

Make leather name signs to hang on a door. Use the following materials:

Scrap of leather, cut to desired size
Rotary leather punch
Leather tools and initials
Permanent-type leather markers
1½ yards of ³⁄₃₂-inch lacing

LEATHER NAME SIGN

1. Cut the leather to desired size and shape; 2-by-8-inch makes a good size.

2. Very carefully, mark places for holes all around the leather, keeping the holes evenly spaced.

3. Use the ³⁄₃₂-inch punch to make holes.

4. Evenly space the name in the center of the leather. The outer sides can be tooled as desired.

5. Lace all around the name plate, starting and ending at either upper corner. Add a length of lacing to the opposite corner for a hanger.

POCKET KNIFE SHEATH

For this practical project, you'll need the following:

Scrap of leather big enough for the knife
Paper for pattern
Knife to cut leather
Rotary punch
About 2 feet of leather or vinyl lacing
Leather tools or initials

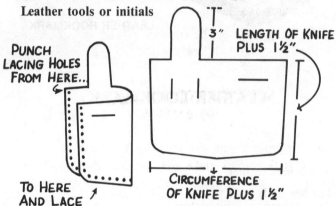

POCKET KNIFE SHEATH

1. Make a paper pattern to fit the knife, allowing the extra length and width as shown. Evenly space marks for the holes. Cut leather by the pattern and mark holes.

2. Cut the slots as shown. Be certain the two vertical slots will fit the belt.

3. If desired, tool a design or mark with initials.

4. Fold over. Hold edges together securely. Punch through both layers at once.

5. Use a whip stitch to lace the two edges together, beginning at the top and ended at the bottom as shown.

6. Slip knife sheath onto belt through the slots in back. Insert knife, fold tab over top of it, and slide tab into front slot.

Plastic Bottle and Carton Crafts

Plastic bottles and milk cartons come in different sizes and shapes and can be used for a variety of craft projects. They are waterproof, strong, easy to cut, bend, and decorate. The list of things you can create from plastic is limited only by your imagination.

Some tips on working with plastic:

• Before beginning any project, wash and dry cartons thoroughly.

- Clear silicone glue is best for plastic bottles. White glue works well for plastic cartons.

- Paint with a mixture of liquid detergent and powdered tempera. Acrylic paint is also suitable. If using spray enamel, sand surface of plastic lightly first so paint will adhere.

- Punch small holes in plastic bottles with a hot ice pick or nail. (*Caution: An adult should do this*). Punch larger holes with an eyelet punch found in sewing departments.

- Plastic cartons can be cut with regular scissors. Cut plastic bottles with heavy scissors or kitchen shears.

MILK CARTON HANGING PLANTER

Plastic milk cartons make excellent planters. Use these items:

One half-gallon milk carton
One gallon milk carton
Plastic bowl or container
Chain, paper clip

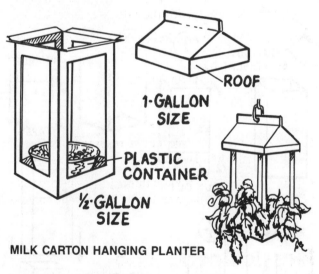

MILK CARTON HANGING PLANTER

1. Mark cutting lines on carton with felt-tip pen. Cut off top of half-gallon carton, folding back top edges as shown. Cut out sides.

2. Cut gable roof from gallon carton. Punch hole through top and insert paper clip hanger to hold chain.

3. Fit the pieces together and fasten with white glue. Paint if desired.

4. Attach chain to clip.

5. Insert plastic container, such as a 1-pound margarine tub to hold the plant.

MILK CARTON BIRD FEEDER

This easy-to-make bird feeder can be assembled quickly from these items:

Half-gallon milk carton
Paper clip
Two brass paper fasteners
Wire coat hangers

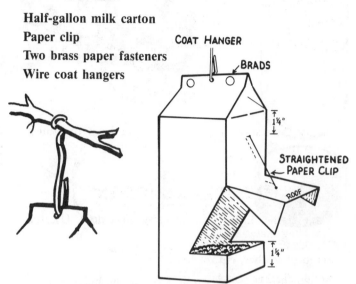

MILK CARTON BIRD FEEDER

1. Mark cutting lines for opening with felt-tip pen. Bottom of feeder is 1¼ inches deep. Cut out, leaving top to be folded back for roof.

2. Straighten the paper clip and push it through carton about 1¼ inches from gable. Bend clip inside carton to secure. Insert other end of clip through feeder roof and bend back to hold.

3. Push paper fasteners through peak to seal top of feeder. Punch hole in peak to hold coathanger hook.

4. Punch a few small holes in bottom of feeder to let out moisture. Hang from a branch.

5. Fill with mixed bird seed and sunflower seed. Birds also like bread crumbs, nutmeats, and dog biscuits.

PLASTIC BOTTLE TERRARIUM

Use the following to make this simple terrarium or bell jar:

2-liter soft drink bottle (clear with dark bottom section)
Charcoal, soil, plants

1. Remove label and plastic bottom from bottle by soaking in hot water about 10 minutes. It may be necessary to pry bottom gently before snapping it off with the fingers. Use paint thinner, fingernail polish remover, or rubber cement thinner to remove glue from label and bottom.

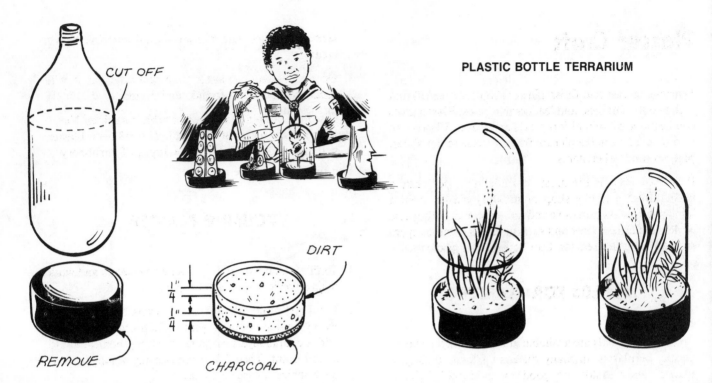

CUT OFF

REMOVE

DIRT

CHARCOAL

2. Cut top of bottle off just below the bulge, leaving about two-thirds of the bottle. Wrap a piece of tape around the bottle to aid in cutting a straight line.

3. Pour ¼-inch charcoal into black bottom. Then fill with potting soil to within ¼-inch of top.

4. Plant with slow-growing plants. Water throughly.

5. Turn the two-thirds bottle upside down over black bottom to form a clear dome.

6. This terrarium never needs water. It creates its own moisture through condensation. Plants live in the environment you have created. If it fogs up, remove the top for a short time. Do not place in direct sunlight.

This bell jar can also be used as a container to show off collectibles.

MILK CARTON PERISCOPE

With this periscope, boys can hide behind a wall, tree, fence, or bush and observe birds and animals unnoticed. Make it from the following:

Two one-quart milk cartons
Two mirrors, about 1 ⅞-by-2 ⅞-inches
Masking tape

1. Cut off top of one carton. Cut out near bottom, as shown.

2. Tape over back of mirror so if it breaks it will not shat-

ter. Place mirror on a slant, in lower back of carton. Adjust angle until you can see straight out the top of the carton when you look through the hole in the side. Tape mirror in place. (If mirror is wider than the carton, cut slits in sides of carton.) This is half of the periscope.

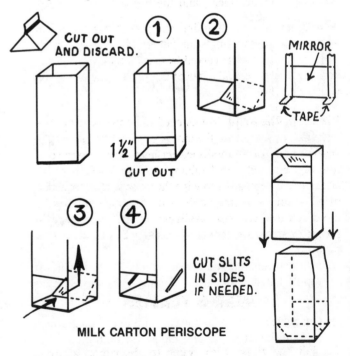

CUT OUT AND DISCARD.

① ②

MIRROR

TAPE

1½"

CUT OUT

③ ④

CUT SLITS IN SIDES IF NEEDED.

MILK CARTON PERISCOPE

3. To complete the periscope, cut the top off another carton and repeat the same steps. Put the two cartons together, squeezing the top of the bottom carton so the other will slide down on top of it.

4. Periscope can be painted or decorated.

Plaster Craft

Learning to cast and finish plaster projects is a skill that Cub Scouts, families, and leaders will enjoy. Plaster casts can be made of animal footprints and leaves. Plaster can also be used to make picture frames, neckerchief slides, plaques, and other items.

Plaster of Paris is the most common type, but casting plaster from a hobby shop or molding plaster from a lumberyard is less expensive and more durable. Orthopedic or dental plaster is finer and stronger, but it is more expensive. All can be used for Cub Scot plaster projects.

MOLDS FOR PLASTER

Commercial molds are available in flexible vinyl or latex, plastic, or plaster, in many different sizes and shapes. Plastic candy molds are good for neckerchief slides. Plastic or waxed tubs or cartons make excellent molds for candle holders with a bottle top as a mold insert. Picture frames and plaques can also be molded in plastic or waxed cartons. Wooden, plastic, or cardboard frames are needed for casting tracks and leaves. Coffee and dry beverage mix scoops make excellent molds for circular objects: bicycle "wheels," "smiley" faces, and the like.

A commercial latex molding compound is available at hobby stores for making your own molds. A design made from modeling clay or carved from soap or soft wood can be covered with several coats of liquid latex and the result is a rubber mold.

Preparing The Mold. Molds need to be prepared to prevent sticking and to aid the cast in slipping out easily. Use vegetable oil for all molds except latex. Use a soap solution of 1 cup water to 1 tablespoon liquid detergent for latex molds. Remember to wipe the mold lightly; an excess of oil or soap will cause defects in the cast. Commercial mold releases are also available. It isn't necessary to prepare wax carton molds, since the wax will serve that purpose.

MIXING PLASTER

1. Fill the mold with water to determine amount required. Pour this water into a disposable mixing container such as a paper cup or small aluminum pan.

2. Sprinkle plaster slowly into water until a peak forms above the surface. Allow to set for 1 minute. Then, using a wooden or plastic spoon, stir gently to pre-

vent air bubbles. The mixture should resemble heavy cream.

3. Do not mix more plaster than you need, as it will harden quickly and cannot be thinned.

4. Discard extra plaster in a disposable container. Never pour it down a sink or dump it near shrubbery. Plaster will clog drains and kill some types of shrubbery.

POURING PLASTER

1. To fill small molds, pour plaster immediately and work it into crevices with a toothpick.

2. Fill larger molds about three-quarters full, flex mold with your hand or tap it gently against table. You may add a couple layers of gauze to strengthen the mold at this point. Then fill to top and tap again to allow air bubbles to rise to surface.

3. If cast needs a ring, such as for a plaque or neckerchief slide, insert it now.

4. Allow to set before removing it from mold— approximately 15 to 30 minutes for small molds, 1 to 2 hours for large molds.

5. Remove cast from mold. It should slip out easily. Scrape or sand rough edges.

6. Allow cast to dry completely—a day or more—before painting.

Note: To speed up the hardening process, add a few grains of table salt to dry plaster before mixing or use a commercial hardening product. To slow down normal hardening process, add 1 teaspoon powdered borax to each 8 teaspoons of dry plaster.

PAINTING PLASTER

Most paint will soak into plaster, so it is best to seal the cast with a commercial spray sealer, gesso, or thinned latex wall paint. After the sealer is dry, any type of paint can be applied—tempera, acrylic, oil, or enamel. Tempera will leave a dull finish unless it is given a final coat of clear shellac or spray varnish.

For an antique finish, paint the object with bluegreen tempera. Allow to dry. Then coat object with dark brown shoe polish and polish with a soft cloth. This will leave an old copper finish.

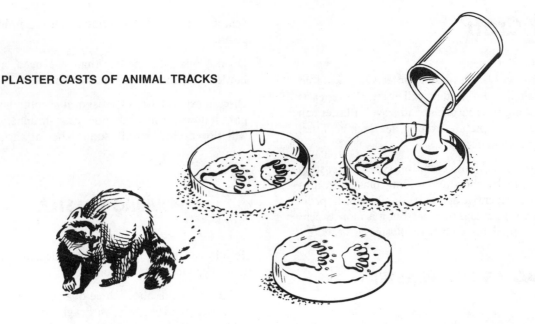

PLASTER CASTS OF ANIMAL TRACKS

CARVING PLASTER

One of the best ways to teach boys to whittle with a pocketknife is by using soap or plaster as the whittling material. When they have mastered this technique, they can go on to wood. Mold plaster in a quart-size milk carton or other disposable container. When ready to whittle, let plaster chunk soak for a while in water. Plaster is porous. The water which is absorbed by the hardened plaster will make it easier to work with.

———— PLASTER PROJECTS ————

PLASTER LEAF PRINTS

For this project you'll need the following:

Plastic lid

Leaf to be printed

Vegetable oil or petroleum jelly

Plaster

1. Grease or oil lid and vein side of leaf.

2. Place leaf, vein side up, in bottom of lid.

3. Pour plaster in gently. Let set until hard.

4. Remove cast from mold. Remove leaf. Let dry thoroughly.

5. Wash off oil. Paint leaf print if desired.

PLASTER CASTS OF ANIMAL TRACKS

The best tracks for casting are found near streams, muddy banks, or on beaches. Materials needed are:

Plaster/water

Strip of cardboard 1½-inches wide, or strip from paper cup or quart milk carton

Paper clip

Empty can for mixing plaster

Stick or spoon for stirring

1. After you have located the tracks you wish to cast, brush away all twigs, stones, or dirt on the ground around the tracks.

2. Surround the tracks with a cardboard circle fastened with the paper clip. Push the cardboard part way down into the mud.

3. Put about a cup full of water into can. Pour dry plaster over water, stirring with a stick until the mixture is thick and smooth.

4. Pour plaster slowly from one side to the other over the tracks inside the cardboard ring. This way the plaster has time to push the air out and no bubbles will be left.

5. After about 15 minutes, the plaster should be hard enough for the cast to be removed. While the cast is still damp, scratch the date and name of the animal in the plaster. When it is throughly dry, remove the cardboard.

If you will be doing the plaster casting while on a hike, have each Cub Scout carry a small sandwich bag with ⅓ to ½ cup of dry plaster. When you find tracks, have the Cub Scouts *slowly* and *gradually* add a little water from their canteens. Knead until smooth. Pour into prepared track as above. No bucket, no mess, and the "empties" can be easily carried home for disposal!

PLASTER PAPERWEIGHTS

Use your imagination to create novel paperweights. You'll need the following:

Mold for paperweight
Plaster/water
Container and spoon for mixing plaster
Paint

PLASTER PAPERWEIGHTS

1. Use plastic or metal margarine containers as molds for larger paperweights. Use paper cups for smaller ones.

2. Give mold a light coat of vegetable oil.

3. Mix plaster as directed above. Pour into mold and let harden.

4. For a turtle paperweight, use mold to make the body about 1-inch thick. Use old measuring spoons as molds for feet and head. When plaster is set, carve head and feet to desired shape. Glue feet and head to body, then glue turtle to felt base. Paint turtle in bright colors.

5. Use your imagination in creating other shapes for paperweight.

SAND CASTING

For this project Cub Scouts need the following materials:

Wood or sturdy cardboard box filled with sand
Plaster/water/container for mixing
Spoons, tongue depressors, etc.

1. Line box with foil or paper before adding sand. Fill box with sand at least ½-inch deep—more for a thicker design.

SAND CASTING

2. Dampen sand with water.

3. Use spoon, pencil, tongue depressor, etc. to make design in sand. Dig out excess.

4. Mix plaster as directed above. Pour it into the sand mold. If sand casting is to be hung, add a string loop or paper clip on the back by inserting it in the wet plaster.

5. When plaster has hardened, remove from sand.

NECKERCHIEF SLIDES

Make neckerchief slides appropriate to the monthly theme. Choose a suitable mold; mix and pour the plaster. Insert a metal or plastic ring in wet plaster for the neckerchief to slide through. When dry, remove from mold and paint.

PLASTER SCRIMSHAW

The Eskimos made whale-bone carvings called scrimshaw, and this same technique was used by sailors. Cub Scouts can use plaster to make carvings that look like scrimshaw to wear as pendants or use as paperweights. You'll need these items:

Plaster/water
Waxed paper
Nail or sharp tool for scratching
Dark tempera paint, shellac
Thong for pendant

1. Mix plaster with water as described earlier. Drop globs of plaster on waxed paper. Flatten them with your fingers.

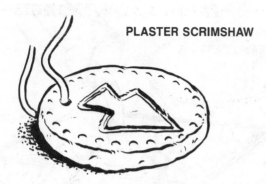

2. Use the nail or a toothpick to make a hole in the plaster if it is to be a pendant.

3. When plaster is hard, scratch a design in it.

4. Thin dark tempera and brush one coat on the plaster. When paint is dry, shellac.

5. For pendant, add thong or heavy cord to tie around the neck.

Papier Mâché

Papier mâché is a modeling material made by mixing wallpaper paste with absorbent paper, such as newspaper, paper towels, paper napkins, or tissue. Cub Scouts love the messiness of papier mâché, but leaders should not hesitate to tackle it since some useful items can be made. Trays, bowls, animals, figures, relief maps, napkin rings, masks, candleholders, or wastebaskets are just a few. Just spread around lots of newspapers for protection and cover the boys' uniforms with mens' old shirts.

FRAMEWORK

Some type of framework is necessary, such as chicken wire, cardboard tubes or cartons, or coat hangers. A small animal or figure can be made from a framework of newspaper rolls or cardboard rolls taped together. A large mask, a pinata, or any round object can be made on an inflated balloon. Various size balloons can be used to make planets for a model solar system. Larger items can be modeled over a framework of chicken wire crushed to the desired shape. A large candleholder can be made by glueing different shape jars or bottles together and cover with papier mâché. Napkin rings can be made by modeling mâché over cardboard tube sections.

STRIP PAPIER MÂCHÉ

This method is good for making large masks, stage props, and for covering wastebaskets.

1. Mix wallpaper paste according to package directions. It should be the consistency of pea soup.

2. Tear (do not cut) newspaper strips about 1 to 1½-inches wide. The frayed edges will blend smoothly. Use wider strips for large objects.

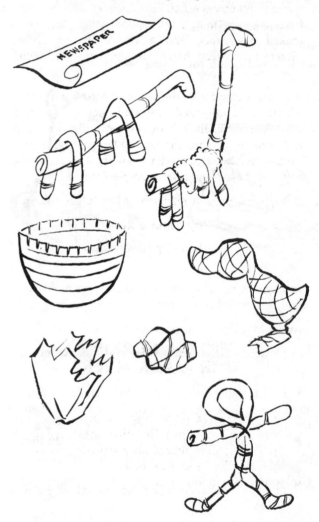

3. Dip the strips into paste mixture and run through the fingers to remove excess paste. Lay them over the framework, overlapping, and in different directions. It is usually best to let each layer dry before applying another. Use alternate layers of regular newspaper and colored comic strip paper so missed spots will show up quickly. The number of layers will depend on the type of object being made and the strength desired. A final coat of torn paper towel strips will give an even-textured surface for painting.

4. Place object in a room where warm air circulates to let it dry.

PULPY MÂCHÉ

This is an instant mâché which is homemade. It can be used to cover tin cans for vases or planters, or to cover a paper bag stuffed with paper to make a mask or animal head.

1. Fill a quart jar with tiny pieces of torn newspaper, about 1-inch square. Cover with water and let soak overnight.

2. Squeeze out excess water. Fill a blender with two cups water, ½ cup flour, 1 tablespoon white glue, 1-cup soaked newspaper, and a few drops of oil of wintergreen to keep the mixture smelling sweet. Blend well, and it's ready to use.

3. Another method is to drop shredded newspaper into a large kettle half-filled with water. Let it soak about a week, then drain off excess. Sprinkle flour and wallpaper paste into the pot and mix it with your hands. Continue adding flower and paste and squeeze and knead until mixture resembles clay.

4. Store excess pulp in refrigerator for future use.

5. Allow project to dry about a week.

6. Sand off rough edges and paint.

TIPS ON WORKING WITH PAPIER MÂCHÉ

1. When using mâché on an object which needs to be removed (bowl, vase, etc.), first oil or grease the object so the dried papier mâché shell will slip off easily. Petroleum jelly works very well.

2. Count on a mâché project lasting through several den meetings.

3. Let object air-dry when possible. Heat tends to make it shrink and buckle.

4. Sand object for a smooth finish before painting. Final finish can also be made by covering with mâché made from paper toweling.

Painting Papier Mâché. If using tempera paint, give project an undercoat of gesso or thinned white latex paint first. Tempera-painted objects should be sprayed with a clear plastic finish or clear varnish for a protective overcoat. Acrylic paint does not require a base coat. Household enamel can also be used.

PAPIER MÂCHÉ PROJECTS

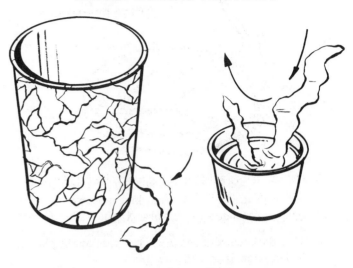

PAPIER MÂCHÉ BOWL

Start your projects with this bowl. Each boy will need:

Bowl for base
Liquid soap or petroleum jelly
Torn newspaper strips
Wallpaper paste
Gesso, paint

1. Apply a thin coat of liquid soap to bowl before starting to apply paper strips.

2. For first coat, apply strips evenly in one direction. Apply next layer evenly, but in opposite direction. Continue until desired thickness is reached. Let dry. Remove bowl.

3. Sand and paint as desired.

WASTEBASKET

For a simple wastebasket you'll need:

A 3-gallon cardboard ice cream carton
Waxed paper
Torn newspaper strips
Wallpaper paste
Gesso, paint

1. Set carton on waxed paper. Completely cover it with papier mâché strips. Also cover the inside of the carton. One or two coats is adequate since the carton itself is sturdy.

2. Let dry completely. Sand any rough edges. Paint and decorate as desired.

TRAY

Make this simple tray out of the following items:

Corrugated cardboard box
Masking tape
Waxed paper
Torn newspaper strips
Wallpaper paste
Gesso, paint

1. Cut two pieces from cardboard box the desired size and shape for the tray. Use masking tape to join pieces together for a double thickness. If you wish, the tray can have low sides by taping on narrow strips of cardboard.

2. Place tray on waxed paper and cover with several layers of overlapping maché strips.

3. Allow to dry thoroughly. To keep tray from warping while it dries, lay a piece of waxed paper on top and weight with books or other heavy objects. Remove weights periodically so air can get to tray.

4. Give tray a coat of gesso, then paint and decorate as desired. Give it a final coat of spray varnish.

HUGE MASKS

Dress up your skits with these simple masks.

16-inch balloon
36-inch length heavy string
Newspaper and paper towel strips
Wallpaper paste

1. Inflate balloon. Tie knot in end and attach string. Suspend balloon by tying string to some object inside or outside. Be sure it isn't near anything that will cause it to burst.

2. Cover balloon with several layers of newspaper maché strips. Let dry.

3. For an animal mask, add framework for nose or ears at this time. Use a paper cup or cardboard roll for the nose, heavy cardboard for the ears. Use masking tape to fasten these to maché-covered balloon, then cover them with paper towel maché strips.

4. When mask is dry, cut out a hole large enough so mask fits over head and remove the balloon. Then cut eyeholes in proper position. Cut out mouth or nose for breathing hole. Also punch some smaller holes in back for air.

5. Paint as desired. Add additional decoration, such as yarn hair, a hat, etc.

PIÑATA

Piñatas are fun, especially when they are colorful animal shapes. They are filled with candy and broken open at holiday parties.

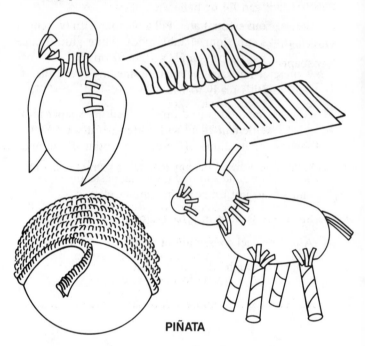

PIÑATA

1. To get the basic body, inflate a balloon and follow the directions above for making the mask. The size and shape of balloons will be determined by the type of animal or figure you are making. Two or three layers of maché is adequate. Let dry.

2. Tape on additional balloons and cardboard pieces for head, legs, ears, wings, etc. Cover with two layers of maché. Let dry.

3. After the piñata is the desired shape and is completely dry, cut a hole in the back to remove balloon and add wrapped candy or favors. Fasten a cord to the top for hanging.

4. If desired, you can add a finishing touch of tissue paper curls which cover typical Mexican piñatas. Fold 3-inch strips of colored tissue paper lengthwise and fringe as shown in illustration. Turn strips wrong side out so they will fluff up. Fold several strips together and cut all at once. Wrap these around the piñata, overlapping each row as you glue it on.

5. Blindfolded people take turns hitting at the hanging piñata with a stick until it breaks and the goodies fall out.

PEDRO MASCOT

To look at this appealing little burro, you'd never think that underneath he's just cardboard rolls and plastic containers taped together and covered with papier mâché. You'll need:

Round cardboard box or plastic bottle (body)

Cardboard rolls (legs and neck)

Plastic spray can lid or paper cup (head)

Cardboard pieces (ears)

Masking tape

Newspaper strips or instant mâché

1. Use masking tape to assemble body parts. Cover any gaps or openings with tape.

2. Cover bottom of legs with cardboard circles, taped in place.

3. Apply one coat of instant mâché or several coats of strip mâché to burro. Let dry completely.

4. Give burro an undercoat of gesso or thinned latex wall paint. Paint with tempera. Use *Boys' Life* magazine illustrations as a guide for assembling and painting Pedro. Add a final coat of spray varnish or shellac.

5. Add a yarn or jute cord mane and tail.

6. Set Pedro in a prominent spot at your den meeting place.

PEDRO MASCOT

Modeling

It's a thrilling experience for young or old to twist and mold a pliable mass into a useful and decorative object. Modeling with clay or other materials gives Cub Scouts a chance to develop self-expression in three dimensions. They become aware of symmetry, texture, curve, and line; they develop a sense of form and increase their ability to shape and reshape objects by working with modeling doughs.

The modeling dough recipes included here have been used successfully by leaders around the country and can be used to make bowls, vases, Christmas tree ornaments, animals, figures, candleholders, paperweights, door stops, napkin rings, and many other useful items. Most of the ingredients for these recipes can be found in the kitchen. Sawdust can be obtained from any sawmill or woodworking shop.

MODELING DOUGH RECIPES

Sawdust Clay. Mix 4 cups of clean, sifted sawdust, 1 cup wallpaper paste, and 2 cups of water. Mix thoroughly to the consistency of modeling clay. Add ½-cup plaster to the basic recipe for added weight to make door stops or paperweights. (This mixture must be used right away.)

Sawdust/Flour Clay. Mix 1 cup flour, 2 cups sawdust, and a teaspoon of table salt together thoroughly. Add water until the dough is thick and pliable.

Sawdust/Cornstarch Clay. Slowly add 3 level tablespoons of cornstarch to 1 cup cold water. Cook mixture in a double boiler until thickened. Allow to cool and empty into a large bowl. Add 1 to 2 cups sawdust, a little at a time, and knead it thoroughly until you get a pliable dough that is thick enough to handle without cracking apart.

Salt/Cornstarch Clay. Mix 2 cups table salt with ⅔-cup water in saucepan. Simmer over medium heat, stirring constantly until mixture is well heated (3 – 4 min.). Remove from heat. Add 1 cup cornstarch which has been mixed with ½-cup cold water and mix. This will make a thick, stiff dough.

Salt/Flour Clay. Combine ½-cup salt and 1 cup flour. Add water, a little at a time, and with your hands, mix and knead until it is a stiff dough. (By adding ⅓-cup water, you can make a soft clay that is good for making relief maps.)

Cornstarch/Baking Soda Clay. Mix 1 cup cornstarch, 2 cups baking soda. Add 1¼ cups water and mix. Bring to boil over medium heat, stirring constantly. This will thicken to the consistency of mashed potatoes. Store in refrigerator. (This clay dries white.)

Bread Modeling Dough. Remove crusts from several slices of white bread. Break up bread into small pieces and mix with white glue. Add a few drops of lemon juice. Mix until it is the consistency of clay.

Baker's Clay. Mix 4 cups flour, 1 cup salt, and 1½ cups water together with fingers in a big bowl. If clay feels too stiff, add a little more water. Knead for 5 minutes. This recipe should not be doubled or halved. After objects are molded, bake them on a cookie sheet in 350 degree oven for 1 hour. Test for doneness with a toothpick.

NOTE: Powdered alum will keep homemade doughs and clays from getting moldy. Add a tablespoon or two to your dough.

TIPS ON MODELING

1. When making tree ornaments or beads, be sure to make a hole in the object before it dries or is baked so that a hanger can be added.

2. If the clay begins to dry and crack as you are working with it, try wetting the cracks with a finger or sponge and rubbing them away as they appear.

3. Unless recipe calls for baking, molded objects should be allowed to air dry throughly. Drying can be hastened by punching tiny pin holes in the object.

4. Leftover modeling clay can be stored in a plastic bag in the refrigerator for later use. Do not store for extended periods, however.

COLORING MODELING DOUGH

All of the modeling doughs mentioned above can be colored with a few drops of food coloring or tempera paint during the mixing process. Or, the plain dough can be painted after model is dry with tempera, enamel, model dope, or spray paint. Add a top coat of clear plastic spray to protect tempera-painted objects.

MODELING TOOLS

In addition to the hands, which are the best tools for modeling, there are other items which can be used for detailing a design. An orange stick is useful for modeling details on small objects—it will do the fine work fingers cannot do.

Nails, screws, spoons, forks, and similar implements can be used to impress designs in the clay. A toothpick or straight pin can be used to punch small holes or make pin-prick designs.

MODELING PROJECTS

TWISTED NAPKIN RINGS

To make these usable gadgets, do the following:

1. Cover a cardboard roll with foil.

2. Roll pieces of modeling dough into ropes, each about ¼-inch thick and 12 inches long. Fold each rope in half and twist.

3. Wrap the twist around the foil-covered tube, dab the ends of the twisted ring with water, and press to seal.

4. Bake or let dry, depending on type of clay used.

5. When dry, slip rings off tube. Give napkin rings a coat of clear shellac or varnish or paint a bright color.

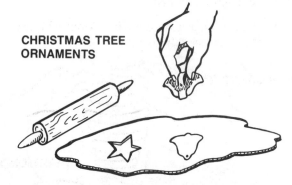

CHRISTMAS TREE ORNAMENTS

CHRISTMAS TREE ORNAMENTS

All you need for these are a rolling pin, a cookie cutter, paint, and shellac.

1. With rolling pin, roll out modeling dough flat between two pieces of waxed paper.

2. Use cookie cutters to cut out stars, bells, or other shapes.

3. Use a toothpick to make a hole in top of ornament for hanger.

4. Let ornaments dry or bake, depending on recipe used. Paint with tempera and add a top coat of shellac.

PAPERWEIGHT

These are simple and easy to make.

1. Shape modeling dough into desired shape—an animal, flower, or geometric shape.

2. Press a lead weight into the bottom of the molded shape to give it weight.

3. Let dry and paint as desired.

MAGNETS

This modeling project can be a gift for mom.

1. Shape modeling dough into desired shape—animal, flower, foot, etc. The back side should be as flat as possible.

2. Let dry. Paint as desired.

3. Glue a craft magnet on the back. Mom will love to stick these on her refrigerator.

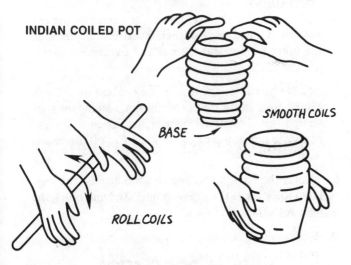

INDIAN COILED POT

Try your luck with Indian pottery by making a coiled pot.

1. Roll baker's clay into a long, thin rope on clean, non-sticky table.

2. Coil clay rope into tight circle for bottom of pot, then begin to lay coils on top of each other to form the sides of the pot.

3. After coiled pot-shape is formed, use dampened fingers and thumbs to press the coils together into a smooth shape. Add a little water at a time to smooth out edges and bottom of pot.

4. Pull and pinch pot into shape you desire.

5. Bake on a cookie sheet in a 350-degree oven for about an hour. Cool.

6. Paint with Indian symbols.

SMALL INDIAN PINCH POT

Have your Cub Scouts try this pottery.

1. Roll baker's clay into a solid ball about 1½ inches in diameter.

2. Place ball in your left palm and slowly push your right thumb into the center to within ¼-inch from the bottom while rotating the clay ball.

3. With both thumbs in the center hole, remaining fingers on the outside, and pot bottom side away from you, press out, revolving the pot in a slow circle.

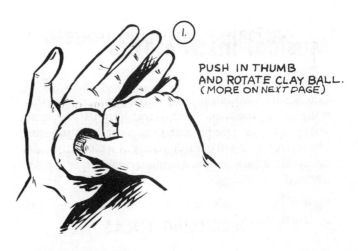

PUSH IN THUMB AND ROTATE CLAY BALL. (MORE ON NEXT PAGE)

4. When sides have been pressed to about ⅜-inch thickness, place the pot on a piece of waxed paper on a table. Work around the edge in a pinching motion with thumbs and fingers until the sides of the pot are smooth and about ¼-inch thick. Be careful not to strain the pot by forcing or pinching too near the bottom.

5. Work from the bottom up, keeping the top edges thick until the very last.

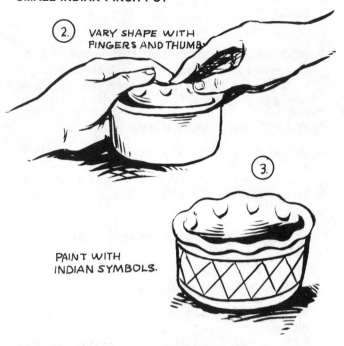

SMALL INDIAN PINCH POT

2. VARY SHAPE WITH FINGERS AND THUMB.

3.

PAINT WITH INDIAN SYMBOLS.

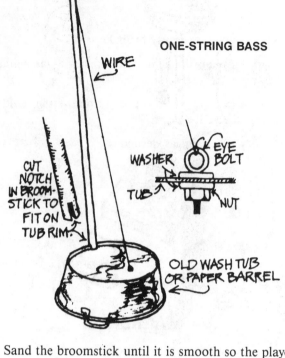

NAIL

ONE-STRING BASS

WIRE

CUT NOTCH IN BROOMSTICK TO FIT ON TUB RIM.

WASHER

EYE BOLT

TUB

NUT

OLD WASH TUB OR PAPER BARREL

6. When the bowl is as even and round as possible, the shape can be varied by pushing the edges inward or outward into the shape desired.

7. Bake on a cookie sheet in 350-degree oven for about an hour.

8. When pot has cooled, paint with Indian symbols.

Musical Instruments

Cub Scouts have fun making musical instruments that really work. Your den might like to form its own band and learn to play a simple tune on homemade instruments. The instruments will come in handy at a Cub Scout circus or fair, a pack or den entertainment night, or just for fun in den meetings.

Most of the materials required for these instruments can be found around the house.

ONE-STRING BASS

This project will add to your den band. You'll need the following:

Old wash tub or paper barrel
Broomstick
Wire
Nail, washers, nut, eye bolt

1. Sand the broomstick until it is smooth so the player won't pick up a splinter as he runs his hand up and down the stick while playing the bass.

2. Cut or file a notch about ½-inch deep in the bottom of the broomstick so it will fit over the rim of the tub bottom. Wrap the broomstick just above the notch with heavy wire to prevent the stick from splitting.

3. Hammer a nail in the top of the broomstick so the top end of the wire can be fastened.

4. Drill a hole for the eye bolt in the center of the tub bottom. Thread on a washer, insert bolt in tub, add the other washer and the nut and tighten, as shown in illustration.

5. Fasten one end of the wire to the eye bolt on the tub. Fit the notched stick over the tub rim, holding the stick straight up, and stretch wire tight. Fasten other end of wire to nail at top of broomstick. Cut off any excess wire.

6. To play the bass, stand and rest tub against the legs. Hold the stick at the top with one hand and pluck the wire with the other hand.

MUSICAL POGO STICK (One Man Band)

To make this unusual instrument, you'll need:

5-foot dowel or broomstick
Homemade drum, bicycle bell, horn or whistle

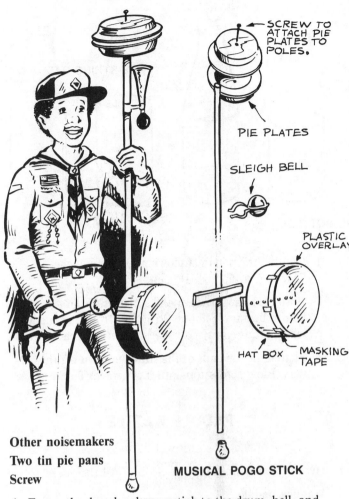

CYMBALS

Your Cub Scouts can really make a bang with this project. Materials are:

Two tin pie pans (not foil pans)
Two spools
15 inches of heavy cord

1. Punch two holes near the center of each pie pan.

2. Run the cord through the holes, tying a spool tightly to bottom of each pan for a handle.

CYMBALS

Other noisemakers
Two tin pie pans
Screw

1. Fasten the dowel or broomstick to the drum, bell, and horn or whistle, and any other noisemaker available.

2. Using a screw, fasten the two pie pans loosely to the top as shown.

3. The player uses one hand to thump the stick on the floor for rhythm, and with his other hand he beats the drum and sounds the noisemakers.

KAZOO

Cover a comb with a piece of tissue paper or waxed paper. Place mouth against the paper and hum a tune through the paper and comb.

COCONUT CLAPPERS

To make this instrument, you need to:

1. Cut a coconut in half with a sharp saw. Drain, pry out the meat, and clean the inside out.

2. Sand the edges of the coconut. Paint or shellac inside and out.

3. Experiment with different sounds and rhythms by clapping the shells together, tapping them on a board, or rubbing them together with a paper in between.

MUSICAL BOTTLES

Your Cub Scouts can have lots of fun with this instrument. All you need to do is:

1. Line up an assortment of bottles of various sizes and shapes. Blow gently across the top of an empty bottle.

SAND BLOCKS

These are easy for Cub Scouts to make and play. All you need is:

Two pieces of wood, 1-by-2-by-4 inches
Sandpaper, thumbtacks

1. Cut pieces of sandpaper the same width as the blocks and about 4 inches longer.

2. Turn the sandpaper over the block ends, with rough sides out, and tack in place.

3. To play, brush the two sandpaper surfaces together briskly for a pleasant "shuffle rhythm."

MUSICAL BOTTLES

2. By adding a little water to a bottle, you can change the tone. The more water, the deeper the tone.

3. Use a straw to tune up the bottles. Insert straw in a glass of water, place a finger over the open end of the straw, and lift water out of the glass. This will allow you to add a little water at a time to each bottle and test the tone.

4. For more accurate tones, use eight 10-ounce bottles. Fill them to the following depths in inches—1⅜, 2, 2⅜, 3, 3⅝, 4, and 4⅛, with one empty. This should produce a fairly accurate musical scale, and with some practice, you can play a tune.

SODA STRAW PIPE ORGAN

For this clever instrument you'll need:

Corrugated Cardboard (with large corrugations), 1½-by-8 inches

8 straws

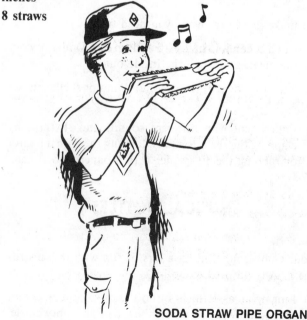

SODA STRAW PIPE ORGAN

1. Cut the straws in the following lengths in inches—8½, 7¾, 7, 6¾, 6, 5¼, 4½, and 4¼.

2. Push the straws between the corrugations of the cardboard, beginning about 1½ inches from one end and leaving four empty corrugations between each straw.

3. Flatten the top ends of the straws and cut off the corners. Blow across tops of straws for different tones.

PADDLE RATTLE

Here's an easy one for Cub Scouts. All they need is:

Wooden paddle
12 bottle caps
Nails

1. Remove the liners from 12 bottle caps and hammer them flat. Punch a hole in the circle of each cap.

PADDLE RATTLE

2. Nail the caps loosely to the paddle board, using three caps to each nail.

3. Shake paddle to play.

SOUP CAN MARACAS

Your den can really go Latin with these. All you need are:

Two soup cans

Pebbles, dried beans or rice (or assortment of nails, screws, washers)

1. Open the soup cans just enough to empty and wash.

2. Put a few pebbles or dried beans in each can, or use the nail and screw assortment.

3. Reseal each can with tape.

4. Fasten the two cans together at ends which were opened, using adhesive or strapping tape. Paint or cover with colored adhesive-back paper.

PAPIER MÂCHÉ MARACAS

Design your own maracas, using the following materials:

Small round balloon
Newspaper strips/wallpaper paste
Pebbles, dried beans or rice

1. Inflate the balloon to about the size of a grapefruit.

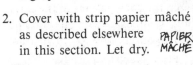
PAPIER MÂCHÉ MARACAS

2. Cover with strip papier mâché as described elsewhere in this section. Let dry.

3. Punch two ¼-inch holes in the mâché on opposite sides of the ball. Insert a few pebbles, beans or some rice. Glue a ¼-inch dowel handle through holes. Let glue dry, then paint and decorate as desired.

Printing

The printing methods included here are simple skills which will delight Cub Scout-age boys. These methods can be used to print Christmas cards, party invitations, blue and gold banquet program covers, flags and banners, T-shirts, shields, table covers, and pictures. Few tools and materials are required.

Printing can be done on paper, paper sacks, fabric, wood, and canvas, using linoleum blocks, wood, wax, sponges, vegetables and fruits, stencils, silk screen, crayons, and other items.

TIPS ON PRINTING

- If design is to be permanent, such as a T-shirt or other fabric which will be laundered, use a fabric paint, oil base paint, or ink. Acrylic paint will also work.

- Otherwise, use tempera paint or water-base inks.

- When printing T-shirts or other fabrics, be sure to place a newspaper pad between the front and back so paint will not run to other parts of the fabric.

INK PAD PRINTS

Make simple ink pad prints by using following materials:

Ink pad
Newspaper
Tweezers
Plain paper
Something to print, such as a leaf

1. Place the leaf, underside down, on the ink pad.

2. Place a piece of newspaper over the leaf.

3. Carefully rub your fingers over the newspaper, pressing all of the leaf against the ink pad, to coat it with ink evenly.

4. Remove newspaper.

5. Pick up the leaf with tweezers and place ink-side down on plain paper.

6. Cover with a clean piece of newspaper.

7. Hold the newspaper and leaf firmly with one hand. With the other hand, rub your fingers over the newspaper, pressing all of the leaf against the paper. Do not move the leaf while doing this or the print will smudge.

8. Remove newspaper.

9. Use tweezers to lift leaf from paper. Wash hands.

10. Let the print dry. Label.

ROLLER PRINTING

Your Cub Scouts will enjoy this novel type of printing. All you need is:

Printing ink, fingerpaint, or tempera
Flat container for ink or paint
Rollers
Paper or cloth for printing
Newspapers, paper towels

1. Select a roller—old rolling pin, bottle, cardboard tube, or piece of dowel or broomstick.

2. Glue a cardboard design on the rolling pin.

3. Roll it on cloth or paper. Try several types to see the different designs.

SPATTER PRINTS

Prints can be made of leaves or ferns collected on a nature hike, or designs can be cut from paper or cardboard. Materials include:

Object or cut-out design for printing
Construction paper
Screen wire, about 8-by-10 inches
Old toothbrush, straight pins
Colored ink, shoepolish, or tempera paint

6"

SCREEN

SPATTER PRINTS

1. Spread working area with newspapers.

2. Place object to be printed on construction paper and secure with straight pins.

3. Dip toothbrush in paint or ink and shake until almost dry. Holding screen about 6 inches above construction paper, brush across screen with toothbrush. Brush away from yourself.

4. Let paint or ink dry, then remove object from paper.

Suggestion: Try using white shoe polish to spatter design on colored construction paper.

OVERLAP SPATTER PRINTS

Lay a leaf on white paper. Spatter with red tempera and remove leaf. Wash screen and toothbrush. When paint is dry, place a second, different shape leaf overlapping the first design. Using a clean toothbrush, spatter with yellow tempera. Allow to dry and lift.

BLOCK PRINTING

Cub Scouts will enjoy this more advanced type of printing, using the following:

Pane of glass or a floor tile
Piece of inner tube, felt, or linoleum
Printing ink or paint
Block of wood
Brayer (roller)
White glue
Rags or paper towels
Paper or fabric to print on

1. Cover work area with newspapers.

2. Draw design on paper and trace it on inner tube, piece of felt, or linoleum. Be sure that it will fit on the block of wood. Design will print the reverse of what you see on the block. If there is lettering or a design that has a right and left, it should be glued to block backwards.

3. Cut out design and glue to block of wood.

GLUE TO WOOD BLOCK.

1.

2.

CUT FROM INNER TUBE OR FELT.

4. Pour a small amount of ink or paint on pane of glass. Roll brayer over glass until it is evenly covered with ink.

3.

GLASS

INK

5. Roll brayer over the design on the block.

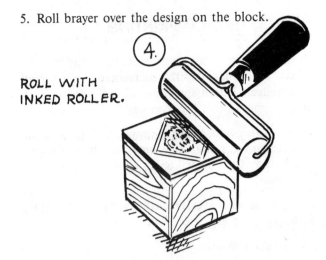

ROLL WITH
INKED ROLLER.

6. Press the block down firmly on paper or fabric to be printed. Design can be repeated or alternated with another design. Roll ink on block each time you print.

7. Wash all tools to clean them with turpentine.

NOTE: A temporary block can be made by cutting a design in a flat bar of soap or a block of wax, or by glueing a cardboard cutout design or one made from string on a block of wood. Or trace a design on a piece of styrofoam meat tray or styrofoam cup and use a pencil or ballpoint pen to make the design deeper, then glue to wood block.

POTATO PRINTS

For this project you'll need:

Large potato
Scratching tool (pencil, nail, toothpick)
Sharp-edged cutting tool (paring knife or pocketknife)
Paper for printing
Tempera paint and paint brush

1. Cover work area with newspapers.

2. Cut the potato in half so that each surface is flat.

3. Draw a design on flat surface of potato.

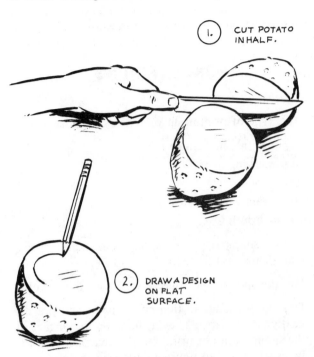

CUT POTATO
IN HALF.

DRAW A DESIGN
ON FLAT
SURFACE.

4. Use scratching tool to scratch design, or cutting tool to cut out design. Cut away all parts that have no design on them. Blot the surface of the potato to remove excess moisture.

CUT OUT DESIGN.

STAMP
WITH TEMPERA
PAINT.

5. Brush design with tempera paint. Stamp on newspaper or paper towel to remove excess. If ragged edges appear on the first imprint, cut away any uneven parts of the potato that cause this.

6. Print design on paper until it begins to fade, then add more paint and repeat.

7. Carrots, turnips, lemons, oranges, and other vegetables and fruits can also be used for printing.

SPONGE PRINTING

Try this type of printing in your den. You'll need:

Flat sponge, about ½-inch thick
Felt tip marking pen
Scissors
Tempera paint, paint brush
Paper for printing

1. Draw a simple design on sponge with marking pen. Cut sponge in this shape.

2. Wet the sponge and squeeze water out thoroughly.

3. Dip damp sponge in thin poster paint and press it gently on the paper. The tiny holes on the surface of the sponge will not print, but the areas between the holes will leave an unusual design on the paper.

STENCILS

Put a design on an item by using these materials:

Cardboard or waxed stencil paper
Sharp hobby knife or scissors
Thick paint (acrylic, latex, heavy tempera, or tube oil paint)
Stiff bristle brush
Paper or fabric to be stenciled

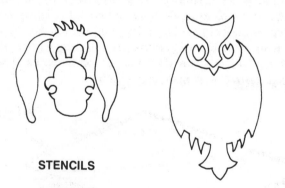

STENCILS

1. If using cardboard for stencil, give it three coats of shellac before using. Or make your own stencil paper by dipping bond paper in melted paraffin several times. This makes the stencil more durable.

2. Select a design and trace it on cardboard or stencil paper. Cut out with a sharp knife or scissors.

3. Paper or fabric surface to be stenciled should lay flat. Stencil should also lay flat so paint will not spread under edges. Fasten stencil to printing surface with tape or pins so it will not move.

4. Using a stiff brush, brush the paint, beginning on the stencil near the cutout edge, onto the fabric or paper. Brush away from stencil edges so paint will not run underneath.

5. Experiment with the stencil on scrap paper before attempting the actual project.

CRAYON RUBBINGS

This is one of the simplest methods of printing. All you need is:

Dark crayons, chalk, or pencil
Thin paper

1. Find a surface with an interesting texture, such as a special tombstone, monument, manhole cover, tree stump, or church door.

2. Hold or tape the paper over the surface and rub hard with the side of the pencil, crayon, or chalk.

3. Another good rubbing material is a heavy, black, waxy mixture called heelball, available from shoe repair shops.

4. These unusual designs can be framed with a piece of poster board or construction paper, or put in a scrapbook.

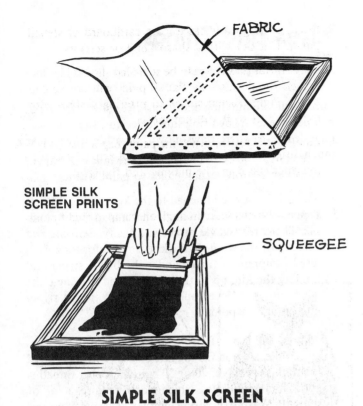

SIMPLE SILK SCREEN PRINTS

FABRIC

SQUEEGEE

SIMPLE SILK SCREEN PRINTS

The silk screen method described here is an easy operation, suitable for Cub Scouts. Use the following:

Silkscreen frame

Design cut from paper

Paper for printing

Fingerpaint or a water base ink

Squeegee or piece of sturdy cardboard

1. A silkscreen frame can be made from an old picture frame. Cut a piece of fabric (silk, cheesecloth, old nylon stocking) 1-inch larger on all sides than the opening of the frame. Fasten it with tacks, or staples, making sure the fabric is stretched tightly.

2. Cut a design from paper. It must be smaller than the opening in the frame. Spread newspapers over the work area.

3. Place the design on the paper for printing and put screen on top.

4. Put some ink or paint on one edge of the screen and spread it across the screen with a squeegee. Lift up screen and remove the paper. The design will stick to the screen. Hang the print up to dry.

5. Repeat procedure for more prints.

6. Clean screen by wiping it with a wet sponge, or rinsing. Be sure to clean screen before using a different color.

HECTOGRAPH
(A Homemade Duplicator)

Many Cub Scout leaders have access to copy machines, but some do not. Making copies in large quantities by commercial methods can be expensive. The hectograph is an old printing method, but it is still an inexpensive and convenient way to duplicate copies at home. The hectograph can be used to print forms, den and pack newsletters, banquet programs, and announcements.

To make making the duplicator, you'll need:

Two boxes unflavored gelatin

1 pint glycerine

1½-cups cold water

Shallow, oblong metal pan (about 9-by-13 inches)

1. Heat glycerine in double boiler for safety.

2. Dissolve gelatin in cold water. Pour hot glycerine on gelatin and stir well to dissolve.

3. Pour into a shallow pan that will not rust and skim off foam by drawing a piece of paper or cardboard across pan from end to end. Place in cool, level place until gelatin sets (about 24 hours).

4. Commercial hectograph filler compound is also available. Follow instructions on package.

Preparing The Master. Hectograph or duplicator carbon paper is available at most office supply stores. The hectograph requires a different technique than machine duplicators. Type through the heco carbon so the print is readable on the back side of the glazed paper. It is best to put the heco carbon between two sheets of paper, so you can read the typing on the top sheet. Corrections are made on the back sheet by carefully scraping off the carbon and retyping.

To transfer the master to the gelatin, wipe the gelatin gently with a moist cloth. It should be only slightly wet so the printing will not bleed. Place the carbon copy face down on the moistened gelatin surface and lightly smooth it. After 3 minutes, remove the paper and discard it. The gelatin plate is now ready for printing.

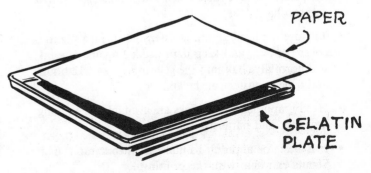

PAPER

GELATIN PLATE

SMOOTH PAPER
LIGHTLY

COPY

Printing Procedure. For best results, use glazed duplicator paper. Simply place a sheet on the gelatin plate, smooth it with the tips of the fingers lightly so that an impression is made. Take care not to rub too hard. Remove the paper. Thirty or more legible copies may be obtained from the master.

Tips On Using The Hectograph

- If gelatin should crack or get rough, it can be reheated right in the pan. The smooth surface will return when it cools.

- The printing surface can be erased by lightly rubbing the gelatin with a moist, clean rag. Take care not to rub too hard.

- To store the hectograph, moisten the surface slightly, cover the pan, and keep until needed again. The ink will normally soak into the gelatin in about 12 hours and a new master can be applied.

- Hectograph pencils and inks are available for making drawings and patterns.

- It is best for an adult to make the hectograph. Cub Scouts can help with the printing.

Kites and Things That Fly

Successful kite-building and flying gives boys a feeling of competence. Start by using simple designs, such as those included here, where flaws in workmanship won't make much difference. The following tips will help leaders who are inexperienced in kite-making and flying.

- The bridle (string attached to the kite) holds the kite face into the wind at an angle that makes flight possible. The correct angle varies with the type of kite and velocity of the wind. If the kite isn't performing well, test by slipping a finger under the bridle string and holding the kite up to the wind to find the angle the wind chooses. Once you find the spot, tie the flying line on at this point.

- Almost any type of string will do for ordinary kites and bridles. Nylon fishing line or heavy string is good for flying lines. No. 20 or 30 cotton crochet thread is good for small kites which don't require a lot of strength. Waxing the string lightly will keep it from rotting in damp weather. Be sure to tie the end to the reel before winding the line on it.

- Use no wire or metal on kite frames. Do not use string with metallic fibers interwoven because of the danger of electric shock if the wire touches power lines.

- Tissue paper is fine for flat kites up to about three feet in length. For larger flat kites, use brown wrapping paper or butcher paper. For bow kites and big flat kites, use a lightweight cloth or plastic cover.

- Readymade sticks for kites are available at hobby shops. They may also be cut from used or new lumber, lath strips or wooden crates. The best woods are spruce, Ponderosa pine, white pine, and cypress. Balsa is all right for small kites. Bamboo is excellent for large or elaborate kites. These sticks for a 36-inch kite should be at least ¼-inch square; for a 48-inch kite, use ⅜-inch sticks; for a 60-inch kite, use ½-inch square sticks.

- If the kite dives or pinwheels, add a tail to stabilize it. Not all kites require tails.

- It's a good idea to have a repair kit handy when you're flying kites. Scissors, cellophane tape, extra paper for streamers, and extra flying line may come in handy.

- Tell the boys that the wind should be pushing against the kite's face. This means that the flyer's back will be to the wind if he's watching it. If he's running with it, he should be running into the wind.

ORIENTAL KITE

Try one of these kites. Ask the boys to design their own, using:

Tissue paper, 12 inches square, and scraps
Four 2-inch-by-5-foot strips of crepe paper (tail)
Rubber cement
Matchstick-thick bamboo reed
Scissors, pencil, ruler
22-inch lightweight string (bridle)

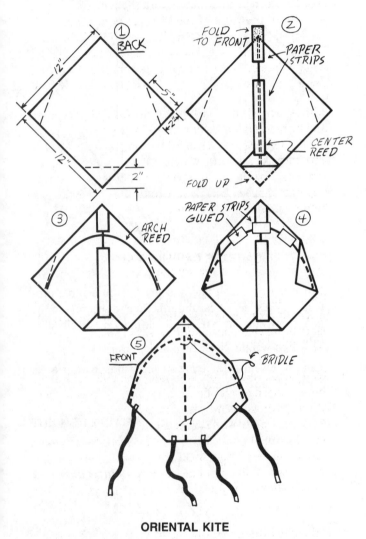

ORIENTAL KITE

1. Cut bamboo reed into one 22-inch and one 15-inch piece.

2. Crease paper on the broken lines as shown.

3. Glue center reed (15-inch) in place by covering with a strip of scrap tissue paper. Trim reed if necessary. Glue bottom flap up over center reed and a narrow strip of paper over the tip, folding corners of this strip to front to act as a reinforcement.

4. Measure and cut reed for arch to fit, as shown. Be sure the reed is strong with a good, natural curve.

5. Glue the left and right corner flaps over arched reed. It's best to glue one side first and let it dry. Then glue the other side, holding until it dries. Glue paper reinforcements over intersections of reeds midway between center and corners. Then turn over kite.

6. Tie bridle string over intersection of bamboo reeds, then over center reed 2 inches up from base of kite. Set angle of bridle by tying loop, as shown.

7. To find correct flying angle, hold kite by the bridle over a table. The center reed (spine) of the kite should be tilted upward at about a 15-degree angle from the horizontal. Add tail.

TWO-STICK FLAT KITE

This old reliable kite is easy to make, using only:

Wrapping paper, strong plastic, or cloth
⅛-by-⅜-inch stick, 36 inches long
⅛-by-⅜-inch stick, 30 inches long
White glue or rubber cement
At least 100 feet of kite string

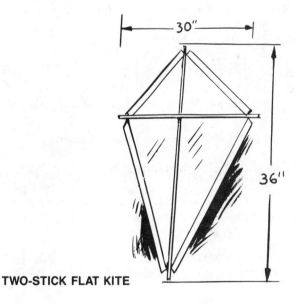

TWO-STICK FLAT KITE

1. Notch sticks in ends for strings. Tie sticks together at right angles as shown.

2. Run framing string around kite and tie.

3. Measure and cut cover with a 1-inch overlap all around, except at sticks, as shown.

4. Lay the frame over the cover and fold all flaps over the frame. Check for fit. Glue one flap at a time.

5. Lengthwise bridle string is about 40 inches long; crosswise string is 34 inches.

6. For tail, tie 4-by-6-inch tissue paper bows about 6 inches apart on 8-foot string.

7. If kite dances too much or is sluggish, add or reduce tail to correct flight. (See Wolf Elective 6 for three-stick flat kite.)

FLYING FISH KITE

Make this attractive kite from the following:

Basketmaker's reed
¼-inch dowel — 3-foot piece and 2-foot piece
Lightweight paper
Glue
Kite string

1. Lay a piece of reed at the top of the wood dowel. Bow the reed, as shown. Glue at top and tie 3 inches from bottom of dowel.

2. Tie on the 2-foot dowel crossarm as shown.

3. Tie a reed to the center stick 3 inches from the top. Bow the reed and glue as shown to form wings.

4. Balance kite frame by resting top and bottom of upright dowel on finger tips.

5. Lay frame on paper and draw around it, allowing a 1½-inch edge for flaps to fold back. Before cutting the paper, decorate like a flying fish. Paint may cause the paper to shrink a little, so be sure to measure again before cutting.

6. Glue paper to frame. Add bridle and line.

GARBAGE-CAN LINER KITE

This is one of the easiest of kites to make and fly. You will need:

Plastic garbage-can liner (3-foot high or over)
Self-adhesive tape
Two ³/₁₆-inch dowels, 3-foot long
String

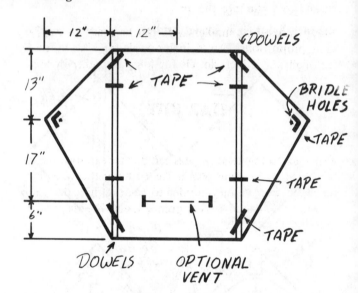

GARBAGE CAN LINER KITE

1. Cut open the trash bag and lay flat on a table protected by a sheet of cardboard. Tape to secure. On the bag, draw kite pattern with a felt marker (see illustration for sizes). Cut out around edges.

2. Cut out a vent if there are strong winds in your area. Securely tape the ends of the cut.

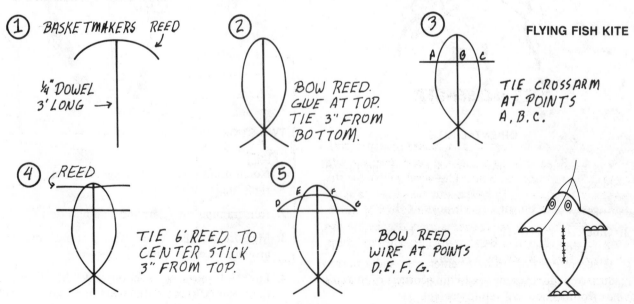

3. Tape dowels to the plastic (see illustration), twice in the middle and at both ends, wrapping tapes over dowel ends. Punch out bridle holes with pencil. Reinforce wing tips with strips of tape on each side, front, and back.

4. Cut a 10-foot length of string for bridle. Tie each end to a bridle hole and tie a loop in the exact center. Tie the flying line to the loop.

5. To launch, stand with back to wind, grasp bridle loop, and toss kite into the air.

NOTE: Larger or smaller kites can be made using the same proportions. Use ¼-inch dowels for kites up to 4 feet high; or ⅛-inch dowels for kites 24 inches or less.

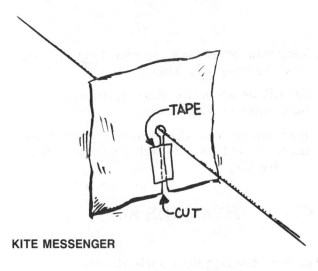

KITE MESSENGER

STAR KITES

Two-stick and three-stick kites can be made in star shape. Sticks are all the same length. Tie them together and glue on paper cover. A tail is needed to balance these designs. Attach tail to one of the star points. Use a three-leg bridle and attach kite line.

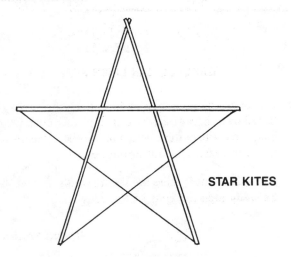

STAR KITES

HANG GLIDER

Your Cub Scouts will enjoy this easy project. Use:

Transparent sticky tape
Thin plastic food wrap
Three plastic soda straws, ⅛-inch diameter
Plastic top (from soft-margarine tub)
Durable, heavy paper such as a file folder

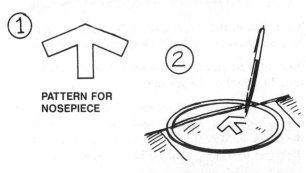

① PATTERN FOR NOSEPIECE

② TRACE NOSEPIECE SHAPE ON MARGARINE TOP. CUT OUT NOSEPIECE WITH SCISSORS OR BLADE.

KITE MESSENGER

Cut a small hole in the center of a square of paper, with a slit to one edge, as shown. Slip the paper over the kite flying line and tape slit shut. The wind will blow the messenger up the kite. To have a kite messenger race, all players send their kites up to a specific length of line—perhaps 50 yards. The messenger is then attached to the flying line and allowed to blow up the kite. The boy whose messenger first reaches his kite wins.

NOTE: Refer to "Kites" elective in the *Wolf Cub Scout Book* for directions for a paper bag kite.

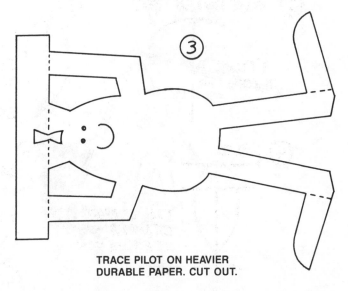

③ TRACE PILOT ON HEAVIER DURABLE PAPER. CUT OUT.

④

**FOLD PILOT AS SHOWN
ATTACH TO CENTER
STRAW 2″ BACK
FROM NOSE.**

⑤ **TAPE
RINGLETS**

1.

2″ STRIP OF TAPE.

2.

**FOLD STICKY
SIDE OUT.**

3.

**CUT ¼″
RINGLETS.**

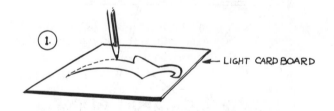

**ALL THREE STRAWS
SHOULD BE OF EQUAL
LENGTH.**

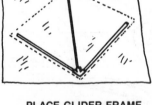

**PLACE GLIDER FRAME
ON THIN PLASTIC
WRAP, TAPE SIDE
DOWN. CUT AROUND
OUTSIDE AS SHOWN
USING STRAIGHT
EDGE AND BLADE.**

⑥

HANG GLIDER

1. Trace shape of the nose piece on plastic top. Cut out the nose piece and insert into the straws. The nose piece should fit tight for better wing support and better flight.

2. Trace pattern for the pilot onto the heavy paper and cut it out. Fold feet forward along dotted lines.

3. Cut a 2-inch piece of sticky tape and fold lengthwise, sticky side out. Cut into ¼-inch rings.

4. Place two rings on each of the straws and one ring on the nose piece. Place straws, rings down, onto the plastic food wrap. Cut around the straws, as illustrated, allowing about ¾-inch extra on all sides. Fold the extra width over the straws and tape down.

5. Attach the pilot to the center straw about 2 inches back from the nose.

HELICOPTER WING

This is easy to fly and make from:

Thin cardboard (from file folder or poster board)
Tissue paper
Paper clip
Transparent sticky tape, ¾-inch width
Rubber band

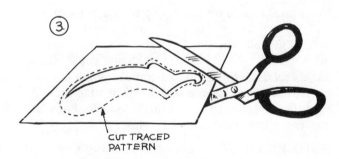

LIGHT CARDBOARD

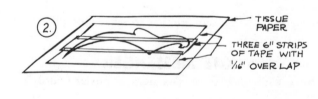

TISSUE
PAPER

THREE 6″ STRIPS
OF TAPE WITH
¹⁄₁₆″ OVER LAP

CUT TRACED
PATTERN

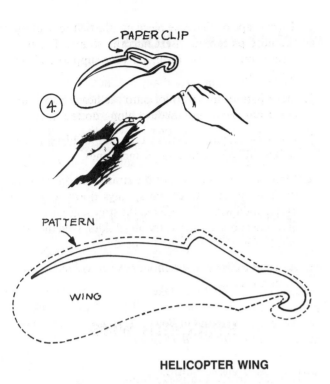

PAPER CLIP

④.

PATTERN

WING

HELICOPTER WING

1. Trace wing strut on the thin cardboard and cut it out.

2. Place strut on the tissue paper. Cover completely with strips of sticky tape as shown in the illustration. Be sure to press down firmly to insure a good bond.

3. Make a pattern for the wing and trace its shape onto the tissue paper. Cut it out.

4. To fly the helicopter wing, slide paper clip onto the wing. You may hand-launch the wing or shoot it into the sky with a rubber band.

SCAT: A CATAPULT GLIDER

This glider will take more time to make, but will be fun. You'll need:

New six-sided pencil with eraser
Stiff cardboard (cereal-box sides or poster board)
Wire nail
7 inches of ³⁄₃₂-inch diameter wire solder
Model cement or craft glue
5-inch length of another pencil or piece of dowel
One or two heavy rubber bands

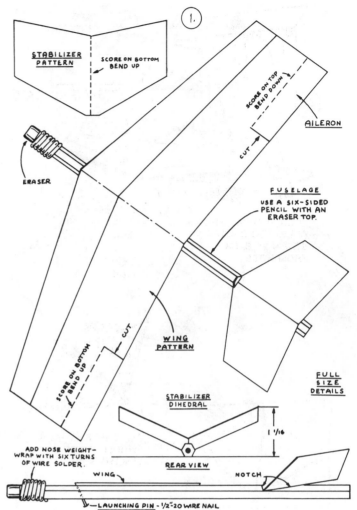

① .

STABILIZER PATTERN — SCORE ON BOTTOM BEND UP

SCORE ON TOP BEND DOWN

AILERON

CUT

ERASER

FUSELAGE
USE A SIX-SIDED PENCIL WITH AN ERASER TOP.

SCORE ON BOTTOM BEND UP

CUT

WING PATTERN

STABILIZER DIHEDRAL

FULL SIZE DETAILS

1 ¹⁄₁₆

ADD NOSE WEIGHT— WRAP WITH SIX TURNS OF WIRE SOLDER.

WING

REAR VIEW

NOTCH

LAUNCHING PIN - ¹⁄₂"-20 WIRE NAIL

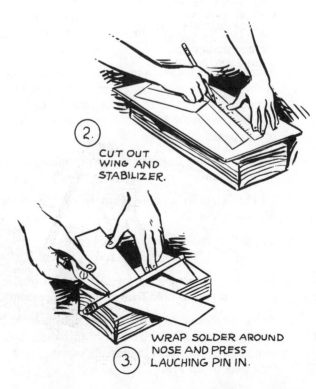

② .
CUT OUT WING AND STABILIZER.

③ .
WRAP SOLDER AROUND NOSE AND PRESS LAUCHING PIN IN.

4. USE A RULER TO CHECK ANGLE OF TAIL.

5. HOLD A CONTEST WITH OTHERS IN YOUR PACK.

SCAT: A CATAPULT GLIDER

1. Enlarge pattern to size indicated and trace onto the cardboard.

2. Cut out the wing and stabilizer. For more accurate cut, use a modeler's knife. Guide cuts with a metal ruler for a straight edge.

3. Notch pencil 2 inches from the end. Score the bottom of the stabilizer on the center line and bend up. Insert stabilizer into the notch. Check that the tips of the stabilizer wings are 1 1/16 inches from the bottom edge of the pencil.

4. Insert launching pin (a ½-inch wire nail) on bottom of pencil, about 1½ inches from the eraser end.

5. To add weight to the nose, wrap with about six turns of wire solder.

6. Cut and score the ailerons at both ends of the wing. Glue wing to the top of the fuselage (pencil).

7. To make a launching rig, notch the small pencil or piece of dowel to hold the rubber band or bands.

8. To fly the glider, attach to launching rig, aim high, and let it go! If the glider dives out of this glide, remove some solder. If it stalls (repeatedly swoops up, dives, then swoops up again), add solder.

Neckerchief Slides

Neckerchief slides can serve many uses in Cub Scouting. They can be used for rewards or incentives, such as presenting a "Jack-O-Lantern" slide to boys who have perfect attendance during October or who wore their uniforms to all meetings; or present a musical-sign slide to Cub Scouts who learn three Cub Scout songs as part of Wolf Elective 11.

Slides can also be used as an aid to completing achievements, electives, and activity badges. For example, glue a small leaf onto a piece of wood while working on Webelos Forester activity badge; or make traffic sign-shaped slides when talking about bike safety.

Neckerchief slides are fun! Make them for various themes, special holidays, sports, or hobbies. More ideas for neckerchief slides can be found in *Boys' Life* magazine, *Scouting* magazine, and *Cub Scout Program Helps*.

LEATHER AND VINYL SLIDES

CLOWN FACE

DRAW FACE WITH PERMANENT MARKER. GLUE ON WIGGLY EYES OR SEW ON BUTTONS.

PLASTIC FLOWERS

CLOWN'S HAIR

INSERT TABS THROUGH SLOTS.

DOG EARS

DOG FACE

LEATHER AND VINYL SLIDES

Use scrap leather or vinyl to make these slides.

1. Cut desired shape. Some possibilities are bobcat, wolf, and bear faces, arrowhead, basketball, baseball glove, elephant, owl.

2. Glue (contact cement works best), staple, or rivet a leather or vinyl loop onto the back.

3. Write on the leather or vinyl with permanent markers or enamel paint.

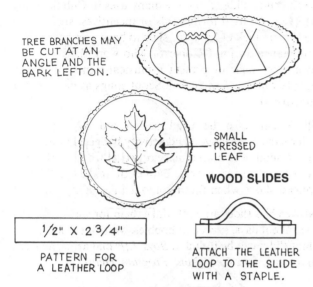

TREE BRANCHES MAY BE CUT AT AN ANGLE AND THE BARK LEFT ON.

SMALL PRESSED LEAF

WOOD SLIDES

1/2" X 2 3/4"

PATTERN FOR A LEATHER LOOP

ATTACH THE LEATHER LOOP TO THE SLIDE WITH A STAPLE.

WOOD SLIDES

These are easy to make.

1. Circles and ovals may be cut from slices of tree branch. Any shape may be cut from thin wood (up to ⅜-inch thick plywood or pine).

2. Cut out desired shape with a coping saw or electric jigsaw. Glue or staple a loop of leather or vinyl to the back side.

3. Sand edges until they are smooth. The slides can be painted with enamel paints, or use permanent markers to color a design on them. Stamps, small pictures, and small articles can be glued onto the slide using a mix of half water and half white glue. Two coats will seal and protect against water.

PLASTER OF PARIS AND RESIN SLIDES

Molds for plaster and resin slides can be found in craft stores, your local Scout distributor, and cake and candy decorating suppliers. Candy molds are just about the right size for many slides and come in many types. Cookie cutters, powdered drink mix scoops, and small containers make good molds also.

1. Follow directions found in this section on plaster casting to cast the molds. If using resin, follow package directions.

2. A pop can ring or small curtain ring can serve as a loop. Insert ring into the plaster or resin before it hardens.

NOTE: Do NOT pour leftover plaster or resin down drains.

PLASTIC CONTAINERS

BLACK PIPE CLEANER WILL BLEND WITH BLACK BODY OF BUTTERFLY.

PLASTIC CONTAINERS

Plastic lids, such as margarine lids, and plastic containers can provide material for neckerchief slides.

1. Use scissors to cut your design from the many colors of plastic containers available. Permanent markers can be used to add details or lettering.

2. Cut a strip of plastic for the loop. Staple loop into place.

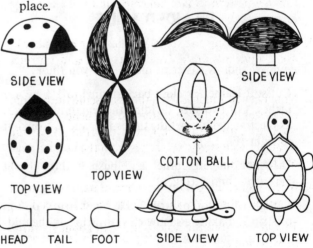

SIDE VIEW

SIDE VIEW

COTTON BALL

TOP VIEW

TOP VIEW

HEAD   TAIL   FOOT   SIDE VIEW   TOP VIEW

WALNUT SHELLS

WALNUT SHELLS

Try these on your Cub Scouts. They'll come up with lots of ideas.

1. The shell determines the shape, but odds and ends of felt, fabric, and pipe cleaners can turn the shell into a lady bug, skunk, or turtle.

2. Glue half a cotton ball into the shell half. Add more glue, then put on a leather loop.

3. Paint details with enamel paint. Let dry thoroughly before adding felt or fabric features.

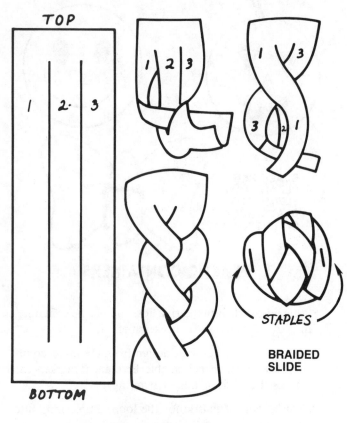

BRAIDED SLIDE

HIKING BOOT

STOP SIGN

WOLF BADGE

HAMMER

KNIGHT'S SHIELD

BASEBALL

BOWLING BALL

BRAIDED SLIDE

This novel slide is easier to make than you think.

1. Cut soft leather or cloth-backed vinyl to 1¼ by 4½ inches. Cut two slits, dividing the length into thirds, as illustrated. Number the thirds 1, 2, and 3, from left to right (Fig. A).

2. Take bottom left corner and push it through slit between 2 and 3 (Fig. B).

3. Put strip 3 on top of strip 2. Then put strip 1 on top of strip 3, making a sandwich with strip 3 in the middle. With fingers, work strip 3 out to left, exposing an open loop (Fig. C).

4. Take bottom end, bring it toward you, then insert it through loop and pull it through.

5. Rework with fingers into a braided strip which looks like Fig. D.

6. Use a small stapler to staple top and bottom ends together (Fig. E).

7. Slide may be made larger by lengthening the pattern.

4 Skits and Costumes

Why We Use Skits

Skits are appealing to boys of Cub Scout-age. Acting comes naturally to many boys, and often they make little distinction between make-believe and the world of reality. Skits help channel a boy's imagination. He doesn't just play he's a pirate. He *is* a buccaneer, sailing under the Jolly Roger. Or he *is* an astronaut, flying to a faraway planet. Play-acting is important in the growth of a boy because it:

- Gives him an outlet for the "let's pretend" part of his character. It gives him a chance for creative expression rather than imitation.

- Develops his powers of observation, coordination, and timing.

- Helps him gain self-confidence and personal satisfaction.

- Allows him to play the parts he has always dreamed of.

- Shows the importance of teamwork and cooperation.

- Improves speech and voice projection.

- Helps him develop an appreciation for other people and their abilities.

Once in a while there is a shy boy who would prefer not to take part in skits. Sometimes a costume or mask will help hide his shyness, or he can be given other important responsibilities, such as handling sound effects or lighting offstage. Each boy should be recognized as an important member of the group, and everyone should take part in some way.

Role playing, pantomime, and charades, help the boys gain self-confidence and build enthusiasm for dramatics. These are a good foundation for planning and presenting den skits at pack meetings.

Role Playing

Role playing is the spontaneous, unrehearsed acting out of a situation with words and gestures. It is putting one's self in another person's place to try to understand that person better.

Role playing lets a boy show how he would handle a particular situation rather than just telling how it should be done. It helps develop an appreciation of other people.

To get the boys in the den interested in dramatics, try these things:

- Describe a situation that a Cub Scout might find himself in and let the boys take turns acting it out. Lead a discussion with such questions as: Which was the best solution? Are there other solutions?

- Suggest that the Cub Scouts watch other people during the week and come to the next den meeting with an idea to role play. Talk about each of these situations as they are acted out.

- With the boys' help, make up a short story, weaving together the characters acted out by the Cub Scouts.

- Ask the boys to act out the story in pantomime (actions without words).

- With the boys' help, add words to the story. Decide how the characters would look and behave in that situation.

- Ask the boys to act out the story using their own words to fit the situation.

Avoid these things:

- Role playing undesirable characters.

- Allowing a boy to role play a character that is too difficult for him, causing him to be discouraged.

- Unfair criticism of people or events with no attempt to show a better way or to recognize improvement.

Pantomimes

Pantomime is acting without using words. Facial expressions, hand gestures, and body movements tell the story. Since long, memorized dialogue is discouraged in Cub Scout skits, pantomime is a good method to use. To show the boys how to pantomime effectively, let them try some of the following.

How would you act:

- If you had a nail in your shoe?

- If you were scared?

- If you slipped on ice?

- If someone pinched you?

How would you lift:

- A baby?

- Something very fragile?

- Something very hot?

- Something heavy?

- Something big and bulky?

How would you look:

- If you saw a ferocious lion?

- If someone gave you a surprise?

- If your report card was all A's?

- If you smelled something bad?

- If you heard a strange sound?

- If you were watching an exciting game?

- If you tasted bitter medicine?

- If you heard a sudden crash?

Another way to use pantomime in the den is to fill a Cub Scout hat with slips of paper which have written instructions. Each boy draws a slip and pantomimes the instructions.

Here are some suggestions:

- Crawl through a jungle full of hanging vines and branches.

- Walk a tightrope in the air.

- Follow a buzzing fly around the room and finally swat it.

- Pretend you are a cat, waking up from a nap.

- Pretend you are a dog, sitting up and begging.

Or, put several articles into a paper bag, one for each boy—a pencil, a clothespin, an eraser, an empty chewing gum wrapper, a paint brush, etc. One by one, the boys remove an article from the bag and pantomime a short scene, using the prop. The others try to guess what he is doing.

Charades

Charades are fun. Boys enjoy both the acting and the guessing. It's an opportunity for them to use their imaginations.

To play charades, divide the group into two teams. One team is given a piece of paper which has a word or title written on it. They leave the room and plan their action. After a quick rehearsal, they return and put on their act for the second team, in pantomime.

Each word or each syllable can be acted out separately. Two-syllable words are good for Cub Scouts. Try the following list, and let them suggest others:

air gun	billboard	cattail	birdcall
checkbook	basketball	fullback	football
garter snake	mousetrap	bookend	downpour

Resources for Skits

Skit books can be found at the public library, school libraries, book stores, and stores that carry teaching aids. Guard against using skits that are too long or with too much memorized dialogue. Skit ideas may also be found in *Cub Scout Program Helps, Boys' Life* magazine, and at the monthly Cub Scout leaders' roundtable and the annual pow wow. Leaders can also adapt and write their own skits to fit the monthly theme.

Here are additional resources for skits and costumes:

Fun With Skits, Stunts and Stories, by Helen and Larry Eisenberg

Handbook of Skits and Stunts, by Helen and Larry Eisenberg

Instant Fun For All Kinds of Groups, by Lorell C. Burns

The Pleasure Chest, by Helen and Larry Eisenberg

Fun Encyclopedia, by E. O. Harbin

Cokesbury Stunt Book, by A. M. Depew

The Right Play For You, by Bernice Carlson

101 Masks, False Faces and Make-Up For All Ages, by Richard M. Gardner

101 Costumes for All Ages, by Richard Cummings

Writing Your Own Skit

Sometimes it's hard to find a written skit that fits the monthly theme and your den of boys. If that's the case, the best thing to do is to adapt a skit to fit or write one of your own. You already know three of the most important things: (1) the facilities available, (2) the number of boys in your den, and (3) the subject. Now, jot down the following information:

- Subject of the plot.

- The title (it can be serious or funny).

- The number of actors.

- The kind of actors (Cub Scouts or puppets).

- Amount of time allowed (write a skit timed for 20 minutes, then boil it down to 5 minutes, saving only the best lines).

- Your stage (is it an open floor, a platform at one end of the room, or a real stage)?

Remember: The audience must like your skit, so write it to fit them. Keep scene-changing to a minimum.

MAKE AN OUTLINE

Follow these simple steps:

1. Boy wants something (friendship, a gold mine, a prize, to find a lost planet, etc.).

2. Boy starts to get it (by canoe, plane, horseback, foot, or some other way, etc.).

3. Obstacles stop boy (a secret enemy, a crocodile, false friend, weather, etc.).

4. Boy achieves goal (through an act of kindness, bravery, wisdom, magic, unexpected help, or some other way).

THINGS TO REMEMBER

1. Keep it simple.

2. Keep it short (3–5 minutes at the most).

3. Avoid long memorized dialogue. Pantomimes are good for Cub Scouts. (If exposition is necessary, the den chief may be narrator while the boys pantomime the action.)

4. Scenery, props, and costumes should be simple, if used at all.

5. Let every boy take part.

6. Use stage directions liberally—tell who goes where and does what.

7. Stimulate interest and surprises as you go along. A "walk on" (someone hunting a rabbit or bird, blowing up a balloon, or engaging in some other nonsense) in each scene sparks interest.

8. Be sure the audience can hear. Boys should be coached to speak slowly, clearly, and loudly. If the audience laughs or claps, actors should pause before continuing their lines.

9. Let the boys help write the skit. They will have some great ideas, and that's part of the fun.

10. Avoid skits that ridicule persons or groups. They are in bad taste.

SIMPLE SCENERY

Making Your Own Scenery

SIMPLE SCENERY

This is a good den project for Cub Scout skits. Scenery can add to the mood of the skit and make it more believable. It isn't necessary for scenery to be too detailed or complicated. Scenery should provide only an idea or suggestion of what it represents. Scenery isn't necessary for every skit. Use it only if you and the boys think it will add to the interest.

Scenery can be made from large pieces of corrugated cardboard. Check with furniture stores, appliance stores, grocery stores, or warehouses for large furniture and appliance cartons. Cardboard can be used for mountain ranges, bushes, trees, lamp posts, forest outlines, picket fences, houses, tents, cabins, or even a sun, moon, or stars to be suspended overhead. Wooden laths nailed to the back of the scenery will make it more sturdy and keep painted cardboard from curling.

Heavy cardboard should be cut by an adult. The boys can do the painting after guidelines are drawn with heavy pencil to show what colors go where. Latex wall paint or tempera is good for painting scenery. Tempera can be used to tint latex paint to a different color.

When painting large areas, use a roller. It is wise to paint on the blank side, so the printing will not bleed through. Felt-tip marking pens can be used to emphasize certain details or to outline a design on the painted cardboard.

Create a mood with color. Paint scenery in grays if the skit is spooky or sad; use bright colors if the skit is happy or funny.

Children's coloring books are a good source of patterns for simple cut out scenery. Just enlarge them to the desired size, using the instructions for enlarging patterns found in the "Crafts" section of this book.

Always keep in mind that the audience will see the scenery from a distance. Be sure it is distinctive. Small details or fine lines will not be visible. To give the appearance of distance, make scenery short.

Sound Effects For Skits

A flash of lightning, a loud crash, a train chugging down the track—all of these and many other special effects can be created by Cub Scouts for their den skits with a few simple preparations. Unusual and comical sounds can be created by using bells, drums, gongs, cymbals, castanets, whistles, horns, rattles, coconut shells, and even pots and pans.

Sound effects can add to the appeal of some Cub Scout skits. One of the Cub Scouts or the den chief could be the "sound effects man" and stand offstage to make the sounds at the appropriate time. Another alternative is to prerecord sounds on a cassette recorder.

Knock at the Door. Hit a half-gallon plastic bottle sharply on the end with a rubber spatula.

Thunder. Grasp a metal cookie sheet at one end, placing your thumb on the underside. Shake the tin so that it vibrates. Bang it against the knee for an occasional loud thunderclap.

Lightning. Flash a white light off and on, or use a photographic flash, along with thunder sound.

Hail. Pour rice on a pane of glass (near a microphone, if you have one).

Rain. Fill a tin can full of dry peas or beans. Rotate the can slowly (in front of a microphone, if you have one).

Crashes. Fill a wooden box with broken glass and a few stones, then nail on the top. Tip the end of the box to create various kinds of crashes.

Train. Place small wire nails inside a flat box, such as a band-aid box. Move it back and forth in rhythm . . . chug, chug, chug, chug . . . .

Creaking Door or Animal Roar. Use a coffee can or two foil pans taped together. Tie a string in the center of a pencil and rub string with resin. Punch a hole in the container, place the pencil inside and pull the string out through the hole. Drag fingernails along the string to produce noise into microphone.

Hoofbeats. Clap two half coconut shells on a wooden board to produce the sound of horses walking or galloping on a hard road.

Auto Brakes. Slide a drinking glass across a pane of glass (in front of a microphone, if possible).

Sword Fight. Holding an aluminum cookie sheet in one hand, hit it with a metal spoon.

Fire. Crumple and twist cellophane into a ball and then release it (near a microphone, if possible).

Campfire. Cover a flashlight with red cellophane or tissue paper, with wood piled on top to create a red glow, and use the fire sound above.

Other special effects are described in the "Puppets" section of this book.

Sample Skits

TOSSED SALAD

Characters: Farmer in the Dell, Cucumber, Tomato, Carrot, Celery, Onion. (Farmer dressed in overalls, straw hat, plaid shirt, with rake or hoe in hand and a very large green thumb made by stuffing a green balloon with cotton and tying it on thumb. Vegetables are boys hidden behind large cardboard cutouts of the appropriate vegetables.)

Farmer: I'm the farmer in the dell and you know me well, cause I grow good things to eat. That's easy to be seen, since my thumb is green. (*Holds out green thumb which was hidden behind his back*). And I have some friends I want you to meet.

Cucumber: I'm a long cucumber, cool and green, and people like me to eat. I'm really tickled, 'cause raw or pickled, they all say I'm a treat.

Tomato: I'm a ripe red tomato, juicy and round, and you'd better not squeeze me, you betcha'. 'Cause if you do, I'll squirt on you and I won't be tomato, I'll be catsup!

Carrot: I'm a bright orange carrot, tall and wise. I'm a health food for lads and lasses. They say, and it's true, that I'm good for your eyes. Did you ever see a rabbit wearing glasses?

Celery: You know me, I'm one of the bunch, and I'm very good for your diet. But I always crunch, whenever you munch, so I'm not too good for your peace and quiet.

Onion: Whatever would a salad be, without poor little me. For that distinctive touch that adds so much, chop me up and see.

All: (*Sing to the tune of "Friendship"*) — Friendship, friendship, just a perfect blendship. When other salads have been forgot, ours will hit the spot. La-de-da-de-la-de-da-da-da. (*Curtain*)

ROBOT INVENTORS

Scene: Table covered with old sheet or other cover reaching to floor at front. Fishbowl or other glass bowl, test tubes, flasks, and a black top hat are on table.

Characters: Six scientists in lab jackets (women's blouses, collars turned inside, put on backwards) stand at both ends and back of table. Scientist 2 is reading a large book, plainly titled, *How to Invent a Robot*. Scientist 3 is looking over his shoulder. Scientist 4 is stirring liquid in a bowl with a wooden spoon. Another boy, a robot with a bunny tail, is hidden behind the table.

NOTE: If seven boys are not available, some could take more lines.

SCIENTIST 1: It doesn't seem to be working.

SCIENTIST 2: I can't understand it!

SCIENTIST 3: We'll have to change the formula.

(*Scientist 4 adds soda to vinegar water in bowl — the mixture fizzes.*)

SCIENTIST 4: Wait a minute. What did you say your friend's name was?

SCIENTIST 5: Magisto the Magician. He says he's pulled a robot out of a hat lots of times.

SCIENTIST 4: That's rabbit, not robot!

(*Scientist 2 raises book, Scientist 4 raises spoon, Scientists 1, 2, 3, and 4 chase Scientist 5 offstage left. Scientist 6 starts to follow, stops, and looks at hat.*)

SCIENTIST 6 (*shrugging shoulders*): It might work! Abracadabra 1-2-3. (*Takes hold of hat with left hand, tips it toward himself at edge of table, reaches "in"—really reaches behind table—grabs and pulls robot out of hat*).

SCIENTIST 6: Hey! It worked! Now I'll just push this button (*pushes button on robot—robot drops to all fours, hops offstage, showing bunny tail bobbing at back*).

PUSH-BUTTON RADIO

Scene: One person is pushing buttons (thus changing stations) on a pushbutton radio. Offstage, five people read the parts below. The following radio programs are mixed up with hilarious effects—a talk on Cub Scouting, a prize fight, a soap opera, a political speech, and a commercial on cornflakes. (It will help for the person pushing the buttons to have a copy of the script so he can push the buttons at the right time.)

NOTE: Since this skit requires quite a bit of reading, it will be best for Webelos Scouts or adults to perform. Rehearse at least twice. The first and last part of the lines are the most important. The second reader should begin immediately after the first reader finishes, etc. This is one time the actors should be instructed not to wait for laughs.

CUB SCOUT: Good evening, friends! Tonight, I am going to tell you about Cub Scouting. Cub Scouting is a home-centered program for boys, their leaders their families, and . . .

POLITICAL (*passionately*): . . . scoundrels in high places! I say to you, we must send to Congress men and women of integrity who will stand up to temptation and say . . .

SOAP OPERA (*with feeling*): . . . let me hold you in my arms, darling! Yes, sweet, come close . . . closer still . . . and let me put my strong arms around you, and then . . .

FIGHT (*hard staccato*): . . . a hard looping right to the stomach! Wow! Whatta fight this is, folks! Murphy swings a left to the jaw, a right to the head, a left, a right, another right, and the Butcher goes down. He drops straight back on his . . .

COMMERCIAL (*loud and brassy*): . . . large, economy-size package. Yes, friends, ask your grocer today for this big, family-size box of Chlorophyll's Crummier Cornflakes . . . the only cornflakes with the built-in crumb! Once you have tasted Cholorophyll's, you'll say . . .

POLITICAL: . . . how in the world can they do it? How can these men, these elected servants for the people, put politics before principle in such a brazen and outrageous effort to advance their own selfish cause? There is only

one thing I know that will put a stop to their selfishness. I mean none other than . . .

CUB SCOUT: . . . a group of overworked den leaders. The answer to this, of course, is to select assistant den leaders who can help out where needed. When you ask someone to be a den leader, just walk right up and say . . .

SOAP OPERA: . . . take your hands off me! Don't come near me! I cannot stand you . . . do you hear? I hate you! . . .

CUB SCOUT: . . . in this way, of course, a person is more likely to say "yes." And then there is only one thing to watch out for . . .

FIGHT: . . . another hard right to the stomach! Now the Butcher is moving in, and Murphy's looking bad . . . very bad. He has a cut on his forehead and his left eye's swelling fast. In fact, he reminds me of . . .

COMMERCIAL: . . . a soggy bowl of leftover cornflakes. So accept no substitutes! Always choose Chlorophyll's cornflakes for the crumminess you love to crunch. Start your day with a big bowl full of Chlorophyll's, swimming in heavy cream and covered with strawberries . . . and a large heaping of . . .

POLITICAL: . . . crooked politicians! Yes my friends, I repeat to you again and again that dishonesty in government, whether local, state, or national, is a shame and a disgrace to our fair land. There is only one thing we can do about it. Only one thing will save our proud and mighty nation . . .

CUB SCOUT: . . . four full dens in every pack! More boys in your pack means more boys to enjoy the fun and benefits of Cub Scouting, as well as more families to share in the leadership. With a full pack, a Cubmaster can look the den leaders in the face and say . . .

SOAP OPERA: . . . Kiss me, you fool! All I ever expected from you was . . .

FIGHT: . . . A hard right to the stomach! And I can see what's coming now . . .

COMMERCIAL: . . . another bowl of soggy, leftover cornflakes. So remember, always use Chlorophyll's . . .

POLITICAL: . . . because they're poison . . . yes, poison. The best solution to political dishonesty is . . .

CUB SCOUT: . . . more and better Cub Scouting everywhere! (*Curtain*)

FITNESS CHAMPS

Characters: Six Cub Scouts in uniform, holding props as described below.

Setting: All boys come on stage and speak their lines.

ALL: We all excel in fitness. We're champs as you can see. Just listen to our stories, and I'm sure you will agree.

CUB SCOUT 1: I hold the title of the strongest in our den. Do you suppose that it's because of my friend? (*Holds up toy skunk, while others hold their noses.*)

CUB SCOUT 2: I'm known as the den's muscle man of the year. But most of my muscles are between my ears. (*Pulls out a small hat and tries desperately to put it on his head.*)

CUB SCOUT 3: I hold the title of the fastest one of all. I'm always first in line for the refreshment call. (*Pulls out bag of cookies and begins eating them.*)

CUB SCOUT 4: I'm known as the champion of the high jump. One time I missed and got a big lump. (*Rubs head, with painful expression on face.*)

CUB SCOUT 5: To keep in good shape, I exercise each day. I wonder why my muscles turned out this way. (*Removes shirt to show colorful padding on arms.*)

CUB SCOUT 6: I'm the champion at making things disappear, you see. Watch us all disappear as I count to three. (*Slowly counts 1 . . . 2 . . . 3 . . . as curtain closes.*)

THE SPIDER'S PLEA

Characters: Four Cub Scouts in spider costumes with eight legs sewn on. Four Cub Scouts in uniform.

Setting: Spiders line up on stage. Each steps forward to speak his lines.

SPIDER 1: We lowly spiders aren't all bad. As a matter of fact, it's really quite sad. We wish to tell you now our story. You be the judge and also the jury.

SPIDER 2: No neck, no arms, no feelers have we. But eight legs, a body, and eyes to see. Our American family often, you realize, is half cobweb, half hunter, and quite good size.

SPIDER 3: We the hunters, are runners and jumpers. Some, being patient, are really good stalkers; living among the flowers and grass, to prey on insects that come to pass.

SPIDER 4: We, as cobwebs, are very bright. Catching our prey is sheer delight. Spinning our own silk in making a web, gives us protection, food, and a bed.

ALL SPIDERS: Men and birds give us quite a fright. Is it because you don't like our sight? Ridding the world of flies and bugs, and all you do is exterminate us!

(*Uniformed Cub Scouts enter, armed with oversize spray guns and chase spiders into the audience*).

HIGH-LOW BRAVES

Characters: Chief High, Chief Low, and any number of Braves, all in Indian costume; Narrator.

Setting: Chief High and Chief Low are on opposite sides of stage with their Braves.

NARRATOR: Chief High and his tribe lived down in the valley and Chief Low lived up on the mountain. Every morning Chief High would go out, look up at Chief Low's camp, and call out.

CHIEF HIGH: Hello, Low (*waving*).

CHIEF LOW: Hi, High (*answering*).

NARRATOR: This went on for many moons and everyone was happy. Then one day Chief High's Braves began to wonder why High was low and Low was high, and they became confused and unhappy. Soon Chief Low's Braves were saying the same thing, and they became confused and unhappy, too. (*All braves pace in a circle.*)

NARRATOR: When Chief High and Chief Low heard about the problem, they laughed and said . . .

CHIEFS (*together, laughing*): We can soon fix that!

NARRATOR: And so the next morning Chief High called up the mountain.

CHIEF HIGH: Hi, Low!

CHIEF LOW: Hello, High!

NARRATOR: But the Braves were still unhappy and more confused than ever. (*All braves pace in circle.*)

NARRATOR: So the two Chiefs got together and talked it over. (*Chiefs move to center of stage and talk.*)

CHIEF HIGH: We've got a problem!

CHIEF LOW: You betcha! What should we do?

CHIEF HIGH: We exchange camps.

NARRATOR. Now, every morning Chief High calls out . . .

CHIEF HIGH: Hello, Low!

CHIEF LOW: Hi, High!

NARRATOR: The Braves are happy and wonder why they were ever unhappy in the first place.

ALL BRAVES (*smiling, say together*): So, whether you're high or whether you're low, you can be happy wherever you go. Whether you're up or whether you're down, it's as easy to smile as it is to frown. (*Curtain*)

ENERGY SAVERS

Characters: Six Cub Scouts in uniform; one den leader in uniform.

Setting: Den meeting place, decorated as desired. Den leader sits at a table. As skit opens, all Cub Scouts arrive together and sit down.

DEN LEADER: Today, let's take turns and tell how we can help to conserve energy in our homes.

CUB SCOUT 1: I know a good way. My mom doesn't use her clothes dryer as much as she used to. She uses a new solar energy device called a clothesline and hangs her laundry outside to dry in the sunshine.

CUB SCOUT 2: My dad said that if we filled a plastic bottle with water and put it in the tank in the bathroom, it would cut down on the amount of water used for flushing.

CUB SCOUT 3: Did you know that if you take showers you use a lot less water than if you take baths? Mom even uses a timer, and we have learned to take 3-minute showers at our house.

CUB SCOUT 4: We keep the drapes closed on summer days and keep them open for light and warmth in the winter.

CUB SCOUT 5: We keep the damper in our fireplace closed whenever we aren't using it. If it's left open in the winter, the warm air in the house escapes up the chimney and that's a waste.

DEN LEADER (to last Cub Scout): Johnny, do you have anything to add about saving energy? (*She turns to see that he is fast asleep.*) I guess Johnny is the best energy saver of us all. (*Curtain*)

THE OPERATION

This is a pantomime skit which involves leaders and parents.

Characters: Narrator, one boy in Cub Scout uniform, a boy in a white lab coat, two leaders in uniform, two other adults in ordinary clothes. Additional boys could be dressed in lab coats and assist in surgery.

Setting: The uniformed Cub Scout lies on a large table, covered with a sheet. The props indicated below are taped to the back of the table out of sight. The doctor holds a large cardboard knife and stands behind the table. His assistants stand at both ends and back of table.

NARRATOR: We are about to show you how to make a new Cub Scout in one easy operation. To do this, we need a boy . . . (*Doctor points to patient on table.*)

NARRATOR: . . . a den leader . . . (*Uniformed leader enters and stands near table.*)

NARRATOR: . . . a cubmaster . . . (*Other uniformed leader enters.*)

NARRATOR: . . . and a family. (*Two adults in ordinary clothes enter.*)

NARRATOR: First he needs to be covered with fun and good times. (*Doctor and assistant raise sheet, taking care not to reveal the boy on the table. In large letters on the sheet is written "FUN AND GOOD TIMES."*)

NARRATOR: We use laughing gas for anesthetic. (*One of assistants uses tire pump or suction cup labeled "Laughing Gas."*)

NARRATOR: We take out hate and put in love. (*Doctor removes a big rock from under the sheet and puts in a big red paper heart labeled "LOVE" which is handed to him by an assistant.*)

NARRATOR: We take out selfishness and put in cooperation. (*Doctor removes a sign marked "ME" and puts in a sign marked "WE."*)

NARRATOR: We put in some good citizenship. (*Doctor puts in a cutout of U. S. flag.*)

NARRATOR: We add some reverence. (*Doctor adds a cutout of a church.*)

NARRATOR: Our operation has been a great success! Just look at the results! (*The uniformed Cub Scout throws off the sheet, gets off the table, stands at attention and gives Cub Scout salute. The Cubmaster holds up a sign labeled "SUCCESS."*) (*Curtain*)

LAMP POST

Characters: Any number of uniformed Cub Scouts; one boy playing part of lamppost.

Setting: A boy stands on stage holding a lighted flashlight. He wears a sign marked "Lamppost." The stage lights are dimmed. As skit opens, first Cub Scout comes on stage and begins to look for something near lamppost.

CUB SCOUT 2 (*enters*): What are you looking for?

CUB SCOUT 1. I've lost a dollar and I just have to find it. (*Cub Scout 2 helps look, as Cub Scout 3 enters*).

CUB SCOUT 3: What are you looking for?

CUB SCOUT 1: I've lost a dollar and I just have to find it. (*Cub Scout 3 begins to look as next boy enters. Continue this procedure until last person enters.*)

LAST CUB SCOUT: What are you looking for?

CUB SCOUT 1: I have lost a dollar and I just have to find it.

LAST CUB SCOUT: Where did you lose it?

CUB SCOUT 1: Down the street.

ALL (*looking disgusted*): Then why are we looking here?

CUB SCOUT 1: Because this is where the light is! (*Others chase Cub Scout 1 offstage.*) (*Curtain*)

DAD'S WORKBENCH

This could be a puppet skit or performed with live actors.

Characters: Dad (den chief); Cub Scout in uniform; Hammer, Saw, File, Screwdriver (boys wearing large cardboard cutouts of tools).

Setting: Dad and Cub Scout are standing near a table (workbench).

DAD: Has anyone seen my hammer?

CUB SCOUT: Did you look on the workbench?

DAD: It's not there. No one ever puts anything back where it belongs!

HAMMER (*peeking in from offstage*): No, I'm not on the workbench. I'm over here behind the door where he used me to drive the door hinge pins down and left me here.

DAD: Now where in the world is my saw?

CUB SCOUT: Look on the workbench. It should be there.

DAD (*angrily*): It isn't here! No one puts my tools away.

SAW (*peeking from behind curtain*): Here we go again. I'm lost because he didn't clean me and put me back after I was used on the garage roof to spread the tar, because I was bigger than a putty knife.

DAD: Good grief! Now my file is lost!

CUB SCOUT: I haven't seen it.

FILE (*standing to one side of the stage*): I knew he'd forget that he left me out in the yard when he sharpened the lawnmower last fall. He'll find me when I get caught in the lawnmower as he's mowing the grass next spring.

DAD: Now I can't find my screwdriver! Did you borrow it, son?

CUB SCOUT: Yes, Dad, but I gave it back to you.

DAD: Now where could that screwdriver be?

SCREWDRIVER (*standing on other side of stage*): He dropped me on the floor and forgot to pick me up. (*Dad continues to grumble, shuffling things on the workbench. All tools come on stage and stand together.*)

TOOLS: Why can't people remember to put us back where we belong?

CUB SCOUT (*to audience*): And it's just as important to use tools properly. (*Just then Dad takes a big swing with a hammer and pretends to hit his thumb.*

He lets out a yell, sticks his thumb in his mouth and hops around stage as curtain closes.)

THE MUSIC MAKERS

This skit can be performed with hand puppets or live actors.

Characters: Violin, Cello, Drum, Cymbals, Clarinet, Flute. Cub Scouts can wear costumes made from boxes, with instruments painted on front.

Setting: Cluttered room with chairs, sheet music, music stands scattered around. The instruments walk onstage, mumbling and grumbling to each other.

VIOLIN: Well, everyone knows the importance of strings! As head violin, my lovely tone rings.

CELLO: Really, my friend! Your strings are a riddle! You call yourself a violin, but to us you're just a fiddle!

DRUM: Now, now, all you strings, just go take a seat. For without my rhythm, you'd not have a beat!

CYMBALS: As a kettle drum, you're more kettle than not. And what's a kettle but an empty pot?

DRUM: If I were you, Cymbals, I think I'd keep hid, or else we'll replace you with garbage can lids.

CLARINET: Honestly, Drum, I'd really rather that all of us just learned to play together!

FLUTE: Well, what about flutes? Or don't we matter? I've never heard such endless chatter!

DRUM: You know, I've been thinking . . .

CYMBALS (interrupting): Where would you get a thought? We know you're as hollow as when you were bought.

VIOLIN: Cymbals, Cymbals, I do declare! For ugly manners, there's none to compare!

CELLO: Now listen to me . . . and maybe you'll see that we're all important and necessary.

CLARINET: It's true that we all are necessary. But without players, not a tune could we carry!

ALL: He's right! It's true! Without the boys, we wouldn't know what to do!

DRUM: Let's all learn a lesson from this little fuss. The boys are what's important . . . and then comes us!

(If additional boys are available, two or three uniformed Cub Scouts could enter and pretend to play instruments as curtain closes.)

BOBCAT'S BIG CATCH

Characters: Grey Squirrel, Running Deer, Small Bear, Little Wolf, Bobcat, and Chief Akela. (All dressed in Indian costumes. Akela wears chief's headdress).

Setting: A clearing in the forest. All characters except Bobcat and Chief Akela are seated in a semi-circle, facing the audience, with arms folded. Grey Squirrel is slowly beating a tom-tom. Bobcat is offstage with a small bow and arrow.

RUNNING DEER: This is a big day in Bobcat's life. He'll become a brave if good with a knife.

SMALL BEAR: To our tribe he will belong, if nothing in the forest goes wrong.

LITTLE WOLF: Hope he catches heap big prey, to make Chief Akela happy today.

GREY SQUIRREL (*stops drum, cups hand to ear*): Hark my brothers! A sound I hear! I think brother Bobcat must be near. (*Offstage continuous loud sneezing is heard. Bobcat and Chief Akela enter. Chief holds Bobcat by back of shirt. Bobcat continues to sneeze.*)

RUNNING DEER: Brother Bobcat, what did you fetch? We waited here to see the big catch.

CHIEF AKELA: Bobcat is headed for his father's tepee. The hunt has made him tired and sleepy. He'll have to hunt where the buffalo play, another time, another day.

SMALL BEAR: But Chief Akela, where is the catch that brother Bobcat went to fetch?

CHIEF AKELA: Brother Bobcat is plenty bold! He waded the creek and caught a cold! (*Chief gently pushes Bobcat offstage as he continues to sneeze. All seated braves laugh, then quickly clap hands to mouth and refold arms. Grey Squirrel starts to beat drum again as curtain closes.*)

ALL'S WELL THAT HAUNTS WELL

Characters (*name cards hung around necks*): Three witches named Scary Ellen, Elizabat, and Hagret Rose, a Fire, and a Narrator.

Setting: Witches' cottage in Haunted Forest. (Long table, center; rocking chair, left; and a washtub on floor in front of table).

Props: Broom, tub with stirring stick, clock, magazine with "Seance Fiction" pasted on front; strip of crepe paper with "Evening" crayoned on it; calendar; fake hand (or 8 to 10 playing cards); basket containing boxes and bottles marked as follows: "Instant Headaches," "Brown-and-Serve Bats," "Quick-Cooking Mothers' Goats," "Minute Mice," "Ever Ready Smoke-O," "Just-Add-Water Snake Mix," "Quick Frozen Toad Stools," "Concentrated Acorn Juice," and "1 Gallon Lake Eerie Water."

Sheet music marked as follows: "In My Sweet Little Alice Blue Shroud," "Sleepy Time Ghoul," "When I Grow Too Old to Scream," "Spook to Me Only With Thine Eyes," "When My Dreambat Comes Home," "The Shriek of Araby." (*Narrator reads the script, others pantomime according to direction. As curtain opens, Fire is rocking in rocking chair, witches are stirring tub.*)

NARRATOR: There once were three darling witches who lived in Haunted Forest. Their names were Scary Ellen, Elizabat, and Hagret Rose (*witches curtsy as names are read.*) Every year on Halloween, these witches sprayed their forest with magic potion which took 6 weeks to make and was absolutely guaranteed to haunt-up the place for a full year. (*Witches continue to stir.*) This magic potion contained such delicacies as pickled cat's feet on mice, gray smoke a la goblin, and apple cry with whipped scream on top. One Halloween, when it was almost dark, the three witches started their annual spraying job . . . (*Witches lift tub, Elizabat stumbles, tub spills on Fire*) . . . when Elizabat tripped over a black cat and spilled the magic potion on Fire. (*Fire stops rocking, stands, puts hands on hips, sighs, exits.*) Fire went out. "Now you've done it," said the other two witches (*Scary Ellen and Hagret Rose shake fists at Elizabat.*) "If we don't haunt this forest tonight, all of our fiends will desert us. And our phantom football team will join another league.

"Never mind, my pretty little darlings," croaked Elizabat (*Elizabat picks up broom, straddles it*), "I'll fly into the stupor market at the magic city shocking center, and pick up more supplies; meanwhile, you two get the fire started again." (*Elizabat exits. Scary Ellen and Hagret Rose pull Fire back onstage with much effort, sit him in rocking chair, push chair several times to start it rocking; after awhile it does.*) With a lot of gentle coaxing, Scary Ellen and Hagret Rose finally got the fire going, then they settled back to wait for Elizabat. (*Scary Ellen and Hagret Rose stand behind table.*) Time passed slowly. (*Witches pass clock back and forth in slow motion.*) They read their favorite magazine, Seance Fiction. (*Witches hold up magazine and read.*) They wonder how Elizabat could hope to make another magic potion in one night.

As the evening grew longer . . . (*Scary Ellen holds up crepe paper marked Evening, then stretches it*) . . . Hagret Rose began to feel a little weak. (*Hagret Rose holds up calendar and runs fingers back and forth over a short week.*) They thought their cause was lost. (*Witches look under things and all around for Lost Cause.*) They almost decided never to spook their sister again, when who should float right through the door . . . (*enter Elizabat with a basket of groceries*) . . . but Elizabat. "What took you so long?" they said. "I ran into an old boyfiend," Elizabat replied. "Did he kiss you?" "No," answered Elizabat, "but he gave me his hand." (*Elizabat pulls dummy hand out of basket, holds it up, throws it in tub.*)

Elizabat's basket was full of goodies, and she laid them on the table one by one. (*Elizabat holds up each article for audience to read before placing it on table.*) Instant Headaches . . . Brown-and-Serve Bats . . . Quick-Cooking Mothers' Goats . . . Minute Mice . . . Ever Ready Smoke-O . . . Just-Add-Water Snake Mix . . . Quick Frozen Toad Stools . . . Concentrated Acorn Juice . . . and 1 Gallon Lake Eerie Water. (*Witches take each item one at a time.*)

Quickly, the witches went to work to make their instant magic potion (*each turns a complete circle before placing item in the tub.*) They took turns . . . adding the ingredients . . . and stirring the kettle. (*Witches then take "turns" before stirring.*) As the magic potion boils, the three witches gathered around for a good old songfest. They sang those sentimental favorites, "In My Sweet Little Alice Blue Shroud" . . . (*Witches hold up sheet music for each song as it is mentioned, throw it into the tub and stir, etc.*) . . . "Sleepy Time Ghoul" . . . "When I Grow Too Old to Scream" . . . "Spook to Me Only With Thine Eyes" . . . "When My Dreambat Comes Home," . . . and "The Shriek of Araby."

When the instant magic potion was finished, Scary Ellen, Elizabat, and Hagret Rose went out to spray the forest . . . (*Witches pick up tub and exit slowly*) . . . and promised themselves never again to cook the old-fashioned way. (*Exit Fire, blowing on name card.*) Being left unattended, the Fire blew itself out. (*Curtain*)

Costumes

Costumes can help set the theme or mood for the skit. They have a magical ability to transform a boy into a man from outer space, a pirate, an astronaut, a clown, an Indian, an exotic animal, or anything else his imagination suggests.

Costumes for Cub Scout skits should be kept simple and inexpensive. More than likely they will only be used once.

Sometimes a simple sign to identify a character is as effective as a costume. A sign can turn a boy into a tree, a lamppost, an animal, or other object. Simple props, such as a cardboard mustache, eye patch, bandana, and cardboard sword for a pirate will be sufficient to set the mood for the skit.

Several types of simple costumes are described below. Most of the materials can be found around the house.

CREPE PAPER COSTUMES

Crepe paper is an inexpensive costume material. It can be glued, stapled, sewn, draped, and folded. Its ability to stretch is also an important factor. Simple tunics, vests, shirts, and hats can be fashioned quite easily. With its wide range of colors, crepe paper has many possibilities.

OLD CLOTHING

Costumes can be made from tights, T-shirts, robes, pajamas, hats, jackets, and other discarded clothing items. Mens' and boys' ski-type pajamas can be made into many different outfits. Save feathers for sparkly trim for knights' costumes. Broken toy guns, foil for deputy badges or for covering belt buckles, vinyl scraps for vests and chaps will be useful for cowboy costumes.

CARDBOARD BOX COSTUMES

Costumes for clowns, animals, vegetables, robots, musical instruments, etc., can be made from cardboard boxes. Cut holes for the head and arms, then let the boys paint them with latex, using felt-tip marking pens for highlights.

PAPER SACK COSTUMES

Grocery sacks and brown wrapping paper can be used effectively for both costumes and masks. They can be painted with latex paint (to add strength) or with tempera. For a leather-like appearance, crush and re-crush brown paper sacks or brown wrapping paper until it is soft and wrinkled. Then press with a lukewarm iron. This works well for Indian and western costumes.

BROK LEE
DARK GREEN
LIGHT GREEN

BILL PEPPER

SAM SQUASH
YELLOW
DARK GREEN

Q. CUMBER
DARK GREEN
LIGHT GREEN

PAUL BEAN
DARK GREEN
LIGHT GREEN

VEGETABLE COSTUMES

Nature Costumes

VEGETABLE COSTUMES

These are easy-to-make but effective.

1. Make cutouts of vegetable shapes from corrugated cardboard, or draw vegetable shapes on large paper bags to be worn over the head.

2. Paint with tempera or latex paint.

3. Hand holds can be attached to back of cardboard cutouts. The boy's lines can be printed on the back side of his cutout.

4. Boys can wear shorts with green socks.

3. Try on the mask to determine where eye holes should be cut. Cut these large.

4. Add other details for each particular animal (ears, nose, tail, etc.) using construction paper and paint.

GIANT PAPER SACK ANIMALS

GIANT PAPER SACK ANIMALS

Use giant-size paper sacks for these costumes. You'll also need cellophane tape, masking tape, colored construction paper, scissors, tempera paint, and glue.

1. Look for heavy-weight paper sacks. If these are not available, glue two sacks together for reinforcement.

2. Cut oval-shaped arm holes, about 4 inches wide and 12 inches long in each side. Reinforce openings with masking tape.

INSECT OR TURTLE COSTUMES

Use cardboard, poster board, and heavy paper for these.

1. Cut front and back shell from poster board. Attach together at top with bias tape or cord so it can be worn sandwich board style.

2. Make head mask from cardboard box or paper sack.

3. Wings are cut from paper or cardboard.

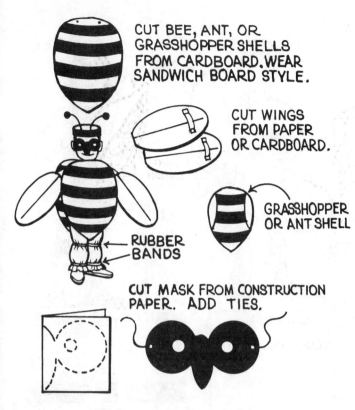

CUT BEE, ANT, OR GRASSHOPPER SHELLS FROM CARDBOARD. WEAR SANDWICH BOARD STYLE.

CUT WINGS FROM PAPER OR CARDBOARD.

GRASSHOPPER OR ANT SHELL

RUBBER BANDS

CUT MASK FROM CONSTRUCTION PAPER. ADD TIES.

INSECT OR TURTLE COSTUMES

PIONEER COSTUME

Shirt and Pants. The basic costume is an old brown shirt and slacks. Cut collar and cuffs off shirt. Sew or glue on a fabric or crepe-paper fringe as shown in illustration. A fringe can also be added down outside seams of pants.

Musket. The musket is a broomstick, nailed to a handle which has been cut from ¾-inch plywood.

Powder Horn. A powder horn can be made as shown, following the directions for papier mâché found in the "Crafts" section of this book.

ASTRONAUT COSTUMES

Use household items, scrap material, and old clothing to make these.

Astronaut Uniform. The basic costume can be a pair of coveralls, an old sweat shirt, and pants or ski-type pajamas which have been spray painted or dyed electric blue or gray.

Helmet. The helmet can be made from a 3-gallon cardboard ice cream carton. Glue on paper cups or typewriter spools for earphones. Cut out face opening. Helmet can be covered with aluminum foil or painted white or silver.

Astronaut Boots. Astronaut boots can be made from ski boots or galoshes, covered with aluminum foil.

Astronaut Gloves. The astronaut can wear a pair of old work gloves which have been spray painted silver.

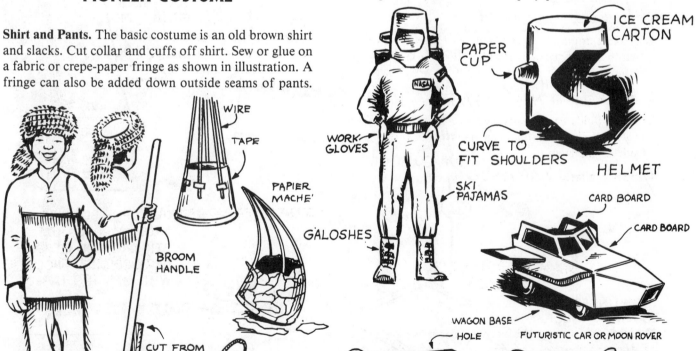

WIRE

TAPE

PAPIER MACHE'

BROOM HANDLE

CUT FROM PLYWOOD

ADD CORD

PAINT

PIONEER COSTUME

WORK GLOVES

SKI PAJAMAS

GALOSHES

ICE CREAM CARTON

PAPER CUP

CURVE TO FIT SHOULDERS

HELMET

CARD BOARD

CARD BOARD

WAGON BASE

HOLE

FUTURISTIC CAR OR MOON ROVER

HOLE

TAB

ASTRONAUT COSTUME

RAY GUN

GLUE TAB TO HANDLE

PILGRIM COSTUMES

Paper, cloth, and cardboard will help to make these.

Tunic. This costume is made from gray or brown crepe paper or fabric. Cut and assemble as shown in illustration, adding bias tape ties at neck and on sides. Cut a collar from white paper or fabric.

Shoes. Cut shoe buckles from cardboard. Cover with foil and stick to top of dark colored shoes with masking tape.

Belt. Cut a cardboard buckle and cover with foil to be worn over a regular belt.

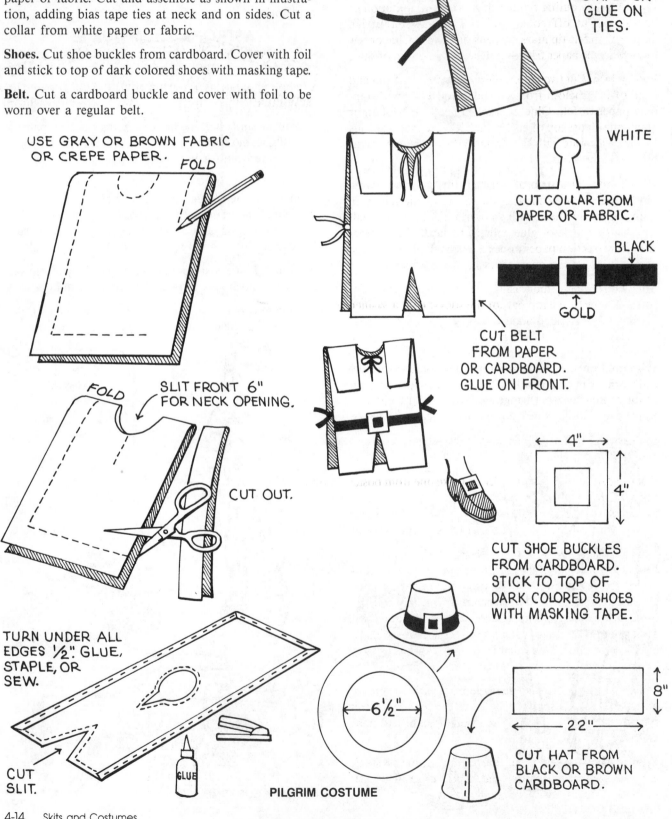

BIASTAPE TIES

STAPLE OR GLUE ON TIES.

USE GRAY OR BROWN FABRIC OR CREPE PAPER.

FOLD

WHITE

CUT COLLAR FROM PAPER OR FABRIC.

BLACK

GOLD

SLIT FRONT 6" FOR NECK OPENING.

FOLD

CUT OUT.

CUT BELT FROM PAPER OR CARDBOARD. GLUE ON FRONT.

4"

4"

CUT SHOE BUCKLES FROM CARDBOARD. STICK TO TOP OF DARK COLORED SHOES WITH MASKING TAPE.

TURN UNDER ALL EDGES ½" GLUE, STAPLE, OR SEW.

GLUE

CUT SLIT.

6½"

8"

22"

CUT HAT FROM BLACK OR BROWN CARDBOARD.

PILGRIM COSTUME

INDIAN COSTUMES

These are the most popular and easy-to-make costumes for den skits.

War Shirt. Use a man's old shirt as a basis for the war shirt. A heavy outing flannel shirt is a good imitation of buckskin. Cut off collar and cuffs. Draw on Indian designs with felt-tip marking pens or crayon. Glue or sew fabric or crepe paper fringe on sleeves and bottom of shirt.

Breechcloth. Cut two panels the size needed for front and back of breechcloth from crushed, ironed brown wrapping paper or felt. Glue or staple a length of ribbon or seam tape across top of each panel, leaving excess at ends for ties. Decorate with felt-tip markers or crayons. Wear over jeans or trousers.

Headband. Cut a strip of crushed, ironed brown wrapping paper about 2 inchs wide and long enough to fit around the boy's head with an overlap. Fold strip in half lengthwise. Staple or glue ends to fit head. Cut feather from construction paper or use a real colored feather and glue it between the open edges of the headband.

Moccasins. These moccasins are cut from old brown socks. Cut away the top part of the socks. Fold a ¼-inch hem on the outside to make a casing for the drawstring. Sew hem near edge, leaving an opening in center front large enough for drawstring. Use an old shoelace or piece of colored yarn for the drawstring. If you fasten one end of the drawstring to a safety pin, it will be easier to draw through the casing. Decorate toes of moccasins with beads.

Indian Anklets. Cut 10-inch lengths of yarn and loop over shoelaces as shown. Tie around ankle.

Quiver. Use a cardboard cylinder or make one from poster board. Cover with scrap vinyl or paint. Use brass paper fasteners to attach a cardboard or vinyl loop. Arrows are dowels with cardboard points and fringed construction paper feathers.

Indian Necklace. Make beads from one of the modeling dough recipes found in the "Crafts" section of this book. Be sure to make a hole for the cord. Beads which are molded into uneven chunks and painted turquoise will look like the real thing. Use a waxed thread for stringing. Plastic bear claws are available, or they can be cut from ¼-inch plywood or heavy cardboard and painted.

Indian necklaces can also be made from various types of pasta or seeds, as shown. The easiest way to color this type of necklace is to dip it in a pot of paint and hang it up to dry.

Fringed Wristlet. Cut from felt or vinyl. Glue or staple a 5-inch wide fringe to one end. Add ties to held cuffs in place. Decorate with Indian symbols.

War Shield. Use a round pizza cardboard or cut a circle of corrugated cardboard to desired size. Paint with latex paint and decorate with marking pens. Use brass paper fasteners to attach cardboard handles on back side. Add real or artificial feathers for trim around bottom of shield.

See "Crafts" section of this book for more Indian accessories.

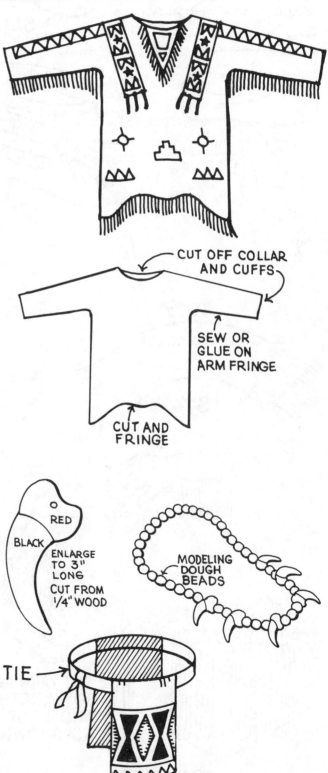

CUT OFF COLLAR AND CUFFS

SEW OR GLUE ON ARM FRINGE

CUT AND FRINGE

RED

BLACK

ENLARGE TO 3" LONG CUT FROM ¼" WOOD

MODELING DOUGH BEADS

TIE

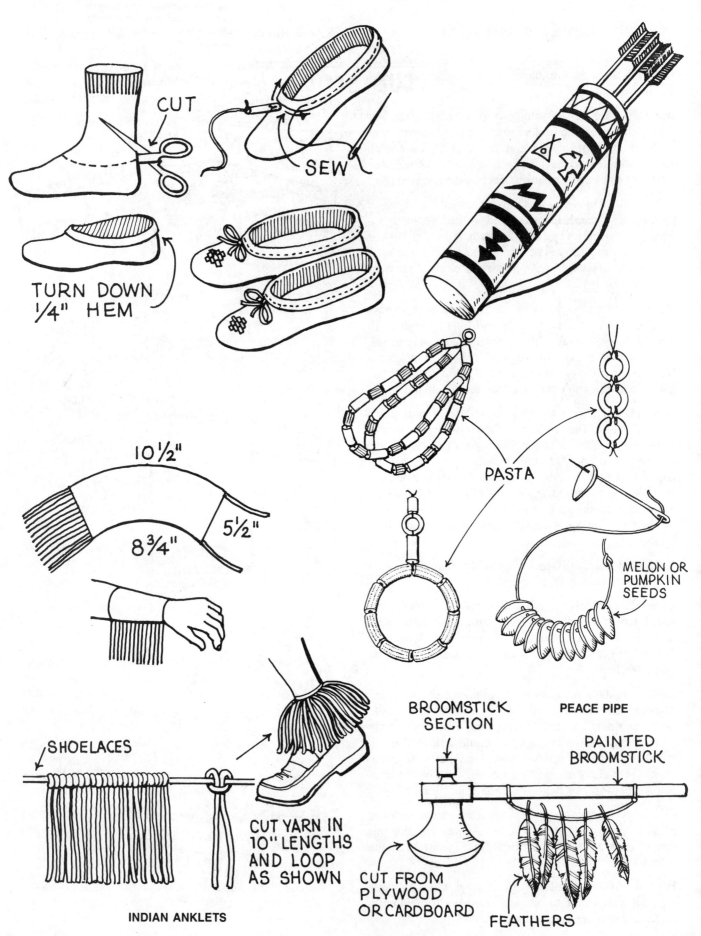

CUT

SEW

TURN DOWN 1/4" HEM

10½"

8¾"

5½"

PASTA

MELON OR PUMPKIN SEEDS

SHOELACES

CUT YARN IN 10" LENGTHS AND LOOP AS SHOWN

BROOMSTICK SECTION

PEACE PIPE

PAINTED BROOMSTICK

CUT FROM PLYWOOD OR CARDBOARD

FEATHERS

INDIAN ANKLETS

You can construct an entrance like this one with just a piece of wall board and some paint. Use an orange crate as a ticket booth.

CUB SCOUT CIRCUS

MAIN~ENTRANCE

FEROCIOUS BEASTS

WILD MEN

WORLDS STRONGEST MAN

CLOWNS

ADMISSION 5 CUDOLAS

1000 LBS

Tiger

An old suit of long underwear dyed pink and padded with cotton makes a powerful strong man.

Decorate an old playpen. It will hold a real cat or dog or one small Cub Scout "animal." Large stuffed animals may also be used for your menagerie.

No circus is complete without one clown who squirts water on the others. Squirter is a small plastic squeeze bottle concealed in a bouquet of construction paper flowers.

CIRCUS COSTUMES

Create the illusion of the Big Top with these simple circus costumes.

Clown. Clowns can be funny- or sad-faced. (*See directions for clown make-up at the end of this section.*) They can wear big, floppy hats, tiny painted hats, straw hats, or even an upturned flower pot hat. The clown can wear a big jacket or shirt and a wide tie cut from cardboard. Make a crepe paper neck ruffle, if desired. Clowns wear oversized pants, held up by a rope belt or suspenders. A pair of swim fins make good floppy clown shoes, or wear a large pair of tennis shoes with paper stuffed in them.

Top Hat (Ringmaster or Lion Tamer). Cut the crown and brim from black poster board as shown. Cut ¾-inch tabs along bottom edge of crown. Overlap sides and staple together. Slip brim over tabs, bend tabs back, and glue to underside of brim. Curl brim on either side.

Acrobat's Cape. Staple a 35-inch length of bright colored crepe paper and contrasting color crepe together at corners. Cut a piece 16-by-20 inches for collar. Fold collar in half, lengthwise. Gather top edge of cape and fit between folded edges of collar. Staple in place. For neck fastener, insert a brass paper fastener on each top edge of cape for buttons. Reinforce inside cape with a piece of cardboard under the buttons and cover rings with masking tape. Hook a paper-clip chain over buttons.

Circus Animals. Use men's pajamas, dyed or painted to appropriate color. Add rope tails and manes. Make papier mâché masks as shown elsewhere in this section. (Also see elephant and giraffe illustrated.)

Tattooed Man. Draw tattoo design on old long underwear with marking pens or crayons. Tattooed man wears this under bright colored shorts.

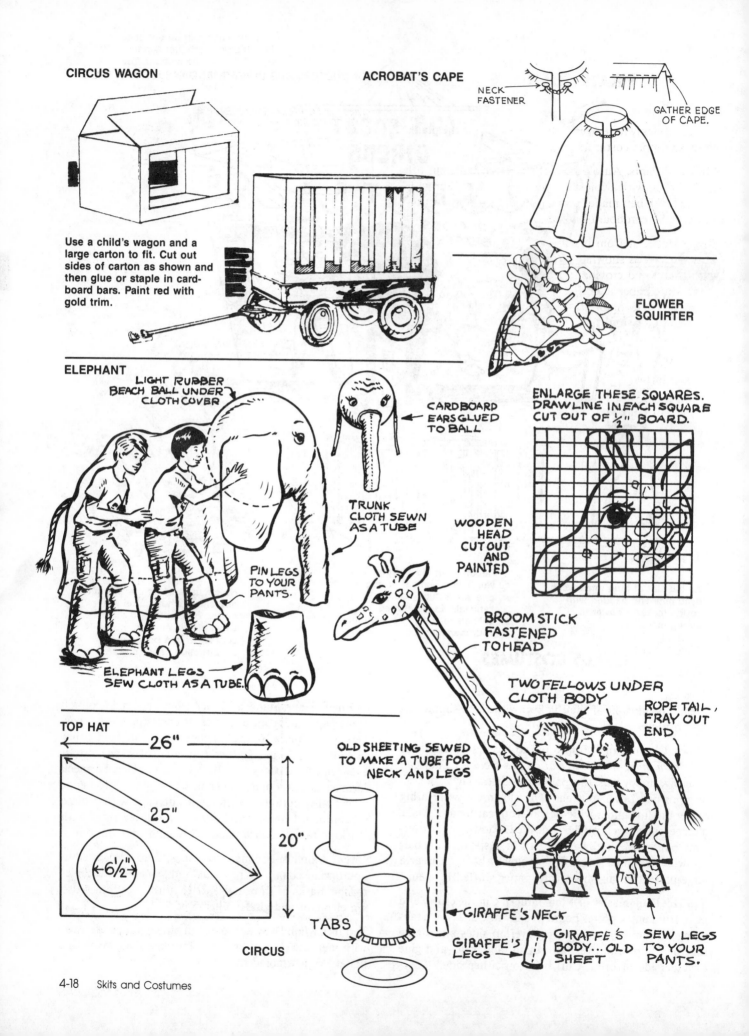

CIRCUS WAGON

Use a child's wagon and a large carton to fit. Cut out sides of carton as shown and then glue or staple in cardboard bars. Paint red with gold trim.

ACROBAT'S CAPE

NECK FASTENER

GATHER EDGE OF CAPE.

FLOWER SQUIRTER

ELEPHANT

LIGHT RUBBER BEACH BALL UNDER CLOTH COVER

CARDBOARD EARS GLUED TO BALL

TRUNK CLOTH SEWN AS A TUBE

PIN LEGS TO YOUR PANTS.

ELEPHANT LEGS SEW CLOTH AS A TUBE.

ENLARGE THESE SQUARES. DRAW LINE IN EACH SQUARE CUT OUT OF ½" BOARD.

WOODEN HEAD CUT OUT AND PAINTED

BROOM STICK FASTENED TO HEAD

TWO FELLOWS UNDER CLOTH BODY

ROPE TAIL, FRAY OUT END

TOP HAT

26"

25"

6½"

20"

OLD SHEETING SEWED TO MAKE A TUBE FOR NECK AND LEGS

TABS

CIRCUS

GIRAFFE'S NECK

GIRAFFE'S LEGS

GIRAFFE'S BODY...OLD SHEET

SEW LEGS TO YOUR PANTS.

PIRATE COSTUMES

You can quickly have your Cub Scouts walking the plank in these simple costumes.

Shirt and Pants. An old pair of slacks or pants cut off at the knees, with a colorful long-sleeve shirt. Wear with a wide black belt made from cardboard or fabric with a foil-covered cardboard buckle.

Pirate Hat. Cut from black poster board as shown. Cut a skull and crossbones from white paper and glue to front of hat. Staple front and back together to fit head.

Crew's Hats. Use a colorful bandanna or cut a square of colored fabric. Tie around head with knot in back.

Colorful Extras. Add a large cardboard eye patch. Paint tattoos on arms with eyebrown pencil or lip liner and draw on a mustache with eyebrow pencil.

Weapons. A cutlass can be cut from cardboard as shown. Glue slotted hand guard between handle and blade. Flintlock pistols can also be cut from cardboard.

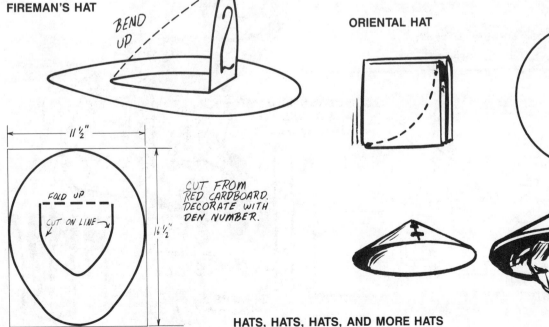

CUT 2

10"

STAPLE

16"

CONDUCTOR, BUS DRIVER, AND POLICEMAN HATS

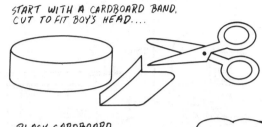

START WITH A CARDBOARD BAND, CUT TO FIT BOY'S HEAD....

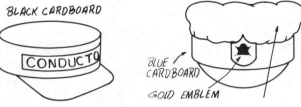

BLACK CARDBOARD

CONDUCTO

BLUE CARDBOARD

GOLD EMBLEM

BLUE TISSUE PAPER

BLUE CARDBOARD

BUS NO. 4

COLONIAL TRICORN

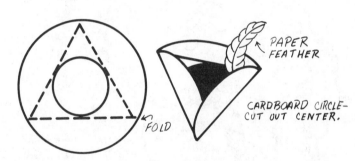

FOLD

PAPER FEATHER

CARDBOARD CIRCLE— CUT OUT CENTER.

FIREMAN'S HAT

BEND UP

11½"

16½"

FOLD UP

CUT ON LINE →

CUT FROM RED CARDBOARD. DECORATE WITH DEN NUMBER.

ORIENTAL HAT

HATS, HATS, HATS, AND MORE HATS

COONSKIN CAP

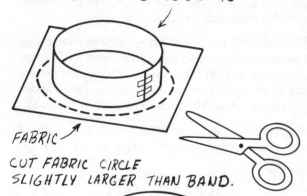

LIGHT CARDBOARD

FABRIC

CUT FABRIC CIRCLE SLIGHTLY LARGER THAN BAND.

GLUE FABRIC CIRCLE TO BAND.

GLUE

CUT TAIL FROM FABRIC. GLUE ON.

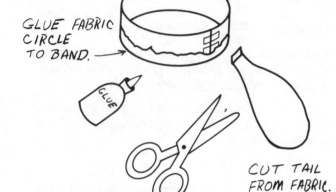

COVER FRAME WITH COTTON.

LET GLUE DRY.

GLUE

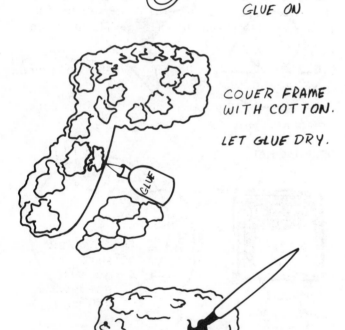

PAINT OVER COTTON. PAINT STRIPES ON TAIL.

CLOWN HAT

KNIGHT'S HELMET

JESTER'S HAT

Stage Makeup For Cub Scouts

The skit is written, the parts assigned, some simple scenery made, and the boys have been busy practicing and making costumes. What's left? How about makeup?

Why use makeup? It helps to show the audience what the character is like. It makes the character more real to the other actors, and as a result, everyone plays their roles better. It can hide an actor's features, make him larger or smaller, younger or older, and change his appearance completely.

Theatrical makeup is expensive, and most Cub Scout leaders work on a limited budget. Following are some inexpensive substitutes and some tricks for using makeup to its best advantage.

MAKEUP BASES

1. Combine equal parts of liquid cleansing cream and sifted confectioner's sugar. Mix well. The result is a white base which can be used for clown white. Tint with a few drops of green food coloring or tempera paint for monster makeup. Tint with a mixture of red and blue for a purple Martian. Or, mix red, yellow, and blue separately for Indian war paint.

2. Mix together 2 teaspoons white vegetable shortening, 5 teaspoons cornstarch, 1 teaspoon flour, a few drops of glycerin, and any food coloring desired. For brown, add 2 tablespoons unsweetened cocoa. This makeup gives a soft skin-like texture and is easily removed.

3. Tempera paint can be used as a makeup base, without fear of allergy problems. It can be washed off.

ADDED TOUCHES

- Use lipstick for both lip and cheek color.

- Eyebrow pencil can be used to darken or change the shape of eyebrows, to line the eyes, to make freckles, mustaches, sideburns, and wrinkles.

- Cornstarch powdered into hair helps age characters. Hair usually begins to gray at the temples first, and in streaks.

- The more light on stage, the more makeup necessary.

- Apply makeup after the character is in costume, using a makeup cape or towel to protect the costume. This way, the makeup won't be smeared while putting on the costume.

- Keep plenty of tissues and cleansing cream handy for makeup removal.

- Remember . . . boys like to pretend, but they don't want to be sissies!

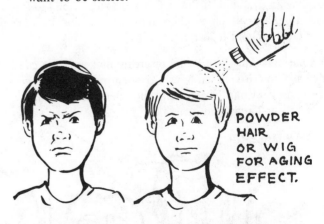

POWDER HAIR OR WIG FOR AGING EFFECT.

HOW TO AGE A CHARACTER

Have the actor frown and wrinkle his forehead. Use gray eyebrow pencil to mark in the creases. More lines add more years. Powder the hair, or use a wig. For a bald head,

HOW TO AGE A CHARACTER

use an old bathing cap, cut to cover hair. Glue on pieces of yarn hair for a fringe just above the ears.

CHARACTER MAKEUP

Clown makeup. For a classic clown face, apply clown white base all over face from hairline to neck. If you are planning to attach artificial eyebrows, clean off white makeup from eyebrows. Spirit gum or rubber cement will hold eyebrows in place. Use an old white bathing cap with holes cut for the ears to cover the head. Use bright red lipstick to paint long triangles on cheeks, extending above and below the eyes. Apply red lipstick around mouth, about 1 inch wide. Use a black eyebrow pencil to outline an oval mouth shape. Cut a red rubber ball to fit the nose, and attach a rubber band which slips around the head to hold it in place.

Indian makeup. Dark liquid or cream makeup base can be used on fair-skinned boys. Cover entire face and ears, neck, and any part of chest and shoulders that will show. Also cover hands and arms.

Hobo Clown. Use black eye liner to fill in wrinkles on forehead while the actor is frowning. Have him smile and do the same thing to wrinkles on both cheeks. Lightly powder the cheeks. Chewed black gum can be used to simulate missing teeth. A false nose, oversize ears, and an old battered hat will add a final touch.

HOBO CLOWN

Wigs

White Hair. Use an old nylon stocking. Pull the stocking down over the hair and ears. Tie it off at the top and cut off the excess. Use cellophane tape or glue to fasten white cotton balls all over the stocking.

Curls. Cut pieces of paper in strips. Curl each strip by holding one end between your thumb and a long pencil. Press lightly with the thumb and pull these trip over the pencil with the other hand. Repeat several times for a stiff curl. Glue curls to a stocking cap base.

Braids. Stretch about three strips of crepe paper, ¾-inch wide. Twist each strip around and around. Braid the three strips together. Use black crepe paper for an Indian wig.

Witch's Wig. Glue several uneven lengths of black yarn to a stocking cap base. Trim across forehead in uneven bangs.

Scarecrow's Wig. Glue uneven lengths of heavy cotton rug yarn or crepe paper to a stocking cap base, or glue to the inside of an old hat.

Try using untwisted wool or rope for wigs, or use an old mop, dyed to desired color.

INDIAN MAKE-UP

RED WITH WHITE OUTLINES

RED

YELLOW AND RED

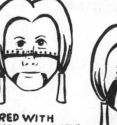

RED WITH YELLOW DOTS

RED

GREEN WITH YELLOW DOTS

YELLOW

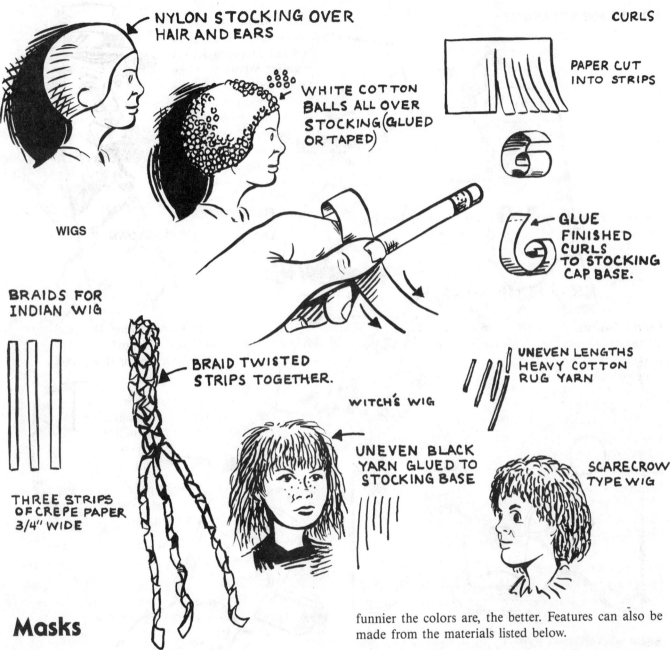

NYLON STOCKING OVER HAIR AND EARS

CURLS

PAPER CUT INTO STRIPS

WHITE COTTON BALLS ALL OVER STOCKING (GLUED OR TAPED)

GLUE FINISHED CURLS TO STOCKING CAP BASE.

WIGS

BRAIDS FOR INDIAN WIG

BRAID TWISTED STRIPS TOGETHER.

UNEVEN LENGTHS HEAVY COTTON RUG YARN

THREE STRIPS OF CREPE PAPER 3/4" WIDE

WITCH'S WIG

UNEVEN BLACK YARN GLUED TO STOCKING BASE

SCARECROW TYPE WIG

Masks

Masks can be made from almost any container and any type of material. Let your imagination be your guide. Try cardboard cartons, paper sacks, foil pie pans, poster board, or plastic bottles. Masks can be used for many Cub Scout themes—Indian, circus, space, holiday, nature, historic. Masks have almost as many uses as there are ways to make them.

funnier the colors are, the better. Features can also be made from the materials listed below.

Hair. String, yarn, rope, crepe paper, strips of fabric, paper curls, kinky wire, cotton balls, an old mop, or even soda straws.

Noses. Rubber balls, cardboard, paper cups, plastic containers, egg carton cups, spools.

Ears. Paper cups, plastic containers, spools, cardboard.

DECORATING MASKS

Most mask materials can be painted with tempera paint. Features can be drawn with colored marking pens. Use heavy, bold lines and splashes of color. The brighter and

CARDBOARD CYLINDER MASKS

This is one of the simplest and most effective ways to make a mask. Use a rolled-up section of poster board.

GIRAFFE

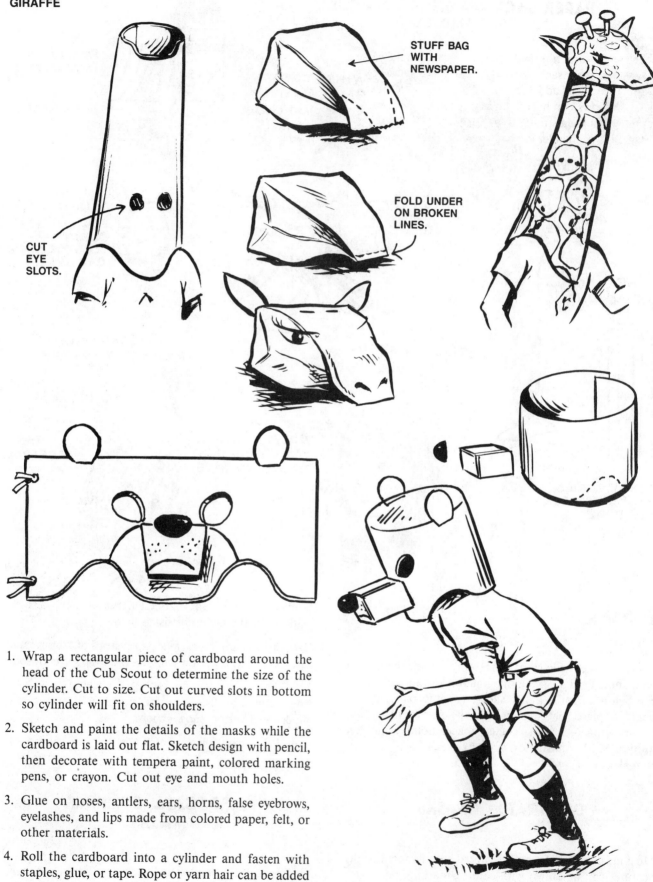

STUFF BAG WITH NEWSPAPER.

FOLD UNDER ON BROKEN LINES.

CUT EYE SLOTS.

1. Wrap a rectangular piece of cardboard around the head of the Cub Scout to determine the size of the cylinder. Cut to size. Cut out curved slots in bottom so cylinder will fit on shoulders.

2. Sketch and paint the details of the masks while the cardboard is laid out flat. Sketch design with pencil, then decorate with tempera paint, colored marking pens, or crayon. Cut out eye and mouth holes.

3. Glue on noses, antlers, ears, horns, false eyebrows, eyelashes, and lips made from colored paper, felt, or other materials.

4. Roll the cardboard into a cylinder and fasten with staples, glue, or tape. Rope or yarn hair can be added to cover seam and give the mask more depth.

CARDBOARD CYLINDER MASKS

PAPER SACK MASKS

These masks are fun and inexpensive to make. Use grocery-size paper sacks large enough to fit over a boy's head. For realism, add construction paper or felt ears, noses, eyebrows, or horns, and hair made from yarn, paper, or even soda straws. Experiment with some of the designs shown, then let the boys pick out their favorites.

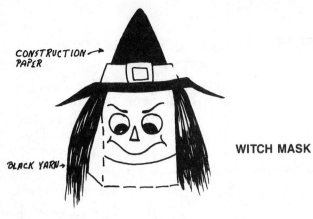

WITCH MASK

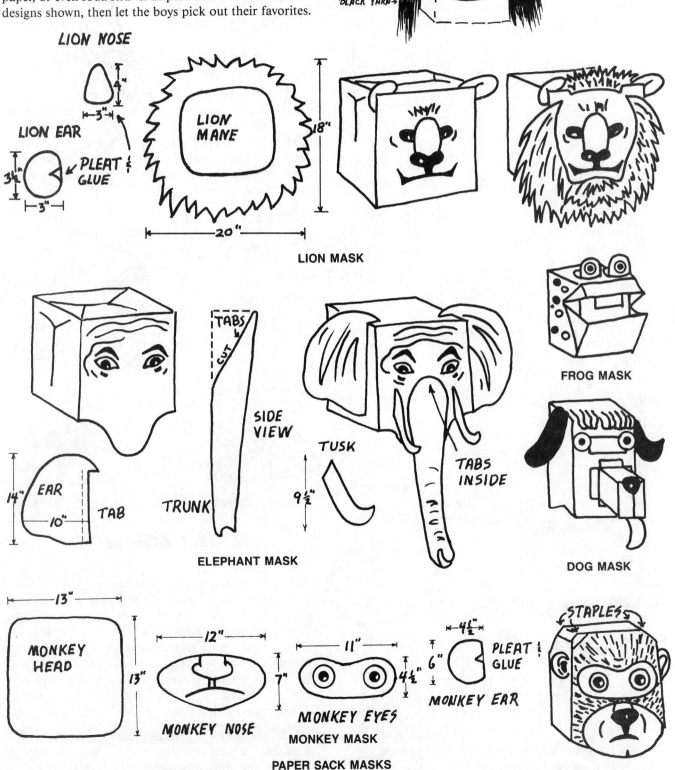

PAPER SACK MASKS

FLAT CARDBOARD MASKS

Large masks can be cut from poster board or corrugated cardboard with designs painted on. Draw details with marking pens in heavy, bold lines and cut out eyeholes. A mask of this type usually doesn't require any other type of costume with it.

CARDBOARD BOX MASKS

CARDBOARD BOX MASKS

Cardboard boxes make good animal masks. Fit carton over boy's head and mark place for eye holes to be cut out. Sketch on details and decorate with paint or colored markers. Horns, ears, noses, and manes can be cut from cardboard, heavy paper, or plastic and stapled, glued, or taped in place. Hair or fur can be added. Broomstraws make good whiskers.

PAPER MÂCHÉ MASKS

CARDBOARD EARS

CUT OUT EYES. PAINT ON OTHER FEATURES.

COVER LARGE GREASED BOWL.

ATTACH ELASTIC.

PAPIER MÂCHÉ MASK

Make strip papier mâché as described in "Crafts" section of this book. Use a large bowl as a base for modeling. Turn the bowl upside down. Grease the bottom and sides of the bowl so the mâché won't stick to it. Apply two layers of mâché, then add any features that are to stand out—nose, eyebrows, ears, etc. These can be made from egg carton cups, paper cups, spools, etc. Cover with two more layers of mâché. After it's dry, remove the bowl and paint the mask with tempera. Add hair or other touches.

(**NOTE:** Also see the big papier mâché mask molded over an inflated balloon described in the "Crafts" section of this book, and Bear Elective 10.)

FLAT CARDBOARD MASKS

5 Puppets

Why We Use Puppets

Puppetry is an ancient art that appeals to boys of all ages, perhaps more to boys of Cub Scout age than any other. Puppets can be used in connection with several achievements and electives and with many of the monthly themes. Webelos Scouts may expand their knowledge of puppetry while earning the Showman activity badge.

No one knows when or where puppets first appeared. They have been found in Egyptian tombs, in China, and in India in very early history. They were used widely during the Middle Ages for teaching the Bible. Puppets have acted before royalty. They have been made and enjoyed by scholars, poets, and artists.

Puppetry can help Cub Scouts to:

- Improve enunciation and voice projection.

- Develop coordination and a sense of timing.

- Gain self-confidence and personal satisfaction.

- Release fears and frustrations in an acceptable way.

- Recognize the importance of teamwork and cooperation.

- Develop creativity.

- Improve listening habits.

- Learn the lessons of everyday living, good health habits, getting along with others, and good sportsmanship.

- Learn and appreciate the effects of light, sound, and movement.

- Experience the enjoyment of entertaining others.

In addition, teachers and leaders of the handicapped find puppets very useful in helping children to overcome stuttering, relieve tensions, strengthen weak muscles, develop coordination, and overcome inhibitions.

Types Of Puppets

Several types of puppets are suitable for Cub Scout age boys, including those made from paper sacks, socks, cardboard cylinders, boxes, egg cartons, and gloves. Most of these fall into the category of hand puppets, which are worn on the hand and manipulated with one finger guiding the head and two other fingers guiding the puppet's hands. They are described in detail in this section.

Jointed puppets, or marionettes, require more detailed construction and operation and are not covered in these pages.

Tips For Puppeteers

- Let the boys decide on the play they wish to present and the type of puppets that will be used. They can plan the dialogue themselves and say their lines informally, even if it comes out a little differently each time. It is difficult for some boys to manipulate a puppet and recite memorized lines at the same time. An alternative is to have a reader backstage so the boys need only operate the puppets.

- Keep the theater and the puppets in proper scale. Small puppets on a big stage lose their appeal.

- Be sure there is plenty of room behind the scenes for all puppeteers.

- Plan frequent exits and entrances of puppets to hold interest and to avoid having too many puppets on stage at one time.

- Keep actions clear, simple, and exaggerated. An excited puppet should be wildly excited, while a tired puppet should groan and sag so wearily that the audience knows immediately how tired he is.

- The puppet should speak and act according to the kind of person, animal, or object he represents.

- Sometimes it's good for the puppet to speak aloud to himself as he goes about his actions. For example, he might say while looking for something, "I'll look under this tree for the treasure."

- Avoid hiding one puppet behind another.

- Hold the puppets vertically.

- Let the puppets walk off the stage, not sink out of sight.

- Puppeteers should remember to wait for laughs so the audience doesn't miss any lines.

- Use music during the production, if possible.

- Keep it simple, make it fun (KISMIF).

Resources For Puppets

Many books on puppetry can be found at public and school libraries and at stores that carry teaching aids. In addition, ideas for puppets can be found at the monthly roundtable and Cub Scout leaders' pow wow and in *Cub Scout Program Helps.*

You should be able to find most of the following books at your public library:

Act It Out, by Bernice Carlson

Easy Puppets, by Gertrude J. Pels

Fun-Time Puppets, by Carrie Rasmussen

Fun With Puppets, by Sylvia Cassell

Simple Puppetry, by Sheila Jackson

101 Hand Puppets, by Richard Cummings

Puppets for Dreaming and Scheming, by Judy Sims

Creating With Puppets, by Lothar Kampmann

Making Puppets Come Alive, by Larry Engler

Puppet Plays for Children, by Antonia Ridge

Beginner's Puppet Book, by Alice M. Hoben

Paper Bag Puppets, by Deatna M. Williams

Puppets for Beginners, by Moritz Jagendorf

Puppet Playwriting

It is usually best to decide on a story or situation to act out and let the Cub Scouts develop their own lines, rather than having a written script with dialogue. They may run into difficulty if they try to read a script or remember lines while they are operating puppets.

A simple comic story is best for Cub Scouts. Exaggerated actions and slapstick comedy are fun for both audience and the puppeteers. A few misplaced lines or mistaken actions may help rather than hinder the play. Grunting, groaning, sniffing, wheezing, and coughing in large quantities add to the value of a funny play. Puppets can dance, hug each other, sing, jump, fight, or clown around. Adaptations of children's stories are a good basis for a puppet play.

Music also adds much to a play. It sets the mood for the characters and adds a professional touch. A record player or tape recorder will come in handy.

When making assignments, to select someone to act as stage manager to be responsible for the props, scenery, music, and lighting. This could be the den chief, one of the Cub Scouts, or a parent.

Follow these simple steps in developing your puppet play:

1. Read the play or story carefully. Pick out the important parts — or develop your own story.

2. With the boys' help, develop an outline, such as the one found in the "Skits and Costumes" section of this book.

3. Keep the play short—5 to 8 minutes at the most.

4. Keep the puppets in mind. How many will there be? Where do they fit into each scene? What will they be doing and saying? Plan entrances and exits carefully, so the puppeteers won't be climbing over each other.

5. Keep dialogue short and simple, or use a reader offstage.

6. In adapting a play, change the number of characters to fit the number of boys in the den by giving some boys more or fewer lines.

Choose scenes that:

• Sustain action and further the plot.

• Build up an important character.

• Have comedy possibilities.

• Add suspense.

• Offer unusual effects—scenery or lighting.

• Have fast action and good dialogue.

Puppet Plays

YOU WERE THERE

Characters: Three Pilgrim puppets and two Indian puppets. Narrator and Sponsor offstage.

NARRATOR (*offstage*): Good evening, ladies and gentlemen of the television audience. Den (No.) of Pack (No.) presents, "You Are There." Now here's a word from our sponsor.

SPONSOR (*offstage*): Friends, this program is being brought to you by Mother Fletcher, who is famous for such products as Rattlesnake Oil Shampoo, Corn Pone Corn Sticks Mix, and Dainty Doggie Biscuits. Be sure to look for these products in your neighborhood store. And now, back to "You Are There."

Scene 1: Early new England coast with rocks, trees, and ship in background.

NARRATOR: We'd like to take you back to the year 1621 and the first Thanksgiving. Several events of great importance have led up to this momentous day. Last year, in 1620, the Pilgrims landed at Plymouth Rock. Let's look in on this scene and talk to some of the people who were there. (*Three Pilgrims come on stage.*) Sir! you look like the leader of the group. What is your name?

FIRST PILGRIM: William Bradford, your servant, sir!

NARRATOR: And how was your voyage, Mr. Bradford?

FIRST PILGRIM: Rough, man, rough!

NARRATOR: And you, sir. Did you find the Mayflower comfortable?

SECOND PILGRIM: Are you kidding? It wasn't exactly the Queen Mary, you know!

NARRATOR: Ladies and gentlemen, here are some Indians coming on the scene. (*Two Indians enter.*) Will they be friendly to our Pilgrims or will they be hostile? Let's watch closely and see what happens. This is a tense moment. (*Indians stand pointing and talking to each other. Pilgrims advance towards Indians, hands outstretched. Suddenly the Indians turn and run offstage.*)

THIRD PILGRIM: Well, they certainly didn't seem very glad to see us!

NARRATOR: No one knows why the Indians ran. Maybe someone called them for dinner. At any rate, the Pilgrims spent a hard winter that first year in the New World. Their crops failed, the people grew ill and starved (*Pilgrims lie down*) and the snows came early and stayed late. (*First Act curtain*)

NARRATOR: Now we interrupt this sad scene to bring you a word from our sponsor.

SPONSOR: Friends, are you bothered with loose and falling teeth? Try Mother Fletcher's Guaranteed Gum Glue for the tightest teeth in town. It's on sale right now at your neighborhood pet shop! And now back to our program.

Scene 2: Background with cabins and trees. Pilgrims are on stage as curtain opens.

NARRATOR: The winter has passed and things look brighter for our little band of Pilgrims. The Indians have come to visit. (*Indians enter.*)

FIRST INDIAN: Welcome! Me Squanto!

SECOND INDIAN: Me Somoset. Who are you?

SECOND PILGRIM (*stepping forward*): I am Captain Miles Standish. We want to be your friends.

FIRST INDIAN: Me friend. You friend. We dance big dance for you. (*Indians dance and sing wildly.*)

FIRST PILGRIM (*stepping forward*): Friends! Friends! This is the Sabbath. We must think of serious things. It is no time for dancing!

FIRST INDIAN: You come. We show you how to plant Indian corn. Make big harvest! (*Pilgrims and Indians leave.*) (*Second Act curtain*)

NARRATOR: Before we see the last act of our show, here is a word from next week's sponsor, the Boy Scouts of America.

SPONSOR: Cub Scouting is a family program, designed to get boys and their families working and playing together. Just try it! You'll like it! Back now to the final act.

Scene 3: Indians and Pilgrims seated at table with heads bowed.

NARRATOR: With the help of the Indians, our Pilgrim friends planted and harvested a bountiful crop. Being deeply religious people, they have planned a great feast to thank God for their good fortune, and they've invited the Indians. Let's listen to their prayer of thanks.

THIRD PILGRIM: Dear God, we are grateful for these good things. Help us to be worthy in the year to come. Amen.

NARRATOR: What kind of a day was it? A day, like all days, filled with those events that alter the course of human destiny . . . and you were there! (*Curtain*)

WHO'S ZOO?

Cereal box puppets are perfect for dramatizing animal plays. Each puppet appears, reads his lines, and asks: "Who am I?" The audience calls out the answer.

ANNOUNCER: We bring you now some animals who come from near and far. Listen to their stories and then guess who they are.

LION: It's evident that although I'm a cat, you would never call me a kitty. I'm a king of renown, with a mane for a crown, and my roar is ferocious, not pretty!

ELEPHANT: Your piano key may be made of me; I need a whole tent for a bunk. If your ride on may back, I hope that you'll pack peanuts, not clothes, in my trunk.

LEOPARD: At the sound of a shot, I can change my spot, when hunters are out to pursue me. But I can't, so they say, change the spots I display. They seem to be glued right to me!

WALRUS: On a hot summer day, you'll envy my play, as I swim for my recreation. My tusks and my skin bring good money in, and my mustache is quite a sensation!

RHINOCEROS: Some folks feel I lack appeal because my complexion is horrid. I must confess, I'm a clumsy mess, with horns on my nose and my forehead!

ZEBRA: Is it true that I'm white with stripes of black? Do you find that amusing? Or am I black with white rickrack? It's really most confusing.

HORNED OWL: My horns you can see when I'm up in a tree, wearing a dark brown suit. But as soon as it's dark, I'll fly on a lark and I'll start out my toot with a hoot.

ALL: We're happy to have met you, but we must leave you now. We bid you all farewell and take a final bow. (*Curtain*)

LITTERBUGS BEWARE

Puppets: any number of Litterbug and Tidy Bug sack puppets.

Setting: Park or countryside backdrop. (Litterbug puppets come on stage and begin littering stage area with pieces of paper, candy wrappers, etc.)

NARRATOR: We are Litterbugs, it's true, and oh, what we Litterbugs can do! We clutter the country with papers and trash. At making a mess, we're really a smash. The roadsides and parks are scenes of our folly. We really enjoy it and think it's quite jolly to leave behind garbage, bottles, and paper, as little mementos of our daily labor. (*Litterbug puppets exit and Tidy Bug puppets enter and begin to clean up litter.*)

NARRATOR: We are Tidy Bugs of the Tidy Bug clan. We work to keep everything spic and span. We pick up the litter wherever we are, and always carry litter bags in our car. We'll squash the Litterbugs as fast as we can and make America a beautiful land, free of litter, clutter and trash. If you will help us, we'll be a smash! (*Curtain*)

KNIGHTS OF YORE

Hand Puppets: Sir Galahad, Sir Trueblood, Servant, The Black Night, and any number of Friendly Knights carrying swords.

Setting: Inside a medieval castle. The servant is on stage. A knock at the door is heard. The Servant goes to one side of stage to answer door.

SIR TRUEBLOOD: Kind sir, pray let me spend the night. I am weary and long for rest. (*Droops wearily.*)

SERVANT (*motions knight to come in*): Enter and rest thyself. Pray tell me, why do you travel so late at night?

SIR TRUEBLOOD: I am the King's messenger and I must take a message to Sir Galahad in a far country.

SERVANT: You are in luck, sir. Sir Galahad is at this very moment resting in this castle!

SIR TRUEBLOOD: Will you please call him? I must

speak with him right away. (*Servant exits to get Sir Galahad.*)

SIR GALAHAD (*coming onstage with Servant*): You wish to speak to me, sir?

SIR TRUEBLOOD: I have a message from the King, sir. You have an enemy who is trying to do you harm.

SIR GALAHAD (*surprised*): Impossible! I have no enemies.

SIR TRUEBLOOD: But this enemy is looking for you right now. He plans to slay you! (*A knock is heard at the door.*)

SIR GALAHAD (*urgently*): Arise! Arise, Knights of Galahad! Make ready to do battle! (*Friendly Knights come onstage in armor, ready to fight.*)

SERVANT (*from side of stage*): No! You may not enter! (*Black Knight rushes onstage with sword drawn.*)

SIR TRUEBLOOD (*fearfully*): It's the Black Knight! (*The knights fight. The Black Knight is knocked down.*)

SIR GALAHAD: We have fought a good fight. Before we go our separate ways, let us promise to use our swords to fight only the battle for truth and honor. (*All Friendly Knights point swords upward and repeat the last line.*)

ALL: Be always ready with your armor on. (*Curtain*)

THE PIRATES' BIG DECISION

Hand Puppets: Any number of Pirates, one Cub Scout.

Setting: A pirate ship. Pirates are on stage when curtain opens.

NARRATOR: Here are some Pirates, brave and bold. Many times you've heard their story told. They sail the seas on their homemade raft. Listen now, and you'll hear them laugh. (*Pirates laugh heartily.*)

NARRATOR: Let's sneak in closer, and what do we see? They seem to be happy . . . listen to their glee. (*Pirates laugh again and say "ho-ho-ho" in pirate fashion. Cub Scout comes on stage and stands in center of Pirates.*)

NARRATOR: Oh dear, a Cub Scout. I can't see his rank. What if those Pirates make him walk the plank? (*Pirates draw closer to Cub Scout.*)

NARRATOR: Wait just a minute. Something's not right. Look at that Cub Scout. There's no sign of fright! (*Cub Scout begins shaking hands with Pirates and pretends to talk to them.*)

NARRATOR: What we see here leaves us no doubts. Our Cub Scout is asking the pirates to become Scouts. (*Cub Scout motions to Pirates and leads them offstage.*)

NARRATOR: So with this happy ending, we'll drift out of sight. For our brave Cub Scout, this was a happy night! (*Curtain*)

WILFRED, THE WOODY WOODPECKER

This is a narrated play with lots of special effects. Two boys may be used for the sounds and actions. A microphone will be helpful.

Hand puppets: Woody Woodpecker family— Mother Woodpecker and four Young Woodpeckers, one with a huge beak.

Setting: Forest backdrop; big nest in foreground with loose strips of newspaper hanging that will blow in the wind. The Young Woodpeckers are in the nest.

NARRATOR: Once upon a time many years ago, there lived in the deep forest a very famous family of Woody Woodpeckers. Down through the ages, this family increased in numbers, in strength, and in wisdom . . . until we come to the day when we find the hero of our story— Wonderful Wilfred! (*Fanfare sounds offstage. Wilfred takes a bow from nest.*)

NARRATOR: Now wonderful Wilfred was no ordinary woodpecker. (*Sound-effects boys shout, "No!"*)

NARRATOR: He was smart—in fact, he was the wisest of all the Woodpeckers. While the soft breezes blew out-side . . . (*blowing or fanning movement offstage causes nest and trees to rustle*) . . . you could hear Wilfred's brothers and sisters tapping away. (*Offstage two wooden blocks are tapped to together. Three Woodpeckers make tapping motions on nearby tree.*) But not Willy! He just sat there and rubbed his beak back and forth. (*Rubbing sound made offstage by rubbing blocks together as Wilfred rubs his beak on a nearby tree.*)

NARRATOR: And when the winds blew . . . (*blowing or fanning movement again*) . . . and the rains rained . . . (*gentle handclapping offstage*) . . . and the owls hooted . . . (*hooting noise offstage*) . . . you could hear the brothers and sisters tapping (*same as above*). But not Willy. (*Boys offstage shout, "No!"*) He'd just sit there and rub his beak back and forth. (*Same sounds as above.*)

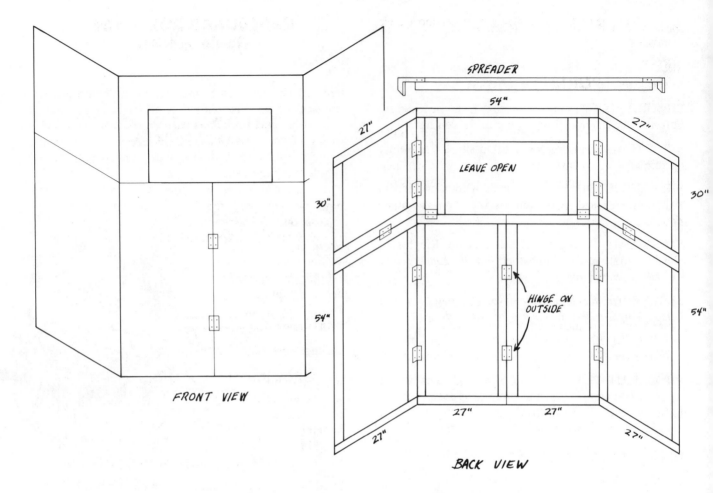

SPREADER

54"

27"   27"

LEAVE OPEN

30"   30"

HINGE ON
OUTSIDE

54"   54"

27"   27"

27"   27"

FRONT VIEW

BACK VIEW

PORTABLE PUPPET STAGE

Hand-Puppet Stages and Theaters

Hand-puppet theaters may be as simple or complex as desired, but for Cub Scouts, the simple stage is best. The simplest stage consists of a table set on edge. A cardboard carton with a window cut in one side works well also. A large piece of wallboard with an opening for the puppets is an excellent stage.

Several hand-puppet stages are described and illustrated here. Stages for finger and bib puppets and a shadow puppet screen are included later in this section.

PUPPET STAGES

Many things can be used as temporary puppet stages so the boys can practice in den meetings. For example, turn a table on its side. The boys kneel behind the table and operate puppets above their heads.

A doorway will serve as a temporary puppet stage. Drape a cloth across it at the necessary height so the boys can

NARRATOR: When their Mother would bring them food, you could hear Wonderful Wilfred's brothers and sisters close their beaks hard on the food. (*Mother Woodpecker comes onstage pretending to give young food. Offstage, hands are clapped together sharply as young woodpeckers close their beaks.*) But not Will. (*Offstage "No!"*) He would close his beak quietly . . . (*Offstage "Shhh"*) . . . and then sit there and rub his beak back and forth. (*Same sound and action as above.*)

NARRATOR: At last came the day for them to leave their nest, and you could hear Willy's brothers and sisters take their last peck at the tree before they left home. (*Sharp tap with wood block offstage as each brother and sister makes a final tap on the tree and exits. Willy remains in nest.*) Willy looked around and picked the biggest tree in the forest and flew directly to it. He didn't waste any time. Once more he rubbed his beak back and forth until it shone so it could be seen for miles around. (*Rubbing sound offstage*) He reared back, and with one mighty swipe of his beautiful beak, he cut the huge tree in two! (*Boys offstage yell, "Timber!" as tree collapses. Willy takes a final bow and exits. Curtain.*)

stand behind the curtain and operate puppets above their heads.

PORTABLE STAGE

The den chief or an adult in the pack who likes to build things can construct this seven-panel puppet stage. Besides being easy to set up, take down, and transport, it will help give den and pack puppet shows a more professional look.

The stage is a wood frame, covered with fabric or other lightweight material.

Upper Section

2 side panels, 27 inches wide by 30 inches high

1 center panel, 54 inches wide by 30 inches high

Lower Section

4 panels, 27 inches wide by 54 inches high

Spreaders

1 1-by-1-by-54-inch spreader to fit across top front

1 1-by-1-by-78-inch spreader to fit across top back

1. Cut frame and assemble each of the seven panels separately.

2. Cover all panels except for upper front panel, as shown in illustration. Staple on fabric or other lightweight material.

3. Fasten upper panels together with 2-inch back-flap hinges.

4. Fasten lower panels together with 2-inch back-flap hinges.

5. Fasten upper and lower sections together with pin hinges. To take down, remove the pins and fold up the sections. (**Note:** All hinges except the two in lower front are placed on inside of stage. Those two are placed on outside to allow stage to fold up.)

6. Make spreaders to keep the screen in place. Fasten a 2-inch angle-iron bracket at the end of each spreader as shown. In addition to these two, additional spreaders can be made for hanging scenery and backdrops.

7. A draw curtain can be added, if desired. Attach a curtain rod to top inside of opening.

CARDBOARD BOX STAGE
(Table Model)

Table model stages can be made from cardboard boxes. The sides of the stage should be about 24 inches high. Cut out back of box, then cut an opening in the front, leaving a frame at least 4 inches wide. Decorate as desired. Set on a table which is draped with a floor-length cloth to hide the puppeteers.

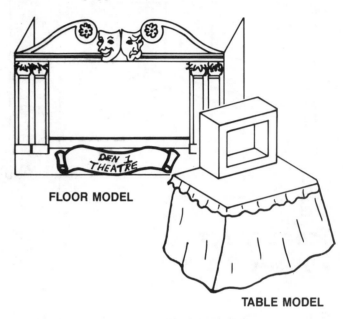

FLOOR MODEL

TABLE MODEL

CARDBOARD BOX STAGE
(Floor Model)

Use a large cardboard carton, such as a refrigerator carton, approximately 42 inches high. This will be about the right height for Cub Scouts to operate puppets above their heads.

1. Cut off the top and bottom of the carton.

2. Cut back panel in half and fold back to form wings, as shown. Add ¾-by-1-inch wood supports at top and bottom to hold stage in place. Or, make wood spreaders as used for portable theater.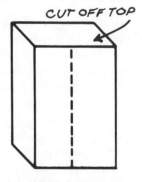

3. Cut an opening in the front.

4. Paint and decorate as desired.

5. Add a curtain, if you wish.

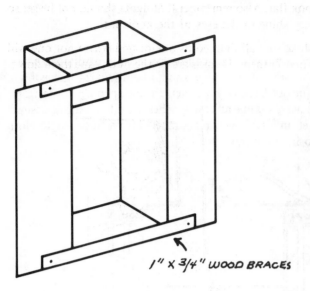

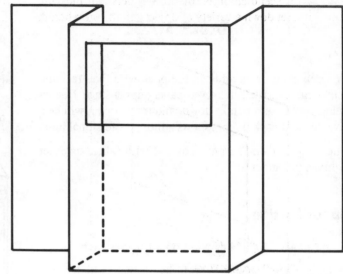

CARDBOARD BOX STAGE

Scenery For Puppet Plays

Scenery not only makes a puppet play more believable, it also helps set the time and place of the story. It can be as simple as a single flower, or as complex as a jungle. Use only what scenery is necessary to suggest the setting and let the audience imagine the details. Elaborate scenery may detract from the puppets.

Backdrops are recommended, and often a solid color backdrop is all that is needed. Scenes can also be painted on backdrops, or scenery pieces cut out and pinned on. Cloth or paper backdrops are easily rolled up for storing or transporting. Remember that except for shadow puppets, lighting of a puppet stage will be from the front, so the puppeteers can see the puppets clearly through the backdrop, but the audience cannot see the operators.

In making a backdrop, it is best to first make a miniature sketch. Then make an enlarged pattern of the desired size and transfer it to the backdrop. In using color on backdrops, keep in mind the mood of the play, the color of the puppets' costumes, and the lighting.

SCENERY PIECES

In addition to backdrops, small scenery pieces can be cut out of cardboard, attached to a rod and held in place by

a boy's free hand. Such things as trees, bushes, fences, boats, houses, tables, chairs, or even bathtubs can be used in this way.

SCENERY PIECES

PROP BOARD

This is a device for holding furniture, scenery, and other props on the stage without a platform. To make a prop board, glue and nail four ½-by-1-inch square blocks to the inside of the crosspiece at the bottom of your stage opening. To these, attach a ½-by-2-inch wood strip the length of the opening. This makes a channel the entire width of the stage. The props will slide into place and out quickly for scene changes, or the puppets can pick up, carry, and set down a variety of objects on the prop board.

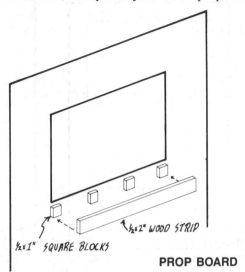

½x1" SQUARE BLOCKS

½x2" WOOD STRIP

PROP BOARD

Lighting For Puppet Plays

Darkening a room and illuminating the puppets with spotlights or stage lights helps the audience see the show and adds a theatrical atmosphere. The simpler the play, the simpler the lighting.

Let the boys experiment with lighting in different ways and from different angles—above, below, in front, and to the sides of the puppet stage opening to find out which type of lighting throws unwanted shadows, and which kind gives the desired illumination. The best way to learn how to use lighting properly is by trial and error, during practice, before the actual show.

Strong flashlights, goose-neck lamps, light sockets with clamps, electric lanterns, shaded bulbs, lightbars, and small spotlights are good sources of lighting for puppet plays.

Special lighting effects can be obtained by using black lights, colored cellophane over lights, dimmer switches, flickering Christmas lights, etc. Housings for lights can be made from tin cans.

LIGHTING ON FRONT STAGE

Remember that the lights must be on the front of the stage and directed toward the puppets. Too much light will wipe out the puppets' features. They will lose their shape and look flat. Also remember that lights should not be set so they shine in the eyes of the audience.

Make sure all light cords are located where not one will trip over them. If cords are on the floor, tape them down.

LIGHTING ON FRONT STAGE

Special Effects for Puppet Plays

Sound effects and other special effects make a puppet production more lively and vivid. The audience always remembers the scene where something unusual happened—such as when the soup burned and smoke billowed everywhere.

The boys will enjoy inventing ways to make special effects for puppet skits. A tape recorder can be used to record needed sounds like street noises and animal sounds. In addition to the suggestions which follow, see the sound effects described in the "Skits and Costumes" section of this book.

Smoke, Steam, Fog, Magic Dust. Blow excess powder off a powder puff.

Snow. Throw white confetti.

Mist, Rain. Spray water from atomizer bottle.

Wind. Blow a fan on the set.

Lightning. Flick lights off and on quickly, or use flash attachment on camera.

Door Slam. Slam two books together.

Crickets Chirping. Run a fingernail over a small piece of fine-tooth comb (near a microphone, if available).

Rustling in Underbrush. Crush broom straws (near a microphone, if available).

Gurgling Stream or Boiling Liquid. Put a straw in a cup of water and blow hard (near a microphone, if available).

Fire. Create dancing shadows in front of a red light by placing something that moves in front.

Wilting Flower. Make flower stem from curtain spring; insert rod, then, when wilting is to happen, pull rod out.

Constructing Hand Puppets

You can be inventive and original in making puppets. Try these materials for puppet starters.

MATERIALS

Before starting to construct puppets or build scenery or props, it helps to be familiar with a wide range of possible construction materials. Have a place for organizing and storing scrapbasket odds and ends. The list below is just a beginning of items which might be collected.

- Old bottle brushes, scouring pads, steel wool, fly swatters, wooden and plastic spoons, and hair curlers.

- Broom handles, dowels, popsicle or other wooden sticks, coat hangers, umbrella parts, bicycle spokes, and chopsticks.

- Plastic containers, small boxes such as egg cartons, plastic and wood baskets and trays, rubber balls, table tennis balls, and tennis balls.

Use a shoebag to hold your props.

- Buttons, beads, sequins, glitter, costume jewelry, bits of glass.

- Corks, sponges, lids and caps, spools, weights, and fishing floats.

- Socks, stockings, gloves and mittens, felt and other fabric scraps, polyfoam, cotton, and materials for stuffing, such as old nylon stockings.

- Lace, fringe, pom-poms, trimmings, fur pieces, feathers, raffia, ribbon, string, shoe laces, yarn, rope.

- Pipe cleaners, chenille, toothpicks, wire, and tinsel.

- Styrofoam balls and pieces, wood scraps, sponges, leather scraps.

- Doll clothes, doll house furnishings, and stuffed toys.

- Construction paper, crepe paper, cardboard, cellophane, paper plates, bags and cups, cardboard and plastic tubes.

PUPPET HEADS

More than any other part of the puppet, the head must express personality. This should be done simply, since small details will go unnoticed by the audience. It is usually best to keep the facial expression neutral and let the voice and movements of the puppet show emotions. However, if removable features are used, the facial expression can be changed as often as desired. The puppet head should be no smaller than one-sixth the body size.

For puppet heads, try the following:

- **Ball or Egg.** A styrofoam ball, rubber ball, or plastic egg-shape.

- **Papier Mâché.** Cover crinkled-up newspaper ball, styrofoam ball, balloon, or a clay model with papier mâché as described in the "Crafts" section.

- **Sock.** A sock can be stuffed and decorated or pulled over another shape such as a ball or plastic bottle.

- **Sponge.** This makes a good puppet head and can be shaped with scissors.

- **Polyfoam.** One-half or ¾-inch sheets can be cut and formed into any shape—use heavy-duty glue or contact cement to join.

- **Cloth.** Felt, muslin, and fake fur are among the types of cloth most frequently used for puppet heads. Stuff to shape.

OTHER PUPPET HEADS

Try puppet heads made from paper plates, paper cups, fly swatters, blocks of wood, boxes, and plastic containers.

Consider how the puppet's head will be attached to its body. In some cases a rod or finger hole can be poked into the head; in others, a sturdy cardboard tube neck-

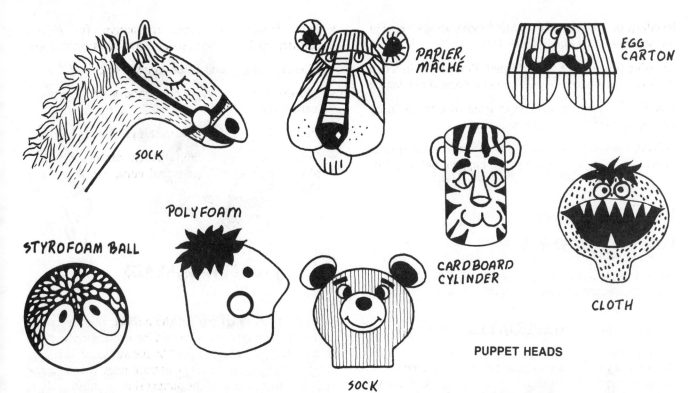

SOCK

PAPIER MÂCHÉ

EGG CARTON

STYROFOAM BALL

POLYFOAM

CARDBOARD CYLINDER

CLOTH

SOCK

PUPPET HEADS

band should be attached to permit good control of the puppet's head.

Some puppet heads must be painted; others, because of the material from which they are made, can be used as is. For white flesh-colored paint, mix varying amounts of white, red, brown, and a touch of yellow. After the base coat dries, touch up cheeks and lips with pink. Use grey or blue for eye shadow. Some paint will need an overcoat of shellac, varnish, or clear nail polish for protection.

PUPPET HANDS/PAWS

Hands or paws add to the versatility of the puppet if they allow it to pick up items. Hands can be made from leather, wood, heavy cardboard, felt, or other fabric. They can be an extension of the costume sleeve, or made separately and attached. Some puppet hands are stuffed, others are not. Above all, the hands or paws should be exaggerated.

HAIR AND EYES

The most effective puppets have simple, clearly defined, and exaggerated features. The size and position of the features will help develop the character of the puppet, as shown by the illustrations.

Hair in the form of wigs, beards, mustaches, and eyebrows can be pinned, taped, glued, stapled, or sewn onto a pup-

HAIR AND EYES

pet head. Narrow streamers of crepe paper, strips of scrub pads and steel wool, fur pieces, wood shavings, feathers, string and yarn can all be used for hair, depending on the effect that is desired.

The puppet's eyes should sparkle! Use a touch of glitter, the head of a pin or tack, a sequin, or a shiny button for the puppet's pupils. Eyes can also be made from stick-on dots available in various sizes and colors at office supply stores, or cut from paper or felt. A black felt-tip pen can be used to make a dot for the pupil.

For some puppets, loosely attached moveable plastic eyes will be effective. These are available at hobby and crafts stores. Buttons and table tennis-ball eyes can be attached so they will move when the puppet moves.

Pinned-on eyes, eyebrows, and mouths can be changed during a puppet performance to show different expressions.

COSTUMES AND BODIES

Puppets can be people, animals, a musical instrument, a tool, or even a tooth! The simplest hand puppets have a handkerchief, piece of shirt sleeve, or other piece of cloth for a costume. Baby or doll clothes can also be used. A basic costume can be used with interchangeable heads and removable accessories.

Remember these important things about puppet costumes:

- Make the costume long enough to extend to the end of the puppeteer's forearm.

- Use a material that hangs well when the puppet is still and moves easily without restricting the puppeteer's hands.

- Select a texture and color that suits the puppet's personality.

- Hats, vests, sashes, scarves, bandannas, and eyeglasses can be added and removed.

Operating Hand Puppets

Operating a puppet is called "manipulation." The basic movements are simple. A puppet can nod, shake his head, clap, scratch his head, bow, twist, sit down, walk, jump, limp, climb, dance, and perform many other actions. He can show his feelings and personality by his actions.

HAND POSITIONS

Two basic ways of holding your hand inside a puppet are illustrated here. The first position gives the puppet arms a longer reach and better grip on the props, but it tends to tilt the puppet to one side. The second position results in better balance, but the little finger may restrict the arm movement and make it more difficult to hold props. The first position is usually best for small hands.

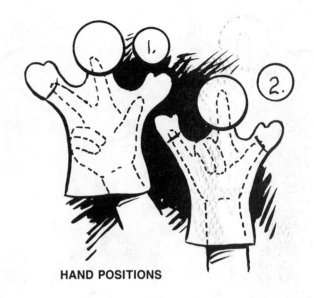

HAND POSITIONS

PUPPET ACTIONS

It is important to move the puppet every time he speaks or reacts to what another puppet says, and keep him still the rest of the time. If a puppet is moved around too much or at the wrong time, it will detract from other puppets and make his own movements less effective.

The best way to learn how to manipulate a puppet is by going through the various movements in front of a mirror. Try some of the following:

Walking. The puppet should not pop out of thin air, but enter at the side of the stage or come up or down stairs in view of the audience. Raise and lower the entire arm slightly and at the same time, turn the wrist from left to right. The wrist motion is slow or fast depending on the speed the puppet is walking. Try to avoid jerky movements.

SITTING

Talking. If the mouth is movable, it is simple to indicate talking. Otherwise, move the head up and down rhythmically when the puppet is talking. The puppet should look at the one to whom he is speaking.

Listening. Puppets should have good listening manners and face the puppet who is speaking.

Sitting. Bend the wrist forward and drop your arm a little. This pushes the back of the puppet out and looks as if he is about to sit down.

DANCING

Climbing. Lower the tree, beanstalk, fence, ladder, or whatever the puppet is climbing, slowly while the puppet remains at stage level. Its only movement would be grasping the tree branches or beanstalk at intervals.

Piano Playing. Use a toy piano that has been muffled so that no sound is heard when the keys are struck. Puppet pretends to play piano as a tape recording is played offstage.

Dancing. Two puppets can dance together or make kicking movements by using the index finger of the opposite hand to make kicks underneath a full costume.

Clapping Hands. Bring thumb and second finger together. Practice touching the puppet's mouth, ears, and forehead with his hand.

Kneeling. Drop your arm down and allow the legs or skirt of costume to fold under the puppet.

Standing. Let the puppet place his hands on a nearby table or chair and pull himself erect.

Lying Down. Drop the puppet to kneeling position and place puppet hand on stage, as if bracing himself. Turn your wrist slowly around until the puppet is on its back. Move your entire hand as if puppet is settling himself in bed or on the floor.

Yawning. Place puppet's hand over his mouth.

Picking Up. Grasp the object firmly between fingers operating the puppet's hands. To pick up an object, first look at it, then touch it, and finally, pick it up.

Fighting. This can look like the real thing as puppets hit each other about the head and body and lead with their left, bring their right back, head forward, and chin in. They can wrestle—first one on top and then the other. They can fight with swords or baseball bats. They can end the fight by collapsing in each other's arms panting and exhausted.

A puppet can show feelings and personality by the tone of voice used and with these actions:

Excited. Clasp hands, jump up and down.

Sad. Put hand to face, droop head.

Angry. Bang hands or clench them together; beat head with hand.

Afraid. Tremble, clasp hands to body.

Tired. Slow, languid movements.

Old. Shaky, slow movements.

Just for fun, let the boys try these actions with their puppets:

- March to music
- Lead an orchestra
- Sweep or scrub the floor
- Stack blocks
- Wash dishes
- Hop like a rabbit
- Cough, hiccup, sneeze
- Walk with a limp

Paper Sack Puppets

Paper sack puppets are the easiest, least expensive, and fastest type of puppets for Cub Scouts to make. Use small paper sacks (lunch bag size). You'll also need crayons, felt-tip pens or paint, scissors, and a pencil. Additional materials such as felt, construction paper, yarn, buttons, etc. can also be used.

TALKING PAPER SACK PUPPET

1. Leave the sack folded (with fold on top) and mark lightly where features will go. Eyes and nose should be on bottom of sack; top of mouth on bottom of sack, and bottom of mouth on side of sack, as shown.

2. Lift bottom of sack and finish filling in the mouth.

3. Glue on hair, ears, clothing, etc.

4. Operate puppet by placing hand in sack with fingers over fold in bottom. Open and close hand to make the puppet talk or sing.

TALKING PAPER SACK PUPPET

STUFFED SACK PUPPET

STUFFED SACK PUPPET

1. Stuff a small paper sack with newspaper to form the head. Tie the head to a small stick. Add features — eyes, nose, mouth, ears.

2. Make a costume from a square of crepe paper or fabric. Make a hole in center so fabric will slide up on stick. Tie or glue fabric just under puppet's head.

3. Hold puppet rod in hand to locate proper spots to make slits in the fabric, just large enough for your thumb and index finger to slip through. These become the puppet's hands.

4. Operate puppet by holding rod in hand.

Sock and Other Puppets

Two types of sock puppets are shown here — one where the heel or toe of a sock is stuffed to form a round puppet head; the other where the entire foot of the sock is used to form an elongated animal head. Several other types of special puppets are included.

ANIMAL SOCK PUPPET

1. Any old sock will do, but a fleecy or wool one will work best.

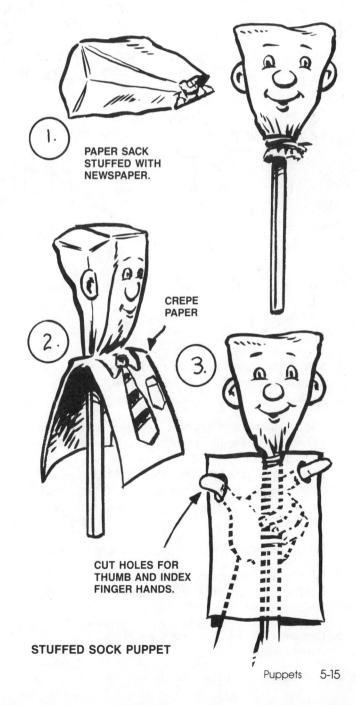

1. PAPER SACK STUFFED WITH NEWSPAPER.

CREPE PAPER

CUT HOLES FOR THUMB AND INDEX FINGER HANDS.

STUFFED SOCK PUPPET

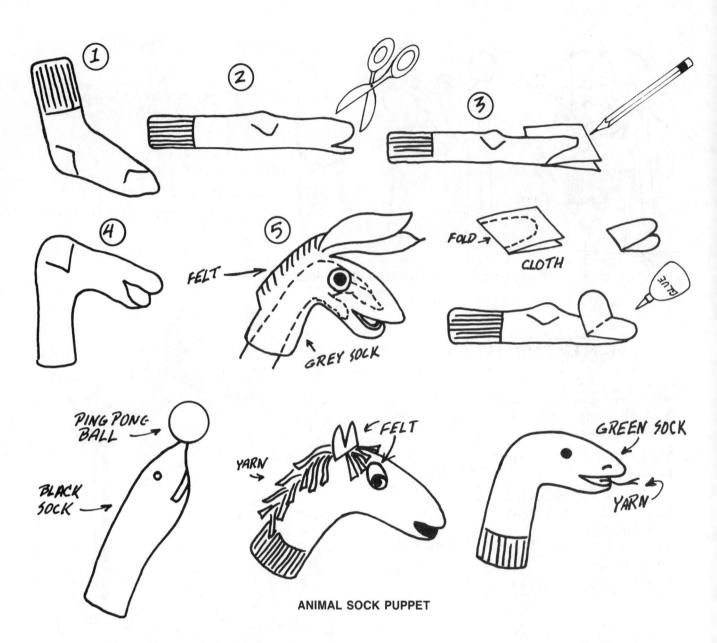

ANIMAL SOCK PUPPET

2. Spread the sock out flat so the heel is on top. Cut around the edge of the toe and back, about 2 inches, as shown.

3. Use a small piece of red, pink, or orange felt or cloth, folded in half for the inside mouth. Fold and insert in open part of sock so the folded edge fits all the way back against the edge of the opening. Mark the cloth to fit, then cut it to the proper shape. Turn the sock wrong side out and sew or glue the red cloth inside the opening.

4. When the glue is dry, turn the sock right side out.

5. Glue or sew on features. Glue a pad of cotton on the inside heel of the sock to give shape to the animal head.

6. Operate with thumb in lower lip and all fingers in upper lip.

STUFFED SOCK PUPPET

1. Make a cardboard tube ¾-inch across and 2 inches long. Fasten with tape.

2. Cut the heel or toe from an old sock (white or tan is usually the best color). Place a ball of stuffing material (cotton, piece of nylon stocking, or tissue paper) over end of tube and slip sock over stuffing. Pull it down and tie securely near the bottom end of the tube.

3. A nose can be made by pulling out a small piece of the sock and stuffing and tying it with a strong thread. Or glue on buttons or beads for nose, eyes, and ears.

4. Use tempera paint for rosy cheeks, eye shadow, eyebrows, mustache, etc. It's a good idea to shellac over the paint after it is well dried. This adds luster to the finish and keeps the puppet cleaner.

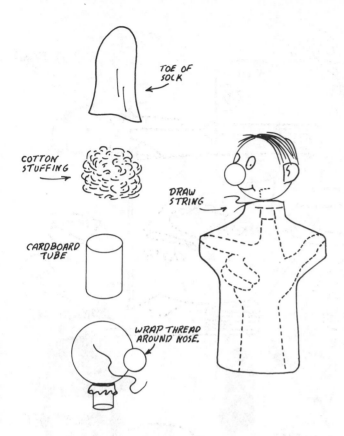

TOE OF SOCK

COTTON STUFFING

CARDBOARD TUBE

DRAW STRING

WRAP THREAD AROUND NOSE.

DOUBLE-BOX PUPPET

1. Use two boxes—the same size or different sizes, depending on the puppet. Or cut one large box (such as a cereal box) in half.

2. Tape the boxes together, as shown, so the back side of the puppet is open and hinged.

3. Add features and decorate as desired.

4. Add a fabric skirt which will cover the puppeteer's hand.

5. Operate by inserting thumb in lower section and fingers in upper section.

DOUBLE-BOX PUPPET

CARDBOARD BOX PUPPETS

Boxes are a good material for making puppets. For small puppets, use Jello boxes; for large ones, cereal boxes work well. For unusual shaped puppets, try spaghetti boxes, egg cartons, and other types of boxes.

If boxes have a waxy surface, add a small amount of liquid soap to tempera before painting. Scratch the surface lightly before gluing on trim. Or cover the boxes with construction paper or adhesived-back paper. Features can be drawn on with felt-tip pens, painted on, or felt or paper cut-outs glued on.

BROOM STRAWS

HINGE WITH TAPE.

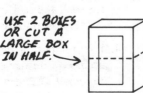

USE 2 BOXES OR CUT A LARGE BOX IN HALF.

CUT OUT BACKS OF BOXES.

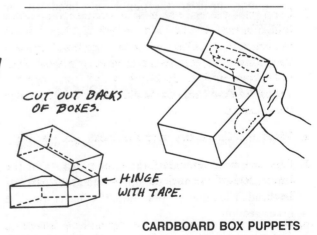

HINGE WITH TAPE.

CARDBOARD BOX PUPPETS

CARDBOARD CYLINDER PUPPETS

These small puppets, made from cardboard rolls, are best suited to a table model theater.

1. Cut roll to desired length. Cover top with construction paper or crepe paper.

2. The entire roll can be covered with colored paper or painted as desired.

3. Add features made from construction paper, yarn, buttons, etc. Or paint on features.

4. Glue on a fabric skirt or costume to cover the puppeteer's hand.

5. To operate, insert two fingers in bottom of roll, or tape a stick on back of puppet to be held by the operator.

EGG CARTON PUPPET

1. Use large scissors to cut an egg carton into thirds, as shown. Each third becomes a puppet mouth. Reinforce the hinge with masking tape to make a durable puppet.

2. Decide whether the puppet character needs the bump side up or down. The holes controlling the puppet will be placed in whatever is the top half of the puppet.

3. The egg carton flaps can be cut off or turned into teeth or lips.

4. Poke finger holes in the top back part of the puppet, directly above the hinge. Finger holes made in this way will last longer than ones that are carefully cut.

5. Add features and decorate as desired.

6. Staple or glue a cloth body to the back underside of the puppet head so the puppeteer's hand will be hidden.

STYROFOAM CUP PUPPETS

These small puppets are best suited to table-model stages.

1. Use a whole cup to make the puppet head. Cut the cup lengthwise to make the upper and lower parts of the head. The upper section should be bigger than the lower section.

2. Cut mouth linings to fit from cardboard and glue in

COTTON

STICK

CARDBOARD

FELT

YARN

CARDBOARD

YARN

FELT

CARDBOARD CYLINDER PUPPETS

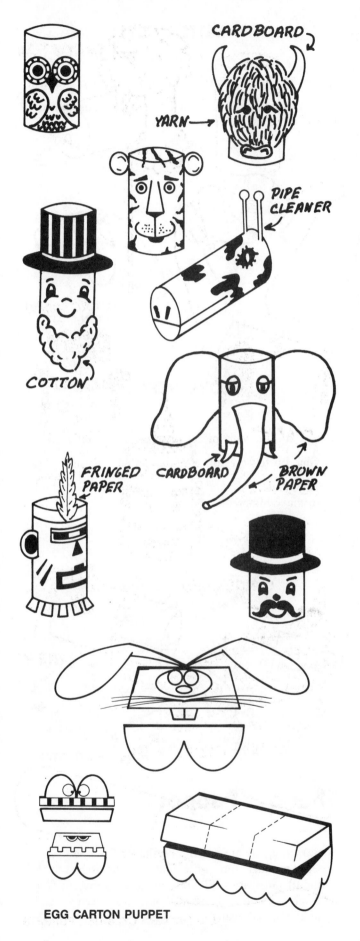

place, as shown. (Tape will hold these in place until the glue dries.)

3. Tape the upper and lower parts together at the back, making a hinge.

4. Paint as desired.

5. For body, cut a hole in the center of a paper napkin or square of fabric. Slip the napkin or fabric over the hand and forearm, then put the puppet head on the hand.

6. To operate, insert fingers in top of head and thumb in bottom part.

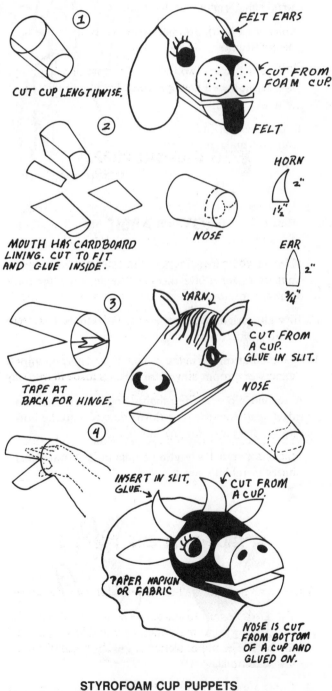

EGG CARTON PUPPET

STYROFOAM CUP PUPPETS

Glove And Mitten Puppets

This is a good way to use those worn-out or outgrown mittens and gloves.

MITTEN DUCK PUPPET

1. Stuff a mitten with tissue or any stuffing material.

2. Turn mitten so thumb becomes a beak. Sew or glue on button eyes.

3. Tie a string or ribbon around the duck's head.

4. To operate, put index finger into head and make a fist with other fingers.

MITTEN DUCK PUPPET

GLOVE RABBIT

1. Turn an old glove inside out. Cut off index and smallest finger. (Save these to use as feet.) Sew up openings in glove.

2. Turn glove right side out, except for thumb. Leave it turned inside for the rabbit's mouth.

3. Sew on button eyes and a felt nose. Glue on pipe cleaners or broom straws for whiskers.

4. A second glove is the rabbit's body. Stuff the two fingers cut from the first glove and sew onto the bottom of this glove for the rabbit's feet.

5. To operate, put body glove on hand, and put three fingers in rabbit's head.

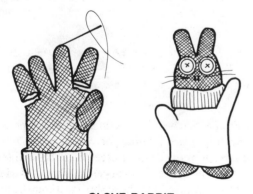

GLOVE RABBIT

MITTEN MUTT

1. Sew or glue button eyes and felt ears on an old mitten.

2. Put on mitten. Thumb is lower jaw of dog. Move it up and down to make him talk or bark.

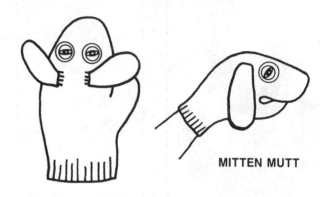

MITTEN MUTT

GLOVE MONSTER

1. Sew or glue yarn pieces on back of an old glove.

2. Glue on felt eyes or use table tennis balls for eyes.

3. To operate, put hand in glove; put fingertips on table to make him walk.

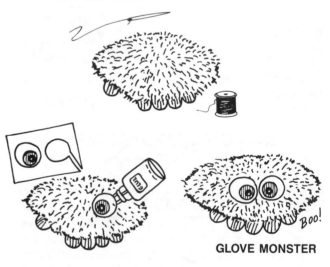

GLOVE MONSTER

Shadow Puppets

Shadow puppets are one of the simplest puppets. They are easy to make, fun to use, and lend themselves to the telling of tall stories. Figures and scenery are cut from lightweight cardboard and held next to a screen which is lighted from the rear.

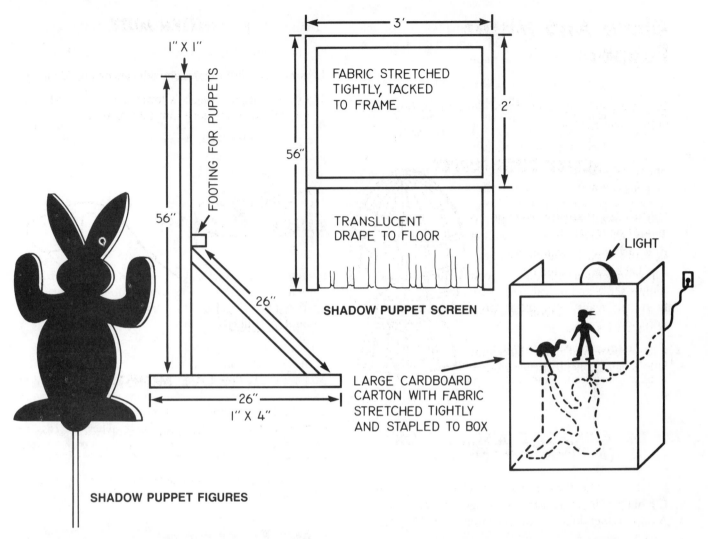

SHADOW PUPPET FIGURES

SHADOW PUPPET SCREEN

The story can be narrated offstage while the shadow puppets perform, or they could perform to a song that the boys sing, such as "Old MacDonald's Farm" or "The Twelve Days of Christmas."

SHADOW PUPPET FIGURES

1. Select patterns of figures, props, and scenery which will fit the story. Chidren's coloring books are a good source for such patterns. About 12 inches is a good height for figures. Few details are necessary since only the outline of the puppet will show. (See the "Crafts" section of this book for information on enlarging patterns.)

2. Cut the figures from lightweight cardboard. Black poster board is recommended since it will eliminate all reflected light, making a sharper shadow.

3. Mount each cutout on the end of a pencil, dowel, or meat skewer with a thumbtack. The shadow puppet is a rigid figure, held straight up against the screen by the handle at its base.

4. Shadow puppet figures grow large or small as they move toward and away from the screen. They can vanish quickly or make an instantaneous appearance on the screen. They can be transformed from humans to animals or the reverse by pulling one puppet back out of the light while another is put in its place.

5. Body limbs can be jointed by various types of hinges to enable them to move independently. A rod must be attached to each limb so movement can be controlled.

6. Scenery can be changed quickly and easily. A car, bicycle, wagon, or other prop can be pushed or pulled across the screen.

7. Scenery which will not be moved during the show can be attached to the screen with cellophane tape or fitted between the frame and screen.

Shadow Puppet Screen. The screen material can be white cotton sheeting, glazed chintz, or oiled paper (butcher paper or newsprint oiled with linseed oil or vegetable oil, which makes the screen translucent). This material is attached to a frame, such as those shown. It may be made from 1-by-2-inch lumber or a large cardboard carton with a window cut in one side. For 12-inch puppets, the screen should measure about 24-by-26 inches with a curtain hanging below to conceal the puppeteers.

Whatever type of frame is used, it should have a footing for the figures. This is a ledge 1 to 2 inches wide, fastened all across the bottom of the screen on the inside. This will provide something for the shadow puppets' feet to touch so they will not seem to be floating in air.

Shadow Puppet Lighting. A light source is placed behind and slightly above the puppet screen, about 3 to 4 feet away. The source may be a 150 watt unshaded bulb, a 300–400 watt reflector spotlight, or special stage lights. These lights can be placed on a dimmer and the illumination varied for special effects.

The room should be as dark as possible during a shadow puppet show, and the puppeteers should be cautioned to keep their heads below the screen so their shadows will not show.

Two or three rehearsals prior to the performance will ensure that the lighting is properly situated. The lighting is of primary importance in the shadow puppet play.

THE ANIMALS' CHRISTMAS STORY
(A Shadow Puppet Play)

Cut out the 25 figures listed in the play and attach to rods. As each is mentioned by the Narrator, it is held up to the screen.

NARRATOR: Everyone has Christmas wishes. We all dream about the things we may find under the tree. Did you know that animals dream too? Den (No.) will show you what I mean.

"I want a CANTELOUPE," said the ANTELOPE.

"I want a FISHING LINE," said the PORCUPINE.

"I want a WAGON," said the DRAGON,

"Underneath the CHRISTMAS TREE."

"I want an OVERCOAT," said the BILLY GOAT.

"I want a NEW FRONT DOOR," said the DINOSAUR.

"I want a VIDEO GAME," said the GREAT DANE,

"Oh, how happy I would be!"

"I want a BARBEQUE," said the KANGAROO.

"I want a PHONOGRAPH," said the BIG GIRAFFE.

"I want a ROCKING CHAIR," said the GRIZZLY BEAR,

"To rock all winter long."

"I want a PRETTY HAT," said the KITTY CAT.

"I want some MISTLETOE," said the BUFFALO.

"I want a HAPPY TUNE," said the BIG BABOON,

"To sing all winter long."

As you can see, each animal has his own special wish, just like you do. Merry Christmas to all and to all a good night!

Finger Puppets

Finger puppets give a Cub Scout another way to express himself and be creative. They are easy to manipulate, even by the inexperienced. They can be simple cardboard cutouts or padded puppets.

The index and middle fingers serve as the legs and feet of the puppet, so his body must be small. Since these puppets are small, they are not suitable for a production at a large pack meeting; however, they are ideal for use in den meeting, at home, on hikes, or for entertaining in a children's hospital or nursing home. They are easy to transport, require little equipment and can even be used without a stage.

Simple Finger Puppet

1. Place your index and middle fingers on a piece of poster board and trace around them. This will be where the legs (your fingers) will be located on the puppet and will help determine the size of the rest of the puppet. Turn the picture around and finish the drawing, adding a head, body, and arms.

2. Color or paint the figure. Cut holes near the base of the puppet's body for your fingers to fit through, as shown.

3. Cut out the puppet, insert two fingers, and practice walking forward and backward, kneeling, jumping, kicking.

4. Shoes or boots can be made from small cylinders of

SIMPLE FINGER PUPPET

cardboard to fit over your fingertips, and yarn hair added, if desired.

PADDED FINGER PUPPETS

1. Make head from a rubber ball, a table tennis ball, styrofoam ball, spool, or cork. Paint and add features. Hair can be made from yarn or colored string.

2. Cut a small hole in the bottom of the head and glue in a wooden peg for the neck.

3. Cut body from 1-by-2-inch lumber, about 2½ feet long. In the center of one end, make a hole about 1-inch deep to fit the neck peg. Also make 18-inch diameter hole from side to side for arm wire to slip through. Round off top corners of body to form shoulders.

4. Insert a double arm wire, twist, and shape a loop at each end for hands.

5. Glue and tack a piece of elastic on back near lower edge, forming loops for the fingers to slip through, as shown.

6. Pad the arm wire with cotton and wrap the arms tightly with muslin. Cut puppet hands from felt and glue on. Padding can also be added to the body to shape it as desired.

7. Add a shirt made from felt or crepe paper.

8. A simple pair of trousers can be made from felt.

Attach to puppet body at front only, leaving room in back for the fingers to slip down through the trouser legs. If you wish, attach a pair of cardboard shoes to the bottom of the trouser legs.

9. To fasten the figure to your hand, slip a rubber band over your wrist, insert fingers into the puppet, then slip the band around the puppet under his arms.

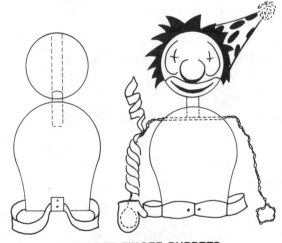

PADDED FINGER PUPPETS

GLOVE FINGER PUPPETS

Fingers of gloves lend themselves to forming finger puppets.

1. Cut the fingers off an old glove.

2. Sew on button or bead eyes and nose.

3. Cut ears, mouths, tails, etc. from felt and glue on.

4. Glue on yarn or fur for hair.

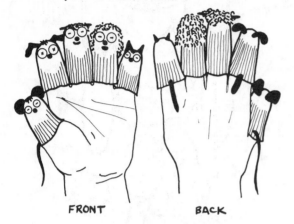

FRONT   BACK

GLOVE FINGER PUPPETS

EGG CARTON FINGER PUPPETS

Cut the cups from an egg carton. Decorate puppet head as desired with paint, felt, or construction paper. Plastic movable eyes add to the appeal of these puppets. Or, use a felt-tip marking pen to draw on features. Animal head puppets can be made by gluing two egg carton cups together, as shown. A piece of rolled cellophane tape on the tip of the finger will help the puppets stay in place.

EGG CARTON FINGER PUPPETS

FINGER PUPPET STAGE

1. Use a cardboard carton, 14 to 16 inches tall. Cut off the top and cut an opening in one side. The opening should be low enough to hide the top of the back of the carton. Paint the inside of the box black. Paint or decorate the outside of the box as desired.

2. So the puppeteer's hands will be concealed, he should wear a long black stocking over his arm, with holes cut for the index and middle fingers which operate the puppet.

3. Strong lights from either side of the stage will give good light and help eliminate arm shadows. Flashlights inserted in the sides of the stage will work well.

4. A draw curtain can be added to the stage if desired.

FINGER PUPPET STAGE

FLASHLIGHT

Bib Puppets

Part boy, part puppet—it moves, it breathes, and it steals the show. A Cub Scout will win the heart of the audience with a bib puppet. He just ties it around his neck and performs actions that will delight the audience.

A bib puppet is actually a cardboard or wood puppet without a head. It is tied around the boy's neck like a bib. The boy, dressed in black, stands in front of a black backdrop and operates the arms and legs of the puppet with wire rods which have been inserted at the elbows and knees.

This is a good opportunity to enlist the help of other adults—someone to cut out the bibs, someone to sew the arms and legs, and someone to make the stage.

CONSTRUCTING A BIB PUPPET

1. Enlarge pattern and cut out bib from cardboard or plywood. Cut four slots in bib, as shown, for attaching arms and legs. Drill two holes for the cord used to tie the bib around the neck.

2. Make patterns for the arms and legs, allowing ¼-inch for seams. Cut four of each from unbleached muslin. Sew, turn seam in, and stuff with kapok or polyester stuffing. Sew a tab to each arm and leg. Slip each tab through the proper slot in the torso. Fold back, forming a loop, and sew into place. Stitch these loops securely, because they will get quite a workout. Make the loops loose enough to give freedom of movement to the arms and legs.

3. The hands can be made from doll gloves or cut out of cloth and stuffed. Insert two iron washers along with the stuffing to add weight. If hands are cut from plywood and painted, drill hole for rod to be inserted.

4. Cut shoes from ⅜- or ½-inch plywood. Drill hole for leg rod to slip through and starter hole on bottom side of shoe for the end of the rod. It will help to tack a staple over the rod to hold it in place.

5. Make the operating rods from clothes hanger wire. Cut two 11-inch pieces for the arms and two 14½-inch pieces for the legs. Bend as shown in the illustration. Always dress the puppet before putting the rods in place. After the puppet has been costumed and the arm rod has been inserted, put end of rod in hand and glue or sew into place. (If hands are plywood, make no loop in rod.) When the leg rod has been inserted, slip on the shoes, bend the rod into a U shape, and force the end back into the shoe.

6. Insert a ¼-inch sash cord or black bias tape through holes at top of bib to tie around neck.

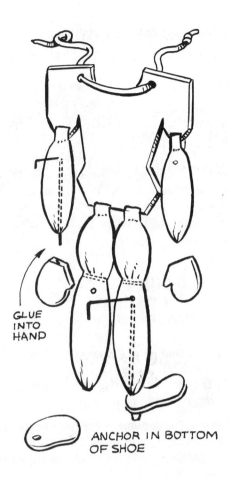

GLUE INTO HAND

ANCHOR IN BOTTOM OF SHOE

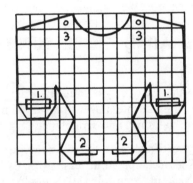

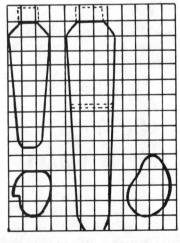

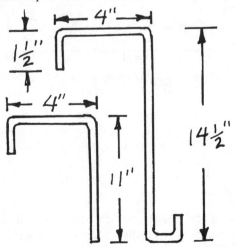

CONSTRUCTING A BIB PUPPET

BIB PUPPET COSTUMES

Lay the puppet on a piece of brown wrapping paper and trace around it for shape. Using this pattern, and allowing ¼-inch for seams, cut costume fronts and backs from fabric. Leave an opening in back of costume so puppet can be easily dressed.

Tape padding on puppet where shape is needed. Dress the puppet and fasten costume in place in back. Add tiny holes at the back of the knees, add elbows for the leg and arm rods to go through. Then insert rods and fasten hands and feet in place.

BIB PUPPET ACTOR COSTUMES

The costumes, including gloves or mittens, must blend with the background. A dull black fabric that doesn't reflect light is good for costumes. For the best results, make backdrop of the same material.

A cape is the simplest costume. Make two slits for the boy to put his hands through to operate the puppet. Stitch black mittens or gloves made of the same material to these slits.

OPERATING THE BIB PUPPET

The boys should practice by holding an arm rod in each hand and learning all the moves that can be made. Try patting hands, saluting, and scratching.

Then practice with the leg rods—walk the puppet, have it kick, cross its feet, spread its legs, swing its foot, and tap its foot. Next, practice doing steps and hand motions together in time to music.

To make the puppet sit, the boy walks it in front of the seat and bends down slightly. The puppet will double at the hips and appear to be sitting.

Boys should remember to keep their heads in line with the puppet body.

BIB PUPPET STAGE

Hang a backdrop of black material from a wall 2 feet behind the puppet stage. The stage can be a table with a drape or cloth covering the front. It should be low

enough to allow the boys to bend over slightly so the puppet will swing free and be more easily operated.

Complete the stage by adding two 24-by-42-inch wood scenery frames made from 1-by-2-inch lumber, as shown. These can be clamped to either side of the table. Tack cardboard scenery to frames.

The stage should be lighted with natural, indirect light. Black out the back of the stage. Have lights on in the room in front of the stage. Avoid overhead lights, footlights and bridge lamps that are directed at the actors.

BIB PUPPET STAGE

6 Songs, Stunts, and Stories

Songs

For many boys, singing is as natural as talking. Most boys and adults have a basic rhythm urge—they will often respond by tapping a foot, humming to themselves, or even gently swaying to a lively song or the beating of a drum. Singing helps people relax, improves attitudes, and sets the tone for what is to come.

Most den and pack meetings will include at least one song. The secret to good singing in the den and pack is fun and enjoyment. If the songs are ones the boys enjoy and are sung with a smile and happy heart, singing can become one of the important elements of a den or pack meeting.

Many packs have enough copies of the *Cub Scout Songbook* to pass out at den and pack meetings. The *Songbook* contains a wide variety of songs and some good tips for songleaders. Anyone can lead songs, but to be successful, it is best to follow the proven methods found in that book and in the *Cub Scout Leader Book*.

Songs In Den Meetings

A lively song provides a change of pace in den meeting activities and helps the boys release stored-up energy. A quiet or patriotic song helps to set the mood for more serious activities.

The den leader, assistant den leader, or den chief might be the regular song leader for the den, but don't overlook the possibility of a potential songleader among the Cub Scouts. If anyone plays a guitar, this will help enhance singing in the den.

The boys may know some of the old familiar songs like "Old MacDonald Had a Farm," "Row, Row, Row Your Boat," and "She'll Be Comin' 'Round the Mountain." These are good for den meetings. The *Cub Scout Songbook* contains many songs which the boys can easily learn. Singing at pack meetings will be better if the songs are practiced in the den.

Songs In Pack Meetings

The song leader at pack meetings should be someone who can start a song on the right pitch and with proper tempo. This person needs enough contagious enthusiasm to get the adults to sing along with the boys and should be familiar with the tips for leading and teaching songs found in the *Cub Scout Songbook* and *Cub Scout Leader Book.*

The choice of songs depends on the mood and theme of the pack meeting. A patriotic song is good at the beginning or end. During the meeting, lively action songs can be used to lift spirits.

When teaching new songs, it will help if the boys practice in den meetings. Then, at the pack meeting, have the words written large on a blackboard or big sheet of paper so everyone can see. This will encourage adults to join in.

Using Songs Creatively

Songs can be used in various ways. Try some of these at pack meetings:

- Divide the pack into two groups and have one group sing the first line, the other group the second, and so on. Or have one group sing while the other group claps or hums.

- Leave some words out and use handclaps instead. For example, when singing "The More We Get Together," have the audience clap hands each time the word "together" would be sung. Or ask them to stand on a certain word in the song.

- Add musical instruments or rhythm instruments.

- Sing "contra songs" where two or more different songs are sung together with a pleasing effect. Divide audience into two groups and have each group sing a different song. For example, "Row, Row, Row Your Boat" with "Are You Sleeping," or "Little Tommy Tucker" with "Three Blind Mice."

- Make up your own songs to fit the theme or special occasion, using familiar melodies such as "Yankee Doodle" or "Clementine."

- Songs are sometimes found in *Cub Scout and Webelos Scout Program Helps.* New songs may also be introduced at your district roundtable and the annual pow wow.

Writing Your Own Songs

It isn't necessary to be a professional songwriter to write your own songs. Just fit your own words to the tune and rhythm of a familiar song.

Some dens make up their own song to be sung at den meetings or on special occasions. Or someone in the pack might make up a theme-related song for all the dens to learn before the pack meeting. Some examples are shown in the *Cub Scout Songbook.*

RESOURCES FOR SONGS

In addition to the *Cub Scout Songbook,* song ideas can be obtained from *Cub Scout and Webelos Scout Program Helps,* and at the Cub Scout leaders' roundtable and pow wow meetings.

Den Yells

Den yells help build den spirit and enthusiasm and can be used to help the boys let off steam at den and pack meetings.

Den yells are usually simple and rhythmic and often end on a word or phrase which the boys can shout. Many high school and college cheers can be adapted for den yells. When the boys help develop the den yell, they feel it is really theirs and will enjoy using it.

Here are sample den yells.

Den One! Den One!
Is there a better den? None!
What den has the most fun? One!
Den One! Den One!

We'll do our best for the gold and blue!
We ARE the best! Den Two! Den Two!

We're the Cub Scouts from Den 3,
And no Cubs could be prouder!
If you can't hear us now, we'll yell
a little louder!
(*Repeat twice, louder each time.*)

One, two, three, four,
Which den do you cheer for?
Which den can you hear more?
Den Four! Den Four! Den Four!

Which den is really alive?
Which den has all the drive?
Den Five! Den Five!
We're the den that is alive!
We're the den that has the drive!
Den Five! Den Five!

T-H-R-E-E
The den that's best for you and me!
Watch us go and you will see!
It's T-H-R-E-E!
Den Three! Den Three!

Stunts

Stunts are a way to achieve one of Cub Scouting's important purposes—fun! They are used to add sparkle to meetings and put the group in a happy, lively frame of mind.

There are many types of stunts. Some get the whole group involved in doing something together; others are performed by a small group for the entertainment of others. Some are used as icebreakers to get the meeting off to a good start or to help people get acquainted. Others are used as an element of surprise or for a change of pace during a meeting.

RESOURCES FOR STUNTS

Ideas for stunts may be found in *Cub Scout Program Helps, Den Chief Handbook,* and *Group Meeting Sparklers.* Sometimes stunts are introduced at Cub Scout leaders' roundtable, the annual pow wow, and workshops.

Public and school libraries have books of stunts. These are a few suggestions:

Instant Fun For All Kinds of Groups, by Lorrell C. Burns

Handbook of Skits and Stunts, by Helen and Larry Eisenberg

Fun With Skits, Stunts and Stories, by Helen and Larry Eisenberg

The Fun Encyclopedia, by E. O. Harbin

Cokesbury Stunt Book, by A. M. Depew

WHY STUNTS? (A Poem)

The pack meeting seemed to drag that night,

And people were tiring fast;

The Cubmaster sensed the feeling

And he hoped through the meeting he'd last.

Then came a lull in the action;

The Cubmaster wiped sweat from his brow;

If only he could perk things up—

He sure wished that he knew how!

Then suddenly quite like magic,

His assistant appeared on the stage;

He held up a book called *Sparklers,*

Opened to a certain page.

With enthusiasm he made the announcement

That the whole audience would help out.

He divided them into groups

And tested each one for their shout.

Before they knew what was happening,

They had all joined in the fun;

Each group was doing its best

To out-do the other one!

Right then and there the meeting perked up;

Things moved along in style,

And the Cubmaster heard people murmur, "Best meeting we've had in a while."

So remember the words "group participation";

That's a very special key,

And your meetings will be filled with fun,

The way they ought to be!

Audience Participation Stunts

Audience participation stunts add variety, action, and fun to den and pack meetings. Some get the people on their feet, going through motions under the directions of a leader. In others, the audience is divided into groups which respond to a key word in a story read by a leader.

Several examples follow.

A MUSICAL STORY

This stunt requires a Narrator and pianist. The audience is divided into groups. The narrator begins to read the story. When he comes to a song title, he stops and the pianist plays the song, or enough of it to give the audience a chance to identify it. The first person to name the song gets a point for his team, and the game continues.

NARRATOR: This story takes place in "America." Many years ago "Old MacDonald Had A Farm." He liked to fish, and so he built his house "Down by the Old Mill Stream." Behind his house there was a "Long, Long Trail." After a hard day, he liked to sit and relax "Under the Spreading Chestnut Tree."

One day a letter came from his brother, who said, " 'I've Been Working on the Railroad,' and I want to take a vacation 'Deep in the Heart of Texas.' " Sometime later, the farmer was waiting "Down by the Station" for his brother to arrive, and he asked the stationmaster when the train was due. The stationmaster replied, " 'She'll Be Comin' 'Round the Mountain' any minute now." A little girl was sitting on the station platform crying, " 'Where, Oh Where Has My Little Dog Gone?' " The farmer said, " 'Ain't She Sweet?' "

Just then the train arrived and his brother stepped off. His brother asked him how things were on the farm, and the farmer replied, " 'It Was a Very Good Year,' except for a few days when we had 'Stormy Weather.' "

On the way home, the men began to talk about their "School Days." That evening, they sat on the porch "By the Light of the Silvery Moon" and talked about their "Home on the Range." A few days later, the brother left, and the last thing he said was, " 'I'll Be Seeing You.' "

THE HOUSE WHERE SANTA CLAUS LIVES

Practice the following actions with the audience so they can respond correctly when the story is read.

HOUSE (hands over head in inverted V).

SHED (hands in front of chest in inverted V).

SLED (hands together in waving motion from left to right).

REINDEER (hands, palms out, on sides of head).

PACK (both hands over a shoulder as if carrying a pack).

LITTLE GIRLS (females, young and old, stand).

LITTLE BOYS (males, young and old, stand).

DOLL (hands with palms together on cheek, with head slightly bent).

LION (extend both hands and give deep growl).

SOLDIER (stand at attention, give Cub Scout salute).

TRAIN (make figure 8 with hand).

SANTA CLAUS (pat stomach with both hands and say, "Ho, ho, ho.").

NARRATOR: This is the HOUSE . . . where SANTA CLAUS lives. This is the SHED . . . behind the HOUSE . . . where SANTA CLAUS lives.

This is the SLED . . . that is kept in the SHED . . . behind the HOUSE . . . where SANTA CLAUS lives.

These are the REINDEER . . . that pull the SLED . . . that is kept in the SHED . . . behind the HOUSE . . . where SANTA CLAUS lives.

This is SANTA CLAUS . . . who guides the REINDEER . . . that pull the SLED . . . that's kept in the SHED . . . behind the HOUSE . . . where SANTA CLAUS lives.

This is the PACK . . . all filled with toys for good LITTLE GIRLS . . . and good LITTLE BOYS . . . that is carried by old SANTA CLAUS . . . who guides the REINDEER . . . that pull the SLED . . . that is kept in the SHED . . . behind the HOUSE . . . where SANTA CLAUS lives.

This is the BOX . . . that is kept in the PACK . . . all filled with toys for good LITTLE GIRLS . . . and good LITTLE BOYS . . . that is carried by SANTA CLAUS . . . who guides the REINDEER . . . that pull the SLED . . . that is kept in the SHED . . . behind the HOUSE . . . where SANTA CLAUS lives.

This is the DOLL . . . that is in the BOX . . . that is in the PACK . . . all filled with toys for good LITTLE GIRLS . . . and good LITTLE BOYS . . . that is carried by SANTA CLAUS . . . who guides the REINDEER . . . that pull the SLED . . . that is kept in the SHED . . . behind the HOUSE . . . where SANTA CLAUS lives.

This is the LION . . . that frightened the DOLL . . . that is in the BOX . . . that is in the PACK . . . all filled with toys for good LITTLE GIRLS . . . and good LITTLE

BOYS . . . that is carried by SANTA CLAUS . . . who guides the REINDEER . . . that pull the SLED . . . that is kept in the SHED . . . behind the HOUSE . . . where SANTA CLAUS lives.

This is the SOLDIER . . . that shot the LION . . . that frightened the DOLL . . . that is in the BOX . . . that is in the PACK . . . all filled with toys for good LITTLE GIRLS . . . and good LITTLE BOYS . . . that is carried by SANTA CLAUS . . . who guides the REINDEER . . . that pull the SLED . . . that is kept in the SHED . . . behind the HOUSE . . . where SANTA CLAUS lives.

This is the TRAIN . . . that runs on the track and carries the SOLDIER . . . forward and back, who shot the LION . . . that frightened the DOLL . . . that is in the BOX . . . that is in the PACK . . . all filled with toys for good LITTLE GIRLS . . . and good LITTLE BOYS . . . that is carried by SANTA CLAUS . . . who guides the REINDEER . . . that pull the SLED . . . that is kept in the SHED . . . behind the HOUSE . . . where SANTA CLAUS lives.

THE THING

Divide audience into six groups. Assign a part to each group and have them practice. Narrator reads story, and groups respond to appropriate words.

CRICKET—"Krick, krick"

DUCK—"Quack, quack"

SNAKE—"Hiss, hiss"

FROG—"Croak-it, croak-it"

BROOK—"Babble, babble"

THING—"Knock-knock-knock"

NARRATOR: Once upon a time a Cub Scout went walking along the shore. The first one he met was Johnny CRICKET. "Good morning, Mr. CRICKET," said the Cub Scout. "What are you doing here?" "Oh," said the CRICKET, "I'm singing so the THING won't catch me." "Where is the THING?" asked the Cub Scout. "Oh, he's around," said the CRICKET mysteriously.

Soon the Cub Scout met a DUCK. "Good morning, Mrs. DUCK," he said. "What are you doing?" "Oh, I'm swimming so the THING won't catch me." "Where is the THING?" asked the Cub Scout. "He's under the blue," answered the DUCK.

The Cub Scout wondered if that meant under the sky. He walked along a little further and soon met a SNAKE slithering along the shore. "Good morning, Mr. SNAKE," said the Cub Scout. "What are you doing here?" "I'm sneaking away so the THING won't catch me," replied the SNAKE. "Where is the THING?" asked the Cub Scout. "Under the gold," replied the SNAKE.

And the Cub Scout thought he meant under the sun. Soon he met the FROG sitting on a lily pad. "Good morning, Mr. FROG," said the Cub Scout. "What are you doing here?" "I'm sitting on the lily pad to keep the THING from catching me," answered the FROG. "Where is the THING?" asked the Cub Scout, who was beginning to be a little afraid. "In the blue," answered the FROG.

The Cub Scout walked on and said, "I wish somebody could show me the THING." "Good morning, Cub Scout" said the BROOK. "I can show you the THING. Just look in my face." The Cub Scout looked into the BROOK, and he saw the . . . Cub Scout!

THE THREE TREES

Divide audience into seven groups, assign each a part, and have them practice their sounds. As Narrator reads the story, they respond to the appropriate word.

BIG TREE—"Plunk!" (in deep voice)

MIDDLE-SIZED TREE—"Plank!"

BABY TREE—"Plink!" (in high voice)

BABBLING BROOK—"Gurgle-gurgle"

RABBIT—"Clippety-clip, clippety-clop"

HUNTERS—(bugle call)

GUN—"Bang!"

NARRATOR: Once upon a time in the deep, dark woods, there stood three trees—the BIG TREE . . . the MIDDLE -SIZED TREE . . . and the wee BABY TREE . . . and through the trees ran the BABBLING BROOK . . . and hopped the little RABBIT. One day a group of HUNTERS . . . came into the forest where stood the three trees . . . the BIG TREE . . . the MIDDLE-SIZED TREE . . . and the little BABY TREE . . . and through the trees ran the BABBLING BROOK . . . and hopped the little RABBIT. As the HUNTERS . . . wandered through the forest, one of the HUNTERS . . . spied the little RABBIT. He raised his GUN . . . at the little RABBIT . . . and sadness reigned in the forest, in which stood the three trees . . . the BIG TREE . . . the MIDDLE-SIZED TREE . . . and the little BABY TREE . . . and through which ran the BABBLING BROOK . . . but no longer hopped the little RABBIT . . . the BIG TREE . . . the MIDDLE-SIZED TREE . . . and the little BABY TREE . . . were all very sad. Even the BABBLING BROOK . . . was sad. But all of a sudden, out from the thicket hopped the little RABBIT . . . The HUNTER'S . . . GUN . . . had missed! And once again happiness reigned in the forest where lived the three trees . . . the BIG TREE . . . the MIDDLE-SIZED TREE . . . and the little BABY TREE . . . and through which ran the BABBLING BROOK . . . and hopped the little RABBIT.

CAR TROUBLE

For a small group, write several of the items below on 3-by-5 cards and give each person one or more cards. For a large group, write only one item on each card, so more people can participate. The narrator reads the story, pausing at the blanks. In turn, the players read one item on their cards to fill in the blank words.

a loose tooth	a short pencil
3 boiled eggs	4 sour pickles
a tall pine tree	a juicy watermelon
a fat onion	a swarm of bees
a green tomato	a can of dog food
2 snowballs	an ice cream bar
a can of tar	a purple crayon
a telephone	6 plump skeletons
a bald eagle	a limping dinosaur
a bar of soap	a can of worms
a cat's meow	a ferocious lion
a butterfly net	a dog's footprint
a rattlesnake	7 pounds of feathers
4 hot rocks	a used firecracker
3 raisins	7 pounds of feathers
a bike horn	a red kite

NARRATOR: One fine day, two little old ladies decided to drive out of town for a picnic. Miss Bingley loaded a basket with _____ , _____ , and _____ , and other tasty things. They took their lunch and drove off in an old car that belonged to Miss Arbuckle. The radiator cap was decorated with _____ , and the holes in the roof had been patched with _____ and _____ .

As they drove along, Miss Bingley pointed to the side of the road and said, "Oh, look at that bush with the _____ growing on it." "Let's stop here," said Miss Arbuckle.

They carried their picnic basket to some shade cast by _____ and spread out _____ to sit on. Nearby, _____ sang gaily in a tree. They noticed that some low bushes had _____ growing on them. The two friends were having a wonderful time.

"There's nothing as delicious as _____ with mustard and pickles," said Miss Arbuckle, as she brushed the crumbs off her lap with _____ . "Yes," sighed Miss Bingley. "But it's getting late. We'd better start for home."

Unfortunately, their car refused to go. The motor made a noise like _____ and then stopped. "Oh dear!" said

Miss Arbuckle, looking under the hood. "I think I see _____ and _____ caught in the fan belt. "Impossible!" said Miss Bingley. "Could the tank be empty? Are you sure you put enough _____ in it before we left home?"

"Of course, I did!" said Miss Arbuckle. "It must be the wheels. We'll jack them up with _____ and then replace them with _____ . She covered her dress with _____ and took _____ to loosen the bolts.

Just then a farmer drove up and asked if he could help. "Looks like _____ in the engine," he said, tightening a bolt with _____ . Then he stepped back and the car started. "I just connected the _____ to _____ which had come loose." The two old ladies looked in their picnic basket and gave him the rest of their _____ to show their appreciation, and they drove home happily again.

JOHNNY MIXUP

Prepare a set of 3-by-5 cards with each of the three-phrase sets below, 54 cards in all. Deal all of the cards to the Cub Scouts and parents, who keep them face down. Each person may get more than one card. Then start to read the story. When you come to a space, pause, and let each player, in turn, read one of the lines on his top card. The crazier the better, although sometimes it's just as much fun when one of the objects on the card happens to fit perfectly.

some dirty dish water	a push cart
a rusty nail	a rattlesnake
a bottle of jam	a rhinoceros
a banana skin	a sourpuss
a bad dream	a battleship
some axle grease	a roaring lion
a toadstool	a shovel full of coal
a pumpkin vine	a black cloud
a skyscraper	a can of red paint
a streetcar	a broken umbrella
a loud noise	a cake of soap
a swarm of bees	a silly giggle
a bathtub	a puff of smoke
a tiny speck	a monkey-faced baboon
a beautiful sunset	a bucket of slop
a toothbrush	a crazy bedbug
some hot pepper	a carload of fish
a loud sneeze	a leaky pail
an old radio	a squeaky pushcart
an old shoe	an old egg
a sock on the nose	a cross-eyed cat

an old setting hen
an elderly porcupine
a Dutch farmer

a pink ghost
a three-legged stove
a dish of beans

a tall hat
a stuffed pig
an energetic turtle

a frowsy bird
a green snake
a pan of milk

a flashlight
a cactus plant
some red ants

a Ford V8
a buggy bumper
a gas stove

a piece of ribbon
a rainy day
a race horse

an ear of corn
a chunk of wood
a spare tire

a tin can
the hot sun
a painted Indian

a skittish kitten
an old road map
some spotted ink

a broken umbrella
a pair of garters
an old spinning wheel

a scrub brush
a head of old cabbage
a corncob pipe

a cross-eyed peanut
a bowlegged horse
some limburger cheese

a pigtail
a wild man from Borneo
an old tin horn

pink lemonade
a bundle of shingles
a bag of rags

a camel's hump
a rubber-neck
a black cat

a hunk of cheese
a heap of pancakes
a high-tone tramp

a wise owl
a bobtailed donkey
a wet cat

a black mustache
a wall-eyed fish
a sinking teakettle

some rain
an old hay rack
a red necktie

a secondhand sponge
a young earthquake
a glass eye

a bent hairpin
an exclamation point
a runaway pussy cat

a trolley car
a snapping turtle
a rusty horseshoe

a bunch of posies
a litter of pups
an inquisitive ostrich

a bucking horse
a purple cow
a red barn

a barrel of tar
three blind mice
somebody's Scout shorts

my suspenders
a yellow parrot
a pile of peach fuzz

a green pair of stockings
a keg of nails
a barrel stove

a green-eyed monster
a hot dog
a set of false teeth

a ton of bricks
a merry widow
Mary's little lamb

a bean shooter
a prickly thistle
your old shirt

a derby hat
a country hick
a yelling baby

a cross-eyed potato
a stick of dynamite
a big fat worm

two fat skeletons
a peanut roaster
a Spanish onion

a military haircut
a brass monkey
a second-hand Ford

a juicy watermelon
a flat car
a blow-out

a crowing rooster
a laughing donkey
your red nose

a rip in your pants
a slice of cold ham
a pain-in-the-neck

a crawling lizard
a bobtailed cat
an old crab

a windy day
Mickey Mouse
a pair of bee's knees

NARRATOR: Once upon a time a little boy named Johnny who lived in Mixup Town. His home was indeed very strange for it had _____ on the roof and _____ on each window sill and _____ with _____ on it planted on each side of the front door to make the house beautiful. The house was painted so that it looked like _____ . Instead of having flowers growing in their garden Johnny's family planted _____ and _____ and over in a corner was a tree with _____ growing on it.

Johnny's father had a pet which was _____ , and he would go for long walks with it, leading it with a chain while it hopped about merrily like _____ . Johnny went with his father on these walks, but he always had to dress up nicely like all the other boys in Mixup Town whenever he went out. This is how he dressed: On his head he wore _____ ; on one foot he had _____ and on the other was _____ . Instead of a necktie, he wore _____ .

One morning Johnny's father told him they were going to the zoo to see _____ and the other things they had there. So Johnny dressed quickly and then washed himself with _____ and dried himself on _____ , which was hanging on the towel rack. He brushed his teeth with _____ and combed his hair with _____ , and he was ready for breakfast. He was very hungry that morning so he took _____ and _____ and put it on his plate and mixed them all up with _____ and ate it all up.

At the zoo Johnny's father had to buy tickets, so he reached into his pocket and pulled _____ and gave it to the ticket seller. The man gave him his tickets and his change, which was _____ . They went inside and in the first cage they saw _____ , which was pacing to and fro and roaring loudly at _____ , which was in another cage, standing on _____ and making faces at him.

That morning when they got to the zoo, the monkeys in their cage were very playful. One of them was hanging by his feet on the trapeze and holding _____ with his hands and tickling another monkey with it. Another monkey with _____ on his head was throwing _____ up like a ball and letting it bounce. A little monkey close to him saw _____ buzzing around in the cage and tried to catch it, but it made a noise like _____ and frightened him; he ran like _____ was after him.

When Johnny tired of seeing the zoo, he went to the aquarium where he saw _____ swimming around like _____ and singing as happily as _____ . Then he went to see the elephants, which were walking around in a pen just large enough for _____ . Johnny reached into a paper sack he was carrying and pulled out _____ and gave it to the biggest elephant. The elephant was so pleased with it that he danced with joy and reached out and gave Johnny _____ .

Now, across the street was a sideshow where a band was playing music that sounded like _____ running after _____ . High up on a platform there was a very strange looking man. His head was shaped like _____ and his body was shaped like _____ . And one ear was as long as _____ . As the man puffed on his pipe, great clouds of smoke came out of his ear. Just as he took an extra deep puff on his pipe, a man slapped him with _____ and out of his ear jumped _____ .

By this time it was time for Johnny and his father to go home so they went to the corner and climbed on top of _____ and rode home feeling as tired as _____ which was pulled out of a mudpuddle.

The following day Johnny, who was an unusual sort of a Cub Scout, had to go to his den meeting. First of all, the Cub Scouts had to sign their names on the back of _____ . Instead of a pencil they used _____ . Their uniforms were indeed strange ones. They were the color of _____ . They had _____ wrapped around each leg. And on their heads they each had _____ , while their neckerchiefs looked like _____ . When they went into their den, they were each given a puzzle which was _____ cut up into several pieces, and they all tried to put it together with _____ .

They sang a song about _____; then they started to work on their handicraft. One Cub Scout was hammering on _____ ; another was busy holding _____ and trying to paint it red with _____ . Still another one was trying to nail an Indian head on _____ but it kept jumping around like _____ . Their den chief was helping the denner to learn his knots achievement. This is what they were doing: the den chief was holding _____ on the table while the denner was trying to tie it up with _____ . Then when they had finished, he showed him how to jump over _____ . Then they all played a game in which each Cub Scout threw _____

as far as he could while he carried _____ in his left hand.

As the meeting closed the den chief lit _____ and told them that it resembled _____ , and all good Cub Scouts should grow up to be like that, too. Then they all went home as happy as _____ , throwing _____ at each other as they sang a beautiful song about _____ , which sounded like _____ that had fallen into a washing machine.

THE AIRSICK WITCH

In this stunt, all of the audience responds to key words by these sounds and actions:

WITCH – "Boo . . . boo . . . booo"

CAT – "Yeooo . . . owl!"

HAT – (pretend to put hat on head)

BROOM – (sweeping motion)

MOON – (big smile, with arms overhead)

NARRATOR: Once there was a young WITCH . . . who lived on the MOON. The WITCH . . . thought she had everything a good WITCH . . . should have. She had a HAT. She had a cape. And she had a BROOM. But one thing was wrong. Whenever the WITCH . . . put on her HAT . . . and her cape and got on her BROOM . . . and flew away from the MOON, . . . she got airsick. The poor WITCH . . . had tried three times, but she never had any fun witching around at all.

So, in desperation one day she decided to go see the oldest WITCH . . . on the MOON . . . and ask her what to do. The old WITCH . . . said, "What's the trouble, dearie?" The young WITCH . . . said, "Every time I put on my HAT . . . and my cape and get on my BROOM . . . and try to fly away from the MOON, . . . I get airsick. I never have any fun witching at all!" and she began to cry.

The old WITCH . . . patted her on the shoulder and said, "Where is your CAT . . . ?" "My CAT . . . ?" replied the young WITCH.

"Why yes, dearie," said the old WITCH. "You need a CAT . . . on the back of your BROOM . . . to hold it steady. Then you will fly smoothly when you leave the MOON . . . and you won't get airsick."

So the young WITCH . . . put on her HAT . . . and her cape; got a CAT . . . and put it on the back of her BROOM . . . and flew smoothly away from the MOON. From that time on, she had lots of fun witching around on Halloween.

So remember, whenever you see a WITCH . . . flying through the air on her BROOM . . . , you can be sure she has a CAT . . . riding along behind her.

THE BRAVE LITTLE INDIAN

The audience follows the Narrator in the actions below as the story is read.

INDIAN — (place hand behind head to make feathers)

WALKS — (make walking sound by slapping leg)

SAW/SEE — (shade eyes and look around)

CROSSES BRIDGE — (pound fists on chest)

JUMPS — (raise hands above head as if jumping)

SWIMS — (swish palms against each other)

SLAMS — (clap hands once)

RUNS — (slap legs as fast as you can)

NARRATOR: Once upon a time there was a brave little INDIAN. He said to his happy little INDIAN friends, "I am going hunting to find a grizzly bear." So he WALKED out the gate and he SLAMMED it. He hadn't WALKED far until he SAW a rabbit. But he didn't SEE a bear. So he WALKED on.

Soon he came to a bridge and he CROSSED the BRIDGE. He hadn't WALKED very far when he SAW a deer. But he didn't SEE a bear. So he WALKED on.

Then the brave little INDIAN came to a ditch. He couldn't step across, so he backed up. He said: "I'll JUMP the ditch," and he RAN, faster and faster. He JUMPED and he landed on the other side of the ditch.

He hadn't WALKED very far until he came to a river. He JUMPED into the river and SWAM across. He got out of the river and WALKED on.

He WALKED up a little hill, and just then he SAW the bear! He quickly turned around and RAN down the hill. He JUMPED back into the river and SWAM across quickly. He JUMPED out of the river and RAN on. He quickly CROSSED the BRIDGE. On the other side he SAW a deer, but he RAN on. When he got home, he RAN through the gate and SLAMMED it. He told his INDIAN friends, "I SAW a bear!" The other little INDIANS just said, "Ha!".

CLANCY TO THE RESCUE

Practice the sounds below with the audience. A Narrator reads the story while the audience responds to key words with motions and sound effects.

CLANCY — (feel your muscles, like a strong man)

HORSES — (slap thighs)

YELL — (Indian fashion, with hand over mouth)

FIRE ENGINE — (High-pitched siren sound)

BELL — (Swing arm like clapper, saying, "Clang-clang, clang.")

HOSE — (shh-sh-sh sound like water from hose)

STEAM — (hissing s-s-s-s sound)

NARRATOR: If you like HORSES, you would have enjoyed living back in the 1800s when they had old-fashioned steam-type FIRE ENGINES, pulled by HORSES. One of these FIRE ENGINES was pulled by the greatest hero ever, CLANCY! Yes sir! CLANCY was a real hero! Every day when there was no fire, he would take the HORSES out for exercise, trotting them gently up and down the streets. If there were children along the way, CLANCY would always stop and let them pet the HORSES.

Sometimes the alarms were in the daytime, but sometimes they were at night. When the alarm sounded at night, one man would YELL up to the firemen above, and the men would get up, stretch, and slide down the pole. Then they would run to the FIRE ENGINE where the STEAM was up, and away they would go to the fire, clanging the BELL, with CLANCY driving the HORSES.

One night most of the men were in bed and the others were playing checkers when the alarm sounded. Where was the fire? At the mayor's big two-story house! Quick as a flash they were there. CLANCY stopped the HORSES and YELLED, "Keep the STEAM up men!" They started the fire HOSE and began to squirt water on the fire.

CLANCY strained to see upstairs where the mayor's wife was trapped. Flames were everywhere! CLANCY YELLED, "You'll have to jump!" The mayor's wife was afraid, so CLANCY threw her a rope and she came right down into the middle of the net.

The firemen kept fighting the fire. They put the HOSE on it and kept up the STEAM In the FIRE ENGINE. Before long, the fire was out, so they turned off the HOSE, got back on the FIRE ENGINE, and went back to the firehouse, clanging the BELL. To CLANCY and the other firemen, it was all in a day's work. The sleepy firemen went back upstairs and soon were sound asleep.

THE FIVE OLD CROWS

Ask the audience to imitate sounds and follow your actions as you tell the story.

NARRATOR: Once upon a time, a farmer's wife stewed a big pan of prunes and set them out on the back porch to cool. Five old crows, perched in the top of the old cottonwood, looked down at the prunes and then at each other and said, "Should we?" (*Everyone stands*). They answered, "Yes"! and they flew down. "Ga lump, ga lump, ga lump," they croaked. (*Flap arms as if flying—audience imitates.*)

They landed on the pan and ate all the prunes. (*Make slurping sounds.*) When the prunes were gone, the crows tried to fly back up into the tree, but they were so stuffed they couldn't make it, so they flew out to the pump and landed on the handle (*everyone sits*) and waited for their food to digest.

After a while, the first crow said, "I think I'll fly east." (*Stand, put hand to forehead, look east.*) The crow took off and flew 20 yards east, saying, "Ga lump, ga lump, ga lump." (*Audience repeats.*) Then he folded his wings and fell down dead. Swish z-z-z-z boom! (*Audience repeats.*)

The second crow said, "I can't fly east. I think I'll fly west." (*Hand to forehead, look east, look west.*) The crow took off, flew 20 yards west saying, "Ga lump, ga lump, ga lump." (*Audience repeats.*) Then he folded his wings and fell down dead. Swish z-z-z-z boom! (*Audience repeats.*)

(*Continue this same procedure with two more crows flying north and south.*)

The last old crow sat there sadly, shaking his head. Rattle, rattle. (*Audience repeats.*) "Well," he said, "I can't fly east, I can't fly west, I can't fly north, I can't fly south." (*Look east, west, north, south.*) "There's only one way for me to go and that's straight up!" (*Point up.*) The crow took off, repeating, "Ga lump, ga lump, ga lump." (*Flap arms, audience repeats.*) The crow went up and up and up and up—up to about 20 yards and fell down dead. Swish z-z-z-z boom! (*Audience repeats.*)

The moral of this story is: "You should never fly off the handle when you are full of prunes!"

Applause Stunts

Applause stunts are short, snappy, and lots of fun for both boys and adults. They are a good way to involve the audience and are often used to recognize a person or den for some accomplishment. A den or pack may have its favorites, which are used frequently. Many applause stunts fit monthly themes. Following are examples.

Popcorn Applause. With one hand closed, cover it with the other hand. Let the closed hand "grow" larger as the other hand moves up. Then spring fingers open and say, "Pop! Pop! Pop!" quickly.

Robot Applause. Walk in place, stiff-legged, saying, "Does not compute! Does not compute!"

Tonto Applause. Leader says, "Where does Tonto take his garbage?" Audience yells, "To de dump, to de dump, to de dump, dump, dump," in rhythm while slapping hands on thighs like running horse.

A Big Hand. Leader says, "Let's give them a big hand!" Everyone holds up one hand with palm open.

Round of Applause. Audience claps while moving hands in large circular motion.

Desert Applause. "Yucca. Yucca, Yucca!"

Motorcycle Applause. Raise foot and kick down three times. Make noise like sputtering motor. Hold hands out as if gripping handlebars. On third try, engine starts. Say: "Varr-oo-omm!"

Flapjack Applause. Pretend to pry a spatula under a pancake. Then throw it up in the air and nod three times as if watching flapjack flip in air, then catch it on spatula as you bring your other hand down with a loud clap.

Turkey Applause. Walk around in a small circle saying, "Gobble, gobble, gobble!" Then rub stomach, saying, "Yum, yum, yum!"

Rudolph Applause. Put thumbs to head with fingers pointing up to form antlers. Wrinkle nose and say, "Blink, blink, blink!"

Woodchopper's Applause. "How, how, how! Chop, chop chop! Timm-berrrrr!"

Paper Bag Applause. Make motions to simulate opening a paper bag, forming a neck, blowing it up, then pop it, saying, "Pop!"

Catsup Applause. Pretend to pound on bottom of bottle six times, saying, "Pop, pop, pop, pop, pop, pop." On the sixth "pop," say, "Squish . . . uh oh, too much!"

Watermelon Applause. Pretend to hold watermelon slice to mouth. Pull it rapidly across the mouth, slurping the fruit, then turn head to one side and give "raspberry" sound of spitting out seeds.

Canteloupe Applause. Same as watermelon except on a smaller scale. The melon is shorter and you spit out only one seed.

Six-Shooter Applause. Point finger in air and say, "Bang, bang, bang!" then blow smoke from the "gun."

Giant Beehive. Group buzzes like a hive of bees. When leader raises hand, volume increases. When hand is lowered, volume decreases.

Handkerchief Applause. Throw a handkerchief into the air with instruction for audience to applaud until you catch it or it falls to the floor. Vary the length of applause—long throw, short, no throw at all. This can also be done with a ball, a Cub Scout neckerchief, or other item.

Walk-on Stunts

Walk-on stunts ("quickies") are similar to skits, but they are usually much shorter and require only one or two people. Walk-ons are good for a change of pace in pack meeting—something to make everyone laugh and relax. They come in handy during pack shows and circuses as fill-ins between acts. They are also used at campfires to fill dead time or to enliven the program.

Stiff Neck. First person enters room, looking up. Second person enters, looks at the first and also looks up in the air. Repeat with as many others as desired. Finally, the last person enters and asks, "What are you looking at?" Each person down the line asks the next the same question, until the first person answers, "I don't know about you, but I have a stiff neck!"

Wrong Feet. One person enters the room with shoes on the wrong feet. Second person enters, looks at the first, who is groaning, and says, "What's wrong?" "My feet are killing me!" replies the first. "Do you have bunions?" "No." "Oh, I see. You have your shoes on the wrong feet!" First person replies, "Well, they're the only feet I have!"

It's All Around Me. First person runs into the room yelling "It's all around me! It's all around me!" Someone asks, "What's all around you?" First person replies, "My belt!"

Loose Rope. A person enters room pulling a rope. The leader says: "Why are you pulling that rope?" The person replies, "Did you every try pushing one?" The stunt can end there or later in the meeting the same person can come back, pushing a rope to the delight of the audience. Just push a wire through the rope so it will be stiff and straight and can be pushed.

You Don't Say! First person pretends to pick up a ringing telephone. He says, "You don't say . . . you don't say . . . you don't say!" (*with more emphasis each time.*) Other person says, "Who was that?" First person replies, "I don't know. He didn't say!"

It's in the Bag. Person comes into room carrying an inflated paper bag which he holds tightly by the top. Another person says, "What are you carrying in that bag?" "Milk", he replies. "You can't carry milk in a bag!" "A cow does!"

The Redcoats Are Coming. Several people run into the room during the meeting at different times, with frightened expressions. Each shouts, "The redcoats are coming! The redcoats are coming!" Later, towards the end of the meeting, two or three adults enter wearing red Scout jackets and say calmly, "We're the redcoats."

I Gotta Cold. Several people enter room tiptoeing cautiously. The first one in line whispers, "That's where I saw the ghost!" and points. This message is passed down the line in loud stage whispers. The last person says, "Where?" This is passed back up the line in whispers. The first one whispers back, "About 20 feet away." (*Message goes down line.*) "How big was he?" (*Message comes back up line and so on, with each additional statement.*) "About 10 feet tall." "When did you see it?" "About two months ago." "Then why are we whispering?" First person says loudly, "I gotta cold!"

There's a Fly in My Soup. Customer says to waiter, "Waiter, what's this fly doing in my soup?" The waiter comes to the table, looks in the bowl, and answers, "It's doing the backstroke!"

An Appealing Stunt. Person enters room carrying a case and states, "I'm taking my case to court!" A little later he enters again carrying a ladder and says, "I'm taking my case to a higher court!" A stranger runs through carrying a suit on a hanger. First man enters, saying, "I lost my suit." He carries a banana or orange which he begins to peel as he makes his last statement, "I'm appealing my case!"

Wrap at the Door. One person says, "Say, wasn't that a rap at the door?" Another person says, "No, I don't think so." First person, "Yes, I'm sure I heard a rap at the door!" "I don't think so." The first one goes to the door and brings back a coat or jacket, saying, "I just knew there was a wrap at the door!"

The Viper. Periodically during the meeting, people run in the room with frightened expressions, shouting, "The viper is coming! The viper is coming!" Each time, the audience becomes more apprehensive until finally, toward the end of the meeting, someone walks in carrying a pail and wiping cloths and announces, "I am de viper. I come to vipe de vindows."

Mixers and Icebreakers

Getting a meeting off to a good start often depends on little things—the greeting at the door, the activity involving people as they arrive, or the opening song or icebreaker. These little things put sparkle and punch into meetings and add to everyone's enjoyment. If "ice" is allowed to form at the beginning of a meeting, valuable time and effort must be spent in thawing it out. Icebreakers help solve this problem.

Also important are mixers—the type of activity which help a visitor get acquainted with others and feel at ease in the meeting. Icebreakers and mixers are used for this purpose, and also for a change of pace during a meeting to keep the audience from becoming restless or bored.

If there are winners for your mixers, they can be recognized early in the meeting with simple, inexpensive, funny prizes or with applause stunts. Several examples of mixers and icebreakers follow.

Name Acrostics. As people arrive, hand them a pencil and card. Ask them to print their full name in capitals vertically at the left of the card. They move about, trying to find persons whose last names begin with those letters. For variation, use the monthly theme or other word along the left of the card.

Paper Heads. As people arrive, give them a numbered slip, a pin, a pencil, a card, and a large paper sack. Each person is asked to pin the numbered slip on the chest, tear eyeholes in the sack and slip it over the head, and move about the room trying to recognize other people. Write the numbers and names on the card.

Who are You? This is a good icebreaker for a den meeting. On the door, hang a sign which reads, "Who are You?" The lower part of the sign is changeable and contains the subject or theme for that meeting. It could be planets, cars, birds, etc. As each boy arrives, he must say, "Today I am Mars" (or a Ford, or a Bluebird, depending on the subject).

What's My Name? As people arrive at a pack meeting, pin the name of a person or object on their backs. For a circus theme, it could be a circus performer or animal (clown, tall man, lion, etc.). For a citizenship theme, it could be the name of a president or statesman (George Washington, Patrick Henry, etc.). They move around the room, asking questions about themselves to try to find out who they are. Answers must be "yes" or "no" only. When the name is guessed, it is removed from the back and pinned on the lapel.

Laughing. Everyone in the audience laughs to a familiar tune, such as "Yankee Doodle" or "Row, Row, Row Your Boat." Use the same rhythm and tune; just sing "ha, ha" instead of the words.

You Never Saw It. Tell the group, "I have something in my pocket that you never saw before and you will never see again. Then take a peanut out of your pocket, crack the shell, show it to audience, and eat it. Say, "You never saw it before and you'll never see it again!"

Dark, Isn't It? Tell the audience that this is a test of intelligence, coordination, and the ability to follow directions. Have each person raise his or her left hand and point left index finger to the right, parallel to the floor. Then have them raise the right hand and hold the right index finger on a level with the left finger, pointing in the opposite direction. Then raise the left hand 2 inches and lower the right hand 2 inches. Now ask them to close their eyes. After a moment, remark innocently, "Dark, isn't it?

Who's Who? As people arrive at meeting, hand them a sheet of paper with the following descriptions printed on it. They are to move around the room and find someone who fits each of the descriptions. That person writes his name in a blank beside the description. A prize may be given to the person with the most blanks filled in.

Someone who wears size 8½ shoes:

Someone with blue eyes:

Someone who has a birthday in January:

Someone who plays a musical instrument:

Someone with red hair:

Someone with a younger sister:

Someone who likes liver:

Someone who speaks a foreign language:

Someone who was born in another state:

Someone who was a Cub Scout as a boy:

By necessity, some of the descriptions must be answered by an adult, which will cause an interchange between boys and adults in the meeting.

Spelling Mixer. Print a large letter on 5-by-8 cards—one letter to a card. Do not use the letters J, K, Q, V, X or Z. Make several cards with vowels on them. Have a card for each person in the group. Three adults act as judges.

On signal, people hold up their cards and rush around to find two letters that will make a three-letter word when added to the card they are holding. The three people lock arms and race to the judge, who writes the word on the back of their cards. Then they separate and rush back to find two more letters. This continues for 5 or 10 minutes. The winner is the person with the most words on his or her card.

Giant Sneeze. Divide audience into three groups. Explain that some people believe that a good sneeze clears the mind. Rehearse each group in one of the sounds.

"O-Hishie!"

"O-Hashie!"

"O-Hooshie!"

On leader's signal, everyone combines into one giant sneeze. The leader responds, "God bless you!"

Stand by Sixes. Audience—boys and adults—stand in large open area. They respond as leader shouts instructions, "Stand by sixes!" "Stand by threes!" "Stand by fours!" Groups of sixes, fours, etc. are quickly formed and stand together with arms around each other's waist. People who cannot find a group to join are eliminated from the game. The action is fast and exciting. Just as soon as groups are formed, leader shouts another command. Eventually most of the players will be eliminated. When there is only one group of six left, the command, "Stand by fours!" will eliminate two more players, and so on.

Prisoner's Escape. This is a good icebreaker for a den or pack meeting. As people arrive, tie a piece of string around the wrists of one person; loop another piece of string over that person's wrist and tie it to another person's wrists. They are now locked together. Challenge them to get away without breaking the string or untying the knot. The solution is to push the center of one string through the loop on the inside of the other person's wrist, bring this new loop back over his hand, and draw it back through the wrist loop. See illustration.

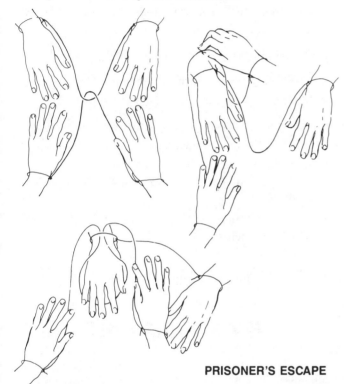

PRISONER'S ESCAPE

The Moon is Big and Round. This is a good campfire icebreaker. The leader says, "The moon is big and round. It has two eyes, a nose, and a mouth." As he says these words, he makes a sweeping circle with his left hand to indicate that the moon is big and round, makes dots in the air with his forefinger for the eyes and nose, and makes a small semicircular motion for the mouth.

Then he invites the audience to do exactly the same thing. Most everyone will fail and wonder why. The secret is that the motions are made with the left hand. Most people will use their right.

Lucky Handshake. Three or four people are secretly supplied with pennies before the meeting. As people arrive, they are encouraged to shake hands with everyone else. The tenth person to shake hands with anyone holding a penny receives the penny. This goes on for a predetermined time, when those holding pennies get to keep them.

Zodiac Madness. Provide copies of the chart and instructions for everyone. The object of this game is to have people get acquainted with as many people as possible.

To Play: Circulate and get acquainted. See if you can get a signature *and* birth date on the chart for each zodiac sign. Additional signatures with birth date and sign can go on the back of the page. If, at the end, *your* zodiac sign has not been filled in, you may put your name in for a score for that sign.

Scoring: Each signature ON THE CHART = 5 Points (60 points maximum).

Each signature on the back = 2 Points

Each birth date which is the same as yours = 10 Points

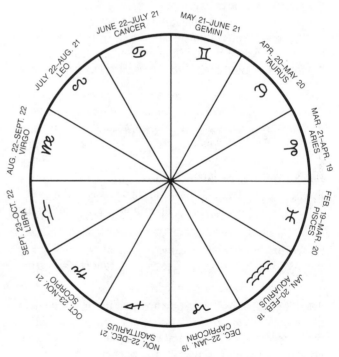

ZODIAC MADNESS

Name: _____ Birth Date: _____ Sign: _____

Score: _____

Stories

Of all the tools a Cub Scout leader can use, none can compare with the art of storytelling. Stories are a lead-in to many other parts of the program. You can tell a story:

- To introduce the monthly theme
- To explain a game
- To introduce a craft session
- While on a hike
- To explain advancement requirements
- To get across a point
- For a change of pace in activities
- For pure enjoyment and fun.

Stories may help boys develop a love of reading. Scouting's founder, Lord Baden-Powell, said, "If you can hand on something of the love of books to your Scouts, you will be giving them friends which will never fail them."

Cub Scout-age boys have great curiosity. They have been introduced to books and reading in school, but not always as a source of entertainment or pure enjoyment. A leader can take a book in hand, read a few well-chosen sentences, then put the book down and tell the story so it will come alive for the boys.

TYPES OF STORIES

Fun Stories. These can be fun for both the teller and the listener. Nonsensical stories lend themselves to the use of actions and sounds. They help everyone relax and enjoy themselves.

Adventure Stories. They always appeal to boys. They include such things as science fiction, fantasy, and true-life adventure.

Teaching Stories. This type can describe a moment in history, an invention or discovery, or a character-building attribute. Stories with a moral will help discipline without actually pointing a finger at any particular boy.

Animated Stories. These can be used to help boys learn pantomime. The leader tells the story while the boys act it out.

"What Would You Do?" Stories. These are action tales where the leader describes some dilemma and the boys provide the solution.

Mystery Stories. They appeal to boys and challenge them to solve the mystery before the story ends. Avoid anything gruesome or gory.

Be sure to use only stories that are in good taste and appropriate for Cub Scout-age boys and families.

HINTS ON STORYTELLING

In addition to the tips on storytelling found in the *Cub Scout Leader Book,* these suggestions will help you become a good storyteller:

- Be completely at ease. Know the story.
- Help put the listeners at ease. Make sure they are comfortable.
- Arouse interest with a catchy or exciting beginning.
- Create a setting or mood by descriptions.
- Make the story move. Maintain suspense.
- Match the speed and pitch of your voice to the action in the story.
- Keep the listeners' attention by varying the speed and tone of your voice and by using gestures where appropriate.
- Don't prolong a story unnecessarily. Decide beforehand how and when to end the story. A good ending is essential.
- Make the story short and to the point.

RESOURCES FOR STORIES

Stories can be found in thousands of books at public and school libraries, in *Boys' Life* and other magazines, and in newspapers. Personal experience is also a good source for story ideas. A Boy Scout may excite younger boys with tales of him camping or Jamboree experiences.

The following books are suggested:

Stories and Storytelling, by Angela Keyes

Story Telling, by Edna Lyman

Indian Why Stories, by Frank B. Linderman

Great Fables of All Nations, by Manuel Komroff

Fun With Skits, Stunts and Stories, by Helen and Larry Eisenberg

Handbook for Storytellers, by C. F. Bauer

Just So Stories, by Rudyard Kipling

Woodland Tales, by Ernest Thompson Seton

Tales for Telling, by Katherine Watson

Grandfather Tales, by Richard Chase

The Gospel of the Redman, by Ernest Thompson Seton and Julia M. Seton

Trail and Campfire Stories, by Julia M. Seton

Sample Stories

AN INDIAN LEGEND

Long, long ago seven boys who lived in a village belonging to the Cherokee Indians became famous because they were more interested in bowling stone hoops on the ground than in tending the cornfields. These boys were very skilled at bowling the hoops. But their mothers thought hoop-bowling was a useless pastime and forgot that by bowling hoops the boys learned many useful things.

In fact, the mothers were so sure that it was a useless pastime that they decided to cure their boys of laziness. They collected several stones, like those the boys used as hoops, and boiled them for their sons' supper instead of the usual corn. Then when mealtime came, the mothers said, "Since you like bowling stone hoops better than working the cornfields, you may eat stones or go hungry!"

The boys didn't like this treatment at all, so instead of being sorry and promising to spend more time working in the fields, they decided they would play all the time. They got together and began to dance around the village. They danced and danced and danced until their mothers noticed that the boys' feet were whirling through space in a circle. As they watched in desperate fear, the boys rose higher and higher. Up, up they went until they reached the sky.

Now, when you look at the sky on a clear night, you will see those seven boys. We know them as a constellation called the Pleiades. But the Cherokees call them the "Antitsutsa" or "The Seven Boys". (*Show a chart of the sky and stars and point out the constellation, or if telling the story outdoors on a clear night, point it out in the sky.*)

BENNY THE FROG

Benny was a big bullfrog who lived in a swamp. This swamp was just an ordinary swamp, with nice big lily pads, nice houses for the frogs to live in, running water, televisions, and a rowboat parked in front of every house. It was just like any other swamp.

One day Benny decided he needed to have something special that would make all the other swamp creatures envy him. He thought and thought and finally decided he would like to have a beautiful, long, white beard. He wished so hard that one day the Fairy Frogmother appeared and said, "Benny, I will grant your wish. But if I give you a beard, you must promise never, never to shave it off. For if you do, I will turn you into an urn!"

Benny promised he would never shave it off, so the Fairy Frogmother waved her magic wand, and "Poof!". . . a big, long, beautiful white beard appeared on Benny's chin.

After a while, Benny's neighbors heard about the beard and came to see it. Everyone came—the alligators, the muskrats, the snakes, the raccoons, the turtles, and even the dragonflies. Benny was very proud of his beard. For days and days the creatures came from everywhere in the swamp. And then after a while fewer and fewer came to see his beard, until finally, no one came at all. Benny wasn't so proud of his beard now as he had been at first. He was always tripping over it.

Finally, Benny just couldn't stand it any longer. He shaved! Suddenly the Fairy Frogmother appeared and said, "Benny, I warned you what would happen if you shaved your beard. Now I'm going to turn you into an urn!" So she waved her magic wand and "Poof!". . . Benny was turned into an urn.

That just goes to show you that a Benny shaved is a Benny urned!

THE GIFT OF TREES

The Indians believe that the secret of happiness comes from giving to others. Many, many moons ago when the Great Spirit first put man on the earth, man was frightened. "Where will I find food and water?" he asked. The trees laughed softly. "We are your brothers," they said. "We will help you."

The maple tree spoke up: "I will give you sweet water to drink and make into sugar." The elm tree said, "Use my soft bark to make your baskets and tie them together with my tough muscles." The hickory tree said, "My cousins and I will fill your baskets with sweet nuts." And he called the chestnut, beech, and walnut to help him. The great pine tree whispered softly, "When you get tired, little brother, I will make you a bed. My cousins the balsam and cedar will help me."

There was sunshine in man's heart as he set out to explore his new world. But soon he came to a deep, wide river. "How will I ever cross the river?" man asked. The trees laughed and laughed. "Take my white skin," said the birch. "Sew it together with the muscles of the elm tree and you can make a boat that will carry you across the widest river."

When the sun crossed the sky to his lodge in the west, man felt cold. Then the balsam fir tree whispered to him, "Little brother, there is much sunfire in my heart. Rub my branches together and you will make a fire." So man made fire. And that night he slept soundly on the branches of the great pine tree. The north wind blew cold, but there was sunshine in the heart of man.

Now when Indian children ask how they can repay their friends, the trees, a wise man answers, "They do not ask for payment. But you can give them care and attention. You can give love and care to every plant and flower that makes your life beautiful."

THE HEADLESS HORSEMAN AND THE CUB SCOUT

It was a dark and gloomy Halloween night in Sleepy Hollow land. The moon cast eerie shadows on the ground. Mike, a Cub Scout, was out trick-or-treating. Now Mike wasn't afraid of witches or goblins or ghosts, but those eerie shadows made him a little nervous.

All of a sudden, he heard the sound of hoofbeats coming near. He tried to reassure himself. "It's probably a friend," he thought, "but just in case it's not, I'll hide behind this tree." Mike picked out the biggest tree he could find and crouched behind it. The hoofbeats grew louder and sounded closer. Mike trembled in the dark. Just then a horseman came into view. He was dressed all in black. And Mike wished that he was home, safe in bed.

As he peered out from behind the tree to get a better look, he saw to his horror that something was terribly wrong with the rider. There was nothing where his head should have been! The horse reared up and the rider shouted, "Where's the crook who stole my head?"

Mike cringed and tried to make himself smaller, but the rider spied him behind the tree. Mike knew the must be brave, and he tried with all his might. He stood up tall and stepped from behind the tree. The rider pointed his long, bony finger at Mike and said in a fierce voice, "Are you the one who stole my head?" Mike answered in a strong voice: "A Cub Scout wouldn't steal!" The rider stomped and shook his fist in a fit of anger—in fact, he was shaking all over!

Mike couldn't help but laugh at the headless horseman. He said, "You have a terrible temper, sir, and your manners are even worse. If you'd learn some patience, maybe you would grow another head!" With this, the rider quickly turned his horse around and rode off into the night. Mike sighed with relief. He was still all right!

So remember this story, Cub Scouts. Try to have good manners wherever you are, or you too may lose your head!

I REMEMBER DAVY

This might be told by an old-timer dressed in frontier clothing, speaking slowly with a drawl.

I was a friend of ol' Davy Crockett. He was quite a man. Why, I remember Davy when he was knee-high to a milk cow. 'Course that was Davy when he was a baby—lyin' down! His cradle was 14 feet long. His ma had to put it up in a tree so the wind would rock little Davy to sleep.

I remember the day I was tryin' to drive some fence posts. Ground was frozen. Young Davy, he jumped along the tops of the posts, poundin' 'em with his feet. He kept goin' in one direction, 'cause if he jumped on 'em comin' back, those fence posts would have gone clean under the frozen ground!

I remember Davy's tame bear, Ol' Death Hug. That was some bear! One day he and Davy were ridin' in a log Davy had whittled out, racing a steamboat up the river. Davy was paddlin' and Ol' Death Hug was sittin' in the back, steerin' with his tail. Shame about that bear! Davy taught him to close doors and churn butter and the like. Blamed thing got so civilized that he caught the whoopin' cough and died.

One day Miz Crockett said Davy couldn't go huntin' till he finished grindin' a hundred bushels of corn. Davy saw a hurricane comin' so he grabbed holda that hurricane and hitched it up to his grindin' mill in nothin' flat. Why that cornmeal was so fine, Miz Crockett had to nail the corncakes to the table so they wouldn't float away.

I remember Davy the mornin' daybreak was frozen. Everything was frozen! That mornin' was dark as midnight. Davy climbed to the top of Daybreak Mountain and he saw that the whole world was frozen on its axis. Just wouldn't turn. Now Davy just happened to be carryin' a ton o' bear grease along, and he blew on that bear grease and melted it. Then he poured it on the earth's axis, and sure enough, the world started turnin' again and we got daybreak!

Then there was the time Davy ran fer Congress. We were all fixin' to vote fer him. Even the four-legged critters hoped he would go to Washin'ton. When we counted the votes, Davy was elected unanimously—plus 463 votes!

Yeah, I sure remember ol' Davy. He stood mighty tall for a man!

7 Tricks and Puzzles

Tricks and Puzzles in Your Program

Magic and mystery are two surefire ways to capture a boy's imagination. Almost everyone enjoys a trick or puzzle, and no one more than a Cub Scout-age boy.

The den leader or den chief will want to have a new trick or puzzle to show at almost every den meeting. This is a good preopening activity and will be very popular with the boys. The trick or puzzle should be simple enough for them to perform, since they will probably want to show it to a family member or a friend. Tricks can also be used in pack meetings, where the boys and their families can enjoy them together.

One of the most important secrets in doing a trick is to practice until you can do it perfectly several times in a row. It is boring and a little embarrassing to watch someone try to do a trick and barely fumble through it. The tricks and puzzles included here are mystifying at first but are easy to learn and fun to do. Materials needed for them can be found around the house.

Resources for Tricks and Puzzles

In addition to those found here, tricks and puzzles are also shown in the *Den Chief's Handbook, Cub Scout and Webelos Scout Program Helps, Group Meeting Sparklers,* *Cub Scout Magic,* and *Boys' Life.* Ideas can also be obtained at Cub Scout leaders' roundtables, pow wows, and workshops. In addition, public and school libraries have books of tricks and puzzles such as:

The Fun Encyclopedia, by E. O. Harbin

Cokesbury Stunt Book, by A. M. Depew

Be a Magician, by Jay Boyar

Perplexing Puzzles and Tantalizing Teasers, by Martin Gardner

Bet You Can, by Vicki Cobb and Kathy Darling

Bet You Can't, by Vicki Cobb and Kathy Darling

Super Colossal Book of Puzzles, Tricks and Games, by Sheila A. Barry.

Coin Tricks

MAGIC DIME

Break a wooden match half way through, being careful not to break it entirely. Lay it on a milk bottle and put a dime on top as shown in the illustration. Ask someone to make the dime fall in the bottle without touching the coin, match, or bottle.

Solution: Let a drop or two of water fall on the broken part of the match and it will move so the dime falls in the bottle.

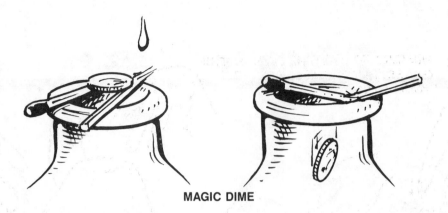

MAGIC DIME

THE EXPANDING HOLE

In the center of a piece of paper, cut a round hole about the size of a dime. Hand the paper and a quarter to a friend and ask him if he can pass the quarter through the hole without tearing the paper or touching the coin. He will be unable to do it.

Solution: Fold the paper in half so the fold bisects the hole. Slip the quarter between the folds. Hold the extreme ends of the paper where the fold is. Raise them upward and toward each other. Shake the paper gently and the quarter will slip through the hole.

NINE COINS

Rearrange these nine coins to form rows of four coins to a row.

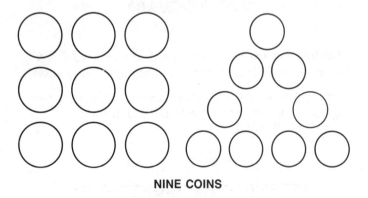

NINE COINS

STACK OF COINS

Make a neat stack of five or more pennies on a smooth table. With finger and thumb, flick a dime along the table so it hits the bottom penny of the stack. The bottom penny will fly out, leaving the rest of the pennies in the stack. You can repeat this, removing the bottom pennies one at a time.

Trick: The moving dime hits only the bottom penny. Its momentum is transferred to the bottom penny only. The rest of the pennies tend to stay in place and the stack just drops down. Notice that the dime bounces back a little. Also notice that if you push the bottom penny slowly with the dime, the whole stack will slide along. The bottom coin must be hit sharply.

FLYING COIN

Take a coin in each hand and stretch out your arms as far as possible. Tell everyone that you will make both coins pass into one hand without throwing the coin or bringing your arms together.

Trick: With your arms still outstretched, place one coin on the table and turn your body around until the hand with the other coin comes to where it lies. You can easily pick up the coin, and both will be in one hand while your arms are still wide apart.

THE DISAPPEARING COIN

Tell your audience that you will make a coin disappear. You drop the coin into a glass you are holding and show them the coin in the bottom of the glass which is in your hand. Cover the glass with a handkerchief and say some magic words. Then hand the covered glass to someone else to uncover. When the glass is uncovered, the coin will be gone.

Trick: Use a clear drinking glass with a flat bottom. When you pretend to drop the coin in the glass, you actually "plink" the glass with your ring. When you show the audience the coin in the glass, it is really under the glass in your hand. While the audience is looking at the empty glass in amazement, you can secretly hide the coin.

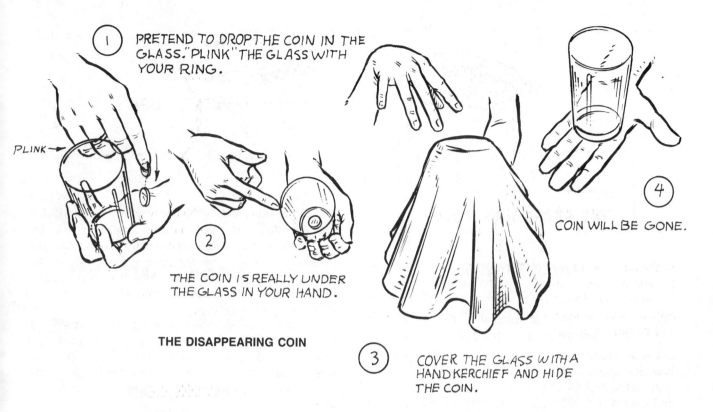

① PRETEND TO DROP THE COIN IN THE GLASS. "PLINK" THE GLASS WITH YOUR RING.

PLINK →

② THE COIN IS REALLY UNDER THE GLASS IN YOUR HAND.

THE DISAPPEARING COIN

③ COVER THE GLASS WITH A HANDKERCHIEF AND HIDE THE COIN.

④ COIN WILL BE GONE.

ANOTHER DISAPPEARING COIN

Show a dime in your right hand. Bend your left arm and put the left hand near your left ear. Put the coin on your left elbow and rub it with a circular motion of your right hand, keeping up a patter about making the coin grow smaller and smaller until it disappears. "Accidentally" drop the coin and pick it up with your left hand. Now pretend to transfer it back to the right hand, but actually keep the coin in your left hand. Go back to the original position with your left hand near your right ear. Resume rubbing the left elbow and keep talking about the coin growing smaller while you put it in your left ear. Now you are ready to show that the coin has disappeared by showing your empty hands. Then say that although it has disappeared, you can make it pass right through your head. Stick the phantom dime in your right ear, and presto! The real dime comes out the left ear.

CARD AND COIN TRICK

Lay a playing card on a glass and place a coin on top of the card. Ask if anyone can put the coin in the glass without picking up the card.

Trick: It's easy! Snap your finger against the card's edge,

sending it flying parallel off the rim of the glass. The coin will drop into the glass.

Match Tricks

MATCH SQUARE

Lay four matches with ends touching to form a cross. Ask someone to form a square by moving only one match.

Solution: Slide only one match out about $\frac{1}{16}$ inch to leave a tiny square opening between the match ends.

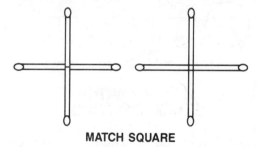

MATCH SQUARE

MATCH TRICK 1

Lay matches in the arrangement shown. Rearrange them to make only three squares by removing only five matches.

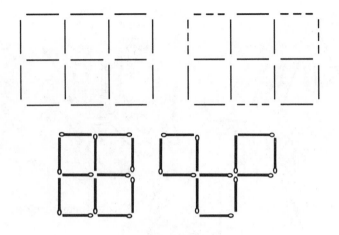

MATCH TRICK 2

Lay matches in the arrangement shown. Rearrange them to make three squares by removing only three matches.

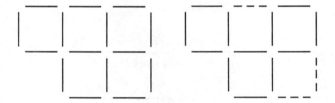

MATCH TRICK 3

Lay matches in the arrangement shown. Remove eight matches so there are only two squares left.

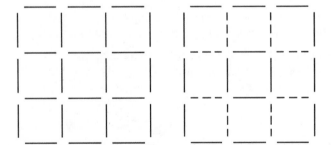

MATCH SWITCH

Hold a pair of matches between the thumb and forefinger of each hand. The stunt is to transfer them to the tips of the thumb and forefinger of the opposite hand.

Trick: Bring the hands together with the palms facing, one thumb up and one thumb down. By bending the thumb and forefinger, the ends of the matches can be reached and the two matches transferred.

Paper Tricks

PAPER ROPE

Twist a paper napkin into a rope and dare everyone to tear it apart. They can't and yet you can

Solution: Merely wet your fingers. When you tear the paper rope, touch the center with the water on your fingers and the napkin will tear easily.

STRONG PAPER

Ask if anyone has seen the new strong paper that will support a glass. Show an ordinary piece of paper and lay it as a bridge between two glasses. Naturally it won't support a glass. Then make ½-inch pleats in the paper and lay it on the two glasses again, and it will support another glass.

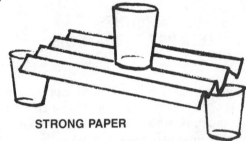

STRONG PAPER

STEP-THROUGH POSTCARD

Would you believe that you can crawl through an ordinary postcard? The answer is yes, if you know how. Fold the card lengthwise and make cuts on the folded side, as shown by the dotted lines in the illustration. Then turn the card around and make cuts in the other direction, almost to the folded edge. Open the card and cut along line A-B. Carefully open out the card and you will have a ring large enough to step through.

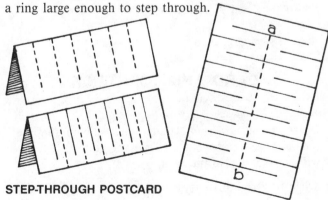

STEP-THROUGH POSTCARD

JACOB'S LADDER

Lay two double-page newspaper sheets together, end to end, overlapping about 5 inches. Starting at the narrow end, roll into a tube, as shown. Flatten the tube and tear a section out of the center of the roll as shown. Fold back the two rolled ends. Put a finger into the top of one of the tube ends and pull up the coiled paper for a few inches. Do the same on the other side. Gradually work the centers out of the rolled ends and the result is a paper ladder.

NEWSPAPER TREE

Make a roll of newspaper, as for Jacob's Ladder. Flatten half the tube and tear it down the center about halfway, as shown. Flatten the torn strips together and tear again down to about halfway. The four torn sections consist of several strips each. Press them down toward the rolled end of the paper so you can see an opening in the top. Put a couple of fingers in the opening and gradually begin to pull the strips out from the top until you have a finished tree.

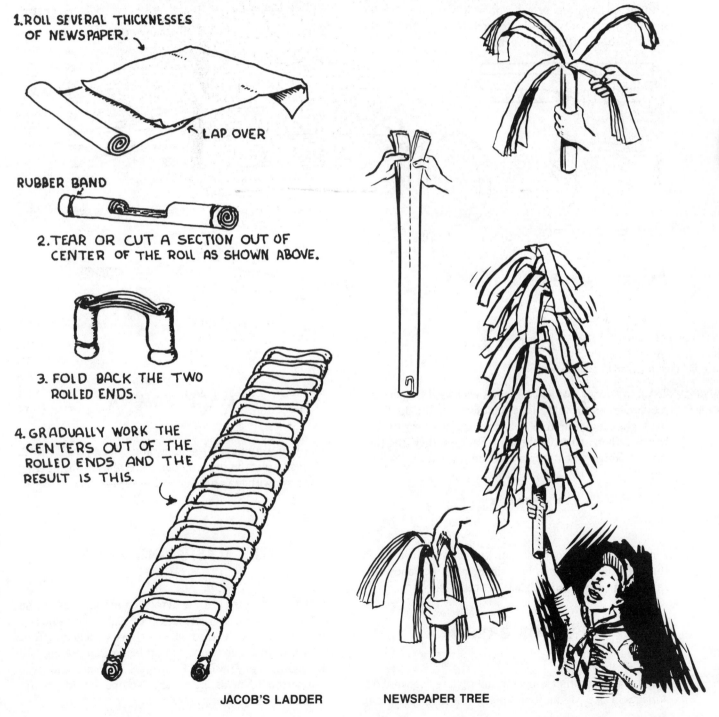

1. ROLL SEVERAL THICKNESSES OF NEWSPAPER.

LAP OVER

RUBBER BAND

2. TEAR OR CUT A SECTION OUT OF CENTER OF THE ROLL AS SHOWN ABOVE.

3. FOLD BACK THE TWO ROLLED ENDS.

4. GRADUALLY WORK THE CENTERS OUT OF THE ROLLED ENDS AND THE RESULT IS THIS.

JACOB'S LADDER

NEWSPAPER TREE

MOBIUS STRIP

Take a long piece of newspaper about one column wide. give it a half-turn and glue the ends together. Split the loop lengthwise and what do you have? Two loops? Surprise! You have one big loop. This looks like magic, but it really isn't. The mobius strip stays together when cut in half because it has only one continuous surface. A German mathematician discovered this principle more than 100 years ago. You can prove for yourself that it is one continuous strip by drawing a line the length of the strip without raising your pencil. You will come back to the starting point and will have covered both "sides" of the paper without lifting your pencil.

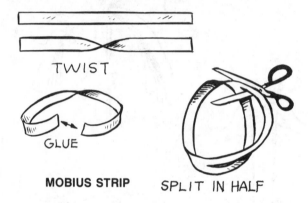

TWIST

GLUE

MOBIUS STRIP   SPLIT IN HALF

Miscellaneous Tricks

IT CAN'T BE DONE

Tell your friends that you can jump backward farther than they can jump forward, if they do exactly as you do. Prove it by grasping your toes and hopping backward a few inches. When assuming the same position, they find they cannot budge when they try to jump forward.

LEAPING SALT

Put a small amount of salt on the table. Run a comb through your hair. Then hold the comb 1 inch above the salt. It will leap up and stick to the comb.

RED OR GREEN?

Cut out a pig or other animal from bright red paper about 4 inches in size. Mount it on a piece of white paper. Hang the picture on the wall. Next to it, hang a large piece of white paper. With the light to your back, look the animal steady in the eye and count to 20, then look directly at the large sheet of white paper. There you will see a green animal. It will surprise everyone.

MAGIC STRAW

Cut a slit in the middle of a straw. Thread a string through it. Tell the audience you can cut the straw in half without cutting the string.

Solution: Bend straw, pull string out the slit, cut straw.

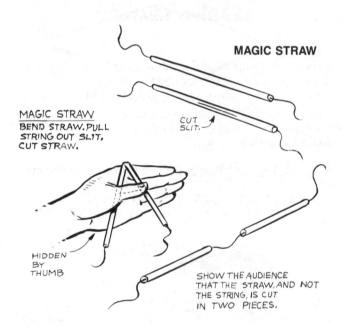

MAGIC STRAW

MAGIC STRAW
BEND STRAW. PULL
STRING OUT SLIT,
CUT STRAW.

CUT
SLIT.

HIDDEN
BY
THUMB

SHOW THE AUDIENCE
THAT THE STRAW, AND NOT
THE STRING, IS CUT
IN TWO PIECES.

MAGIC NUMBER

Think of a number. Double it, add 10, and divide by 2. Then subtract the first number. Regardless of the number you start with, the answer will always be 5.

THE MYSTIFYING PAPER

This is a good trick for a den meeting and requires an accomplice. Give everyone a slip of paper the same size and shape. Ask them to write a short sentence of four or five words. The words should be written plainly and not shown to anyone else. The papers are folded and given to a person acting as "guardian." No one should attempt to read the papers.

Ask the guardian to hand you one of the papers. Gravely close your eyes, place the folded paper against your forehead, and remain a moment in deep thought. Then call out any sentence and ask who wrote it. The boy who is the accomplice, and did not write a sentence, claims authorship. Unfold the paper, as if to verify it, and read the sentence to yourself. Place this paper in your left hand and ask the guardian for another.

Repeat the same procedure, calling out the sentence you just read. This will be a correct answer which one of the boys will have to admit writing. Keep this up until all players' slips have been read. The accomplice must keep your secret.

READING TEMPLES

Select an accomplice and send him from the room. Tell the group that thoughts can be transmitted by feeling a person's head. Have the group select a number between 1 and 10 and call the accomplice back in. Tell him to place his hands on your temples and after "serious concentration," name the number.

Solution: You can transmit the number by tightening and relaxing your jaw the required number of times, giving a movement of your temples that can be felt but not seen.

SEVERED THUMB

Hold the left hand flat with the palm facing toward you and thumb bent. Bend right thumb and slide along left forefinger, giving the illusion that the thumb is cut off.

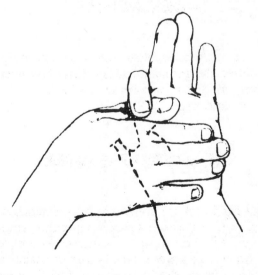

SEVERED THUMB

BAFFLING BANANA

Run a needle and thread under the skin and parallel to one side of a banana. Repeat on each side until a circle of thread is made around the fruit. Hold the needle and end of thread together and pull out the same hole. A cut will have been made through the fruit. Repeat this several times to cut banana in several slices under the skin. The small needle holes will not be apparent, and yet when you peel the banana, it will fall out in slices.

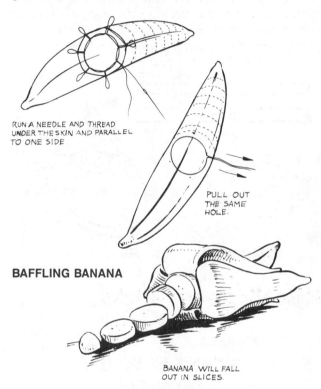

RUN A NEEDLE AND THREAD UNDER THE SKIN AND PARALLEL TO ONE SIDE

PULL OUT THE SAME HOLE.

BAFFLING BANANA

BANANA WILL FALL OUT IN SLICES.

FLOATING BALL

Hold a table tennis ball over the end of a soda straw, tip head back, and blow hard. Release the ball. It will stay suspended above the straw as long as you blow.

TABLE TENNIS BALL

BLOW SOFTLY.

TILT HEAD BACK.

FLOATING BALL

MYSTERIOUS MONEY

It appears that a dollar bill is cut in half, but the bill is returned to its owner untouched!

Solution: Cut a small slit in a small paper bag. Slide the bill into the bag, making sure that half of it goes through the slit. While you distract the audience with conversation, fold the bill over so it won't be seen or cut. Cut the bag in half and it seems the bill has been cut too. Then slide the bill out of the slot and return it to the grateful owner.

CUT SLIT IN SMALL BAG.

SLIDE BILL INTO SLIT...AND THEN FOLD BACK WHILE TALKIN' PATTER.

CUT THE BAG IN HALF, AND THEN GIVE THE COMPLETE BILL TO THE SURPRISED OWNER.

MYSTERIOUS MONEY

IMMOVABLE

Tell a friend you will hypnotize him so he cannot raise a foot. He will think this is impossible. Ask him to stand with his right side close to a wall that has no ledges or handles to hold. His right foot must be parallel to and touching the wall, while his left foot is at a natural standing distance from the right. Then go through various mysterious motions with your hands, making circles in front of his left foot, and announce that now he cannot lift the left foot slowly from the ground and keep it up.

Secret: To balance properly on the right foot so he can raise the left, he must lean to the right, and the wall prevents him from doing this.

PINHOLE ILLUSION

Take two business cards and punch three small holes in one with the point of a pin. These holes should be close

together, and they must not cover an area greater than the pupil of the eye. In the other card, punch a single hole. Hold the card with the three holes as close to your eye as possible and hold the other card about 2 to 3 inches in front of the first. When you look at a light, it will appear as if the far card has three holes in it also.

MAGIC SEED

Drop a grape seed into a glass of water. It drops to the bottom. At your command the seed will rise to the top and then sink to the bottom again.

Solution: What the audience doesn't know is that you are using seltzer water, not ordinary water. The gas in the seltzer clings to the seed and causes it to rise up. When the gas frees itself, the seed sinks. This will continue as long as gas is still in the water. Watch the seed carefully, and when you see it starting to rise or sink, give it that command.

SELTZER WATER INSTEAD OF REGULAR WATER

MAGIC SEED

HANDKERCHIEF TRICK

Tie two white handkerchiefs together, and then tie a colored handkerchief to one of the white ones. Ask someone to put the colored handkerchief between the two white ones without untying any of the knots.

Solution: Simply tie a third knot, making a circle of the three.

HANDKERCHIEF TRICK

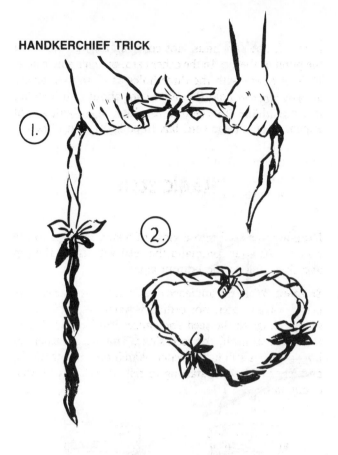

Solution: First move—turn over second and third glasses; second move—turn over first and third glasses; third move—turn over second and third glasses again.

DISAPPEARING KNOT

Tie an 18-inch piece of string so there is a loose, open, overhand knot in the center. Now tie the ends together with several knots so the string makes a loop. Let someone examine the string and explain that you are going to remove the overhand knot without untying the other knots. Place the string behind your back and in an instant produce it again showing that the overhand knot has disappeared from the loop.

Solution: While the string is behind your back, open the overhand knot out wide, and move it up and join all the other knots so it will not be noticeable.

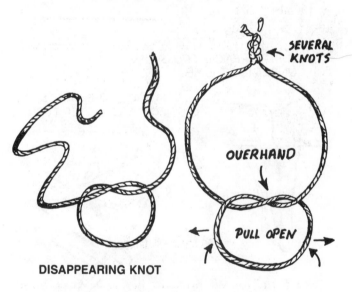

SEVERAL KNOTS

OVERHAND

PULL OPEN

DISAPPEARING KNOT

CANDLE BLOW

Prove you can blow a candle flame toward you by holding a card between yourself and the candle and blowing against the card. The flame will be drawn toward you.

BLACK MAGIC

Your accomplice boasts that he can leave the room and when he returns, name any object that the players have selected in his absence. The accomplice leaves, the players select an object, and the accomplice returns. You name one object after another, saying, "Is it (object)?" The answer is always, "No." You finally name the selected object and the accomplice says, "Yes, that's it!"

Trick: You name the correct article immediately after you name a black object. This is the accomplice's signal that the next one named will be right.

BOTTOMS UP

Stand three glasses in a row with the middle one upside down. Ask someone to turn all glasses bottom up, using three moves and picking up two glasses at a time, turning them over with each move.

BLOW HARD

Place three small bits of paper on the back of your hand. Let anyone select one of the pieces. Claim that you can control your breath so as to only blow away the chosen one. It sounds impossible.

Solution: Place two fingers on the other two bits of paper, then blow the chosen one away.

OBEDIENT STRAW

Tell the audience that you can make an ordinary straw obey your command. Put the straw on a table with your forefinger 6 inches in front of it. As you move your finger away from the straw, it follows.

Trick: As you move your finger, blow softly on the straw.

DISAPPEARING PENCIL

Hold the hands together, fingers extended, with a short pencil crosswise under the thumbs. Rotate the hands a quarter-turn (right fingers up, left fingers down), bending the right fingers over the left half of the pencil and the left hand. Bring the right thumb under the left thumb and palm, and continue the rotation, allowing the hands to turn over so both palms are down and the pencil has disappeared. To make the pencil reappear, reverse the motion by putting the right thumb over the left thumb and pencil and rotating the right thumb toward the left wrist, along the outside of the left thumb. Bring hands together as in the beginning with the pencil again under the thumbs.

① HOLD THE HANDS TOGETHER WITH A SHORT PENCIL CROSSWISE UNDER THE THUMBS.

② ROTATE THE HANDS FOR A QUARTER TURN.

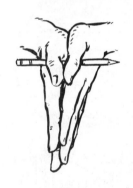

③ BRING THE RIGHT THUMB UNDER THE LEFT THUMB AND PALM.

④ CONTINUE THE ROTATION UNTIL BOTH PALMS ARE DOWN AND THE PENCIL DISAPPEARS.

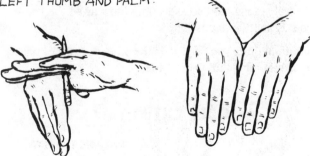

DISAPPEARING PENCIL

MYSTERIOUS ICE CUBE

You may not be able to saw a woman in half, but you can do a similar trick with an ice cube. Balance a ruler between two tall cans. Put an ice cube on the ruler. Twist an end of a long piece of wire around an unopened soup can or other heavy object. Run the wire over the ice and fasten it to the can so it is suspended. Soon the wire will pass through the ice cube. Has it been split in half or is it still in one piece?

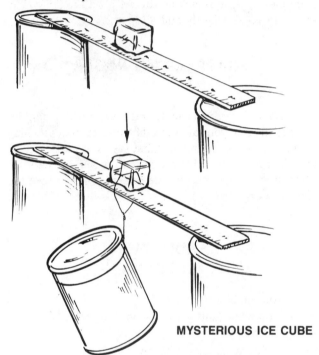

MYSTERIOUS ICE CUBE

MAGNETIZED RULER

Close the fingers of one hand on the ruler and then turn the back of that hand to the audience. With the other hand, take hold at the wrist. Explain that you must hold the hand with the ruler very steady. Slowly open and spread your fingers. The ruler will appear to be sticking to your hand.

Trick: Before you open your hand, slide the first finger of the hand holding the wrist onto the ruler. For added mystery, rub the ruler to your sleeve to "magnetize" it before starting the trick.

BALANCING EGG

This magic egg will stand upright when you hold it on the outstretched palm of your hand. It will balance in many queer ways on any flat surface.

Trick: The egg is a blown egg which contains some salt. To prepare it, pierce an egg at both ends and blow the contents out into a dish. Let the inside of the shell dry. Seal one end by pasting a tiny piece of tissue paper over it. Make a small funnel from paper and pour two teaspoons of salt into the shell. Seal the other end. At the end of your balancing act, place the egg out of sight.

Pick someone from the audience to try to balance the egg as you did, but give him a hard-boiled egg to use. Of course he can't do it. Then you take the hard-boiled egg and give it a little smack as you set it on the table. The shell will break slightly and allow the egg to balance.

DISAPPEARING WATER

Put a glass of water on a table and cover it with a napkin. Tell a friend that you can drink the water without touching the napkin. Walk around the table, say some magic words, and then ask him to lift the napkin to see if the water is still there. When he lifts the napkin, quickly take the glass and drink the water. You didn't touch the napkin, did you?

ELECTRIC DEN CHIEF

A den chief can master this trick with a little practice. When he's ready to perform, he tells the Cub Scouts he can light up a bulb with the electricity from his body.

Trick: Hold a small key-ring flashlight behind the frosted light bulb with the third and fourth fingers of the hand. The fourth finger exerts a twist to turn on the flashlight and make it appear that the bulb has lit. The frosted bulb will hide the flashlight from the Cub Scouts.

MONEY HAS POWER

Have someone hold a wooden pencil at both ends and parallel to the floor. After folding a dollar bill length-wise, announce to the group that you will break the pencil in half with the dollar bill, and ask them to give you three chances to do so. On the first two attempts, use only the dollar bill, but on the third, put your index finger in the fold of the bill and hit the pencil with your finger. The pencil will break if it is held firmly.

MAGIC HAT

Put three pieces of candy on a table and cover each with a hat. Lift the first hat, eat the candy, and put the hat back where it was. Do the same with the second and third hats. Now say, "You have seen me eat the candy under all three hats, but I can use magic so that all three pieces of candy are under one hat. Which hat do you choose?"

Trick: After the hat is selected, pick it up, put it on your head and announce, "Now the candy is under the hat."

Puzzles

BALANCING BAT

Here's a balancing act to mystify your friends. The bat will balance on the tip of your finger, the edge of a table, or the rim of a glass. Enlarge pattern and trace onto black poster board. Cut out bat and tape a penny to the underside of each wingtip. With a little practice you can make it appear to fly by balancing it on your finger and raising and lowering your hand.

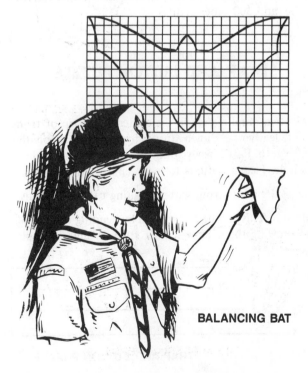

BALANCING BAT

BLOCK PUZZLES

Cut these puzzles from cardboard or plywood as shown. Mix up the pieces and see who can be the first to put them together.

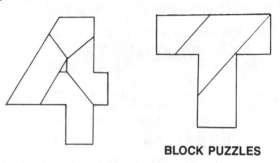

BLOCK PUZZLES

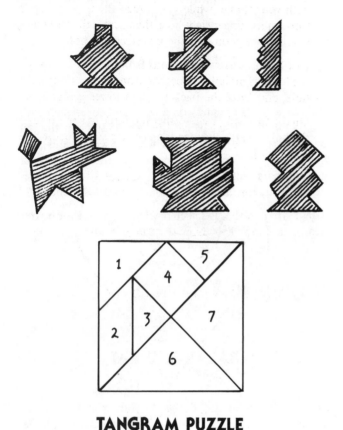

TANGRAM PUZZLE

It is said that this puzzler is over 3,000 years old. From a square of cardboard, cut seven pieces as shown in the illustration. Using all pieces you can make a square, a rectangle, and 100 other figures.

INDIAN WINDMILL

This windmill will amaze your friends. You can make the propeller revolve, stop, and reverse directions. To make the windmill, fasten a light propeller to the end of a notched stick or dowel with a pin or nail. Rub a pencil along the notched edge of the stick to set up vibrations that will cause the propeller to revolve rapidly. The direction can be controlled by light pressure with the thumb or forefinger on one side of the notched stick or the other. Do this without being observed and let people think it's willpower.

STRAP AND BUTTON PUZZLE

Make two parallel cuts in the center of a strip of firm, pliable leather, as shown. Just below this, cut a hole the same width. Pass a heavy string under the slit and through the hole. Fasten buttons to loose end of string.

Puzzle. Remove string without taking off the buttons.

Solution. This can be easily done by bending the leather and drawing the narrow leather strip through the hole.

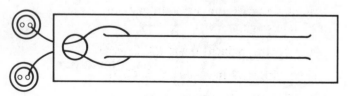

STRAP AND BUTTON PUZZLE

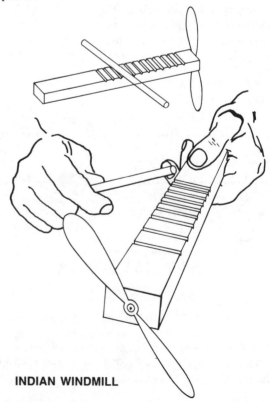

INDIAN WINDMILL

HOLIDAY JIGSAW

Cut up several old greeting cards into jigsaw pieces. Put each in a separate envelope. Boys can work these individually or the den can be divided into teams to see who can finish a puzzle first.

YOKE PUZZLE

1. Cut a strip of ⅜-inch wood, 3½ inches long and ½ inch wide, or use a wood tongue depressor or craft stick.

2. Drill a ¼-inch hole in center of wood. Drill a smaller hole ½ inch from each end.

3. Loop a 9-inch piece of string through the center hole, as shown.

4. Hang two washers on string.

5. Insert ends of string through holes in ends of wood and knot in place.

Puzzle. Move the two washers so they are hanging from the same loop. Do not untie the string, break the stick, or pull the knots through the holes.

Solution. Loosen the string slightly and pull the loop at the center hole straight out about 2 inches. Slide the left washer up the string and through the center loop. Then pull the rest of the center loop through the center hole. Slide washer along the string through center loop onto opposite side. Pull center loop back through hole to its original position. The washer is now hanging on the opposite loop. Reverse this procedure to separate the washers again.

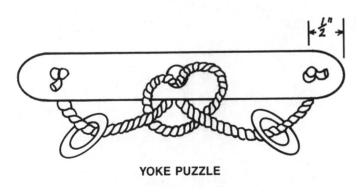

YOKE PUZZLE

HEART PUZZLE

Make a heart-shaped board 3½ inches high and 3½ inches wide. Bore six holes, as shown. Lace a 30-inch string to the heart in this manner:

1. Fold the string in the center and thread the loop from the back through the upper left hole. Hold it in place with your thumb while you thread the two free ends through the upper right hole, then across the front and through the loop and the upper center hole.

2. Next thread the two free ends from the back through the lower right hole, across the front to the lower right hole, and from the back through lower center hole.

3. On the free ends, tie a washer too large to slip through the holes. Make a 6-inch loop of free string below the center hole.

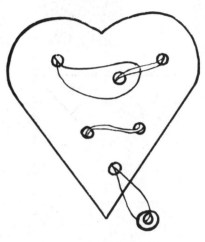

HEART PUZZLE

Puzzle. Remove the string from the heart without untying the washer.

Solution. Draw in all the free string from the washer end, up to the loop end at the upper center hole. Now thread the loop back through the center top hole to the lower right hole, lower left hole, and lower center hole. Don't twist the string. Then slip the washer through the loop, thread the loop back again through the hole, and it will come off.

SLIDING BLOCK PUZZLE

An adult who likes to work with wood can make these puzzles for the boys.

1. Make a box with inside measurements 3⅝ inches square.

2. All puzzle blocks are made from ⅜-inch wood. Cut the following:

   Four blocks ⅞ inch square (D, E, F, G)

   Three blocks ⅞ inch square (B, C, H)

   One block 1¾ inches square (A)

3. Sand all blocks and stain or paint.

Puzzle. Slide the blocks and move the largest one to the diagonally opposite corner and back.

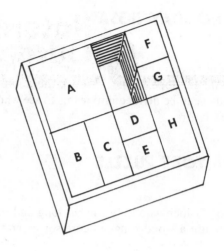

Solution:

1. A right
2. B up
3. C left
4. DE left
5. H Left
6. FG down

7. A right, DE up, H left, FG left
8. F right and down
9. A down
10. D right, E up and right, H up
11. G left and up, F left, A down

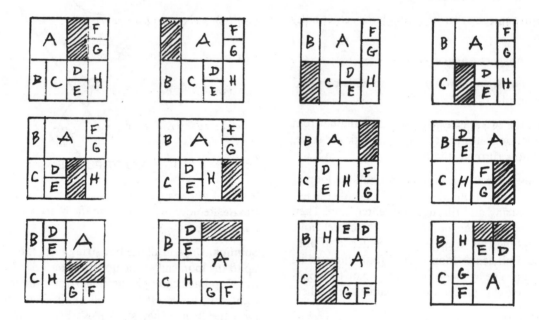

SLIDING BLOCK PUZZLE

8 Nature and Outdoor Activities

Introduction

Outdoor activities are an important part of the Cub Scout program. Cub Scouts learn to appreciate and care for our beautiful outdoors as they hike, explore, and investigate the world around them. The Cub Scout outdoor program is a foundation for the outdoor adventure they will experience when they move on to a Boy Scout troop.

Cub Scouts should be given opportunities to enjoy the outdoors in the spring, summer, fall, and winter. Included in this section are nature and outdoor activities for both the city and the country during all four seasons.

Health and Safety

The health and safety of the boys, leaders, and families must be one of the first considerations in planning any outdoor activity. Try to anticipate and eliminate hazards — or at least warn against them. Most accidents can be prevented. See pages 92–97 in the *Cub Scout Leader Book* for the safety rules for outdoor activities, the Safe Swim Defense, and Safety Afloat.

Also follow these tips when planning and conducting an outdoor activity:

- Always get permission from parents or guardians for activities that are held away from the regular den and pack meeting places. Better yet, take the families with you.

- Be sure to have sufficient adult leaders for the activity planned.

- Check out the site prior to the activity. Find out about gathering places, restroom facilities, safe drinking water sources. Look for hazards such as poison ivy.

- Get permission from the owner to use the property.

- Use the buddy system to prevent anyone from getting lost. Coach the boys in advance what to do if lost.

- Carry a first aid kit and know how to use it. Be prepared with emergency procedures.

- File a Local Tour Permit with the local Scout council office a couple of weeks in advance for trips which will last several hours or are a distance away from your regular meeting place.

- Have adequate and safe transportation. (See pages 95 and 129–130 in the *Cub Scout Leader Book*.)

- When leaving the site, take everything you brought with you. Leave site in its natural condition.

What To Do If Lost

Have boys learn the following five steps which are recommended by the National Association for Search and Rescue. They could save a life.

1. **Hug a tree.** As soon as you realize you are lost, stop walking and "hug" a tree. That is, stay put. Searchers will look for you first at the spot where you were last seen. The closer you are to that place, the faster you will be found.

2. **Take shelter.** It's easy to carry along a shelter that folds up and fits into your pocket. It's a big plastic leaf bag. Cut or tear a hole in the closed end for your head to fit through. Then slip the bag on like a poncho. Be sure to keep your face uncovered so you can breathe.

3. **Save body energy.** If the weather starts to cool off, curl up like an animal in the cold. That will help conserve body heat and energy. Snuggle against a log, a rock, a hill, or anything that will shield you from the wind.

4. **Make yourself "BIG."** Always carry a whistle when you go hiking. If you hear or see rescuers, make a BIG noise. Blow your whistle, shout, or pound rocks together. If you spot a search plane, stretch out on the ground face up and make slow, sweeping motions with your arms as if you are making a snow angel.

5. **Remember that people are searching for you.** The longer you are lost, the more people will join the search. If you hear people yelling, don't be frightened. They're exchanging information over wide areas, doing their best to find you. Remember, the searchers won't give up. They will find you.

For more information about what to do if you're lost, write to Hug-a-Tree, National Association for Search and Rescue, Box 2123, La Jolla, CA 92038.

Resources for Nature and Outdoor Activities

Ideas for nature and outdoor activities can be obtained at the monthly Cub Scout leader roundtable, the annual pow wow, workshops, and in *Boys' Life* and Scouting magazines.

Books on outdoor activities are abundant at public libraries. Here are a few. For more information and BSA catalog numbers see "Resources" section of this book.

Introduction to Family Camping

Introduction to Cub Scout Camping

Growing Up Green, by Alice Skelsey and Gloria Huckaby

Sharing Nature With Children, by Joseph B. Cornell

Foxtails, Ferns and Fish Scales, by Ada Graham

The Kids' Garden Book, by Patricia Petrich and Rosemary Dalton

The Incredible Year-Round Play Book, by Elin McCoy

Golden Book of Nature Crafts, by John R. Saunders

Kids' Outdoor Gardening, by Aileen Paul

Invite a Bird to Dinner, by Beverly C. Crook

Puddles and Wings and Grapevine Swings, by Imogene Forte and Marjorie Frank

Exploring as You Walk in the City, by Phyllis Busch

Collecting for the City Naturalist, by Lois Hussy and Catherine Pessino

Science in a Vacant Lot, by Seymour Simon

Golden Nature Guides (many different subjects)

Background Roughing It Easy, by Diane Thomas

Your Own Book of Campcraft, by Catherine Hammett

Campfire Adventure Stories, by Alan MacFarlan

Creative Campfires, by Douglas R. Bowen

Campfire Programs, by Jack Pearse

Good Times Around the Campfire, by L.A. Thurston

Materials From Nature

Do not take any nature objects without permission. There are penalties for removing some natural items from local, state, and federal properties, and of course taking things from private property without permission is stealing.

Live trees should never be cut without the owner's permission. If you are collecting wood, take only down branches and twigs (with permission).

Cedar is an excellent whittling wood. Its heartwood has a beautiful color.

Hickory is one of the best woods for making coals for cooking. Slender green branches may be bent for making frames and cooking utensils. Nuts are excellent to eat.

Willow shoots are good for weaving baskets. Willow can be used to make whistles.

Bark can be used for pictures, collages, greeting cards, block printing.

Pine Needles can be used for weaving, basketry, and making pillows and brooms.

Pine Cones are used for making Christmas tree ornaments, unusual animals, mobiles, bird feeders.

Berries can be used for dyeing or staining and strung for ornaments.

Cattail leaves can be used for weaving, basketry, or decorative arrangements. The roots can be eaten.

Cornhusks can be used to make braided sandals, baskets, brooms, etc. They can be dyed with fabric or native dyes.

Corncobs can be used for figures, animals, puppets, block printing.

Cornstalks can be used for whistles, animals.

Gourds can be used for dishes, salt and pepper shakers, birdhouses, rhythm band instruments, and decorations.

Nature Rambles, Hikes, Hunts, Games, and Field Trips

Always use the buddy system on rambles, hikes, and field trips for safety and to prevent anyone from getting lost. Buddies remain together at all times.

NATURE RAMBLES

A nature ramble is a short hike. It might be in your own backyard or a nearby park or playground, or even a stroll around the block. The object is for the boys to get a closer look at what they see outdoors every day. Take along a selection of pocket-sized field guides. Talk about why each thing is growing where it is; what eats it or is eaten by it; what the buds on twigs become; the purpose of a tree leaf, etc. (Do not remove growing things from their natural habitat.)

NATURE FIELD TRIPS

For a nature field trip, visit a nature center, natural history museum, fish hatchery, zoo, or game sanctuary. See pages 52 and 84 of the *Cub Scout Leader Book* for information on planning and conducting field trips.

———————HIKES———————

When did you last watch a colony of ants? Or investigate a hollow tree? Or travel an unbeaten path? These are just a few things that you and the boys can do when you go hiking. The fun lies in observing everything around you as you hike, and while observing, talk about what you see.

A hike is simply a long ramble. The boys may gather specimens for their collections and a pack meeting display. Try plaster casting an animal or bird track (see *Bear Cub Scout Book* and the "Crafts" section of this book) or make prints of leaves. There are many types of hikes, some which include nature activities. Several nature hikes are described here. See pages 56-57 of the *Cub Scout Leader Book* for other types of hikes and for hiking safety rules.

EARLY SIGNS OF SPRING HIKE

Hike in an area where there are flowering plants, shrubs, and trees. Make a list of what you see and try to identify them, using field guides. Hike in the same area a couple of weeks later and notice the changes.

BABY HIKE

Look for nature babies—birds, fern, leaf, snail, etc. How are the babies protected? How are they fed? Do not touch baby birds or animals. Look only from a little distance. Most "abandoned" babies really aren't. Mother may be nearby.

TRACKS OR SIGNS HIKE

Look for all types of animal signs. Identify bird and animal tracks. Make plaster casts.

CATERPILLAR HIKE

Take the boys to a secluded spot. Blindfold them and arrange them in a line, caterpillar fashion, with each boy placing his hands on the shoulders of the boy ahead of him. (More than six segments to a caterpillar is hard to manage) With a den chief or adult leading each group, ask them to identify sounds, smells, and touches they experience. The sound of ducks might indicate a pond or marsh; fragrance could mean flowers, etc.

MICRO-HIKE

Lay out several strings 3 to 5 feet long. The boys cover the trail inch by inch on their stomachs, with eyes no higher than 1 foot off the ground. They may see such wonders as grass blades bent by rainbow dewdrops, colorful beetles sprinkled with flower pollen, powerful-jawed eight-eyed spiders, and more. Ask questions to stimulate their imagination: "What kind of world are you traveling through?" "Who are your nearest neighbors?" "Are they friendly?" "Do they work hard?" "What would life be like for that beetle—how would he spend his day?"

UNDERCOVER HIKE

Preparing for this hike creates an atmosphere of suspense which the boys will love. You can camouflage yourselves by wearing clothes to match the colors of the area to be hiked. You may want to darken your faces and hands.

Tell the boys, "We're going on a special mission. Our objective is to search the surrounding area thoroughly, missing nothing. We are to observe and remember everything we can about what we see. It is important that we stay hidden and unseen." On the hike, try to stay under or near cover. Move slowly, pausing every few steps to look around and listen. Avoid walking in the same direction as the wind so your scent won't be carried ahead of you.

BIG GAME HUNT

This will help boys learn to identify animals. See how many different species you can see. Each boy makes his own list to see who can "capture" the most.

TOUCH AND FEEL HIKE

This hike will illustrate how nature is made up of many textures. Boys are instructed to touch and feel, not take, any of the objects found. They are to look for:

- The hairiest leaf
- The softest leaf
- The smoothest rock
- The roughest rock
- The roughest twig
- Something cool
- Something warm
- Something dry
- Something bumpy

Ask questions like: "What did you find that was dry? Why was it dry?" "How might it be different tonight? Next summer/winter?" "How did it get there?" "Does it belong there?" "Did people have anything to do with it being there?" "Has it always been the way it is?"

NIGHT HIKE

In areas where it is safe to go walking at night, try a hike after dark. See how different things look, smell, and sound at night. Don't use flashlights as they will lessen your ability to see and reduce awareness of what is happening out in the dark. Carry flashlights for emergency use only.

GET-TOGETHER HIKE

Two or more dens hike to a location for games, songs, and fun.

BREAKFAST HIKE

Hike to destination in time to see sun rise, then cook breakfast outdoors.

HEADS-TAILS HIKE

Toss a coin each time you reach a crossroad. Turn left if the coin turns up heads, right if the coin is tails.

CRAYON HIKE

Have each boy select five crayons and color an area of each on a piece of paper. Take the paper on a hike and write each object found that matches one of the colors.

INCH HIKE

Find as many objects as possible that are 1 inch high, long, wide, etc. Take small rulers along. This helps boys discover the small things that might otherwise be overlooked.

ABC HIKE

Write the letters of the alphabet vertically on a piece of paper. On hike, find an object, sound, or smell in nature for each letter.

OBSTACLE HIKE

Some boys have never climbed a tree, walked a log, climbed through a fence, chinned themselves on a tree branch, etc. To give them this experience, pick a trail which will provide such an obstacle course.

STRING ALONG HIKE

Take a 36-inch piece of string on your hike. Every now and then, place the string in a circle on the ground. See how many different things you can find enclosed in the circle. Then stretch string in a line and see how many different things touch it.

Described here are some things to do when stopping for a rest while on a hike.

SENSE OF TOUCH

Each boy finds a fist-size rock, remembering where he found it so it can be returned after the game. All sit in a circle with eyes shut, holding rock. They are told to get to know their rocks by the feel, texture, smell, etc. After a few minutes the rocks are collected, mixed, and redistributed in a different order. Now the rocks are passed around the circle and boys try to identify their own rocks with eyes still shut. To help prevent any disagreements, affix a small piece of tape to each rock with the owner's initials. Remove the tape before you leave!

MAGIC LEAF

This is similar to the rock game. Each boy gets to know his leaf by its shape, size, veins, etc. Then put all leaves in a pile and let one boy at a time try to find his.

GRAB BAG

Collect about 15 nature items such as pine cones, nuts, shells, etc. and place each in small paper sack. Pass the sacks around the circle of boys and let them try to identify the object by feeling the bag.

NATURE TRAIL

Make up your own nature lore trail using the features available in your area. If it is a wooded site, tree and leaf identification are possible. If it has a stream, include a station on spotting marine life or water insects. The trail must be prepared in advance. It should have five to 10 stations. At each station the den is to find something, identify something, or otherwise show knowledge of nature lore.

This is a den competition to test nature skills. It is not a race. Dens start at intervals of about 5 minutes. At each station they find a message under a rock which tells them what to do. They have a scorecard on which they write their findings, then move on to the next station. It will help to have an adult at each station to provide assistance and make sure the message is replaced under the rock.

The sample nature trail which follows is suitable for a small wooded park.

Station 1. "Look for the biggest tree you can see from here. What direction is it? Write the direction on your scorecard. Go northwest to a picnic table and look under it."

Station 2. "Within 15 paces of this spot, there are five different kinds of trees. Write the names of two of them. Go south 50 paces and find a small mound of pebbles."

Station 3. "Within 20 feet of here, there is a clump of wildflowers. Write down its name. Go east until you come to a tree with a split trunk. Look around its base."

Station 4. "Somewhere in this tree there is a nest with young birds. Spot it, but do not disturb the nest or birds. Try to identify the name of the birds from the shape of the nest. Write down what kind of birds you think they are. Go north toward the entrance to the park. Near the gate, look for two rocks, one on top of the other."

Station 5. "Within five paces of this spot there is an insect's home. Find it and write down the name of the insect. (Could be an ant colony, beehive, wasps' nest, etc.) Go southeast until you come to a seesaw. Look under one of the seats."

Station 6. "Ten paces due east of this spot is an animal track. What is the animal?" (If there is no real animal track, use a plaster cast of a cat's track.) "Go due east until you come to a weedy patch. Look along its edge."

Station 7. "Pick up a leaf or a bit of grass and toss it in the air. What is the wind direction? Write it on your card. Go north 30 paces and look under the pile of rocks."

Station 8. "Look around you. There is a wooded area, a small pond, and a grassy lawn. Remember that animals need different kinds of places to live. Which of the following animals do you think live near here: Deer, bee, squirrel, rabbit, lion, muskrat, dragonfly, chipmunk, elephant, bear, skunk, frog, ant, mouse, leopard, cricket. Write down the animals you think live around here. Then go southwest until you come to a drinking fountain. Look around its base."

Station 9. "Within 10 yards of the fountain is a bush whose berries and seeds are important food for some birds. Pace off the distance from the fountain. Write down the number of paces. For an extra point, write the name of the bush. Then return to Station 1 and turn in your scorecard."

Have judges ready to check scorecards and post each den's ranking on a chart. Give an inexpensive prize to the winning den, with treats for all dens.

NATURE SCAVENGER HUNT

This hunt is intended to test the boys' knowledge of nature in an exciting competition. It is run like any scavenger hunt, with each den having a list of nature objects and identifying as many as possible in a time limit. Boundaries should be established and a time limit set (10 to 20 minutes). The list should have 20 to 50 objects from nature that can be found within the area. They should be common enough that a Cub Scout can identify most of them.

Your list will reflect the nature items which can be found in your locale. These are some suggestions:

- Anthill
- Oak leaf
- Maple leaf
- Dandelion
- Needle from an evergreen
- An insect
- An animal home
- A cocoon
- A spider web
- Animal track
- Bird's nest
- Barrel cactus

Fun With Collections

LEAF COLLECTIONS

One of the best ways to learn to identify trees is by their leaves. Leaves can be preserved by drying or by sealing them with a wax or glycerine solution. Leaf prints can be made in several ways. Plaster casts can also be made of leaves. (See "Crafts" section of this book.)

DRYING LEAVES

1. Select a leaf that is fully grown and has not been damaged by insects. Keep it in a sealed plastic bag until ready to dry.

2. Lay the leaf between a folded sheet of newspaper. Add several more layers of newspaper underneath and on top. Cover with a board the same size as the newspaper.

3. Weight the newspaper pad with books or rocks. Leave to dry for about 10 days, changing the inside layers of newspapers every few days.

MOUNTING LEAVES

1. Glue the dried leaf to mounting paper, such as cardboard, large index cards, construction paper, or a scrapbook page. Thick stems can be held in place with tape.

2. Label with name and location of tree and date.

3. Dried or fresh leaves can be protected with transparent adhesive-back plastic.

MAKING A LEAF SKELETON

The delicate veins of a leaf can be seen by removing the fleshy part of the leaf. This will allow you to see the network of leaf veins through which the leaf got the raw materials (minerals and water) needed to make food that was carried through the veins to the rest of the tree. Use a fresh, green leaf with tough veins, such as an oak leaf.

1. Place leaf on an old piece of carpet or a pad made from several thicknesses of felt or soft cloth.

2. Tap leaf with a hairbrush and shoebrush. Periodically turn leaf over to tap the other side. Continue tapping until only the veins are left.

3. Dry the leaf skeleton between layers of weighted newspaper. Then mount on paper or between two pieces of glass held together with tape.

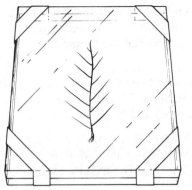

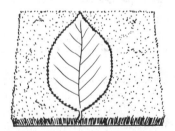

MAKING A LEAF SKELETON

SEED COLLECTIONS

Collecting Seeds. Collecting tree, flower, vegetable, and plant seeds can be an interesting hobby. Seeds come in a variety of sizes, shapes, and colors. Collect seeds at home and while on hikes. To add interest to the collection, also gather seed pods, such as pine cones.

Storing Seeds. Seeds can be stored in glass pill bottles, plastic coin tubes, square and rectangular plastic boxes. For larger seeds such as walnuts, acorns, pecans, Brazil nuts, and peanuts, use plastic or cardboard egg cartons.

Cataloging Seeds. The best way to catalog seeds is to label each jar or box with the name. Self-sticking labels work well. Cardboard tags with strings can be used for labeling pine cones or similar large items. Another way to catalog seeds is by large categories, such as trees, flowers, etc., or group them by the way they are dispersed, such as winged seeds, popping seeds, edible seeds, etc.

Displaying the Collection. To display the collection, the seed bottles or vials can be wired to heavy cardboard or a piece of plywood.

SHELL COLLECTIONS

The study and collection of shells is called conchology. Empty shells are often weather-beaten and chipped. To get perfect shells, it is usually necessary to find and collect live mollusks and clean out the shells. Land snails can be found on dry land, but most mollusks live in fresh and salt waters. Many can be found along rocky and sandy ocean shores.

The best time for collecting sea mollusks is during low tide. Since tides run at different times each day, check the local newspaper or radio for the correct time. Shells will chip easily, so wrap them individually in small pieces of newspaper. To restore the natural luster of shells, rub them lightly with mineral oil.

Tiny shells can be kept in small bottles with screw caps or corks. Medium shells may fit into matchboxes. Larger shells can be kept in cardboard boxes. Shells can be mounted on cardboard with household cement. Each shell should be identified and labeled.

For a special display, glue shells to golf tees with household cement. Then press the points of the tees into a piece of styrofoam.

ROCK AND MINERAL COLLECTIONS

A good place to find rock specimens is in road beds, river beds, roads under construction, and building excavations.

Choose rock and mineral specimens carefully. Don't pick up just anything. Wrap each in a piece of newspaper with a card to show where you found it.

Rocks can be chiseled to standard size (such as 2-by-3 inches) with a geologist's hammer or a regular hammer and a cold chisel. (Be sure to wear protective glasses when chiseling.)

Label rocks by attaching a small label to the underside with transparent tape or by painting a small white spot on which you can write the identification. Show the type of rock, where it was found, and the date.

Small rocks can be kept in pill bottles. Larger rocks may be kept in sectioned boxes or egg cartons.

ROCK AND MINERAL COLLECTIONS

COLLECTING INSECTS

Encourage boys who have insect collections to prepare them correctly, mount them properly, and display them

attractively. This means more than just pinning insects in cardboard boxes with ordinary pins.

Finding Insects

Grasses and weeds contain numerous crawling and jumping insects. Insects can be found feeding on leaves of trees or shrubs or hiding in the bark. Flowers attract butterflies, moths, bees, flies, and other species. Streams and lakes contain hundreds of species—some scurrying over the surface, some swimming, others crawling on the bottom or hiding under stones.

Catching Insects

Try holding an umbrella under a shrub while you beat the branches with a stick. Insects will fall into the umbrella where they are easily captured. Other insects can be attracted to a jar which has a small amount of fruit pulp or molasses inside. Other insects can be captured in a net.

Killing Insects

Insects for collection are killed by exposing them to fumes of various chemicals in tightly closed "killing jars." For a nonpoisonous killing jar, put a circle of cotton batting in the bottom of a jar with a screw-top. Add about ½-inch of nailpolish remover, cover the jar, and allow it to stand for a day. Pour off excess liquid. To use the killing jar, simply drop the insect into the jar and cover it tightly. Remove the insect within an hour and move it to a relaxing box until the legs and wings can be moved freely.

Mounting Insects

Never use regular pins for mounting insects. They are too coarse and may bend and rust. Use insect pins, which are available in different sizes. The pins should be placed in locations that will leave the identifying marks undisturbed. Moths and butterflies must be dried on a spreading board with their wings spread out flat. (See an insect guide for more information on mounting.)

Displaying Collection

Insects can be displayed in Riker mounts (shallow, cotton-filled cardboard boxes with glass covers) or in a homemade version made from a cotton-lined box covered with acetate.

Fun With Plants

MAKE A TERRARIUM FOR PLANTS

A terrarium can be used for a miniature garden which will grow the year round. The "Crafts" section of this book shows a terrarium made from a 2-liter plastic bottle. There is another type, made from a glass container.

You will need:

A large wide-mouth glass jar with lid, or a fishbowl with a cover made by a plain glass dish or plastic film

Fine-to-medium grade gravel

Horticultural grade gravel

Charcoal

Soil separator (piece of nylon or other synthetic material)

Terrarium soil

Plants (ferns, matted mosses, wild strawberry, violets, evergreen seedlings)

Spoon, scissors, tamping tool

1. Clean and dry container. If using a jar, lay it on its side.

2. Spoon ¾-inch gravel into bottom of container for drainage. Sprinkle in enough charcoal to cover gravel. This will absorb odors.

3. Cut the soil separator to fit on top of charcoal. This will keep soil out of the drainage material.

4. Spoon 1 inch of soil on top of separator. Use ready-mix terrarium soil or mix your own by using 1 cup sterilized potting soil, ⅔-cup Perlite and ⅓-cup peat moss.

5. Make a hole in soil and add largest plant. Scoop some soil around base to hold it in place. Add remaining plants in same manner.

6. Add more soil, so that soil layer and drainage material fills about ¼ of the container. Tamp down soil.

7. Water terrarium slowly. Put on cover.

8. Place in bright to medium light, not in direct sunlight.

Check the terrarium the next day to be sure there is a correct moisture balance. It should have a light mist on the inside of the glass, and the soil should be medium dark. Too much water will cause a heavy mist and can be corrected by leaving the cover half-open for a day. If there is too little water, there will be no mist at all. In this case, add a teaspoon or water every other day until terrarium moisture is balanced.

To maintain the terrarium, give it a little fresh air every week or two by removing the top for 15 minutes at a time. Trim the plants when necessary.

SEALED WORLD

This project illustrates how everything in nature depends on something else. It is a self-sufficient world of plants and small animals that will last a month or longer, but you should return your specimens to the pond before they die.

You will need:

A large wide-mouthed jar, 1-gallon minimum

Sand or sandy soil

Water plants

Water from a pond

1. Put about 1½ inches of sand or sandy soil in bottom of jar.

2. Plant five or six water plants, such as eel grass, cabomba, and elodea, which can be obtained from a tropical fish dealer.

3. Fill the jar to where the neck narrows *with water from a pond*. It may look lifeless, but it contains plankton—tiny plants and animals. By the next den meeting, the water will have cleared and tiny animals can be seen swimming about.

4. Add a snail and two minnows not more than 1-inch long. Put the screw top on the jar and seal it with tape.

5. Keep the jar where it will get indirect sunlight. With no further attention, the sealed world should sustain itself almost indefinitely.

What happens? The green plants use light, minerals from the soil, and the carbon dioxide exhaled by the plankton, fish, and snail. The fish eat the plankton, but the tiny plankton keep multiplying so the food supply will last a long time. The snail eats plankton, too, but it is a scavenger that also feeds on the tiny plants growing on larger plants and the glass. This is an excellent demonstration of what scientists call the web of nature.

SPONGE GARDEN

Because a sponge holds water in its many small cavities, it's an ideal surface on which to grow seeds. Soak a sponge and place it in a shallow dish of water. Sprinkle seeds over the top surface of the sponge. Try the seeds of grasses, sweet alyssum, coleus, and any other small seeds. The shoots will make an attractive display. Be sure to keep water in the dish so the sponge never has a chance to dry out. As soon as leaves appear, the food stored in the seeds has been used, so liquid plant food should be added to the water.

SEED GERMINATION TEST

Have each boy dampen a piece of old terrycloth or paper toweling. Scatter 10 bean seeds on it, then roll up the towel. After 3 days, or at the next den meeting, unroll the towel. How many seeds have sprouted?

GROW A GIANT PLANT

The giant sunflower sometimes grows to 12 feet tall. Its blooms are often larger than a child's head. You can grow your own bird food by planting this huge sunflower.

Plant a few giant sunflower seeds outdoors at least 3 feet apart. Keep giving them plenty of water as they grow. After the sunflower has bloomed, you will see hundreds of big seeds in the center. When the seeds have turned black and dry, pick them out. Crack the thin shells with your teeth and you'll find a tasty "nut" inside that can be eaten. Birds like to eat the whole seeds.

PORCUPINE PLANTER

Scoop out an oval opening in the top of a large, firm potato. Insert thumbtacks in front for the porcupine's eyes, and insert four golf tees in the bottom for his feet. Fill the opening of the potato with soil and grass seed. Water. Place the porcupine with his back toward the sun, so the grass will grow at an angle and look like bristles.

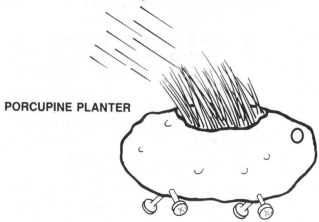

PORCUPINE PLANTER

GROW A MINATURE FOREST

With carrot tops and beet tops, it's easy to grow a color-ful indoor forest of red and green "trees."

For the green "trees," cut off about ½-inch of each top of a bunch of carrots. Remove any old green leaves from the tops so it will grow tender new shoots. Place the tops in a shallow bowl with about ¼-inch water in it. About half of each carrot top should show above the water. Place the dish near a bright window, but not in direct sunlight.

By the next den meeting, green sprouts will have appeared from the carrot tops. The green sprouts will continue to grow if you keep the bottoms in a little water.

For the red "trees," cut off the top leaves of several beets, almost down to the beet itself, leaving stubby stems. Cut the beets in half to make flat bottoms. Plant beet halves in a shallow dish or plastic container which has about 2 inches of soil in it. The top of the beets should be covered so only the stubby stems show. Wet the soil well and water it every few days.

In about a week, there will be red shoots poking up from the beet tops. Soon green leaves will appear on the red stems, making them look like little trees.

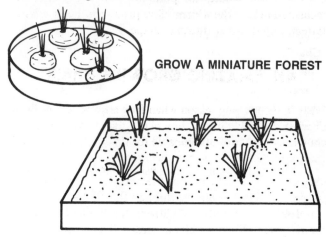

GROW A MINIATURE FOREST

THE BOY WITH GREEN HAIR

Gently puncture the pointed end of an egg. With manicure scissors carefully cut away about ¼ of the pointed end of the shell. Remove egg. Rinse inside shell and let dry. Fill shell with dirt and plant ordinary grass seed. Draw eyes, nose, mouth, and ears on shell with permanent mark-ing pen. Set shell in an egg carton cup. Water every day and soon the boy's green hair will begin to grow. In about a week, he may need a "haircut."

THE BOY WITH GREEN HAIR

THE GREAT PUMPKIN RACE

Give each boy the same number of pumpkin seeds. Choose a starting day and a finishing day. Everyone must plant the seeds on the same day. They can all be planted in one location (with plenty of space between hills) and labeled with the boys' names. Or each boy can plant his own at home.

Each boy is responsible for watering, weeding and caring for his plant. As small pumpkins appear, they should be picked off the vines to allow all the growing energy to go into the biggest pumpkins.

On the ending date, all pumpkins are weighed and measured to find the winner. Give prizes for the heaviest, fattest, tallest, most unusual shape, etc.

AN AMAZING GROWING TRICK

Early in the growing season when fruit trees have tiny fruit or when cucumber or zucchini plants have tiny vegetables, choose a small fruit or vegetable for this trick. Use a long jar or bottle with a narrow neck.

Very gently, place the part of the branch or vine holding the small fruit or vegetable through the neck of a bottle. Carefully tie the bottle to a strong tree branch or lay it on the ground in the vegetable garden. The bottle will act as a hothouse, particularly if you have chosen a sunny spot. Watch the fruit or vegetable as it grows. When it is large enough to fill the bottle, cut it from the vine or tree.

Display this at pack meeting and let people guess how the fruit or vegetable got through the narrow neck of the bottle!

**AN AMAZING
GROWING TRICK**

CUCUMBERS

GROW AN INSECT-EATING PLANT

There are several types of insect-eating or "carnivorous" plants that catch and eat insects. The most common is the Venus Flytrap which is grown from bulbs, available at supermarkets, variety stores, and garden shops.

Plant the bulb in a pot of sphagnum moss, peat moss, or vermiculite. Place the bulb so the roots are facing down and the top is even with the soil. Place the pot on a window sill where it will get lots of sunlight. Keep it heavily watered so the soil doesn't dry out. In about a week, stems like arms will start to grow up from the bulb. In a few weeks the traps will appear at the ends of the stems. In about 8 weeks, the plant should be fully grown with five or more traps ready to catch insects.

Notice that each leafy trap is hinged in the middle and has sensitive hairs on each half. When an insect such as a little fly touches at least two of these hairs, the trap snaps closed and the hairs help hold the insect inside. The plant digests the insect. The trap opens again in a few days for another meal.

The plant will live and grow even if it doesn't get insects to eat. And don't worry—it never eats people!

Fun With Birds

BE A BIRD DETECTIVE

Many questions can be answered by observation. You can observe birds in woods, in a park, or in your own backyard. Even the city birdwatcher can learn many things about pigeons and other birds.

- Choose a spot near your home. It can be a bird feeder in your yard, a patch of ground in a vacant lot, or a quiet spot in a park.

- Visit that spot every day at the same time.

- Leave birdseed or suet, and then sit down a little distance away where you can watch without disturbing your visitors.

- Keep a pad or notebook handy so you can write short descriptions of the birds you see. Write down how big they are, what colors they are, the shapes of their heads, tails, beaks, and wings.

- Get a bird guidebook from the library and look through it until you find the birds that fit your description. Read about the birds to find out their mating and nesting habits, their migration patterns, and their diets.

- After you identify all the birds, keep track of when you see them. If you live in a cold climate, which stay around all year? Which are the first to return after a long winter?

- Make notes of these things:
  - What is the difference in appearance between the male and female?
  - Do they both build the nest?
  - What is the nest made of?
  - Does the male or female hunt for food?
  - How much of the bird's day is spent in looking for food?
  - What kind of food do they like best?
  - How many eggs does the species lay?
  - When do the young birds leave the nest?
  - What sounds does the bird make?
  - How much time is spent in preening?
  - How often does the bird drink?
  - How does the bird react to animals? Which animals does he fear?

FEEDING BIRDS

- Once you start, continue. Birds will get used to coming and finding food in your feeders. Don't disappoint them.
- Birds need water too. If you don't have a regular bird bath, use an old hubcap, Frisbee, or shallow pan on top of an overturned trash can. If temperature is freezing, boil water every morning and pour over pan, taking out ice. Remaining water will cool quickly for birds to use.
- Feed early every day. This is when the birds eat.
- Cracked corn is a good all-purpose bird food. Ask for "fine" or "chick cracked corn" at a poultry supply store or garden center.
- Sunflower seeds are popular with finches, grosbeaks, woodpeckers, and other seed- and grain-eating birds.
- Wild bird seed is a prepackaged mixture sold at many stores.
- Birds like nuts, in or out of the shell, but only birds with strong bills, such as blue jays and titmice can crack the shells. For other birds, shell the nuts and chop them.
- Beef suet gives energy that helps birds stay warm in winter and is a good substitute for the insects they can no longer find. Ask the butcher for "beef suet for

birds". Use it only during cold weather and in a special container so other animals can't eat it.

- Some birds like fruit, such as a cut-up apple, banana, pear, raisins, and other dried fruit.
- Many birds enjoy table scraps such as cheese, cooked rice, breakfast cereal, bits of meat. Use table scraps only in cold weather and keep them well off the ground. Never give birds moldy bread or any other moldy or spoiled foods.

FEEDING BIRDS

BIRD CAKE

Wild bird seed

12-ounce juice can

½-pound suet

Long piece of wire

Piece of mesh vegetable sack

1. Cut vegetable sack to fit inside can with extra sticking up above can top.

2. Cut suet into small pieces and heat in double boiler so it won't burn. Let cool and harden. Remove any pieces of meat.

3. Reheat suet. Mix in 1 cup bird seed. Pour mixture into can. Set in refrigerator to harden.

4. Set can in warm water and carefully run knife around inside to loosen sack. Pull out sack.

5. Tie the ends of the sack with wire, leaving enough to tie it to a tree limb.

6. This same mixture can be molded in a cut-down cardboard milk carton, small foil dishes, or half a grapefruit shell, and the cakes set on a fence post or in a feeder.

BIRD'S DELIGHT

1 cup melted suet	3 tablespoons butter
3 tablespoons cornmeal	¼-cup cracked corn
¼-cup peanut butter	¼-cup raisins

1. Melt suet as described for "Bird Cake," adding the peanut butter during the second heating.

2. After the suet has cooled the second time, add the other ingredients.

3. Pour into containers and set in refrigerator to harden.

EGG CARTON CAFETERIA

The bottom half of a styrofoam egg carton will hold several kinds of food. Birds can select their favorites at the cafeteria.

1. Cut off and discard top of egg carton.

2. Use a small nail to punch a few drainage holes in the bottom of each egg "cup."

3. Fill 2 cups with sand or gravel. This will help keep the lightweight feeder from blowing away and will also provide grit for the birds to eat. If it is to be placed in a windy area, nail the carton to a post.

4. Fill the rest of the cups with cracked corn, wild birdseed, sunflower seeds, etc.

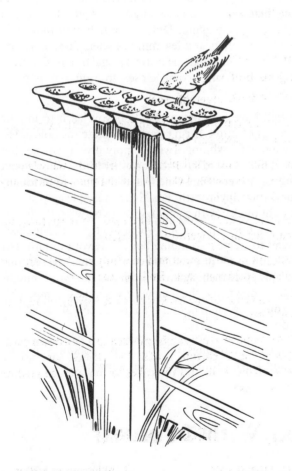

EGG CARTON CAFETERIA

SAFETY TIPS

- Cover anything sharp on the feeder. This is to protect the person handling the food as well as the bird. Cover wire ends and sharp edges of plastic and metal with tape. Sand smooth rough edges of wood.

- Never use thread anywhere on a feeder. Birds can easily become entangled.

- Use only fresh, clean grain and seeds. A deadly fungus sometimes grows in moldy food.

- Be sure the container used to make the bird feeder has never held anything poisonous. Even a tiny amount of a harmful substance can affect a bird.

- Leave the feeder unpainted, or if you must paint, use exterior latex paint.

- Do not use plain peanut butter.

PINE CONE TREATS

Mix together equal amounts of peanut butter and cornmeal—about 2 tablespoons of each. The cornmeal keeps the peanut butter from being sticky and is safer for birds to eat. Tie a piece of wire around a large pine cone for hanging from a tree. Spoon mixture in between pine-cone petals. The birds will love it.

EXAMINE A BIRD FEATHER

As you hike through the woods and across fields in late summer and early fall, you may find quite a few bird feathers on the path or in the grass. This is the time when birds lose their old feathers and grow new ones. They are moulting.

When you take a good look at a bird feather you will see that it has a stiff shaft in the middle. The lower part of this shaft, the quill, is hollow. On each side of the shaft is a flat vane. When you look at this vane through a magnifying glass, you will discover it has hundreds of separate barbs held together by tiny hooks.

Most birds have three types of feathers. The flight feathers of the wings have a curved shaft and the vane along one side is narrower than the vane on the other side. The steering feathers of the tail have an almost straight shaft and the vanes on each side are about the same width. The contour feathers that cover the bird's body are much smaller than the others, and they are usually curved.

The color of the feathers will give a clue to the type of bird. A bright red feather might come from a scarlet tanager or cardinal. A banded light-blue feather may have come from a bluejay. A solid black feather may come from a crow.

Do not collect feathers. Only the feathers of gregarious birds (ducks, geese, chickens, etc.), the English sparrow, starlings, and pigeons may be in the possession of non-native Americans. All other birds are classified as migratory and protected, and it is against federal law to be in possession of their feathers.

NOTE: The National Audubon Society has many books and materials for people interested in birds. It also sponsors a Junior Audubon Society that boys can join. Write to the society at 950 Third Avenue, New York, NY 10022.

CHRISTMAS TREE HOTEL

A discarded Christmas tree makes a good shelter and feeder for birds. It will provide protection during the coldest part of the winter.

1. Stick the trunk of the tree into the ground or snow.

2. Trim the tree with bird cakes (see above), stale donuts, or very stale bread tied on with a string of popcorn, cranberries, or raisins. Have orange or grapefruit shells filled with bird's delight (see above).

CHRISTMAS
TREE HOTEL

BIRD HELPER

This is a way to help birds find materials for building their nests.

1. Bend a wire coat hanger into a square or rectangle.

2. Cover the shape with mesh material, such as a fruit or vegetable sack. Attach securely.

3. Loosely weave short pieces (6 inches or less) of dark-colored yarn, strips of fabric, and white string through the mesh.

4. In early spring, hang the nest-building helper in a tree near your window. Watch as the birds flock to it to choose the materials they need.

5. After the hanger has been emptied, take a walk through the neighborhood and see how many nests you can spot that contain your materials. Remember, a bird's nest is its home, so be careful not to trespass.

CALLING BIRDS

Sometimes birds are so far away it is hard to identify them. Bring them closer by "squeaking." Purse your lips against the back of your hand. Draw in your breath in a long, squeaky kiss. Repeat a few minutes later. The sound you make is very much like the distress signal of a bird in trouble. The birds will come closer to find out what is happening.

You will have even better results if you learn to imitate the songs of birds. It isn't hard to imitate the chickadee, bobwhite, and whippoorwill. Simply give a whistle that sounds like the bird's name. For other birds, whistle with steady or quivering lips, and flutter the tip of your tongue behind your upper teeth. For higher notes, keep your lips in a tight pucker with a small opening between them. For low notes, open up your lips wider and tighten your cheek muscles to create a sounding box inside your mouth. For very deep sounds, use your hands. Cup them together, wet your lips, place them against the knuckles of your thumbs and blow down into the hollow between the thumbs. This way you can learn to hoot like an owl or coo like a mourning dove.

Listening to recordings of bird calls is a good way to practice and learn to imitate various songs.

Fun With Trees

Each tree is a special, individual living thing, just as each person is. So it's fun to try to get to know one tree individually. Walk through a forest, park, or yard and choose one tree—any tree you like.

- Look at the tree from a distance. Where is it growing? What color is it?

- With your fingertip, "trace" in the air the shape of the tree. Start from the ground, go up to the top, and back down to the ground.

- Describe the shape of the tree. Do the branches grow upwards, sideways or downwards?

- Make a telescope with rolled-up paper or your hands. Look through this telescope at the tree from a distance.

- Take a close look at the tree. What things do you notice about it? Write them down. Does it have leaves? Needles? Cones? Blossoms? Nuts? Fruit? Are there birds in it? What kind? Do you see a nest?

- How are you and your tree alike? Different?

- Look at the trunk. Is it straight or bent, single or divided? Is there any moss or lichen growing on it?

- Close your eyes. Press your cheek against the tree. How does it feel? Is it rough? Smooth? Uneven? Even? Is the bark thick or thin?

- Keep your eyes closed and sniff the tree. How does it smell? What does the smell remind you of? Smell the sap, needles, leaves, bark.

- Press your ear or a stethoscope against the tree. Can you hear its heartbeat? What other sounds does the tree make?

- Measure the distance around the trunk 3 feet from the ground.

- How old do you think the tree is? Who are its neighbors? Can you see any roots?

- What plants grow under the tree?

- Make a sketch of the tree.

- How might the tree look 25 years from now, or 100 years from now?

- What do all trees have in common? How are some different from others?

- Make bark and leaf rubbings.

- If you can climb the tree, do. Sit up there and look around to see how the world looks to your tree. What has this tree seen in its life? What does the tree know?

COUNTING TREE RINGS

Find the stump of a tree that has just been cut down. Count the rings to see how old the tree is. Each ring represents a growth season of one year. A wide ring shows a good year of growth for the tree, with lots of rain and plenty of sunshine. A narrow ring shows the opposite; not enough rain and a poor growing season. When a tree is hurt by forest fire, its growth may be slowed down for several years.

BE A STUMP DETECTIVE

Study a tree stump and, by observation and deduction, decide the facts about the tree's life and death.

- What kind of tree was it? There may be dry leaves still lying around the base.

- How old was it when it was cut?

- In what year did it start growing?

- In what year did it grow most rapidly?

- Was the summer 20 years ago rainy or dry?

- How was the weather 12 years ago?

- Was the tree damaged in a forest fire? In what year?

- How was the tree cut? With an ax? With a saw? With both?

LISTEN TO THE HEARTBEAT OF A TREE

A tree is a living, growing thing. It eats, rests, and has circulation just as we do. The heartbeat of a tree is a wonderful sound. The best time to hear it is in early spring when the tree sends the first sap upward to its branches, preparing them for another season of growth.

Choose a tree that is at least 6 inches in diameter and has thin bark. Deciduous trees (those that shed their leaves) are usually better for listening. Some species have a louder heartbeat than others.

Press a stethescope firmly against the tree, keeping it motionless so there will not be interfering noises. You may need to try several different places on the tree trunk before you find a good listening spot.

TREE TAGGING

Divide group into teams. Give each team 20 pieces of 1-inch gauze bandage, 12 inches long, with numbers from 1 to 20 written on them in a different color for each team. The object is to tie the gauze bandages on as many different trees as possible within 100 feet of a starting point. One team member keeps a list of the trees tagged. The team tagging the most trees correctly within the time limit is the winner. Remove the gauze before you leave.

BUILD A TREE HOUSE

A tree house is a shelter against wind and rain and it can also be lots of fun. You can have a meeting there, plan a bike hike, or even stand guard against an attack by "enemy forces."

Find a large tree with sturdy branches. Get permission to use it. Ask the den chief and parents to supervise the project. Draw a plan before doing anything else. This will tell how much lumber is needed. All you need are a floor platform, four walls, and a simple flat roof, plus a rope ladder for climbing up and down. The tree house could be about 6 feet square with walls about 5 to 6 feet high (tall enough for a boy to stand inside). Scrap lumber can probably be obtained from a construction site nearby or from a lumberyard.

A strong rope or cable can anchor the house to the tree. Never drive nails into the living wood of a tree, because that can cause permanent damage. The parents may have some good ideas for anchoring the house to the tree.

A rope for climbing to the house can be made with three strands of clothesline tied together with knots to grip with your feet. Or a rope ladder can be made by binding pieces of wood to the rope at intervals for the rungs.

COLLECT ALPHABET TWIGS

A regular twig collection will tell a lot about trees. But there is a special kind of twig that is fun to collect — the alphabet twig. The idea is to find twigs that grow naturally in the form of letters of the alphabet. Use only dead twigs.

You will have no trouble finding twigs that look like an I, V or Y. T is also fairly common. A part of a curved twig may look like a C. If the curve starts right off a branch, you may find a G or perhaps even a D. Collect as many different letters as you can find, then see what words you can spell with them.

WHITTLE A WOOD WHISTLE

All you need is a 5-inch length of straight green basswood, willow, red maple, or hickory, about ½-inch in diameter.

1. Cut off one end at an angle for the mouthpiece.

2. On the opposite side, cut a small triangular notch ¼-inch deep.

3. Close to the other end, make a circular cut just through the bark, all around the twig. Tap gently to remove bark. Remove by twisting carefully until bark comes off in one piece.

4. Cut the solid inside to form whistle cavity and flatten top leading from whistle cavity to mouthpiece as shown.

5. Replace this inside back into bark.

6. The tone of the whistle may be varied by changing the size of the whistle cavity.

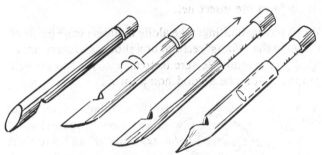

WHITTLE A WOOD WHISTLE

Fun With Insects

KEEP AN INSECT AQUARIUM

Brooks, ponds, lakes and swamps are alive with insects. The water strider walks and runs on spider-like legs across the water's surface. A beetle called the back swimmer clings to the underside of the surface while his hind legs propel him along. Whirligig beetles skate over the surface of the water, chasing one another in a crazy patch of circles. A scuba diver called the water boatman keeps his air supply in a bubble between his front legs, and moves through the water with his oar-like hind legs. Nymphs and naiads swim through the water, catching and eating smaller insects, then finally crawl up onto a log or rock above the surface and turn into dragonflies and damselflies. All of these aquatic insects are common and easily caught.

Take along jars to bring insects home to your aquarium. Put sand, rocks, and plants on the bottom of the aquarium as you would for fish. Cover the aquarium with wire screening. Feed the aquatic insects flies, mosquitoes, mosquito wrigglers, ants, or grasshoppers by dropping them on the surface of the water.

MAKE A PET OF A PRAYING MANTIS

The praying mantis — the tiger of the grass stems — is a very helpful creature. Most of the insects on which it preys damage crops and gardens. In captivity, this insect does things you would expect from a dog or cat.

Speak to a mantis and it will turn its head toward you and seem to respond. Offer your hand; it will alight on it, sit up, and beg. The mantis will learn to eat bits of fresh liver from your fingers or from a toothpick. It will even drink milk or watermelon juice from a spoon. Mantises need live food—small insects such as grasshoppers, flies, and beetles.

To capture the mantis and its food, a net is a must. Attach a circle of coat hanger wire to the end of a broomstick with tape. Then attach mosquito netting to the wire circle to form the insect net.

When you go hunting, take along an insect cage (such as shown in the "Crafts" section) or a shoebox to carry home what you capture. Be sure to treat gently whatever you capture and make a good home for it.

BENT WIRE
NOTCH
TAPE
BROOMSTICK
CLOTH BINDING
CHEESECLOTH

MAKING A PET OUT OF A PRAYING MANTIS

WATCH A BUTTERFLY GROW

Watching a cocoon turn into a butterfly is one of nature's greatest now-you-see-me, now-I'm-something-else acts. It begins with moth or butterfly eggs that hatch into a caterpillar that becomes a cocoon or chrysalis. The caterpillar emerges and becomes a moth or butterfly that lays eggs and starts the whole process over again.

Look for cocoons/chrysalises before trees and shrubs leaf out. They are easily spotted, hanging from branches and twigs. Cut away part of the twig to which the cocoon is attached, taking note of the tree or shrub. The butterfly or moth sleeping peacefully in the cocoon will need food—leaves from the same plant upon which you found

it. Shake the cocoon. If you hear a rattling sound, discard it. The pupa inside is probably dead.

Keep the cocoon in a clean can or jar with a tight cover. Punch a few holes in the cover to provide ventilation. Put it in a cool place. When the trees are fully clothed in leaves, make a suitable home for the cocoon. A half-gallon jar with a 1-inch layer of dirt or moss and a couple of sticks inserted is good. The emerged adult will need a place to crawl to dry and spread its wings. Sprinkle the pupa and dirt with water about once a week to keep them from drying out. Once the butterfly has emerged, release it.

MAKE A BEE FEEDER

Bees can dine right at your window with this simple feeder. Punch small holes in the lid of a glass jar lid, using a small nail and hammer. Tape a bridle of string to the jar, as shown in illustration, and fill the jar with honey or thick, well-mixed sugar water. Hang the jar upside down, in front of a second-story window and watch who comes to eat.

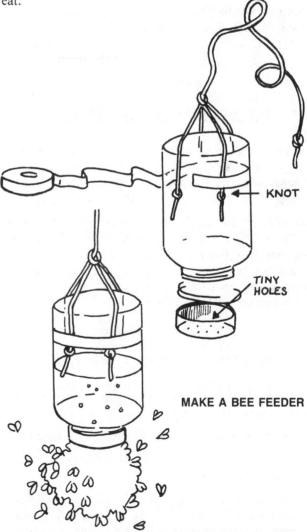

KNOT

TINY HOLES

MAKE A BEE FEEDER

MIDNIGHT SNACK FOR MOTHS

Many beautiful moths can be attracted and observed by giving them a nightly treat. Mix together fruit pulp and sugar. Tie a tennis ball to a length of string and dip ball into the sticky, sweet mixture. Hang it from the top of a window. Soon you should have attracted some lovely, hungry visitors.

Try hanging balls in different locations. Are the same types of moths attracted in all locations? Why?

MAKE AN ANT FARM

Be careful of the types of ants you keep. Beware of fire ants and other stinging ants.

You will need:

Quart or gallon-size jar
Small can to fit inside jar
Jar lid or small, flat dish

1. Insert can in jar, leaving space for the soil, as shown in the illustration. Fill the jar about half-full of slightly moist, sandy soil. Place the jar lid on top of the can.

2. Find an anthill or ant nest under some rocks. Stir up the anthill with a stick. Collect ants in a large-mouth bottle or jar and screw on the lid. Finding the queen may require some digging. As you dig, put the dirt on a white paper or cloth. The queen, larger than the rest, will probably show up. Guide her into a second bottle.

3. Collect some of the soil from the ant nest to put in the ant farm. Fill most of the space left between the jar and can.

4. Put the ants and queen into the jar and cover the top with a piece of cheesecloth or screen. Ants like the dark, so fasten a dark paper around the jar with a rubber band.

5. Place the jar on a block of wood in a pan of water, as shown, to prevent the ants from escaping. Put the jar in a warm place, but not in direct sunlight. It may take a few days for the ants to settle down. Then they will build their tunnels close to the glass where they can be observed.

6. Keep the dish on top of the can filled with water. If the soil gets dry, moisten it with an eyedropper.

7. Feed the ants by putting different kinds of food on top of the soil. Try bread, cake crumbs, bits of meat,

honey, small pieces of vegetables, and dead insects. Always remove unused food before adding any more.

Try These Experiments:

- Take some ants out of the nest for a few days, then put them back and see what happens.

- Introduce some new ants from outdoors and see what happens.

- Set up a regular feeding time and see how soon they learn when it is.

MAKE AN ANT FARM

OBSERVING FRUIT FLIES

Because they multiply rapidly, fruit flies make a good exhibit for the den to watch. A new generation will be born every few days.

To catch fruit flies, place a piece of ripe fruit in the bottom of a small glass jar. Make a paper funnel to fit the top, to make it harder for the flies to escape. Put the jar in the open.

When six to 10 flies have entered, remove the funnel. Plug the opening with loose cotton. There should be both males and females (the males are smaller and have black-tipped abdomens). Soon some eggs will be deposited. Within two or three days, larvae will hatch. Soon they will pupate. The adult insects will come from the pupae. Take the young, adult insects out and start a new colony in another jar.

SPIDER WEB PRINTS

Spiders make their webs from silk, which they spin from a liquid made in their bodies. They use the silk not only to spin webs but to make sacs for their eggs, as anchor lines, and as parachutes or balloons. A young spider launches itself into the air at the end of a long silk thread.

During the summer and fall, spider webs can be found on bushes, in grass, on branches of small trees and on fence rails. On your next hike, take a can of spray paint and a piece of paper with you. The following directions will help you capture some of the most beautiful designs in nature. The print will be so interesting, you may want to frame it.

You will need:

White enamel spray paint
Dark blue or black construction paper
Spider Web

1. Find a spider web. If there is a spider on the web, you won't want to kill him. Try tickling him with a long twig. This will usually cause him to exit to the nearest cover. Don't worry about taking his web. He will quickly spin another.

2. Be careful not to touch the web. Stand a short distance away and very carefully spray the web on both sides with the white enamel. Too much paint will cause the web to sag.

3. Carefully put the dark paper behind the web and bring it into contact so the web will stick to the paper. Then break the supporting lines of the web and remove the paper.

4. Cover the dried web with cellophane or clear plastic for protection.

   Another way to enjoy spider webs is to photograph them. Look for them in the morning. They sparkle in the sunshine. This way, all of the boys in a den or pack can enjoy a single web.

Fun with Fishing

In spite of what old-time fisherman may tell you, there is only one secret to catching fish. That is to have your bait at the right place at the right time. It isn't necessary to use a lot of fancy tackle. Probably more fish have been caught with an inexpensive cane pole than with all the more expensive rods made. It's true that with good tackle you have more fun and perhaps catch fish when other people fail. But the real secret is knowing where and when to fish.

KNOW YOUR LAYERS

A lake or pond is much like a layer cake, except that the icing isn't necessarily on top. (The icing, in this case, is where you find the fish.) The water is in layers, and one thing that makes the layers different is the water temperature. Fish are sensitive to temperature. If the water is too warm or too cold, they won't be very active or eager to eat your bait.

In the early spring, generally, fish are in rather deep water in channels or in holes, where it is warmer than on the surface. As the surface warms, they come toward the top to feed and frequently you can see them dimpling the water as they suck in insects. In streams you'll find them in shallow water, in riffles, or along the edges of deep holes.

In summer, as the surface gets too warm, they drop down again to deep water. As the surface cools in the fall, they come back to feed near the top, dropping down again in the winter.

WHERE THEY FEED

When the water is warm, early morning or late afternoon and evening will usually find fish feeding in shallow water near shore, or near the top of deep water. But during the day they lie in deep holes where the water is cool. So it pays to do some experimenting to find out where to fish.

Look for a spot where there is a sudden drop-off, a place where the water is shallow, then suddenly becomes deeper. Look for a weed bed under water, or a channel or deep hole. Find a spot where a stream runs into a lake or drains out. Look for a gravel or rocky bottom, or a place where there may be old stumps, logs, big rocks, undercut banks, roots, or brush piles under water. Sometimes docks or floats or even anchored boats shelter a big one. Try to find underwater springs or steep banks where ground water may seep into the lake, These are all good spots to fish, so try them first.

Some stream fish will lie just on the upstream side of big rocks, waiting for food to come along. Others will lie behind a rock on the downstream side.

Fish along the edges of the weed bed, rocky bottom, or deep hole. Fish usually swim along the edge, trying to find food, and will come upon your bait. Fish hide during the bright part of the day and feed best at dusk or dawn. But plenty of big fish are caught in the middle of the day by fishermen who know where fish like to hide and have their bait at the right place at the right time.

CATCH AND RELEASE

Keep only those fish which are going to be used. Release all the rest.

To release fish easily, use snelled hooks. These are hooks with the leader already attached. It requires that a snap swivel be used. If a fish is caught that is well-hooked and cannot be taken out, the hook can be unhooked from the line and then the fish is released. The hook will be dissolved by the fish and fall out. The cost of the snelled hook is minimal and is well worth it to save the life of a fish.

BAIT

Worms. One of the best all-round baits for most fish is the good old worm. Worms can be found under decaying leaves and in rich garden soil. Night crawlers and dew worms can be found on the lawn at night after the dew has fallen. Small worms are good bait for sunfish and rock bass. Use a small hook—size No. 6 or No. 8—with long shank. Medium-size and large worms are good for perch, catfish, bullheads, crappies, or bass. Use a No. 4 hook for perch, crappies, and bass; use a No. 6 or No. 8 for bullheads.

Minnows. Fish such as large perch, crappies, and bass sometimes prefer minnows and will not take anything else. Minnows can be caught in a minnow trap baited with bread or rolled oats. Place the trap in shallow water near the weeds and wait.

Crayfish. Bass sometimes like crayfish. Use small ones for bait, hooking them through the tail.

Insects. Many kinds of insects make good bait for sunfish, perch, bass, or trout. Grasshoppers, crickets, roaches, grubs, and caterpillars all make good bait.

NO FANCY TACKLE NEEDED

One good thing about bait fishing is that you don't need fancy tackle. A cane or willow pole, 10 to 20 feet of line, a few feet of leader material, a cork, a sinker, a few hooks, and bait are all you need to catch sunfish or perch.

But if you have a baitcasting rod, fly rod, or spin-casting outfit, you can use it with live bait or artificial lures.

Hand Line. The simplest tackle, and the best for some purposes, is a hand line. All you need are line, leader, cork, sinker, and hooks. Wind the line around a stick or block of wood to keep it from becoming tangled. Tie a 4- to 5-foot piece of leader to the line, tie a hook to the leader, fasten on the cork and sinker, and you're ready to fish. This kind of fishing can be done from a steep bank, dock, pier, jetty, or from a boat.

Cane Pole. The next simplest equipment is a cane or willow pole, 7 to 9 feet in length. Use the lightest pole you can find so you won't get tired handling it. Tie a piece of line (slightly longer than the length of the pole) to the small end of a clove hitch or other suitable knot. Tie a 4- to 6-foot piece of light nylon leader (4- to 5-pound test) to the line, and tie the right size hook to the leader, a little below the sinker. If you use a cork for a bobber, cut a slot lengthwise through the cork and slip the line into the slot. Then you can slide the cork up and down the line to raise your bait off the bottom or drop it down lower.

Fly Rod. To rig a fly rod for bait fishing, use the same method as with a cane pole, except the line will be on a reel and strung through guides instead of being tied to the end of the pole.

Bait- or Spin-Casting. If you have bait or spin-casting equipment and use it for bait fishing, you will have a few advantages. You can fish almost anywhere and cast your bait to places you might not be able to reach with a cane pole or fly rod.

Evening and Nighttime Outdoor Fun

STARGAZING

Billions of stars shine in the sky. Although they are millions of miles away, we can see many of them. The library has many excellent guides for stargazing.

- Choose a clear, dark night. A night with no moon is best for beginners, since the constellations are easier to see. Find a place that is dark, away from street and house lights. Moonlight, as well as city lights, will blot out all of the fainter stars.

- Lie on your back and enjoy the whole display of stars before looking for specific ones.

- Start with a star group you already recognize, such as the Big Dipper, and use it to star hop. Move to the Little

STARGAZING

LOOK FOR ORION.

- In winter months, look for Orion, the Mighty Hunter. You will recognize him by his belt, a row of three bright stars. Try to locate the bright star, Betelgeuse, that marks Orion's shoulder.

Dipper, nearby. The star at the very end of the curved handle is Polaris, the North Star. It is almost directly above the north geographic pole of the earth. Sailors and travelers have used it for centuries to tell which way is North.

- Cassiopeia is easy to find and remember because of its shape: a "**W**" formed by five bright stars. To find Cassiopeia, draw an imaginary line from the star where the handle joins the Big Dipper's bowl through the North Star and beyond. Cassiopeia and the Big Dipper are on opposite sides of the North Star and rotate around it. They are always above the horizon and can be seen any time of the year.

LOOK FOR CASSIOPEIA.

START WITH A STAR GROUP YOU KNOW.

- Follow the belt stars upward and you will find the constellation Taurus.

- With these as a beginning, go on to locate others. Work your way around the night sky, using a star guide to help you locate and identify stars, planets, and constellations.

- You might be able to see Venus just after sunset. It is very bright. Mars has a steady, reddish light. Jupiter is steady and more white than stars. Saturn has a yellow light.

- If a "star" moves steadily, it may be a satellite or plane instead of a star.

- A flashlight, covered with red cellophane, will come in handy to help you read your star guide. Red light will not blind your eyes as white light will.

MAKE A STAR UMBRELLA

Use an old black umbrella. Make a large map of the night sky the same diameter as the umbrella, with Polaris in the center. Use a star guide for the proper locations. Transfer the map to the umbrella, painting the stars with white paint. Connect the stars into constellations with white crayon. Use the star umbrella outdoors to help identify constellations by opening it and pointing its tip toward Polaris. The umbrella can be used indoors to show the movement of the stars by turning it slowly in a counter-clockwise direction.

MAKE A STAR UMBRELLA

MOONWATCH

As the moon orbits the earth, its appearance seems to change. A full orbit takes about 29½ days. During the first part of this time, the moon is waxing and appears to be increasing in size. Because the moon shines only with reflected sunlight, we see different parts of its sunny side as it moves around the earth.

Find out from an almanac, a calendar, or the local weather station when the next new moon will be. Make a calendar that begins with that day and continues for 30 days. Each evening, write on the calendar what time the moon rises and draw a picture showing how it looks. The calendar should tell you these things:

- How many days the waxing takes

- How many days the waning takes

- How many days the moon is full

OBSERVING WILDLIFE AT NIGHT

Many animals are active at night. To see them, try these tips:

- To make yourself less noticeable, wear dark clothes.

- Cover your flashlight's beam with a piece of red cellophane so its light will not be visible or threaten-

ing to many nocturnal animals. Use the flashlight sparingly, as it will actually lessen your night sight. After several minutes in the dark, your eyes will adjust and you will be able to see as well as some animals.

- Before starting the observation period and during the daylight hours, select a spot where you can remain motionless and quiet for an extended period. Go where you have seen evidence of an animal trail or eating or drinking place and which provides a clear view of the wildlife to be observed.

OBSERVING UNDERWATER NIGHT LIFE

If there is a stream or lake nearby, take the den out to see what fish do at night. Seal a two-cell flashlight in a watertight plastic bag. Tie strong twine or a light rope around the center of the flashlight so it hangs level. After dark, lower the light slowly from a pier or boat into 6 to 8 feet of water. Turn the light slowly. It will attract many fish, crabs, and crayfish of various species. See how many the boys can identify. If a pier is not available, a walk around the pond will reveal as much or more wildlife. Silence is a must. (For observing these creatures in daytime, use a waterscope, such as the one described in the "Crafts" section of this book.)

FUN WITH FROGS AT NIGHT

Visit a pond at night. In the spring, the voices of frogs and toads may lead you right to it.

To see one of the most beautiful sights in nature, place the battery end of a regular flashlight at your nose tip while you bend over until the light shines in a bullfrog's eyes. As the frog moves its eyes slightly, you will see brilliant flashes of topaz, emerald, ruby, and sapphire.

Try a "frog raft." Fasten a lighted candle to the middle of a 1-foot piece of 1-inch board with candle drippings. Tie a rope or twine to the board so that it can be retrieved. Float it in the water and watch for passengers.

TRY A FROG RAFT

ATTRACTING INSECTS AT NIGHT

Tie a white sheet between two trees. Shine a flashlight on it. Many insects will be attracted to the light. Move the light around and see what happens. The insects will probably follow the light.

BLIND EAGLE

This is a good nighttime stalking game to play in a large open area. One player, the Eagle, is blindfolded and stands in the middle of the area, holding a flashlight. Be sure the blindfold does not cover his ears, since he will depend on hearing to protect himself. A Spotter stands next to him to assist.

The other boys form a large circle around the outer edge of the open area. On signal, they begin to stalk toward the Eagle as quietly as possible. If the Eagle hears anything, he aims his flashlight in the direction of the sound and shouts, "Freeze!" All players must stop immediately. The Eagle's Spotter looks to see if any players have been caught in the flashlight's beam. If so, they are out of the game. The play continues in this way until one of the players is able to touch the Eagle without being spotted.

OWLS GAME

Choose four boys to be Owls and give them a handful of leaves, pebbles, sticks, or other items. Each Owl has a different type of object. The Owls hide within a designated area. As they are hiding, they count slowly to 20. Each time they reach 20, they must give a loud "hoot" like an owl. The other players try to locate the hidden Owls by their noises. Each time an owl is found, he must give up one of the objects he is carrying.

The winner is the first player to return to the leader with four different objects (one from each owl). Set a time limit and a signal for all the others to return.

SPIDER SNIFFING

First off, this is not a "snipe hunt." It really works! At least it works for spiders on the ground.

Spiders have complex eyes that are excellent light reflectors. The way you can "sniff" them out at night is to put a narrow-beam flashlight to the bridge or end of your nose and look down the beam to where spiders are likely to

be. A small bright green glint (reflection) will signal the presence of a spider. When you see this green glint, slowly walk toward the spider, always keeping the glint in sight, to the point where you can actually see the full body of the "critter." You'll be surprised—it works and it's fun! You may even see a female wolf spider with dozens of little "glints" on her back—which are the young she carries.

Don't try this when the ground has dew on it or is otherwise wet. The water droplets will reflect as well. If you are really lucky, you may even catch the reflective eyes of a mouse, deer, raccoon, or a host of other animals.

SPIDER SNIFFING

Fun for All Seasons—Spring

THINGS TO LOOK FOR

Look at the buds on trees and bushes. Many will be swelling or opening. Notice how the leaves are folded into the bud. Which kinds of trees begin to leaf out first?

Does the weather have anything to do with the time the trees leaf? What happens to leaves on a cold spring day?

Search for dandelions and other early season flowers. Which emerge first—native plants or introduced plants? See if bees and other insects are attracted to them. Watch how the insect burrows into the flower to eat the sweet nectar. At the same time, the insect is picking up pollen to carry to another plant so it can be fertilized.

See if you can find any seedlings in bare batches of soil. By late spring, there will be few bare patches left.

Birds are migrating northward now. You may see some stopping to hunt for insects and other food. Write down their descriptions so you can identify them later.

ROOT OUT RAGWEED

In many places in cities, near buildings, and on vacant lots, weeds are a fire hazard and should be removed. One specific weed, ragweed, is a major health hazard and should be eliminated wherever possible. Many people suffer from hay fever, which is often caused by ragweed pollen.

One mature ragweed plant can product 3600 seeds and a billion pollen grains. Ragweed plants removed in May will reduce the pollen during August and September (pollen seasons).

Conduct a ragweed elimination project by identifying it and cutting it down. Check with the local health department and find out what your pack can do to help eliminate this health hazard and air pollutant.

BEAUTIFICATION PROJECTS

Improving the environment can begin in your own neighborhood. For example, clean up an empty lot, cemetery, park, or school yard; cut and uproot unsightly weeds; plant flowers in yards, window boxes, traffic circles; paint fences and garbage cans; plant trees and shrubs; make and distribute car litter bags.

Before beginning such a project, get the advice of a local, county, or state conservation officer. You don't want to destroy endangered species of plants or the habitat of wildlife.

FUN ON A WINDY DAY

Listen to the wind. Try to hear all the different sounds it makes as it blows through the trees or past buildings. Try to imitate the sounds of the wind. Capture some of the sounds on tape.

Watch what the wind does. Look at trees, bushes, people walking. See how the wind changes things. What things do you see blowing around in the wind?

Lean into the wind. Will it hold you up? Turn around. Does the wind push you along?

Shout into the wind. Have a friend stand about 100 feet away and shout to him. Can he hear? Are you shouting against the wind or with the wind? Can you hear him shout back? Measure the distance you can hear each way.

Bat into the wind. Try batting a ball with the wind. Measure the distance it flies. Then bat against the wind. How far does it go?

COLLECTING SPRING SOUNDS

Sit very still with your eyes closed and listen to the sounds around you. Can you hear rustling? Whistling? Swishing? Screeching? Sighing? Scampering? Singing? Thumping? Buzzing? Write the sounds in your notebook or record them on a tape recorder. Decide which sounds are natural and which ones are man made. Listen for the sounds above you, beneath you, around you. Put your ear to the ground, against a tree, near a fire hydrant, beside a stream.

MAKE SOME WIND CHIMES

You'll need:

Circle of heavy cardboard or foil pie tin
Twine
Nail or ice pick
Metal canning jar rings, large nails, some old keys, or shells

MAKE SOME WIND CHIMES

1. Use the nail or ice pick to punch holes about 1 inch apart in the cardboard or pie tin.

2. Attach a double thickness of twine through the center hole for the hanger.

3. Cut several pieces of twine about 6 to 8 inches long. Thread one through each hole and tie a knot on top.

At the end of each piece, tie on a jar lid, nail, key, or shell.

4. Hang the chimes so the wind can make music outside your window.

MAKE A RAIN GAUGE

For measuring precipitation, the weather bureau uses an 8-inch diameter funnel on top of an overflow can, a measuring tube with a cross-section area one-tenth the size of the funnel, and a measuring stick. When 1 inch of rain falls into the funnel, it fills the measuring tube to a depth of 10 times as much. You can make a simple rain gauge as follows:

1. Fasten a strip of masking tape vertically on the outside of a tall jar with straight sides, such as an olive jar.

2. Pour water into a No. 10 tin can until it measures 1 inch, then pour it from the can into the jar.

3. Mark the height on the tape for 1 inch of rain, then divide the tape into tenths.

4. To use it, put the measuring can in the bottom of a pail and set it 2 to 3 feet above the ground in an exposed location. After a rainfall, measure the amount of rain by pouring the contents of the can into the measuring jar.

MAKE A RAIN GAUGE

BURY A TIME CAPSULE

This is an activity which would be fun for the den or pack. Collect items which represent everyday life today. You might include dated items such as a copy of *Boys' Life* magazine and a daily newspaper; a current edition of *Wolf Cub Scout Book;* a current fad item, a popular toy, etc. Include some identification of your den or pack, sponsor, etc. Put items in an airtight, non-perishable container with a synthetic seal, such as a 5-gallon plastic pickle barrel or paint container.

Select a spot to bury the capsule. Be sure to get permission. Let the boys help dig the hole. Bury it so there is at least 18 inches of soil on top. Then sit back and think about how exciting it will be for Cub Scouts 100 years from now to dig up your time capsule. Or the boys might like to sign a pact that the first one who becomes a Cubmaster when he is grown is permitted to dig up the capsule.

MORE THINGS TO DO IN THE SPRING

• Plant a vegetable garden.

• Go on a fishing trip.

• Have a kite-flying contest.

• Go on a nature hike.

• Visit a greenhouse.

• Build a tree house.

• Make a tent for backyard camping.

• Have a marble contest.

• Take a bike hike.

• Have a breakfast cookout.

• Take a walk in the rain.

• Plant a tree.

• Photograph wild flowers.

• Visit the desert to observe spring flowers.

Fun For All Seasons—Summer

THINGS TO LOOK FOR

Summertime is insect time. Look and listen for insects. You may hear a cricket in the early evening. Crickets chirp faster when the temperature is higher. There is a formula for finding the temperature by counting the number of cricket chirps in 15 seconds and adding 40. Try this on both warm and cool nights to see if it works.

Examine some growing plants. Look at some of the same plants you saw in the spring. How much have they grown? Do any plants show signs of lack of water? Too much water? Too much heat? What kind of flowers are in bloom now?

On a hot day feel the temperature of the sidewalk and compare it to the temperature of a grass-covered spot. Which is hotter? Plants absorb some of the sun's rays and keep the ground cooler than the unprotected sidewalk. Can you tell why the city is usually hotter than the country in summer?

Watch for sparrows and other birds bathing themselves in water after a rain. During dry periods, birds dust themselves with dry loose soil to get rid of the insect pests in their feathers. They flutter in the dust just as they do in the water.

Look for little mounds of earth on top of the soil. These are earthworm casts. Earthworms tunnel through the soil, eating plant material. The casts are remains of an earthworm's meal. The earthworm helps to mix the soil and make it better for plants.

LITTER BRIGADE

Involve the whole pack in a litter clean-up campaign. Have the boys bring wagons, carts, large bags, and boxes for collecting. Divide into groups and cover the neighborhood, picking up paper, cans, bottles, and other trash.

Bring all litter to one location for sorting. Separate the paper, cans, and glass to be taken to a recycling center, if there is one in your community. Use the remaining litter to build a litter scarecrow or make litter prevention displays to make the community aware of this problem. Be sure to dispose of all litter properly or it is still litter.

SIDEWALK FRIED EGG

Grease a piece of aluminum foil with margarine and place it on the hottest spot on the sidewalk. Break an egg directly on the foil to cook. The temperature of the sidewalk will determine how fast the egg cooks.

DEN COOKOUT

The lowly hot dog and hamburger take on the aroma and taste of costly delicacies when they are cooked outside by Cub Scouts. A cookout for den families is a fine summer evening activity. It can be held in a backyard or in a park.

Use a charcoal grill, outdoor fireplace, or a tin can stove as described in the "Crafts" section of this book. Follow fire safety rules found on page 97 in the *Cub Scout Leader Book*.

COLD BANANA TREAT

This is a nice treat from the freezer on a hot day. The recipe makes six servings.

1. Peel three bananas and cut them in half crosswise. Stick a skewer in the flat end of each piece and freeze them on individual pieces of waxed paper.

2. When the bananas have been in the freezer about 30 minutes, start the chocolate sauce. Fill a small saucepan half-full of water and heat it on medium heat. Fill a 6-ounce juice can with ¾-cup of chocolate chips and 1 ½ tablespoons vegetable oil. When the water is hot, set the can of chips into the water to melt the chocolate.

3. One at a time, remove banana pieces from freezer and dip into hot chocolate. Give each a turn as you pull it out of the chocolate.

4. While chocolate is still wet, roll coated banana in chopped nuts. Wrap in waxed paper and return to freezer for another hour.

SUN-DRIED FRUIT LEATHER

With a little help from you, the sun will dry fruit into tasty, natural snacks that will last for months. Choose a dry, sunny day for this project. You need:

2 quarts ripe, fresh fruit (peaches, plums, apricots, berries)
Collander, blender, or food processor
Waxed paper, tape

Here's how to make it:

1. Wash the fruit. Remove the stems and pits. Cut any large pieces in half.

2. Put the fruit through a collander or blender to turn it into a thick puree.

3. Heat the puree over medium heat until it is almost boiling. Stir to keep it from sticking. Let cool until lukewarm.

4. Lay out a large piece of waxed paper on an outside table or other flat surface. Tape it on the corners so it won't blow away.

5. Pour the mixture on the waxed paper and let it dry in the sun all day. Bring it inside at night and keep in dry place. Do not put in refrigerator.

6. It will take two or three days for it to dry into fruit leather. When it peels away from the paper easily, it is ready to eat.

7. Cut the fruit leather into pieces and roll them up in waxed paper or plastic wrap. Store it in a jar in a cool place.

MAKE FRIENDS WITH A WORM

Earthworms can be found close to the surface of the soil at night. Or they may be found crawling on the ground during a heavy rainfall.

To make a home for the worms, use an old fish tank or other large, deep container. Put layers of dirt, dead leaves, and sand in the bottom. Sprinkle water on each layer. Keep the outside of the glass covered with dark paper except when you are observing the worms. Keep the container covered, but be sure there are air holes in the cover.

Feed the worms bits of lettuce, dead leaves, grass clippings, or bits of table food. Remove uneaten food before adding more. Keep the soil moist by adding a little water each day.

Watch the worms tunnel through the dirt. Take a worm out of its home and look at it under a magnifying glass. See how it moves by expanding and contracting its muscles. Look at its head. Does it have eyes? Ears? Look behind the first segment to find the mouth.

To learn the worm's age, count its segments. Adult worms have about 110. Try playing music near the worm house to see if they come to the surface. They can feel vibrations from the music.

WATCH SOME ANTS

When you see ants scurrying around, in and out of a hole, they are probably looking for food. An ant scout finds the food and leaves a trail so the others can find it. Lay some bread crumbs nearby and see what happens.

Lay a pencil across the ants' trial. Do they go over it or around it? Rub your finger over the trail to erase the chemical that guides them. How do they react? How long does it take for them to find their way to the food again?

Try to tempt the ants with other foods. Scatter some sugar or other bits of food and watch them discover it.

During the winter, the ants stay underground. When the weather warms, they clear a passage to the outside world. Grain by grain the soil is brought up and deposited in a little pile around the opening.

To study ants more closely, capture some and make them an ant farm such as the one described earlier in this section.

HOW TO MAKE A SUNDIAL

Most animals and plants use the sun as their natural time teller. Cub Scouts can too, by building their own sundial.

1. Cut a piece of wood about 11 inches square.

2. Use a compass to draw the largest circle that can fit inside the square. Mark the center of the circle with a dot.

3. Drill a hole in the center and glue in a long, thin stick, knitting needle, or wood dowel. This will be the pointer (gnomon) that casts a shadow on the sundial.

4. Draw a line straight through the center of the circle, perpendicular to the top of the wood block. This is the 12:00 marking.

5. Attach the sundial to the top of a post and put it in a place that gets full sunlight. Set it so the 12:00 mark points north, or at noon (standard time) rotate sundial until shadow of gnomon fall on the 12:00 mark.

6. From 6:00 a.m. to 6:00 p.m., make a dot each hour where the shadow hits the outside of the circle.

7. Now you can tell the time of day by simply glancing at the sundial to see where the sun casts its shadow.

HOW TO MAKE A SUNDIAL

TELLING TIME BY THE SUN

Early sailors used the following technique to estimate how long it would be until sunset. Hold your hands out at arm's length so your palms are facing you and your fingers are parallel to the horizon. Keeping your fingers close together, let the sun rest on your index finger. Each finger between the sun and the horizon equals approximately 15 minutes.

PREDICTING THE WEATHER

The skies help to predict the weather. Check the following folklore predictions with your own observations to see how many are true.

- Red sky at sunset is a sign of a fair tomorrow. (A sunset sky is air which will reach you tomorrow. Dry air produces a red glow, while wet air produces a yellow-gray sky color.)

- Dull moon and stars foretell rainy tomorrow.

- Lightning from the westerly sky is from a storm that is on its way toward you.

- Towering, ragged clouds predict a rainsquall and wind.

- Sky full of cirrus or webby clouds foretells rainy spell on its way.

- A halo around the sun or moon means a warm front is on its way, with rain.

- Dark clouds against lighter ceiling foretell windy rainstorm.

- The higher the clouds, the finer the weather. Lowering clouds foretell rain.

Wind direction also helps forecast the weather.

- The west wind generally brings clear weather except when it blows off the ocean.

- The north wind brings clear, cold weather.

- The south wind brings heat and sometimes showers.

- The east wind brings rain east of the Rockies.

When rain is near, nature gets excited. Look for these signals:

- Tree frogs cry

- Fish swim near the surface

- Flies sting

- Low clouds move swiftly

- Gone-to-seed dandelions close up like an umbrella.

- Clover leaves fold together.

MEASURING WITH SHADOWS

Shadows can be used to measure trees, buildings, and other tall objects. You will need two 12-inch rulers and a bright, sunny day.

Hold one ruler straight up next to the tree or building. Use the other ruler to measure the ruler's shadow. Write down the measurement. Now measure the shadow of the object and write down that measurement.

Multiply the shadow of the tall object by 12. Then divide that answer by the length of the shadow's ruler. That will

give you the height of the tree or building.

It's also fun to measure your own shadow. Stand in the morning sun while a friend measures your shadow with a measuring tape. Make a mark on the ground with tape or chalk. Stand in the same spot at noon, late in the afternoon, and again before sundown and measure your shadow again at those times. What happens? Why?

SEND A SUN MESSAGE

By letting the sun's rays bounce off a small mirror, you can send messages to friend. First you need to decide on a code. One flash might mean, "Come over to my house;" two flashes, "Meet me on the corner;" and three flashes, "I can't come right now."

Each boy will need a small pocket mirror and a piece of cardboard larger than the mirror. Catch the sunlight on your mirror. Hold it to reflect a spot of light on the ground or a wall. Then aim that spot of light at your friend. Keep the mirror steady and cover and uncover the mirror with the cardboard to send the message. Each time you uncover the mirror there will be a flash of light.

HAVE A BEACH PARTY

This can be either a den or pack activity. It could be a picnic lunch, fish fry, or clam bake. Include swimming and games, collecting shells and rocks, building sand forts, fishing, crabbing, clamming, boating. Be sure to follow water safety rules.

While you're at the beach you could include a conservation project in the activities. Plan and carry out a beach-clearing project and pick up litter.

TREASURE HUNT ON THE BEACH

The beach is a good place to look for "treasure." The action of the sea or lake brings ashore bits of wreckage, old coins, bottles, and other things. You may not be lucky enough to find a handful of Pieces of Eight from a Spanish galleon, but you will find some interesting things that have been washed ashore.

The best time to search for this kind of treasure is after a storm. Walk along the high tide line and keep a sharp lookout for rocks, shells, bottles, coins, etc. The boys may find things to add to their collection. And while you're at it, pick up paper, cans, and other litter, and dispose of it properly.

PRINT A FISH

This is a good way to preserve the one that didn't get away, and still eat it. The fish should be printed before it is cleaned and still have its head and tail. A flat fish is easiest to print.

Rice paper makes a nice print. For many centuries, the Japanese have used rice paper to make fish prints. Some are so beautiful they are in museums.

1. Wash the fish in a mild, soapy solution. This will remove any surface slime. Dry it thoroughly.

2. Study the parts of the fish you want to print. Look at its shape, placement of fins, and pattern of scales. Plug up the gills or any other openings with cotton so they will not leak.

3. Squeeze some water-soluble printer's ink on a pane of glass. Roll a brayer (printing roller) over the ink until it sounds sticky.

4. Roll the ink across the surface of the fish, from head to tail, so scales will not be disturbed. Be sure head, fins, and tail are inked completely.

5. Lay a piece of rice paper over the fish and run your fingers around the head, over the scales, and along each fin. Then lift the print and examine it. You may be surprised by its detail.

6. Continue making prints, using more or less ink and more or less rubbing, until you get the results that please you. If the scales become clogged with ink, wash it off and try again.

7. When you are finished printing, wash off the ink. Then clean, cook, and eat the fish.

OBSERVATIONS AT THE SEASHORE

Can you see any of the following?

- Tracks in the sand. Are they made by man? Animals? Birds?

- Homes of burrowing animals in the sand.

- Compare the colors of beach animals with their surroundings.

- Is there evidence that salt water has affected trees and shrubs?

- Watch a hermit crab choose a new shell.

- Watch the behavior of hermit or fiddler crabs.

- Look for animal hiding places — under rocks, in grasses and reeds, attached to other things.

- Watch a tide pool. Do you see a starfish? A barnacle collecting food?

- Measure the tide's advance and fall.

- Turn over wet seaweed and see what is underneath.

SAND SCULPTURE CONTEST

This is a good way for boys to use their creativity at the beach. Sand can be molded, packed, and carved into many interesting shapes. Pails, bowls, milk cartons, cans, plastic containers, spatulas, boxes, and other items can be used in sand sculpture.

To mold it, pack wet sand into a container. Carefully turn the container upside down and gently lift off the container. If the sand sticks, tap the container gently.

To pack it, make a pile of wet sand and pack it into a mound with your hands. Use spoons, rulers, spatulas, or other objects to carve the mound into a shape.

Set a time limit and have a contest. Let the boys build anything from sand castles to dinosaurs to spaceships. Award every boy a prize — most unusual, tallest, funniest, most realistic, etc.

More Things To Do In Summer

- Make leaf blueprints.

- Have an ice cream social.

- Go fishing.

- Have a swimming party.

- Go berry picking or fruit picking.

- Have a treasure hunt.

- Have a Fourth of July celebration.

- Visit a farm.

- Go family camping.

- Explore a new area: forest, desert, lake, mountain.

Fun For All Seasons—Fall

THINGS TO LOOK FOR

Look at the autumn leaves. The leaves of most deciduous trees turn a certain color. See if you can identify the color of oak and maple leaves. Warm days and cool nights are

MINI-WORLD

necessary for a good leaf display in the fall. Notice which trees lose their leaves earliest, which latest.

Look for insect eggs and cocoons on bushes and beneath rocks and logs. Eggs are all different shapes. It is hard to tell what kind of insect will hatch from them. Some way be from a spider, slug, or other small animal.

Collect seeds of different kinds from bushes, trees, and grasses. Many seeds will come in packages. Open one of these seed packages and count the number of seeds inside. Do you think most of these seeds will grow into plants? Could all of the seeds turn into new plants? Why not?

Look at the buds on trees and bushes. How are they protected against winter? Open one of the buds and notice the leaves or flowers that are folded inside. Most buds must go through a long period of cold weather before they will burst into bloom in the spring. This keeps them from blooming during a short spell of warm fall weather and then dying when winter comes.

Animals are getting ready for winter now. Look for squirrels gathering and storing acorns and other foods. Look for birds migrating south. Sometimes you can see flocks of migrating birds or geese in the fall.

MINI-WORLD

Lie on a lawn or in grass, face down. Make a circle by stretching your arms out in front of you on the ground, with your hands come together. Or use a 36-inch length of rope, string, or other material. Spread the grass apart and describe what you see. How many different kinds of plants can you find in this circle? What tiny animals do you see crawling through the grass? If there are none, ask yourself, "Why are there no animals here?" Do you see any dead leaves, twigs, or litter? How do these things help or damage your mini-world?

How is a grass plant like a tree? How is it different? What do we get from grass?

What might be different about your mini-world tonight? Next summer/winter?

FUN WITH LEAVES

When fall winds blow and the autumn leaves begin to fall, sweep up some leafy piles and have some fun. Never build your leaf pile in a street or alley. Make sure you know what is *under* the leaves!

Try pile jumping. Build the pile of leaves as high as possible. Jump over it and into it.

Have a tug of war over a leaf pile. The losers wind up in the leaves. Sweep up a pile of leaves and make a castle, a dungeon, a spaceship, or anything else you want.

Have a leaf relay. Divide into two teams. First player on each team starts with approximately the same amount of leaves held loosely in his arms. He runs to a goal line and back and passes the leaves on to the next player. The winning team is not the one that finishes first but the one with the most leaves left.

Play leaf bag hot potato. Fill a plastic trash bag with leaves. Tie it shut. Toss it back and forth. Periodically the leader blows a whistle or calls, "Stop!" Don't get caught holding the bag!

GO NUTTING

October and November are the best months for finding edible nuts. The ideal time is just after a heavy windstorm. If you can beat the squirrels and chipmunks, you will find plenty of nuts on the ground beneath the trees. Be sure you have permission to gather the nuts.

A small, slender tree can be shaken to break loose some of the nuts. You may need to use a stick to shake the nuts loose from low-hanging branches. A small stick can be tossed into the tree to loosen nuts from the higher branches. Hazelnuts and pine nuts are often within arm's reach.

Depending on where you live, there may be several varieties of nuts available—pecans, hickory, walnuts, butternuts, beechnuts, pine nuts, chestnuts, and hazelnuts. You may need a hammer to crack open some of the harder nuts.

Most nuts have more flavor after they have dried and seasoned a while. Toasting or roasting usually improves the flavor.

FUN IN A NUTSHELL

Turn a nutshell into a racing car, a frightened mouse, or a fast beetle. You will need some large walnuts, small marbles, and materials for decoration. Carefully crack a large walnut. The entire half-shell is used for the "nutkin." Scrape out the nut meat and hard membrane inside. Decorate the outside of the shell with paint and bits of felt or paper for eyes, ears, etc. See illustration for ideas. The nutkin moves because of a marble under the shell. When it is placed on a sloping surface, it runs downhill. Make a ramp from any smooth, tilted surface.

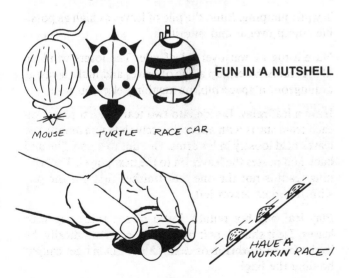

MOUSE   TURTLE   RACE CAR

FUN IN A NUTSHELL

HAVE A NUTKIN RACE!

MAKE A SPORE PRINT

Mushrooms are one of nature's most interesting and mysterious creations. They grow in damp, dark places and can pop through the ground overnight. They have no roots, no leaves, and no flower, but they come in bright fiery reds and oranges or in snow white puffs.

Early autumn is a good time to look for mushrooms in the woods. *Never eat a mushroom that you find in the woods.* Some are very poisonous.

A mushroom sends out hundreds of tiny, fertile bodies called spores. Like flower seeds, spores are the mushroom's way of reproducing. You can capture these spores on paper.

1. Choose a fresh mushroom with a flat cap. Old, dried mushrooms have already dropped their spores. Cut off the stem close to the cap.

2. Pour a little white glue in a paper cup and mix in two or three drops of water. Paint a circle of glue (a little larger than the mushroom) in the center of a piece of colored construction paper. Lay the paper on a piece of corrugated cardboard.

3. Press four straight pins into the outer rim of the mushroom. Hold it over the glued area, but do not let the mushroom touch the glue. Press the pins through the paper and into the cardboard.

4. Quickly place a bowl over the mushroom, and leave it for several hours.

5. When you remove the bowl and the mushroom, you will find the spores have dropped in a fascinating design on the paper. Each species of mushroom makes a design of its own. Some spores are white, others are brown.

LOOK FOR FOUR-LEGGED ANIMALS

On one of your hikes, you may be lucky enough to see some four-legged animals. In an open field, a rabbit may jump up in front of you and scurry off with its fluffy tail bobbing. A woodchuck may sit up for a quick look around, then hurry back into its burrow.

As you walk in the woods, a deer may bound up before you, then quickly disappear into the brush. Or you may spot some squirrels playing in the leaves. When they see you, they will probably rush to the nearest tree, run up the trunk, and hide among the branches.

Even if you don't see any of these animals, you can look for their homes and hiding places. Look up. You may see squirrel nests or raccoon or opossum dens in hollow trees. Look around. You may discover a muskrat house made up of reeds and twigs or a beaver house of branches and mud. Look down and you may see where rabbits bed down or spot the entrance to a fox's den or a skunk's hiding place.

Chewed-off twigs may be where deer have been feeding. You may see shells of nuts left behind after a mouse party, or the remains of pine cones where squirrels have bitten off the petals to get to the seeds.

Animals tracks show where animals have walked slowly to their feeding places or have hurried off at full speed to get away from some enemy. Keep your eyes open and you will learn a lot about mammals.

MAKE A NEIGHBORHOOD TREASURE MAP

1. Use a large sheet of paper or cloth.

2. Begin by drawing a square in the center to show where you live. Label it "home."

3. In one corner of the map make a circle with four compass points. Mark them North on top, South on the bottom, East on the right, and West on the left.

4. On a separate sheet of paper, make two lists. One includes all your favorite places in the neighborhood—baseball diamond, ice cream store, movie theater, park, etc. The other includes danger spots—the house where a ferocious dog lives, a poison ivy patch, a dangerous intersection, etc.

5. Mark each favorite and dangerous spot on your map in the proper location from your house. Use stars for the favorite spots and **X**'s or skulls and crossbones for the danger spots.

6. Choose one or two landmarks near each favorite and danger spot—a lake, a church, a school, a cemetery, a large tree, etc. Put these on your map in the proper location by drawing simple pictures of them.

7. Now visit each landmark and count off the number of paces between it and the favorite or danger spot. Make notes as you go. When you get home, add these measurements to your map.

MORE THINGS TO DO IN THE FALL

- Plant a tree.
- Plant bulbs.
- Have a leaf-raking tournament.
- Have a top-spinning contest.
- Go on a weiner roast.
- Have a Halloween party.
- Go apple-picking.
- Go on a hayride.
- Visit a county fair.
- Make a leaf collection.

- Take a nature hike.
- Visit a historic spot.
- Go to a football game.
- Play touch football.

Fun For All Seasons—Winter

THINGS TO LOOK FOR

Look for birds during winter. What kind of food do they eat? Many depend on people feeding them. Watch how their feathers fluff out on cold days. The feathers are full of tiny air pockets that act as insulators so the birds will stay warm. Look for abandoned bird nests. The branches of trees are bare and you can see the nests more easily. But don't remove the nests because birds may use them next spring.

Look for tracks of birds and other animals in the snow. What kind of animal made the prints? How do the tracks go—in a straight line, stopping, zigzagging? Was the animal looking for food or just walking?

Go outside after a snowstorm. Notice how the trees and bushes are loaded down by the weight of the snow. Have any branches been torn off by the storm? Branches snap more easily when they are frozen than at other times. As the sun comes out and the snow begins to melt, the branches may become covered with sheets of glistening ice.

The ground is warmer under a blanket of snow than it would be if exposed to air. If you have an outdoor thermometer, check the ground temperature under the snow and compare it to the air temperature. Also check the temperature beneath a pile of rotting leaves. Leaves and snow are good insulators. They protect the ground below the surface from freezing solid. This helps keep the animals and plant roots in the soil from freezing and dying.

COLLECTING SNOWFLAKES

Sometimes snow is fine and dry; other times it is heavy and wet. And sometimes it falls in big fluffy flakes. No two flakes are exactly alike.

To collect snowflakes you will need glass slides or any small pieces of glass, a flat piece of wood to hold the glass, an eye dropper, and a 2 percent solution of polyvinyl formal resin dissolved in ethylene dichloride. These can be obtained at a drug store.

1. Place the solution and glass outdoors in a spot protected from dirt and falling snow. Both must be very cold before they can be used to collect snowflakes.

2. Using the eye dropper, cover the glass with the solution.

3. Carefully catch a few snowflakes on the coated glass. Put the glass in a spot protected from falling snow.

4. If any of the snowflakes are not completely covered by the solution, place a small drop of the solution on the flake.

5. Let dry for 15 minutes.

6. After the glass is dry, bring it indoors and examine the snowflakes with a magnifying glass. They are delicate, so handle gently. The collection can be stored in a small box.

TAKING SNOW TEMPERATURES

Tie or tape an old outdoor thermometer to the end of a yardstick. Do not tape over the bulb. Gently push the thermometer end in a snowdrift. It will take a little time for the thermometer to adjust to the snow's temperature, so leave it there for a few minutes. Measure the temperature in deep snow and shallow snow, in shady spots and in sunny spots. What is the difference?

Is snow always colder than air? To find out, hold the thermometer in the air for a few minutes, then read it.

MEASURING A SNOW DRIFT

Push a yardstick into a snowdrift until the end touches the ground. Measure the drift next to trees, up against buildings, next to fences, on driveways, and in other spots. Find the deepest drift. Is it in a shady, sunny, or windy spot?

MAKE A SNOW GAUGE

Use a snow gauge to measure how much snow falls in your yard. Use a ruler and permanent marking pen to mark lines on the inside of a 2- or 3-pound coffee can. Make a line for each inch and lable 1", 2", etc. from the bottom up.

When its starts to snow, put the can on the ground in an open spot away from trees and buildings. Check to see how many inches have fallen when the snowstorm is over.

Does 1 inch of snow make one inch of water? To find out, let the snow melt in the can. Does the water measure the same as the snow? Different kinds of snow contain different amounts of water. Loose snow has less water than wet, tightly packed snow.

SNOW SCULPTURE

Snow sculpture can range from a simple snowman to animals, birds, forts, and comic book characters. Make your sculpture in a place where it can be admired by passersby.

Select a location, subject, and general layout. Make a framework of light wood or chicken wire to strengthen the figure. Pack in the snow roughly, then carve it to shape with spoons, spatulas, etc. Sprinkle the finished sculpture with water to set and preserve it.

BUILDING WITH SNOW BRICKS

Snow bricks can be used to build houses, castles, forts, walls, and other structures. A metal bread pan makes a good mold. Pack snow into the mold, turn it upside down, tap the bottom of the mold lightly, and you have a snow brick.

If the snow doesn't pack well, it is too dry. Sprinkle it lightly with water before packing it in the mold.

Build each wall layer by layer. Stack the snow bricks with long sides together so the wall will be sturdy. Pack snow lightly in the gaps between the bricks.

WINTER NATURE HIKE

Look for these things:

- Deer tracks
- Raccoon tracks
- Mouse tunnel in snow
- Squirrel nest
- Cattail
- Dormant tree
- Moss
- Plant with blue bark
- Owl home in dead tree
- Winter birds
- Squirrel tracks
- Muskrat house
- Cocoon
- Brown leaf
- Open milkweed pod
- Dead tree
- Plant with red bark
- Frozen water

BIRDFEEDER SNOWMAN

Make a snowman. Give it a pine cone stuffed with suet and birdseed mixture for a nose, dates for eyes, a line of raisins for mouth, and apple pieces for buttons. String cranberries on strong thread to make a belt. Add an old straw beach hat with a wide brim and sprinkle birdseed and sunflower seeds on the brim. Make arms for the snowman from thick branches so the birds will have a place to perch while they are eating. Set a pail of water nearby to give them something to drink.

CASTING OF ANIMAL TRACKS IN SNOW

Follow instructions for making plaster casts of tracks found in the "Crafts" section of this book, with these additions:

1. Dust dry plaster into all parts of the track.

2. Use a plastic squeeze bottle to spray a mist of water over the dry plaster. Let it freeze.

3. Mix plaster as usual, adding a little snow to lower the temperature. Then proceed to make the cast in the normal manner.

GO SNOW BOWLING

Smooth a path (the lane) in the snow. It must be very smooth and icy. Set five or more upturned plastic drinking glasses at the end of the lane for pins, about 15 feet away. Make a pile of bowling snowballs. They should be hard and round so they will roll.

Take turns knocking down the "pins" with the snow balls.

SNOWBALL GUESSING

Make five snowballs. Place each in a different location—one on a snowy rock, one on ground, one under a bush, one on the hood of a car, etc. Try to guess which will melt first and why. Keep checking until one of them has melted. Were you right?

SNOWBALL PELOTA

Make scoops from plastic bottles as shown in the "Crafts" section of this book. Then make some snowballs. Toss the snowballs back and forth, catching them in the scoop.

MORE THINGS TO DO IN WINTER

- Have a snowball throwing contest.
- Go ice skating or sledding.
- Go on a sleigh ride.
- Shovel and clear sidewalks.

- Build bird feeders.
- Go ice fishing.
- Play some winter games (see "Games" section).

Backyard Camping

The Boy Scouts of America encourages backyard camping by younger Cub Scouts. A boy is not likely to run into problems beyond his depth when his family is close by.

Backyard camping is simply sleeping out with a buddy or two in someone's backyard, either under the stars or in tents. The boys may try to cook their meals outdoors, too, but they will need some supervision. Someone should be ready with emergency chow. They may need it.

BACKYARD TENT

A tent is a big plus for backyard campers, although they can do without it if necessary because shelter is so close by. It can be a family tent, an old pup tent, a tarp, or even an old rug. With some help, a boy can make a simple but serviceable tent from almost any heavy material. Unbleached muslin is good and inexpensive. When it is completed (dyed and decorated as desired), take it to a dry cleaner for waterproofing or buy a nonflammable waterproofing mixture and do it yourself.

The tent can be set up with poles, or it can be hung over a clothesline or fence as illustrated. Use a plastic groundcloth for protection. (A large plastic bag slit on side and bottom makes a good ground cloth.)

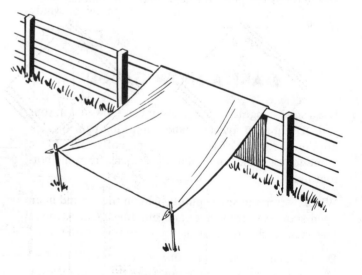

BACKYARD TENT

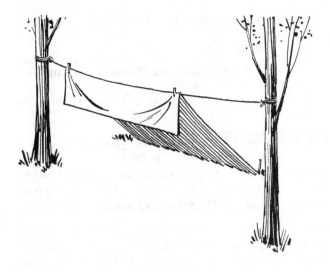

Family Camping

Family camping has become a very popular activity and is encouraged by the Boy Scouts of America. A family camping trip can be rewarding for Cub Scouts and every member of the family.

Family camping may also be a den, or pack activity. Den or pack family camping trips should include Cub Scout or Webelos Scout activities as a part of the program. Remember, overnight and long-term camping are not permitted for 7-, 8-, or 9-year old Cub Scouts, except as a part of family camping. That means that a parent or other adult must accompany and supervise each Cub Scout.

COOKING

With supervision, younger Cub Scouts can cook a simple meal on an outdoor grill, or on a tin-can stove, like the one shown in the "Crafts" section of this book. Some sample recipes are given later in this chapter.

BEDDING

A bed for backyard camping doesn't need to be elaborate. A ground cloth and a sleeping bag are adequate. An air mattress adds comfort. If these are not available, make a ground cloth from an old shower curtain, a plastic bag, or other plastic material. An envelope bed can be made from blankets as shown in the illustration. In the summer, one blanket is often enough. Fold it so there are two layers under you. In cooler weather, you will need at least two blankets. Fold the first blanket with two layers under you, then bring the bottom up over your feet. Swing half of the second blanket over you, and fold the bottom under your legs. Safety pins will help hold it in place.

WHERE TO CAMP

There are many places to camp, both public and private. These include national and state parks and forests, privately-operated campgrounds, and Scout camps. A campground usually has improvements such as running water, sanitary facilities, and platforms floors for tents. A campsite can also be set in an undeveloped area.

State and national parks operate on a "first come, first served" basis, with no reservations. Entrance charges vary, but they are usually moderate.

SELECTING A CAMPSITE

Look for these things when selecting a campsite:

• South or southeast exposure.

• Protection from wind.

• Level and reasonably smooth ground. (Even a shallow depression can collect water in a heavy rain.)

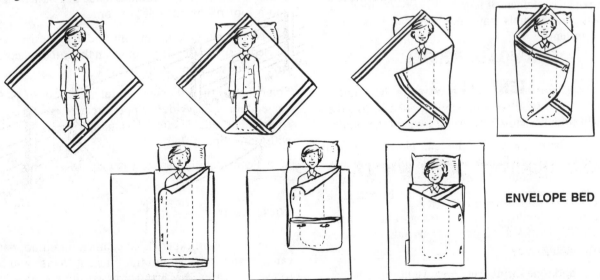

ENVELOPE BED

- No gullies or ravines nearby. They can be dangerous in flash flooding.

- Avoid trees with dead or dying branches.

- Check water supply. Piped, well, and spring water is usually safe.

- Don't camp near swamps, tall grasses or watery meadows.

SETTING UP CAMP

- Pitch a tent on smooth and level ground with tent back to prevailing wind. The slope of the stakes will depend on the condition and texture of the ground. Usually stakes driven at an angle toward the line of pull will hold in either hard or soft ground. Use taut-line hitch on guy lines.

- Make a door mat of plywood or heavy cardboard, to help keep the inside of the tent clean. When possible, leave shoes outside.

- If campsite does not have toilet facilities, locate your latrine well away from tents and water supply.

- Many campers take along a large tarp or dining fly and set it up as a shelter to provide a covered area for cooking, eating, and other activity outside the tent.

- Keep an adequate supply of drinking water on hand. It's a good idea to keep a thermos bottle full of water in the tent at night, especially for children.

- Always gather firewood during daylight and stack it under shelter. Don't count on firewood being available. Bring wood or charcoal or stoves.

- Before turning in for the night, be sure everything is secure and covered for protection from rain or animals. Be sure food is well covered or hung out of reach. Don't leave open containers of food in the car—the food may be safe, but animals may scratch the car. Don't store food in tents.

TENT LIVING

Living in a tent is enjoyable if you prepare for it.

- Keep all flames away from the tent. Never use liquid fuel stoves, heaters, lanterns, lighted candles, matches, or other flame sources in or near tents. Be fire safe. *No flames in tents* is a rule which must be enforced.

- Tent ropes should be clean, strong, and securely attached to tent. Keep extra ropes available for quick storm rigging.

- Canvas and rope shrink when wet. Tight ropes can rip your tent in a storm. If it rains, loosen the tent ropes a little.

- Never pile dirt and leaves against lower walls of tent.

- Never use flammable chemicals near tents (charcoal lighter, spray paint, insect repellent). These may remove the water-proofing.

- Clean and dry the tent thoroughly before storing. Carry and store tent in a bag, if possible.

CAMPING IN COMFORT

Sleeping Bags

Sleeping outdoors has always been half the fun of camping. The sleeping bag makes it easy, and an inflated air mattress will add to comfort. Foam pads keep you warmer and don't deflate. Some campers use a sleeping bag on a cot. Choose a sleeping bag that suits the season and area.

Down bags are the warmest and lightest, but the most expensive, and they do not insulate when wet. Several other types are available. Be sure the cover fabric is sturdy. Your Scout distributor will have various bags approved by the Boy Scouts of America.

Tents

Allow about 20 square feet per person for tent living. Straight-walled tents provide more living area. All-cotton or cotton/polester drills and ducks are durable and water-resistant but are prone to mildew. Synthetics are strong, lightweight, and mildew-resistant, but the water-resistant urethane coating keeps air from passing through. A good combination is a tent with walls made of synthetic fabric and a roof of "breathable" cotton.

Remember that by law, tents must be flame-resistant and labeled as such. This does not mean they are flameproof, so use fire safety precautions.

Some tent features that are helpful are a floor of plastic-coated fabric; heavy-duty zippers; reinforced stitching at stress points; double stitched seams and screened windows with inner-zipper flaps.

Your Scout distributor can show approved tents.

Equipment

If you are not an experienced camper, an outdoorsman can give you some helpful tips on what to take and how to use it. Nearby Boy Scout troops will be glad to help with advice and suggestions. Some families borrow or rent the large equipment until they know what purchases they need to make.

In addition to a tent and sleeping bags, the list will include cooking and eating equipment, food and food containers, some tools, and personal equipment.

The dishwashing problem can be solved by using paper plates, and cups. These can be burned, leaving only the cooking utensils to be cleaned.

Always bring plastic garbage bags. They serve many useful purposes in addition to holding trash. Be sure to include a first aid kit.

FIRES

Be careful when building fires on open ground. Pick a spot away from low overhanging branches. Before building the fire, clear a circle 10 feet in diameter of everything that will burn—litter, leaves, sticks, pine needles, etc., right down to bare ground. Build the fire in the center, and there will be less chance of it spreading. Keep the fire away from dead logs and stumps.

Always break burnt matches before throwing them away, and be sure the matches are "cold out."

Never leave a fire unattended. A breeze may come up while you're gone and spread the fire. Keep a bucket of water, dirt, or sand handy for emergency use. An unattended campfire or sparks from a fire can cause an entire forest to burn. Be campfire safe.

Be sure the fire is out—*dead out*—before breaking camp. Spread the coals and ashes and drench the fire and ground around it with plenty of water. Or mix soil and sand with embers so fire will go out. Continue adding and stirring until all material is cold enough to feel with your bare hand. Don't just bury the fire—it may smoulder and break out again.

DISPOSING OF TRASH

Burn all garbage and rubbish that will burn. Wet garbage can be dried beside the fire, then burned. If there are garbage disposal facilities at the campsite, they should be used. If not, wash bottles and flatten tin cans and take home for disposal. Do not bury garbage; animals may dig it up. Never leave any broken glass around your campsite. Don't burn plastics—they may melt and change shape, but never decompose.

Outdoor Cooking

COOKING FIRES

The first and most important requirement for outdoor cooking is fire safety. Follow fire safety rules and heed the flammability warning found in the *Cub Scout Leader Book*. Careless use of fire can cause a disaster.

Start with crumpled paper, shavings, or small dry sticks. In wet weather, split a log and cut slivers from the dry, inside part. Or, use one of the fire starters described below. Use dry hardwoods (oak, maple, walnut, or birch) for the fire rather than evergreen branches. Keep the cooking fire small. A good bed of coals with a low flame, surrounded by rocks, gives plenty of heat for cooking. Tamp the coals flat with a stick if you wish to make it level. Make the fire only large enough to serve its purpose.

Be sure to build the fire out of the wind. Remember to start the fire early, since it will take a while to burn down to coals.

FIRE STARTERS

In addition to natural tinder and the buddy burner found in the "Crafts" section of this book, here are some other simple fire starters:

French Candles. These are also called paraffin logs or "fire bugs" and are useful in building wet-weather fires. Tear several thickness of newspaper into 2-inch strips. Roll to make a log about 1-inch thick and tie with a string. Melt paraffin in a double boiler. Holding the newspaper roll with tongs, dip it into the melted paraffin. The saturated string becomes a wick. French candles produce a high, steady flame to help get the fire going.

FRENCH CANDLES

Another way to make "fire bugs" is to roll up four newspaper sheets, beginning at the short side. Tie strings 2 inches apart. Cut between the strings to make 2-inch bugs." Soak in paraffin as directed above.

To provide a little more burning area, create a candle effect with the "fire bugs" by using your finger to push out some of the middle. When completed, you can use the string for a wick and also light the small "top" end of the candle.

Egg Cup Burner. Mix ¾-cup sawdust with enough melted paraffin to saturate it. Put in a 3-ounce paper cup or a cup cut from an cardboard egg carton. Insert a string in the center for a wick.

SATURATE ¾ CUP SAWDUST WITH MELTED PARAFFIN. ADD WICK.

3 OUNCE CUP

EGG CUP BURNER

Match Bundle. Tie six to eight kitchen matches together with a string and dip in paraffin.

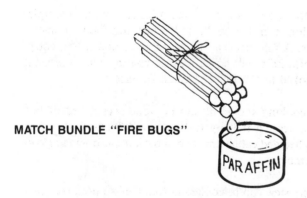

MATCH BUNDLE "FIRE BUGS"

PARAFFIN

STOVES AND FIREPLACES

Besides the tin-can stove and charcoal chimney found in the "Crafts" section, which are helpful when cooking outdoors with Cub Scouts, several other successful techniques are included here.

Newspaper Stove

This stove is easy to make, fast and easy to clean up.

5-gallon can

Wire cookie cooling rack to fit over can

Some newspapers

Spray bottle of water

To make:

1. Remove the top from the 5-gallon can. Cut a 2 ½-by-1 ½-inch vent on one side of the can, above 2 inches from the bottom.

2. Loosely twist and crush lightly four or five newspapers into small "logs" and place them in the stove bottom. Wad up a single sheet of newspaper and set it on top of the "logs" and light. (Do not use newspaper with colored inks, such as comic pages, since they produce toxic flames when burned.)

3. Place the cooling rack over the top of the can as a grill. (Do not use a refrigerator rack; it may be coated with a substance that's toxic when heated.)

4. Any meat not more than 1-inch thick which contains some fat can be cooked on this stove. Fat drippings from the cooking meat will keep the paper burning. If flames get too high, spray them with water to avoid charred, half-cooked food.

5. When cooking is finished, clean rack with steel wool and your stove is ready to use the next time.

SOLAR COOKER

Here's a practical way to cook hot dogs by tapping the sun's energy. A den chief or adult can make one for the Cub Scouts to use all summer.

40-inch piece of 1-by-8-inch wood

1-by-2-foot foot piece of sheet aluminum

Two 4-inch nails and assorted smaller nails

Two 2-inch wood screws

Two metal washers

Steel wool

Household cement

Aluminum foil

10-by-10-inch piece of brown wrapping paper

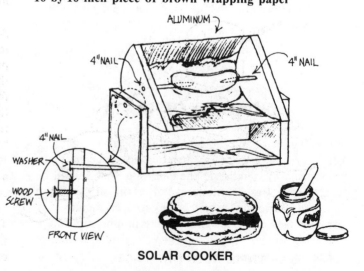

ALUMINUM

4" NAIL

4" NAIL

4" NAIL

WASHER

WOOD SCREW

FRONT VIEW

SOLAR COOKER

Here's how:

1. On wrapping paper, draw grid as shown, with 1-inch squares. On the grid, carefully duplicate the arc shown.

2. Cut out the pattern and trace it on the wood. Cut the side pieces, base, and side support pieces with a coping saw or jigsaw.

3. In each side panel, drill two holes as shown on pattern. The top holes should be slightly smaller than the 4-inch nails; the bottom holes slightly smaller than the wood screws.

4. Nail the base and side supports together. Then nail the aluminum sheet to the side panels to make a "canoe" to fit between the side supports.

5. Polish the inner surface of the aluminum with steel wool and wipe clean. Cement the aluminum foil, shiny side out, to the canoe.

6. Push the 4-inch nails through the holes and fasten them with household cement. Clean the nails with steel wool and rinse with water.

7. Mount the canoe on the support stand with the wood screws and washers.

8. Now you're ready to cook. Skewer a hot dog on the nails. Position the cooker so the sun's rays reflect from the aluminum to the hot dog. In a few minutes you'll have a well-done treat.

SIMPLE ROCK FIREPLACE

Arrange flat rocks into a level "**V**," with the point of the "**V**" in the direction of the wind. The dirt inside can be scooped out to make a deeper bed for the fire. The rocks can be used as warming shelves for pots. Pans can be set at the narrow end of the "**V**." Foil dinners can be cooked in the coals.

SIMPLE ROCK FIREPLACE

RECTANGULAR FIREPLACE

When cooking for a large number of people, build a rectangle of flat rocks not over 10 inches high and large enough to hold a grid from a kitchen range. When the fire has burned down, use a large stick to push the coals to one side of the rectangle. This provides a hot fire on one side for cooking and a warming area on the other side. Replace rocks where you found them when you leave the campsite.

RECTANGULAR FIREPLACE

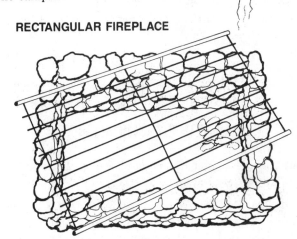

ALUMINUM FOIL COOKING

Outdoor cooking can be great fun. If you like it simple, try aluminum foil cooking. It's fast and food retains its juices. A foil meal can be prepared at home. Foil cooking also helps cut down on dishwashing since the meal is cooked in the foil and eaten from it.

Foil cooking should always be done over a bed of hot coals, never a flaming fire. Start the fire well ahead of the scheduled eating time and allow it to die down to glowing embers.

A tasty stew can be cooked in foil. Cut up potatoes, carrots, onion, and celery. Add stew meat or a hamburger patty. Season as desired. Use heavy-duty foil or a double thickness of the regular kind. Place food on one half and fold over the other half to make an envelope, open on three sides. Fold in each side about three times and crimp the edges to make an air-tight container—(called the "drug-store wrap"). Place packet on coals and cook about 10 to 15 minutes on each side. Timing the meat can be a little tricky until you have experience. Different fires cook at different speeds.

The foil drug-store wrap can be used to cook a fresh fish fillet, chicken, baked potatoes, corn on the cob, and many other types of foods.

Aluminum foil can also be fashioned into cooking utensils and eating utensils. It is a helpful item in outdoor cooking.

ALUMINUM FOIL COOKING

CREATIVE EQUIPMENT

Time-consuming preparation and cleanup can be cut by using this creative equipment:

Plastic Bag "Bowls." Heavy-duty, self-sealing plastic bags will save dishwashing. Use them as substitutes for mixing bowls when you make cake, biscuits, or instant pudding. Carry mixed dry ingredients in these bags. When you're ready to mix, add liquids and depress the bag to get rid of excess air. Reseal the bag and "mix" by squeezing the bag firmly.

These bags can also be used to carry prepared salads or other dishes. When you are ready to serve. simply place the bag in an appropriate size empty can, open the bag, pull the top over the outside edges of the can, and serve from the "bowl."

Frisbee Plate. A flimsy paper plate can spill easily. To solve this problem, use several regular paper plates together or use a Frisbee as a paper plate holder. It is great for "fast-food" service.

Soap Bottle. Before leaving home, fill a plastic squeeze bottle with water and a few drops of liquid detergent. Use to clean hands before, during, and after food preparation. Another alternative is to carry a plastic, self-sealing bag with a damp cloth or damp paper towels inside. There will never be a problem with sticky fingers.

(See "Crafts" section of this book for homemade cooking utensils.)

PACKING TIPS

Keeping hot food hot and cold food cold can be a problem on a trip. Commercial insulated thermos containers, styrofoam containers, and hot boxes come in handy. Before packing your cooler, chill it in the refrigerator.

If you don't have a thermos to keep foods warm, make a "hot box." Use a Dutch oven or heavy aluminum pan to bring a one-pot meal to a boil. Cook to a point just short of the last 10 to 20 minutes of recommended cooking time. Remove from heat and place in a large cardboard box lined with 2-to-3 inches of newspapers. Pack newspapers around the Dutch oven or pan on all sides and top and bottom of box to prevent heat loss. The food will continue to cook in the box and stay hot for hours.

Commercial coolers will keep drinks and salads cool for a longer period of time if you use a large block of ice rather than ice cubes. Freeze water in half-gallon or gallon cardboard or plastic milk cartons.

To carry meats to be cooked later, freeze them in self-sealing plastic bags, then carry in a cooler. They will keep other foods cold and will thaw without leaking.

PLANNING A COOKOUT

- Plan menus carefully and write them down.
- Make a list of the foods and equipment needed for the number of people to be served.
- Pack the food carefully so it won't spoil or spill.
- Store food properly before and after cooking.
- Keep food preparation simple.
- Be safety conscious at all times when working around fire. Have a container of water handy to use in case of an emergency and to put out fire when you are through.

──────RECIPES──────

HEARTY HOT DOG THERMOS SPECIAL

Fill a thermos ¾-full with your favorite steaming hot soup. Tie a string around a heated hot dog and drop it in the soup, leaving the end of the string outside the bottle. Cap the bottle. For a quick meal on the road, open the thermos, pull out the hot dog, place it on a bun spread with your favorite fixings. Serve it with the hot soup, a drink, and cookies or cupcakes.

For a Spanish-flavored variation, suspend the hot dog in a thermos of spicy, steaming hot chili. Serve with corn chips, drink, and dessert.

KABOBS

On a skewer or stick, place bite-sized pieces of meat and vegetables, alternating them. You could use cubed luncheon meat, precooked ham, quartered weiners, or beef chunks. For vegetables, try chunks of onion, potatoes, green peppers, mushrooms or cherry tomatoes. Brush skewered food with melted butter and barbecue sauce. Broil over hot coals. Turn the kabobs occasionally as they cook.

INSTANT TACOS

Pack your favorite taco mixture in a thermos. At mealtime, open the top of a small bag of corn or taco chips and pour the mixture into the bag to mix. Sprinkle with grated cheese and eat from the bag.

CHICKEN AND RICE FOIL DINNER

Place chicken breasts on a 14-inch square of heavy-duty aluminum foil. Mix a can of condensed cream of mushroom soup with ⅔-cup uncooked instant rice. Spoon over chicken. Sprinkle with paprika. Seal the foil package and place on grill 5 inches above coals. Cook about 40 minutes, turning once.

SUBMARINES IN FOIL

Scoop out a "bowl" in the center of a hard roll. Mix together canned luncheon meat, corned beef, or minced ham with pickle relish, diced boiled egg, and grated cheddar cheese. Moisten with salad dressing or undiluted cream of chicken soup. Fill rolls with mixture and wrap each individually in double-thickness foil. Cook 20 to 25 minutes over hot coals.

GRILLED CORN ON THE COB

Strip the husks back over the end of the cob but do not tear off. Remove all silk and soak in cold salted water for 15 minutes. Then smooth on some butter. Bring the husks back over the corn, wrap each ear in a piece of foil, and twist the ends tightly. Lay on coals and cook for 15 to 20 minutes, turning once.

HUNTER'S STEW

Cut ½-pound beef, veal, or lamb in small chunks. Place 1 tablespoon cooking oil in pan and brown the meat. Add

1 cup water, diced carrots, celery, onions, and potatoes. Simmer for 30 minutes. Season with salt and pepper.

WALKING SALAD

Cut the top off an apple and remove the core. Take care not to cut all the way through to the bottom of the apple. Fill the cavity with peanut butter mixed with raisins. Replace the top of the apple and wrap in plastic wrap. Take along for a quick snack on a hike. Create your own filling, using your favorites—cheese, nuts, marshmallows, dried fruit, etc.

PIGS IN BLANKET

Add water or milk to biscuit mix to make a stiff dough. Mold dough around a weiner already on a clean roasting stick. Pinch ends of dough to hold. Roast over coals.

TWIXER BISCUITS

Open a biscuit-mix box and make a depression in the contents so you can pour a little water into the hole. Stir it gently with a clean, pronged stick until it forms an egg-sized ball. Remove the ball from the stick, flatten it, and wrap it around a clean, preheated stick to bake as twisted over the coals. Or, form it into a biscuit shape and bake in aluminum foil, leaving space for the biscuit to rise.

For extra flavor, make a depression in the dough and fill with jam, jelly or cheese.

For pizza, flatten the dough. Spread on some tomato or spaghetti sauce and a sprinkle of oregano. Add thin slices of cheese and pepperoni or salami. Wrap in foil and bake in coals.

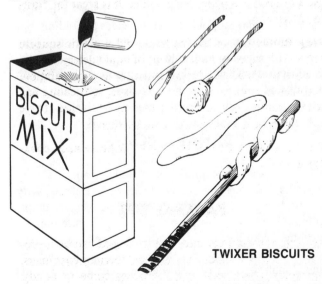

TWIXER BISCUITS

FOIL-CUP EGG

For each egg, make a cup by molding a 7-inch square of aluminum foil around the bottom of a 16-ounce can. Slide cup off can and break an egg into the cup. Place cup on grill and cook 10 minutes, or place directly on coals and cook 2 to 3 minutes.

EGGS ON A RAFT

Grease the cooking surface of a tin-can stove. Cut a hole 2 to 2 ½-inches in diameter in the center of a slice of bread. Place bread on the burner and break an egg into the hole. Season. Turn over once and cook to your satisfaction.

BREAKFAST-IN-AN-ORANGE

Cut an orange in half and carefully remove the meat of the orange without tearing the cup-shaped peeling. Break an egg into one orange cup and fill the other with your favorite muffin batter mixed in a self-sealing bag. Place each cup on its own square of double-thickness foil, then bring the four corners of the foil to the top and twist securely to seal. (Be sure to leave enough room for the muffin to rise).

Set the foil-enclosed cups on hot coals for 10 to 15 minutes, then enjoy a delicious breakfast of orange slices, eggs, and muffins.

HOBO POPCORN

In the center of a 6-inch foil square, place 1 teaspoon cooking oil and 1 tablespoon popcorn. Bring foil corners together to make a pouch. Seal the edges by folding, but leave room for the corn to pop. Tie each pouch to a long stick with a string and hold the pouch over hot coals. Shake constantly until all corn has popped. Season with butter and salt. Make one for each person.

BANANA BOATS

Cut lengthwise a diamond-shaped wedge from a banana. Strip back the peeling but don't remove it. Fill the cavity in the banana with a mixture of milk-chocolate chips, miniature marshmallows, and nuts. Replace the banana peeling. Wrap it securely in foil and place it in the coals for about 10 minutes so the chocolate melts and the marshmallows puff off. Unwrap and enjoy. Or try butterscotch, butter brickle, or peanut butter chips.

For a tropical treat, fill banana cavity with crushed pineapple, coconut, a little brown sugar, and a dab of butter. Bake 5 to 10 minutes on hot coals.

SHAGGY DOGS

Open a can of chocolate syrup and heat it over the coals until runny. Toast a marshmallow on a stick until just golden. Dip the marshmallow in the syrup and roll in coconut or chopped pecans. Easy and delicious!

BAKED APPLE

Core an apple and place it on a square of aluminum foil. Fill the core with raisins, brown sugar, a dash of cinnamon, and a chunk of butter. Seal with drugstore wrap and place on hot coals. Cook until apple is soft.

FRUIT KABOBS

Follow the instructions for regular kabobs, using chunks of banana, pineapple, cherries, etc., alternating with large marshmallows. Toast over coals until marshmallows are golden brown.

SNACKS FOR HIKERS

The following mixtures can be mixed in quantity and divided into individual sandwich-size, self-seal plastic bags. They make welcome treats and provide energy for hikers.

Gorp. Mix salted nuts, dates, semi-sweet chocolate bits, raisins, dried fruit pieces, cubes of dry cheese, and cocktail-size miniature crackers.

Hiker's Birdseed. Mix individual-size packages of sugared breakfast cereals, two small bags of M&Ms, a handful of dried raisins, and ½ handful of dry roasted peanuts.

TIN CAN ICE CREAM

Place one 3 ¾-ounce package of instant pudding mix and two 6-ounce or one 13-ounce can evaporated milk in a clean 1-pound coffee can. Add enough regular milk to fill the can three-quarters full. Mix well. Cover with plastic lid. Tape on lid securely with duct tape so can is airtight.

Place the 1-pound can in a 3-pound or a No. 10 can. Add layers of crushed ice and rock salt around the smaller can until it is surrounded by ice and salt on all sides. Put lid on larger can. Tape with duct tape.

Roll the can back and forth on a table or the ground for 20 to 25 minutes. The boys can form two lines to do this, rolling it back and forth to each other.

Carefully untape the large can and remove smaller one to check ice cream. Wipe off all salt before removing lid from smaller can. Scrape ice cream from insides of can. Put lid back on and tape securely.

Place the smaller can back in the large can and add more ice and salt. Tape lid on large can and continue to roll for about 10 more minutes. By then the ice cream should be ready to eat.

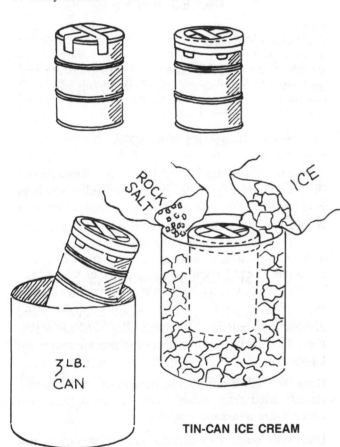

TIN-CAN ICE CREAM

Campfires

Campfires are great fun for Cub Scouts and their families. A well-planned campfire is an exciting and inspirational way to end an evening pack activity. A campfire should be the highlight of the Webelos dad-son overnight campout.

The location and construction of the campfire are important, but most of all, it's the campfire program that counts. To be truly successful, a campfire must be more than just a casual gathering around a leaping fire. It should have purpose and direction.

PLANNING A CAMPFIRE

- Use Campfire Program Planner, Supply No. 3696.

- Decide who does what, when, and how.

- Develop a written plan, even down to the song titles.

- Check all program items in advance. Songs, jokes, or stunts in poor taste have no place in a Scout campfire.

- Select a scenic spot, with good drainage, so ground will be dry for seating. Provide protection from the wind and insects.

- Check the location for fire safety and follow fire safety rules.

RESOURCES FOR CAMPFIRE PROGRAMS

The "Songs, Stunts, and Stories" section of this book will be helpful in planning campfires. In addition, use *Group Meeting Sparklers,* and the *Cub Scout Songbook.*

Your public library may have these books of campfire programs:

Complete Book of Campfire Programs, by LaRue A. Thurston

Creative Campfires, by Douglas R. Bowen

Campfire Programs, by Jack Pearse

Campfire Tonight, by Richard J. Hurley

CAMPFIRE LEADERSHIP

Showmanship is the art of attractive presentation. Without it, the campfire leader and all the songs, stunts, and stories may fall flat. Showmanship is the indispensable ingredient that puts sparkle and life into a campfire program. Here are some suggestions:

- Follow the fire. When it leaps high, the program should be lively and loud. As the fire dies down, the program becomes quieter and deeper.

- Have the best stunt or skit last on the program. Begin with the next-best stunt or skit. Use noisy, lively stunts early in the program.

- Vary the pace by scattering stunts in between the other features on the program. The walk-on stunt is an attention-getter and can be used as a fill-in between other activities.

- Dress up the campfire area. A tom-tom, off in the distance, is an excellent pre-opening mood setter for an Indian program. Ceremony boards, candles, and other props add to the excitement.

- Crowd control with a large group is easier if you insist on silence as the group enters the campfire ring. Make sure there is adequate light in the campfire area for people to find their seats easily.

- Discipline is important. A friendly request for cooperation will usually do the trick. Encourage enthusiasm but maintain control.

- Get everyone involved. Participation by the audience is vital to the success of the campfire program. Songs and audience participation stunts will accomplish this.

- Recognition, with awards or certificates of appreciation should be a part of every campfire program.

- Inspiration contributes to showmanship and is essential to a successful campfire.

- The program should be quieter as the embers die. The group may be asked to leave the campfire circle silently, to add to the mystery and inspiration.

THE FIRE

A campfire program means just that—a program that takes place around a campfire. The fire serves a purpose, but it should not detract from the other program features.

Check the firewood supply and lay the fire in advance. You may need to bring firewood with you. Select a safe location for building the fire.

The council firelay is recommended for campfire programs. (See page 113 of the *Official Boy Scout Handbook* or ask the den chiefs for help.) The fire can be lit when people arrive at the site, or you may want to include the fire-lighting as a part of the opening ceremony. The den chief or an experienced Scouter or commissioner can provide some ideas for special fire-lighting techniques.

Fire safety must be foremost in your mind. Activities around an open fire must be adequately supervised. Never take risks.

INGREDIENTS OF A SUCCESSFUL CAMPFIRE PROGRAM

Before we discuss sample campfire ceremonies, songs, stunts, and games in more detail, let's take a bird's-eye look at the ingredients of a successful campfire:

Song. Scouting, action, quiet, novelty, special occasion songs can all be used.

Stunts, Skits. No campfire program is complete without stunts and skits. These are primarily for fun and entertainment, but they can also include physical or mental contests and educational stunts.

Ceremonies. The opening ceremony sets the tone of the whole program, so it must be good! It should be attractively staged to capture and hold the attention of the audience. The closing ceremony should be quiet, inspirational, and challenging.

Stories. A story can be the high point of the campfire and make it something to remember. It could be an old-timer telling of adventure in faraway places; it could be a Boy Scout telling of his Jamboree experience or tales of the Philmont trails; it could be a storyteller spinning a ghostly yarn. (But remember, many younger boys are easily frightened by "horror" stories and care must be exercised to edit out extremely "ghostly" yarns.)

Games. They help build enthusiasm and help the boys let off some steam so they will be ready for the more serious moments of the campfire.

ALL FIRES SHOULD BE TOPLIGHTED.

FOR A SMALLER GROUP BUILD A **BACKLOG FIRE.** USE BIG, SEASONED LOG FOR BACK.

THE COUNCIL FIRE

Sample Campfire Program

1. Gather the boys in a circle or semicircle around the firelay with parents behind them. A denner or den chief can light the fire while the Cubmaster or other leader declares the campfire open and welcomes the group.

2. Sing one or two lively songs that everyone knows—something like "She'll Be Comin' 'Round the Mountain" or "Row, Row, Row Your Boat." If someone plays the guitar or harmonica, they can accompany the song.

3. Play a campfire game, such as the Laughing Game.

4. Lead an audience-participation stunt such as "Story of the Moor Monster" (*Group Meeting Sparklers*).

5. Sing an action song such as "Head and Shoulders, Knees and Toes" (*Cub Scout Songbook*).

6. Play another game.

7. Tell a story such as "The Gift of Trees."

8. Lead a quiet song such as "Scout Vesper Song" or "Scout's Good-Night Song" (*Cub Scout Songbook*).

9. Close with the Scout benediction, with boys and adults standing around the fire.

CAMPFIRE OPENINGS

Indian Running Opening. A tom-tom beats in the background. A den chief, dressed in Indian costume and carrying a lighted torch, makes his way into the council ring and lights the fire as the master of ceremonies declares the campfire open.

Cub Scout Promise Opening. Three den chiefs in Indian costume assist the Cubmaster, who holds a lighted torch. The Cubmaster says, "We will light our council fire with this torch which represents the spirit of Cub Scouting and a Cub Scout's promise to do his best." He passes the torch to the first den chief, who says, "This fire is a symbol of a Cub Scout's promise to do his duty to God and his country." He passes the torch to the next den chief, who says, "This fire is a symbol of a Cub Scout's promise to help other people." He passes the torch to the third den chief, who says, "This fire represents our pack and a Cub Scout's promise to obey the Law of the Pack." He returns the torch to the Cubmaster, who lights the fire.

Peace Pipe Opening. The peace pipe in this ceremony is not smoked. It can be whittled from wood or made with a dowel and spool, painted bright colors, and decorated with feathers.

Akela, in Indian headdress, takes a central position in the council ring. The fire lighter (a den chief dressed in Indian costume) enters carrying a lighted torch and bows to Akela. Akela says, "Now let the council fire be lighted." While this is being done, another den chief in Indian costume hands the peace pipe to Akela.

Akela steps forward holding the pipe in both hands, arms straight, and says, "To our Father (*hold pipe aloft*), who has given us so many blessings. To the Earth (*extend arms downward*), who has given us rich harvests. To the North Wind (*gesture toward the north*), with its cold breath of winter that gives us endurance. To the East Wind (*gesture to the east*), from the land of the rising sun, sending the morning light across the plains and mountains. To the South Wind (*gesture to the south*), and the warm sunshine. To the West wind (*gesture to the west*), from the land of the tall mountains. I now declare this council fire open!"

Candle Ceremony. All leaders (and other adults, if you wish) are given small candles in advance. Boys and adults gather around the unlighted fire. The Cubmaster says, "All around us is darkness. I light this little candle and it is no longer dark. Although this is a tiny light and lights only a small area, we can all see it. This tiny light can grow. It can be multiplied. (*Several leaders come forward and light their candles from the Cubmaster's light.*) Now the light is brighter and we can see more than before.

"But this is only a beginning. With people willing to share it, it will grow. (*The leaders fan out and light other candles*). See how fast the light can spread. Just as these candles brighten our council ring, our light can brighten the lives of others. That's what the Cub Scout Promise means when it says, 'help other people.' Even the smallest light is very important."

Three or four leaders come forward to light the council fire with their candles as the Cubmaster says, "Now we will light our council fire with the same light that has grown from such a tiny flame. Watch as the fire begins to grow. As we sing "This Little Cub Scout Light of Mine," let's all remember that each of us can brighten the lives of other people."

CAMPFIRE CLOSINGS

Friendship Circle. Everyone forms a friendship circle around the fire while the Cubmaster gives a brief, inspirational "minute." Explain that for centuries men have used a grip or handshake to show friendship and respect for each other. Start the frienship handshake around the circle by gripping the hand of the person on the right. When it returns to the leader, say, "May we all be friends forever. Good night."

Taps Closing. Everyone forms a friendship circle around the fire while a bugler plays "Taps." Or, everyone can sing it. (See *Cub Scout Songbook*.)

Indian Sign Language Closing. Akela repeats the following with actions: "May the Great Father, who has been with you in the past (*points behind him*) and will be with you in the future (*points to the front*), bring you great joy" (*moves hands together in a hopping motion*).

Scout Benediction. "And now may the great Master of all Scouts be with us till we meet again."

CAMPFIRE RECOGNITIONS

A campfire is an impressive site for giving advancement awards. This is particularly important during summer pack activities. Badges should be presented every month, regardless of whether it is a regular pack meeting or an outdoor activity. No boy should have to wait months to receive a badge he has earned. See *Staging Den and Pack Ceremonies* and *Cub Scout Program Helps* for ideas.

Thank-you or appreciation recognitions can also be given around the campfire. This is a good place for the Grand Howl, which shows respect and appreciation for a leader.

Grand Howl

Boys stand in a circle. The person being honored stands in the center. Starting from a crouching position, the boys make the Cub Scout sign, but instead of putting their hands over their heads, they touch the ground between their feet with the two fingers of both hands. Then, wolf-like, they raise their heads and howl, "Ah-h—-kay-y-la! Wee-e'll do-o-o ouu-u-ur best!" As the word "best" is yelled unison, they jump to their feet, with both hands high above their heads in the Cub Scout sign. The hands are held high while a den chief or other leader yells, "Dyb-dyb-dyb-dyb," meaning, "Do your best." On the fourth "dyb," each boy drops his left hand smartly to his side, makes the Cub Scout salute with his right, and shouts, "We-e-e'll dob-dob-dob-dob," meaning, "We'll do our best." After the fourth "dob," the boys drop their right hands smartly to their sides and come to attention.

CAMPFIRE GAMES

Campfire games can be noisy or quiet. They build enthusiasm and interest and involve the audience in the program. They are a good opportunity for everyone to stand and stretch or sit quietly and think. Select games which can be played in the campfire circle. In addition to many suitable games which can be found in the "Games" section of this book, here are a few that are fun for campfires.

Continued Story Game. This is a good campfire game for a small group. The leader begins a story and suddenly quits. The person next to him picks up the story, adding just one sentence. The next person tries to add one more sentence to the story. Continue until one player can't think of anything else to add, or set a time limit.

Simon Says. Everyone stands around the fire. The leader gives instructions. If he precedes his command with, "Simon says . . . " the command must be obeyed. Otherwise, it is ignored. Anyone who makes a mistake must sit down. Commands such as, "Right face . . . ", "Raise your right arm . . . ", and so on, can be used without moving the group away from the campfire ring.

Laughing Game. Players are seated around campfire. The first player says, "Ha." The next says "Ha, ha." The third says "Ha, ha, ha," and so on, with each player adding a syllable until someone makes a mistake or until someone laughs out of turn. Those who do must pay a forfeit.

Variation: The leader tosses a handkerchief in the air and everyone laughs until it touches the ground.

CAMPFIRE STUNTS AND SKITS

The wide range of stunts and skits suitable for campfires includes audience-participation stories, walk-on stunts, applause stunts, and mixers. (See the "Songs, Stunts, and Stories" section of this book for ideas. Also see *Group Meeting Sparklers* and the "Skits and Costumes" section). Some additional ideas are included here.

Frog Pond. Divide audience into three groups. The first group says in a high treble voice, "Tomatoes, tomatoes, tomatoes." The second group says in a deeper voice and slower tempo, "Potatoes, potatoes, potatoes." The third group says in a deep bass voice, "Fried bacon, fried bacon, fried bacon." After each group has rehearsed, turn them all loose at once, to continue until a signal is given.

Cub Scout in a Toy Shop. The group stands around the campfire. The leader tells the following story and asks the group to follow all the gestures. Each gesture should be done continuously to the end of the story. By that time, everyone will be doing several things at once.

LEADER: This is the story of a Cub Scout whose mother left him in a big department store. This boy has been left for some time and so he taps his right foot to show his irritation. (*All players tap right foot and continue tapping.*) The boy becomes tired of waiting for his mother, so he walks to the toy department. Here he sees a small toy lion whose head is nodding up and down. As he watches it, he too, starts to nod his head. (*All nod, and continue tapping foot.*) Then he becomes interested in the other toys. He picks up a trumpet and fingers the keys with his right hand. (*Wiggle fingers and continue other motions.*) He

GRAND HOWL

picks up a drumstick with his left hand and beats a drum with it. (*All pretend to beat drum with left hand.*) He had entirely forgotten his mother by this time, so he climbs up on a hobbyhorse and rocks merrily away. (*All rock.*) Suddenly he sees a jack-in-the-box and he tries to jump just like it. (*Crouch and jump.*)

The Growing Machine. Hang a sheet or blanket in front of the audience. Explain that this wonderful invention is a growing machine. Drop a stick behind the curtain and a big log rolls out. Put a small rock in, and a large rock is tossed out. A person enters carrying a baby (a doll) and accidentally drops it in the machine. Out comes a "giant baby" (a person wearing a big baby bonnet and carrying a baby bottle), crying, "Mama!" This accomplice is hidden behind the curtain and helps by throwing out the large objects.

The Bottle Factory. The leader explains that the group is going to take a tour of a bottle factory. Divide audience into six groups and teach each group the action and sounds they are to make.

- Loading Dock — "Swish, crash, swish." Move back and forth as if loading cases onto a dock.

- Conveyer Belt — "Tug a tug a tug." Hold out arms straight, weaving hands up and down.

- Bottle Washer — "Shh shh shh." Stoop down while turning, as if a brush was being twisted in a bottle. Stand and repeat.

- Capper — "Shh pt! shh pt!" Pound fist in other hand as though capping bottle.

- Shipping Room — "Crash, bang, crash, bang." Stoop and pick up loaded crates and load on truck.

- Tasters — "Burp! Pardon me. Burp! Pardon me." Cover mouth with hand.

When everyone has learned their parts, go through the factory one station at a time, then all perform their actions together.

CAMPFIRE SONGS

People like to sing around a campfire. One of the keys to successful singing is an enthusiastic song leader who beats time and set the pitch. Begin with songs that everyone knows. The liveliest songs should occur early in the program, with the quiet songs saved until toward the end. If someone plays the guitar or harmonica and can accompany the songs, so much the better. If you are teaching a new song, be sure it is easy or that everyone has a copy of the words. A pre-recorded cassette tape and player may help in teaching new songs. (See the *Cub Scout Songbook* for ideas).

CAMPFIRE STORIES

Storytelling is an art that almost anyone can acquire with practice. All you need is a good imagination, an appreciation for good stories, a knack for showmanship, and some experience. (See the "Songs, Stunts, and Stories" section of this book for tips on storytelling and some sample stories).

9 Special Pack Activities

Introduction

This section includes a broad assortment of time-tested special events which have been used successfully by dens and packs. Some are indoor activities, others are outdoors; some are suitable for the summer, some for winter, and others can be used any time of the year.

Many of the activities offer possibilities for Cub Scout advancement. It is important that leaders take advantage of these opportunities so the boys will not only have fun but have a chance to advance in rank.

Most of the activities require a minimum of materials and equipment. Even though they are simple, and within the capabilities of Cub Scout-age boys, all call for some advance preparation by leaders if they are to be successful.

Planning Special Events

Following these guidelines will help ensure the success of the event:

Objective. Why are we having the activity? Does it help to achieve the purposes of Cub Scouting?

Leadership. There should be adequate adult leadership. In major pack activities, the pack committee usually appoints a chairman and an event committee is recruited to carry out various responsibilities.

Facility. What type of facility is needed? Can the event be held in the regular pack meeting place? Is it an outdoor activity? Are reservations necessary? Will there be a charge for the facility?

Physical Arrangements. What type of seating arrangement is needed? How much space is available? If it is outdoors, what is available, and what do we need to provide?

Schedule. A written schedule or program will be helpful. When will the activity be held? What time does it begin? Who does what when? What time does it end?

Alternatives. Plan for backup leadership to fill in for emergencies. If it is an outdoor activity, have a backup plan in case of rain.

Public Relations. Be sure all pack families are informed about the activity. Is this an event that could be publicized in local newspapers and other media?

Rules. For competitive events, establish clear and simple rules that everyone can understand. Be sure everyone knows the rules in advance. This will save many disagreements and help prevent hard feelings.

Judging and Awards. Any special pack activity which takes the place of the regular pack meeting should include advancement awards, so that boys get recognition promptly. If it is a competitive activity, will each boy get something for participating? Or will only the winners be recognized? How and when? What type of awards will be used? Who will do the judging? How?

Health and Safety. The plan should include adequate supervision and insure the proper use of equipment. A harmless object can become dangerous when used in the wrong way. Take the necessary measures to ensure the health and safety of the boys and the others taking part.

Materials and Equipment. What materials and equipment are needed? Who will provide them?

Finances. Estimate the cost of the activity, if any. Will the pack budget cover the expense? If not, how will costs be covered?

Registration and Check-In Procedure. Most competitive events require some type of check-in procedure. How will it be done, and who is responsible?

Transportation. Will transportation be needed? Will each family provide its own? If not, what arrangements need to be made?

Countdown. Does everyone involved know what is expected? Remember Cub Scouting's secret word— KISMIF—Keep It Simple, Make It Fun.

BACK-DATED PLANNING CALENDAR

To ensure that nothing important is overlooked, a back-dated planning calendar such as the one shown here should be developed for each special event. List all of the steps which should be completed before the activity, with a target date for the completion of each phase of the planning.

6 months before	Chairman and co-chairman selected
5 months before	Committee recruited
4 months before	Have a detailed, written plan with specific assignments made.
3 months before	Order materials, awards. Make arrangements for facility.
2 months before	Begin publicizing in pack.

1 month before	Make announcement at a pack meeting and contact other pack families. Contact media for publicity.
2 weeks before	Last-minute check on materials, equipment, and facility.
0	Hold the event. Have fun.
0 – -1 week after	Evaluate success of event. Thank those who helped.

CALL ON THE SECOND TEAM

In planning and conducting special pack activities, don't forget to use your second team — Cub Scout parents and other adults.

At the pack's annual planning conference, select a chairman and co-chairman for each special activity, and identify other adults who would like to assist. This way, the leadership is identified early so planning can begin early. Last-minute planning may be haphazard and incomplete. The chairman and co-chairman work together, so if the chairman is unexpectedly transferred out of town, the plans are not left hanging.

This is a good way to get participation from pack families, to strengthen the pack, and to build spirit.

Cub Scout Sports

Because most Cub Scout-age boys love sports, and because one of the purposes of Cub Scouting is "encouraging good sportsmanship and pride in growing strong in mind and body," your pack will want to take part in the Cub Scout Sports program. The program offers Cub Scouts and their parents a chance to learn the skills and participate in one or more of 14 sports and earn awards for their participation.

More than that, it offers leaders an opportunity to teach the values of good sportsmanship and physical fitness. In contrast to some junior sports programs which place a premium on winning, Cub Scout Sports stresses participation by every boy, competitiveness without high pressure, and fun for all, including leaders and parents.

The 14 sports offered are:

Archery	Skiing
Baseball	Soccer

Basketball	Softball
Bowling	Swimming
Golf	Table Tennis
Marbles	Tennis
Physical Fitness	Volleyball

For each sport, there is a separate booklet which covers the rules and skills, training tips, and the requirements for earning the awards for that sport. The booklet should be used by the boy and his adult teammate, who may participate in the sport and may earn a physical fitness award. The booklets, available from your Scout distributor or Scout council service center are: *Archery,* No. 2153; *Baseball,* No. 2156; *Basketball,* No. 2155; *Bowling,* No. 2154; *Golf,* No. 2157; *Marbles,* No. 2158; *Physical Fitness,* No. 2161; *Skiing,* No. 2159; *Soccer,* No. 2162; *Softball,* No. 2160; *Swimming,* No. 2163; *Table Tennis,* No. 2164; *Tennis,* No. 2166; *Volleyball,* No. 2165.

Pack leaders will need a copy of the *Cub Scout Sports Leader Guide,* No. 2152. This booklet summarizes the value of sports and their proper place in Cub Scouting, tells how to begin and operate an ongoing Cub Scout sports program, and lists the recognition items available. (The awards include a participation belt loop for each sport, physical fitness pins, and a sports letter to be worn on a sweater or jacket. Special Cub Scout Sports T-shirts are also available for team sports.)

USING THE CUB SCOUT SPORTS PROGRAM

Cub Scout Sports may be introduced into your pack in several ways. Here are possibilities:

- At the pack's annual program planning conference, select one or two sports and make them the theme for one or two months during the program year. The pack's highlight for a month would be a tournament in the sport. Den meetings for that month would find the boys training ad practicing the sport under the guidance of a coach — probably an interested parent.

- Use the Cub Scout sports participation awards to recognize Cub Scouts who participate in organized sports outside the pack.

- Use Cub Scout sports in den meetings. Practice in the skills and techniques of various sports might be part of the "While Cub Scouts Gather" and "Activity" periods. For several sports, the booklets explain "lead-up games" that offer practice in the sport without requiring full-scale games.

CHOOSING A SPORT

Although Cub Scout Sports should be decidedly low-key, with absolutely no pressure, they are not informal in the way that the games in the "Games" section of this book are. They are sports wih rules to be followed and certain standard equipment to be used.

Therefore, the pack committee must consider what facilities and equipment will be needed. If you don't have access to safe, suitable bows and arrows or catcher's gear, better not consider archery or baseball. For several sports, incidentally, it is recommended that modified equipment and playing areas be used. (In basketball, a junior-size ball and a lowered basket; in volleyball, lower net and junior ball. Suggested modifications, where recommended, are explained in the booklet for each sport.)

The pack committee should also try to determine the interest of the boys in a particular sport before choosing it. In addition, you will want to be sure that coaches will be avilable as needed.

Another consideration is the number of boys in the pack. Five of the Cub Scout Sports are team sports. Three of them can be played by teams made up of normal-size dens—basketball, volleyball, and socccer (for soccer it is recommended that seven to nine boys make up a team, rather than the 11 in the official rules). Baseball and softball are a different story. Modifications of these sports can be played by fewer than nine on a team, but they aren't really baseball and softball. If you choose to use these sports, consider enlarging dens to make up full teams.

PLANNING A PACK TOURNAMENT

Appoint a sports chairman and committee to:

- Secure equipment and facilities as needed; make sure that each den has access to them for practice.

- Ensure that each den has a coach (who may, of course, be the den leader).

- Provide each den with copies of the booklet for the sport.

- Assign officials, judges, timekeepers, etc. as needed.

- Obtain medals, ribbons, and trophies, as desired.

- Conduct the tournament. For details, see the *Cub Scout Sports Leader Guide.*

The Cub Scout Sports program is designed for competition within a single pack. However, interpack competition is permitted, so if other packs in your community are interested, a community tournament might be held. Guidelines for such competition are in the *Leader Guide.*

Pack Picnic

A picnic is a natural for spring, summer, or fall. It should be an informal family affair. This doesn't mean that no planning is necessary. The location, feeding arrangement, games equipment, transportation, and other details must be thought out ahead of time. With careful planning, the picnic will be fun for everyone.

SAMPLE PICNIC PROGRAM

A sample picnic program is given here. Each family could be asked to bring hot dogs and buns. The paper plates and utensils, drinks, and dessert could be provided by the pack. Have on hand several pair of pliers and unpainted wire coat hangers for weiner-roasting sticks.

3:00 – 4:00	Arrive at picnic site. Gathering-time activity.
4:00 – 5:00	Organized games.
5:00 – 6:00	Unorganized games and play. One adult from each den reports for firebuilding. Other adults set tables with food.
6:00 – 6:30	Meal
6:30 – 7:00	Clean up. Campfire preparation.
7:00 – 8:30	Campfire

————PICNIC GAMES————

TUNNEL RACE

Use den teams with equal numbers of boys and adults. Teams line up side by side behind starting line, with adults in front, boys in back. Adults spread legs. On signal, boys crawl one at a time through tunnel. As each boy gets to the end of the tunnel, he stands up and spreads his legs. Team whose last boy is first to make it to the front of his team wins.

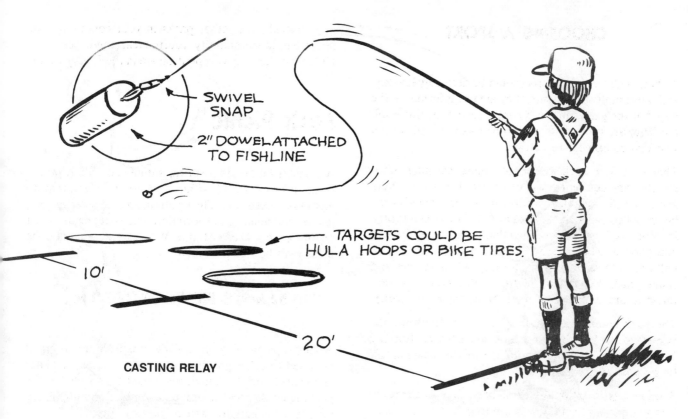

SWIVEL
SNAP

2" DOWEL ATTACHED
TO FISHLINE

TARGETS COULD BE
HULA HOOPS OR BIKE TIRES.

10'

20'

CASTING RELAY

NAIL DRIVING CONTEST

Each den team has an equal number of boys and adults.
For each den, start three 4-inch nails in a block of wood.
Adults and boys then alternate striking the nails with a
hammer, trying to drive them into their block. *This is not
a speed contest.* Winning den is the one that drives all three
nails into block with the fewest strokes.

SIR WALTER RALEIGH RACE

Played with adult teams. Man places two pieces of cardboard on ground for the woman to step on as she walks
toward a goal line.

BALLOON PASSING

Everyone can play this game except very small children.
Divide into equal teams. Give each team a balloon inflated
to about a 6-inch diameter. On signal, first player on each
team tucks the balloon under his chin and without using
his hands, passes it to the next player, who must take it
under his chin. Continue until all have received the
balloon. If the balloon is dropped, the player may pick
it up with his hands but must put it under his chin before
passing it on.

CASTING RELAY

Divide adults and boys into two teams. Set up a target
as shown, or draw a 5-foot circle on the ground. In relay
fashion, members of each team take turns casting with
a rod and reel to hit the target. (A weight is tied to the
end of the line.) First team to finish wins.

COPYCAT TAG

In this game, It is not the tagger. Rather, he's the taggee.
He runs off while the other players count slowly to 3. Then
they chase him, but they must imitate everything he does
while trying to escape. If he crawls, they must crawl; if
he hops, they must hop; if he stops, they must stop, and
so on. The first player to tag him becomes It.

WATER BALLOON TOSS

Any number of two-person teams can play. Teams line
up in two rows, with partners opposite each other about
4 feet apart. All players in one line are given a water-filled
balloon. On signal, each tosses his balloon to his partner. A certain amount of skill is required to keep the
balloon from breaking. When a balloon does break, some-

WATER BALLOON TOSS

one gets a slight shower and that pair is eliminated from the game. Each time the balloons have been tossed down the line, the lines move farther apart. The farther away, the harder it is to toss the balloons without breaking. (Fill the balloons in advance by stretching the necks over a water faucet. Store in large sturdy container until ready to use.)

DIP, DRIP, AND DUMP

Divide group into two or more equally matched teams. In front of each team place a bucket full of water and two small plastic cups, each with two small nail holes in the bottom. About 20 feet away, put two bottles with small necks, such as pop bottles. In relay style, the first player on each team dips the plastic cup into the bucket, runs to the pop bottle and dumps any remaining water into it. He runs back and hands cup to the next player. Continue until bottles are filled to a certain level.

WICKET BOWLING

Set up 10 croquet wickets in a row, with enough space between them for a croquet ball to go through. Make a bowling line 15 feet from the wickets. In turn, each player tries to bowl a ball through the wickets, in order from first to last. If he makes one, he continues to the next until he misses. When he misses, he waits for his next turn and starts at the last wicket he missed.

DODGEBALL

Boys and adults form a large circle, with one boy in the middle. Give the circle players a soft volleyball or other large ball. They try to hit the player in the center with it. When he is hit, he changes places with the player who hit him.

MARBLE GOLF

For holes, bury baby food jars to the rim. Flags are paper triangles glued to craft sticks. Add water hazards and sand traps if you wish. The "golf shots" are made in the approved knuckles-down way for regular marbles. Winner is the player who takes the fewest shots to go around the course.

TWIG HORSESHOES

TWIG HORSEHOES

Use two straight twigs for pegs and four forked ones for horseshoes. Paint horseshoes red and green. Put pegs in ground 4 feet apart with 2 inches above ground. Each player pitches his two horseshoes at a peg. Ringer counts three points, leaner two points. If there are no ringers or leaners, shoe nearest peg counts as one point. Game is 21 points.

Other games could also include such things as horseshoe pitching, croquet, table tennis, tug of war, beanbag toss, etc. See the "Games" section of this book for additional games. Also see the "Nature and Outdoor Activities" section for campfire games.

Pack Treasure Hunt

This treasure hunt can be conducted in a neighborhood park. It can be one of the activities at a pack picnic or other outdoor event.

The trail is laid out in a rough circle with at least five or six stations, preferably out of sight of each other. The sta-

tions are plainly marked, and directions from one to the next are clear. The activity comes in doing something at each station rather than scurrying around looking for the next station.

The dens assemble for instructions from the Cubmaster. Each den receives instructions on how to get to its first station. Den 1 starts at Station 1, Den 2 at Station 2, etc. Each den is given a score card for making notes. Den members stay together and take the stations in numerical order.

An instruction card at each station tells the den what to do there and gives directions for reaching the next station. The den follows the instructions, which may include writing something on its score card.

THINGS ROBINSON CRUSOE DID -	FOR WOLF AND BEAR	FOR WEBELOS ACTIVITY BADGES
MADE HIS OWN UTENSILS, CLOTHING AND TOOLS	WHITTLING, TYING THINGS, HANDICRAFT, MACHINERY, USING ROPE, WOODWORKING, THINGS THAT GO, REPAIRS	GEOLOGIST OUTDOORSMAN ENGINEER FORESTER CRAFTSMAN
PLANTED GARDEN CROPS	CONSERVATION	NATURALIST
KEPT ANIMALS AND PETS	BIRDS PETS WATER AND SOIL CONSERVATION FISHING WILDLIFE CONSERVATION NATURE CRAFTS	OUTDOORSMAN
COOKED HIS OWN MEALS	COOKING	OUTDOORSMAN
BUILT A SHELTER AND LIVED OUTDOORS	OUTING	ENGINEER CRAFTSMAN

TREASURE HUNT SCORE CARD

PACK TREASURE HUNT TRAIL

After the hunt, the score cards are turned in and the scores tallied. The den with the best score for each station wins the treasure for that station. This way, it is possible for all dens to win at least one treasure.

The instructions will be determined by the natural items available at your treasure hunt site. The list below is an example.

STATION 1 (at the bridge over Cub Scout creek). "How many peanuts (or caramels) are in this jar? Guess the number, but do not open the jar. When you have written the number on your score card, go to Station 2 at the flagpole."

Treasure. After the hunt, the winning den gets the peanuts.

STATION 2 (at flagpole). "What achievements, electives, and activity badges could Robinson Crusoe have passed? Write these on your score card. When you have finished, go to Station 3 at the picnic shelter." (Provide boys with a list such as the one shown and let them give the answers.)

Treasure. After the hunt, the winning den gets a bag of marshmallows for roasting.

STATION 3 (at picnic shelter). "Without asking your leaders, tell how many Cub Scouts are in your pack. When you have finished, go to Station 4 at the big oak tree."

Treasure. Winning den gets to be first in line for the picnic supper.

STATION 4 (at the big oak). "How many trees between the path and the creek are the same as this tree? Write the number on your score card. When you have finished, go to Station 5 at the playground swings."

Treasure. Winning den gets inexpensive paperback field guide to trees.

STATION 5 (at the playground swings). "Count and identify all the different birds you can spot within 2 minutes. Write the names on your score card. When you have finished, go to Station 6 at the maple tree near the park's 4th Street entrance."

Treasure. Winning den gets inexpensive paperback field guide to birds.

STATION 6 (at the maple tree). "Write down all the things you see in and on this tree. Write them on your score card. When you have finished, go to Station 1 at the bridge over Cub Scout Creek."

Treasure. Winning den gets a bag of candy.

Pirate Picnic

The pack pirate picnic can be an adventure for Cub Scouts and their families. It can include games, an obstacle course, a treasure hunt, and a picnic supper.

The picnic committee should assign teams to registration, obstacle course, treasure hunt, games, and cookout. Follow the guidelines for planning special events. Pack families can bring simple picnic suppers.

As the families arrive, have the boys "walk the plank" blindfolded (a 2-by-4 board on the ground). Then present them with a bandana to wear to add to the excitement of the afternoon. (Each den could wear a different color bandana.)

SAMPLE PIRATE PICNIC PROGRAM

- Check-in. Walk the Plank
- Obstacle course
- Pirate treasure hunt
- Contests, games, races
- Shipwrecked activity
- Picnic supper— cookout
- Recognition ceremony
- Closing

PIRATE PICNIC

PIRATE OBSTACLE COURSE

Give each Cub Scout who completes the following obstacle course a gold earring (made from cardboard) to complete his pirate costume.

1. Crawl through the "whale." (Three large cardboard cartons taped together and painted to resemble a whale.)

2. Climb up rope ladder and down the other side. (Hang rope ladder from strong branch on a large tree, not too far from ground.)

3. Dodge spring from "island" to "island." (Lay eight auto tires in a row and place a pan of water in the center of every other one. Boy jumps over the tires with pans.)

4. "Man the Lifeboat." (Each boy sits in a dry land rowboat or box and takes three sweeps with the "oars"—two brooms.)

5. Climb through the Jolly Roger (a large cardboard carton with a skull and crossbones painted on it). Cut out mouth section for boys to climb through.

PIRATE OBSTACLE COURSE

PIRATE TREASURE HUNT

Spray several hundred pop bottle caps, cardboard circles, or tiddlywinks with gold paint. In advance, scatter these "coins" around the picnic grounds. The boy who finds the largest number of "pieces of eight" wins a black sash to add to his pirate outfit. Or you might want to present him with a bag of foil-wrapped candy coins to exchange for his other "coins." (Be sure the clean-up crew picks up any stray "coins" before you leave the picnic grounds.)

Another idea is to use a treasure hunt such as the one described elsewhere in this section. Give each den an authentic-looking treasure map to lead them from station to station. Make the maps from brown wrapping paper and char the edges. The instructions could read, "Walk 20 paces toward the flagpole," or "Walk 30 paces to the big oak."

SHIPWRECKED

This could be another exciting feature of your pack's pirate picnic. In advance, select a "shipwreck site" for each den and lay out the necessary materials as described below. The den leaders (or den chiefs) are prompted in advance. They go along with the den and provide the necessary explanations.

Explain that the dens have set sail to the South Seas in search of treasure. Each den is assigned a color (it could be the color of the den's bandanas) and is told to follow the trail of colored yarn to find their treasure island. When they are about to reach their destinations, explain that, just as they were ready to put to shore, their ships are wrecked by a huge wave, and they will have to swim for it! Explain that they will know their island because it is flying a flag the same color.

At each of the "island" sites, leave the following note and the necessary materials. The note can be written on brown wrapping paper and the edges burned or torn to make it look old.

You are now marooned on your island. You will find that many things have been washed ashore and your leader will have saved some items from the wreck. You now have to live on the island and make yourselves comfortable until you are rescued.

1. Build yourselves a shelter. (Have an old blanket, some long sticks, and some rope handy.)

2. Make a national flag for your island. (Provide flag material, crayons, and pole.)

3. Decide on a name for your island.

4. Make some money to use on the island or decide on some other form of currency. (This could be leaves, twigs, stones, etc.)

5. Hide your treasure when you find it. (Treasure could be a "chest" containing gum or balloons.)

6. Draw a map of your island and mark where you have hidden your treasure. (Provide paper and crayons.)

7. Draw a picture of a raft or boat that you could make to travel to the other "islands."

After the dens have completed all these instructions, they can be "rescued" by a team of adults who tell them it's time to eat. At dinner, a team of adults could judge the drawings of the rafts or boats and award prizes for the most unusual, most useful, etc.

After dinner, the dens could exchange the maps they have drawn and search for another den's treasure. Be sure each den winds up with a treasure chest to enjoy.

Field Day

The pack field day is an afternoon of fun for Cub Scouts and their families. In preparing for the field day, the event committee should follow the guidelines for planning special events. Consider such things as location, promotion, signmaking, instructions for events, equipment, marking game areas, scoreboards, decorations, and prizes. Involve a lot of helpers.

Make a final check about two weeks before the event to make sure plans are progressing smoothly. When the big day comes, the committee should arrive early to decorate and set up the games. Large signs inform families of the events and where to deposit their picnic suppers.

Field Day Personnel: Chairman; physical arrangements committee (signs, permits, equipment setup); awards committee; program committee (schedule, ceremonies, decorations); starter; judges; scorekeeper; refreshment committee.

SAMPLE FIELD DAY SCHEDULE

2:00 – 3:00	Gathering-time activities. Informal games such as box hockey, beanbag toss, tetherball, tin-can bowling, etc.
3:00 – 4:00	**Field Events**
	30-Yard Dash
	Crab Race
	Nail-Driving Contest
	Three-Legged Race
	Barefoot Marble Race
	Shoe-Kicking Contest
	Hopping Race

	Sack Race
	Dutch-Shoe Race
	Clothespin Race
4:00 – 4:30	**Den contests**
	Tunnel Relay
	Balloon-Kick Relay
	Other relay games
4:30 – 5:00	Informal period – wash up
5:00 – 5:15	Recognitions
5:15 – 6:00	Picnic supper and clean up

Note: It may be necessary to run each field event in heats unless 15 or fewer are competing. Two heats may be run at the same time to speed things up. Finalists compete for pack championship.

FIELD EVENTS AND CONTESTS

THREE-LEGGED RACE

Man's left leg is tied to boy's right. On signal, they make their stumbling way to a goal line and return to the starting line.

THREE-LEGGED RACE

CUB SCOUT FIELD DAY

SHOE-KICKING CONTEST

Players loosen their shoes, stand at a line, and see how far they can propel the shoes by kicking.

HOPPING RACE

Players line up at a starting line. On signal, they hop on the left foot to a turning line and hop back to the starting line on the right foot.

SACK RACE

Fifty-pound sacks (such as onion or potato sacks) are needed. On signal, each player picks up a sack and pulls it over his feet and legs. Holding it with both hands, he hops from the starting line to a goal line and returns.

BOTTLE-FILLING RACE

Each player has a paper cup. An empty soda bottle is placed 20 yards in front of him and a can of water is behind him. On signal, each player must fill his cup with water, run to the bottle, and pour in the water. He runs back and forth between can and bottle until the bottle is full.

TUNNEL RELAY

Get four fiberboard boxes about 20 inches square and 3 feet high and reinforce the corners. Fold in the top and bottom of each box and lay them on the ground end to end to form two tunnels. Two dens compete to see which can wiggle all its boys through the tunnel first. The tunnels can also be used as part of an obstacle course. (*Note:* It may be helpful to insert the end flaps from one box into the other and tape securely. This will keep the boxes from separating.)

(The other field events and contests mentioned above can be found in the "Games" section of this book.)

Cub Scout Fitness Day

The Cub Scout Fitness Day is a fun-filled family afternoon. It is similar to the field day, except that the contests are aimed more toward developing and testing physical skills. It can close with a picnic supper and awards ceremony.

Follow the guidelines for planning special events. The equipment is simple, but it must be obtained in advance.

Score sheets need to be made and prizes made or purchased. Den leaders should know the events in advance so the boys can practice at den meetings.

Several of the events are also Wolf and Bear badge requirements. Remind parents to pass the boys on these requirements if they do their best.

Fitness Day Personnel: Chairman; physical arrangements committee (permits, signs, equipment setup clean-up crew); program committee (schedule, decorations, makes equipment, conducts the events); awards committee; starter; judges; scorekeeper; picnic supper committee.

SAMPLE FITNESS DAY SCHEDULE

The Fitness Day committee must arrive early to set up the events, registration table, decorations, etc.

1:00 – 1:30	Registration and gathering-time activities (such as those suggested for field day)
1:30 – 1:45	Opening ceremonies
2:00 – 4:30	Events
4:30 – 5:00	Wash up
5:00	Recognition ceremonies and closing
5:30	Picnic supper and clean up

SCORING

Establish a simple scoring system in advance. Cub Scouting encourages competition among dens, so choose an overall den winner. Some of the competition calls for individual winners, too.

Determine den winners by using a simple scoring system such as this: Award 10 points to winner of each race or contest, 5 points for second, 3 points for third. Give the den 1 point for each boy who successfully completes the physical feats course.

PRIZES

Winners could be called to a decorated victory stand to receive their awards. Overall den winners could be awarded olive branch wreaths and trophies. Simple wreaths can be made from coathanger wire circles covered with paper leaves. Trophies can be made from tin cans bolted together and sprayed with gold paint.

Other winners could receive ribbons or medals which can be purchased or homemade. All boys taking part should be awarded certificates of participation signed by the Fitness Day chairman.

See "Prizes and Awards" section of this book for ideas.

PRIZES—FIELD DAY

SUGGESTED OPENING CEREMONY

After a regular flag ceremony, the Cubmaster might say something like this: "This afternoon you meet on the field of honor. May you strive manfully to win, letting courtesy and good sportsmanship guide your behavior. As we light this torch that will burn throughout our Fitness Day, let us remember it is to remind us to be courteous and good sports." *(He lights a simple torch that will burn during contests.)*

Then the Cub Scouts participating in the contests repeat the Olympic Oath (Cub Scout version) together: "We promise that we will take part in the Cub Scout fitness games in fair competition, respecting the regulations which govern them and with the desire to participate in the true spirit of sportsmanship for the honor of our pack and for the glory of sport."

SUGGESTED CLOSING CEREMONY

All Cub Scouts stand and repeat (or read from a card) the Athenian Oath (Cub Scout version): "We will try hard not to bring disgrace to this, our community, by being

SHOT PUT

DISCUS THROW

dishonest or cowardly. We will fight for the ideals and worthwhile things of the community both alone and with our friends. We will respect and obey its laws. We will do our best to do our community duty. In all these ways we will make our community better and more beautiful than it was given to us."

DISCUS THROW

Staple two 10- to 12-inch paper plates together to form a discus. A beanbag can be placed inside for weight, if desired. Use regular form for throwing—plate should be held flat in hand, not between thumb and finger. Count best throw out of three.

─────FITNESS EVENTS─────

MARATHON

It is best to let boys compete against other boys of the same age, with prizes for each age group in each event.

This is a distance relay. The classic 26-mile marathon could be run in 26 yards. Divide each den into two groups, stationed 26 yards apart. Give each den a baton made from a foot-long section of dowel or broomstick. On signal, the first runner races to the other line and hands off the baton. The runner who receives it runs to the first line, and so on, until all boys have raced.

SHOT-PUT

Use a softball as the shot and follow regular shot-put rules for form. Shot must be pushed, not thrown. Count best put out of three for each player. Distance determines winner.

JAVELIN THROW

30-YARD DASH

Use a broomstick. Boys throw for distance. Count best throw out of three.

Run in groups of about 10, picking first-, second-, and third-place finishers to run in the finals.

PENTATHLON

This is a special event. Each den enters at least one and no more than two boys, selected ahead of time. There is no age limit. Five events are run in the order listed below. All contestants enter the first event. There is no rest period between events. As soon as one event is finished, the next starts.

- **Standing Long Jump.** The five boys making the longest jumps compete in the next event. The others drop out.
- **Javelin Throw.** The boy with the shortest throw is eliminated. The others compete in the next event.
- **30-Yard Dash.** The slowest boy is eliminated. The remaining three compete in the discus throw.
- **Discus Throw.** The boy with the shortest throw is eliminated. The other two compete in last event for the pentathlon championship.
- **Shot-Put.** Boy with longest distance is the champion.

TIRE OBSTACLE RELAY

Make two rows of automobile tires, five in each row, placing them on their sides and touching. Station the dens, relay style, about 20 yards from their rows. On signal, first boy in each den runs over the tires, stepping into each one. He then turns to his right and runs back to the den to touch off the next runner. First den through wins.

PHYSICAL FEATS COURSE

Give each boy a card listing each event of the course. Be sure his name is on the card. A parent is at each station to serve as judge and initial the card. Set a minimum standard of performance for each station. The events could include:

- Running long jump.
- Vault fence to 30 inches high.
- Climb tree.
- Walk 2-by-4 rail.
- Throw a ball 20 feet to an adult and catch return throw.
- Do a forward roll.
- Do dodge springs into a series of six auto tires, keeping feet together.
- Do one chin-up.
- Do three push-ups.

Water Carnival

Summertime is swimming time, and a water carnival is certain to be a popular pack activity. If the pack has conducted a Cub Scout Learn-to-Swim program, then most if not all of the boys will already be swimmers. If not, there are several swimming games and activities for non-swimmers in the "Games" section of this book.

The events used during the water carnival will be determined by where you hold it. If the site is along a river or lake, you may be able to include some boating. If it is a swimming pool, you will need to stick to swimming events and games. The suggested program below can be held at any body of water. Adjustments can be made if you are meeting along a river, lake, or at the shore.

When selecting events, be sure to include some activities for all ability groups, as well as all family members. You may wish to designate some of the events as man-boy, women only, adults only, etc.

Be sure to take safety precautions at all activities in or around the water. Follow the Safe Swim Defense plan on pages 92–93 of the *Cub Scout Leader Book*. This includes qualified supervision, lifeguards on duty, separation of boys into ability groups, the buddy system, and other important considerations. If swimming in a home pool, additional safeguards need to be taken. (See the *Cub Scout Leader Book*.)

If boating is included in the program, be sure to follow Safety Afloat, found on pages 94–95 in the *Cub Scout Leader Book*.

As the boys arrive, they are registered for the events in which they wish to take part, divided into ability groups, and paired with a buddy.

SAMPLE WATER CARNIVAL SCHEDULE

2:00 – 2:30	Registration and pairing of buddies.
2:30 – 3:30	Water games and races, such as:
	• Pirate's Gold Hunt
	• Rope Throw Rescue Relay
	• Egg and Spoon Race
	• Bubbling Contest
	• Nail-Driving Underwater
	• Up and Under
3:30 – 4:30	Free swim for families
4:30	Recognition of winners; refreshments

SNAPPING FISH GAME

The water games mentioned above are only suggestions. Many others can be found in the "Games" section of this book.

Fishing Derby

There are two kinds of Cub Scout pack fishing derbies; both are fun for boys and parents. One kind is a parent-and-son fishing trip to a nearby lake or river where adults and boys can fish off the bank or in boats. Small prizes are awarded for the biggest fish and the best string.

The other type is a family outing with games and contests related to fishing. The ideas here are for this kind of derby.

The fishing derby committee should follow the guidelines for planning special events. Planning includes securing a site, arranging for transportation, planning activities and obtaining prizes, and arranging for food and equipment. Try special promotional gimmicks such as invitations in the shape of a fish.

Make identifying signs for each contest area. Use ropes, posts, colored streamers, and colorful signs to mark game areas. Consider using a public address system to control the activities, if necessary, and a tape player to provide lively music.

SUGGESTED FISHING DERBY SCHEDULE

1:00 – 2:00   Gathering-time activities.

2:00 – 3:30   Special contests.

3:30 – 3:45   Awards ceremony.

3:45 – 5:00   Free time for fishing.

5:00 – 6:00   Supper and clean-up. Roast corn and fried fish might be prepared by the fishing derby committee, or a picnic supper, with hot dogs, baked beans, and ice cream might be served.

GATHERING-TIME ACTIVITIES

GUESSING CONTEST

How many fish eggs are in the jar? Use marbles for the eggs. The winner gets the jar of marbles.

JAPANESE FISH KITE CONTEST

Each boy brings a kite he and his family have made and decorated. Kites are attached to 6-foot sticks. Judge the entries and choose winners for the most beautiful, colorful, original, unusual, etc.

CLOTHESPIN FISHERY

Give each person a chance to catch a clothespin "fish" using a pole with a 3-foot string to which is tied a metal nut. Slide the string into the fork of the clothespin so the nut catches. Use a small plastic wading pool to hold the water.

GATHERING OF THE SCHOOLS

Give each person a cutout of a fish. Print the name of the fish on each cutout so there are about 20 bass, 20 swordfish, tuna, trout, etc. Stack the cutouts in a pile, mixed so there won't be two fish of the same kind in a row. Use these as name tags. Tell everyone to find other "fish" of the same kind. See which "school" can assemble first.

SNAPPING FISH GAME

This game requires several fishing poles with sinkers and a piece of foam rubber attached to a 3-by-4-foot line. Also, have several mousetraps set to spring. Object of the game is to set off a trap by hitting it with the foam rubber without getting the line caught in the trap. Player stands about 5 feet away from trap.

—————— SPECIAL CONTESTS ——————

FISHING RELAY

The "fishpond" is a large cardboard box, turned upside down, with slots cut in the bottom. In each slot, insert a "fish" cut from cardboard. On each fish, mark an arbitrary length and weight for it. For each den, you need a cane pole with a 3-foot string and a bent paper clip for the hook. Dens line up relay fashion, with the first boy holding the pole. On signal, he runs to the fishpond and

catches a fish. A judge records the length and weight. If the fish is below legal length, the boy must put it back and try again. The den with the greatest weight total of fish wins.

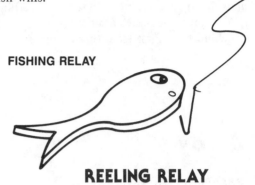

FISHING RELAY

REELING RELAY

Dens are arranged in relay fashion. The first player on each team has a fishing pole and reel. On signal, he places the fishing pole and reel on the ground in front of him, takes the plug, and runs to a line 25 feet away, unwinding the line as he goes. He then runs back, sits on the ground, and reels in the line. The next den member follows and so on, until all have played. First den through wins.

LAND THAT FISH

Dens are lined up in relay style. Each den member in turn runs to a goal line where he picks up a landing net and rubber ball. He bounces the ball and quickly turns completely around and nets the ball before it hits the ground a second time. He places the net and ball on the ground and runs to touch off the next player.

HEAVE-THE-ANCHOR RELAY

Tie a stuffed sock, beanbag, or other soft weight to the end of a 25-foot rope. Each den member in turn throws out the rope, re-coils it, and hands it to the next player. First den through wins.

KNOW-YOUR-FISH RELAY

Line up dens relay style. At a goal line about 20 feet away, each den has a stack of cards with the names of fresh-water and salt-water fish. Each den also has two containers marked "Fresh" and "Salt." On signal, the first boy in each den runs to the goal, takes the top card, reads it, then places it in the proper container. The den with the most correct answers wins.

CASTING RELAY FOR DADS

Teams of dads line up and each one in turn casts a plug at a target. As soon as he scores a hit, he gives the rod to the man behind him. First team through wins.

Kite Derby

A pack kite derby can be one of your best spring or summer activities. It may include various kite contests, followed by a picnic supper. Some kite derbies are held just for fun with no special contests or prizes. Others include contests with prizes for each.

Follow the guidelines for planning special activities. The kite derby committee must consider the location (an open field), the layout of the field, and the meal, if any. If contests are to be included, decide on entry requirements, which events will be held, and the rules and prizes for each. You will need an announcer, a starter, and one or two judges.

The kite derby plan should be developed far enough in advance so the boys and their families will know the types of events and rules for each before they begin making kites. The "Crafts" section of this book contains information on making several types of kites. The *Wolf Cub Scout Book* also has kite plans. The Den meetings leading up to the derby would be a good time to discuss kite flying safety rules with the boys.

SAMPLE KITE DERBY SCHEDULE

- Exhibit Period
  - Registration
  - Display of kites
  - Judging of kites
- Opening ceremony
- Kite contests
- Picnic supper
- Recognition
- Closing ceremony

CLASSIFICATION OF KITES

Kites should be divided into three groups for competition:

1. Bowed or tailless kites
2. Flat kites or those having tails
3. Box kites or combination kites

ENTRY REQUIREMENTS

The kite derby committee will want to set some rules beforehand to help prevent any misunderstanding or disappointment. Here are suggestions.

- All kites must be parent-son made.
- Each kite should be numbered.
- Only one kite per boy may be entered.
- Each boy may have his mom or dad (or other adult) help him get the kite into the air and help catch it when it comes down.
- A kite must fly to be eligible for a prize.
- No restrictions on materials used in construction of kites, except that no fighting kites are allowed. (Glass, razor blades, and metal are not permitted.)
- No wire flight lines are permitted.
- Kites caught in power lines are lost and may not be retrieved.
- Kites may be adjusted and modified any time during the derby.

You may want to measure the kite cords before the competition and mark them at 100 yards to aid the judges in determining how high they are flying. Cords could be provided by the kite derby committee.

JUDGING

You may wish to establish a point system for judging to make it easier to determine the winners of some of the awards. Pre-flight judging can be done for design and workmanship, and prizes could be awarded for:

- Smallest
- Largest
- Most comical
- Most beautiful
- Most unusual

KITE DERBY

- Best craftsmanship
- Most original

During flight, kites could be judged for:

- First kite in the air
- Highest after 5 minutes
- Highest after 15 minutes
- Most stable flying
- Most graceful in air
- Fastest climbing
- Best sportsmanship (boy)
- Most persistent flyer (boy)

In addition, prizes should be given to the winners of contests.

KITE CONTESTS

100-YARD DASH

Contest starts on signal with launching in any manner. Kites must be flown to the end of a 100-yard cord and then wound back to the hand of the flier. An assistant may remain under the kite as it is wound in to catch it before it falls to the ground. The race ends when the flier has rewound all his cord. At the finish, the flier must be on the starting line with his kite wound back to his hand.

ALTITUDE RACE

Fliers start on signal and run out from the flying line, working the kite up to its highest possible altitude. At the end of 5 minutes, all fliers return to the starting line. The kites at the lowest elevation are then ordered down. The judges determine which kite is flying highest.

MESSENGER RACE

All players send their kites up to a specific length of line—about 50 yards. A paper messenger is attached to the flying lines and allowed to blow up the kite. The boy whose messenger first reaches his kite wins the race. (See "Crafts" section for making kite messengers.)

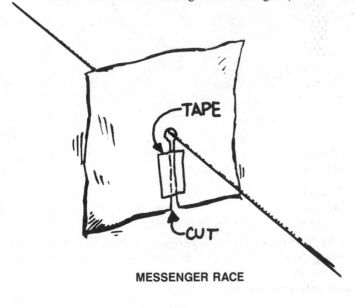

MESSENGER RACE

KITE FLYING SAFETY RULES

• Always fly a kite far from electric or power lines, transmission towers, TV and radio antennaes, and ponds.

• Fly a kite on days when there is no rain. Never fly it in a thunderstorm.

• Use wood, fabric, paper, or plastic in the kite. Never use metal in making a kite.

• Always use dry string. Never use wire for a kite line.

• When flying a kite, avoid public streets, highways, or railroad rights-of-way.

• If your kite gets snagged in a power line, treetop, roof, or on a high pole, never try to remove it.

Glider or Plane Derby

A glider or plane derby can be a very enjoyable pack event when the rules are kept simple and uncomplicated. Follow the guidelines for planning special pack events.

In a glider or plane derby, the object is to keep the craft in the air as long as possible. The most important official is the timer, who must be equipped with a stopwatch. If the pack is large, you may wish to have two or three timers so that several planes can be in the air at the same time.

A simple derby involves only one type of glider or plane. Kits for balsa gliders and rubber-band-powered planes are available at any hobby or variety store. They are put together by the boy, with help from his family, and flown without modification of parts, other than the shifting or bending of wings. The derby committee may wish to purchase all kits at the same time to save trouble and expense and distribute them to the boys before the derby.

GLIDER OR PLANE DERBY RULES

• Timing begins the instant the model is released for flight. Time ends when the model touches the ground, hits an obstruction, or passes from the sight of the timer. The timer may move any direction (not more than 200 feet) from the take-off point to keep the model in sight, so long as he remains on the ground.

• All boys must launch their own models. The model shall not be launched from a height greater than the flier's normal reach from the ground.

• Specify the number of rubber bands permitted for each plane.

• Specify if lubrication of rubber bands is permitted.

• It is suggested, if time permits, that the flier's score be the total elapsed time of three best flights out of five, or best two out of three.

TIPS FOR FLYING PLANES

• Start "flying trials" by gliding the plane gently, pointing down. By adjusting wings back and forth, a long, gentle glide can be achieved.

• Moving the wing forward makes the plane climb. If the wing is too steep and the plane stalls, move the wing back.

TIPS FOR FLYING PLANES

- Start "flying trials" by gliding the plane gently, pointing down. By adjusting wings back and forth, a long, gentle glide can be achieved.

- Moving the wing forward makes the plane climb. If the wing is too steep and the plane stalls, move the wing back.

- Rubber bands may be lubricated with one-half soft soap, one-half glycerine. Don't lubricate near the hooks, or the band may slide off.

- For best results, launch planes almost into the wind, standing with wind blowing on right cheek.

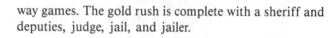

TIPS FOR FLYING PLANES

TIPS FOR FLYING GLIDERS

- A glider should be launched by throwing it as if it were a baseball, except that the hand should be well over the head on release. The glider's fuselage is held firmly with thumb and forefinger. The glider should be held so that the wings are banked 45 degrees or more. This will put it into a right turn (if launched by a right-hander). The nose should be pointed up at a 45- to 60-degree angle. Rudder should be set for a left turn.

- After launching, the glider should start a right-climbing turn. The turn decreases as it climbs, until finally at the top it levels off. Then left-turn adjustments take over, and the model should glide down in a smooth left circle.

- Lifting power can be increased by increasing the camber or arch in the wings. Hold the wing close to the mouth and exhale heavily upon the wood, bending it gently at the same time. This adds moisture to the balsa and tends to keep the camber in.
- If the glider dives, slide the wing toward the nose.
- If the glider dips, slide the wing toward the tail.
- The rudder can be bent in the same way as the wings by moistening the wood with your breath.

Gold Rush

A Cub Scout gold rush makes a fine attraction for an afternoon pack picnic. Cub Scouts are turned loose to search for "gold" nuggets, which they use to play mid-way games. The gold rush is complete with a sheriff and deputies, judge, jail, and jailer.

The gold rush committee should follow the guidelines for planning special activities. Get permission to use about an acre of ground, preferably grass covered. This could be a park, churchyard, playground, or schoolyard. Stake out the "gold field" in an area away from the games and contests area. Boys are cautioned to stay away from this area until time for the gold rush.

Many people must be recruited to help make and run the midway games, run the special contests, fix the meal, etc. It's a good opportunity to involve pack families.

When the gold rush is over, a clean-up crew dismantles the equipment, much of which can be stored for future use. Be sure that the grounds are left clean.

The afternoon program can be arranged in various ways. One suggested program is shown below.

SUGGESTED GOLD RUSH PROGRAM

2:30 – 3:30	Informal games.
3:30 – 4:30	Gold rush.
4:30 – 5:00	Special contests and games.

GOLD RUSH ACTIVITY

5:00 – 6:00	Picnic supper and clean-up.
6:00 – 6:30	Awards and closing ceremony.

PERSONNEL NEEDED

- Starter—with starter's gun or camp pistol.
- Sheriff and several deputies (wearing big hat, vest with a star, gun and holster, moustache).
- Judge (wearing black stovepipe hat, fancy coat and vest, holding gavel).
- Jailer.
- Salter—collects nuggets from midway game operators and replants them in the gold field.
- Midway game operators (one or two for each game).
- Special contest leaders.
- Meal committee.

PHYSICAL ARRANGEMENTS

Gold Field. Stake out area about 200 by 200 feet, using colored flags, cloth triangles, or pennants tacked to 2-to 3-foot stakes. Make a large sign reading, "Gold prospectors caught with more than three nuggets at any time will be arrested by the sheriff, thrown in jail, brought before the judge, and sentenced to the wet-sponge treatment." Make nuggets by spraying gold lacquer on stones about the size of sugar cubes. Fill two No. 10 tin cans with nuggets. This should be enough to scatter over the gold field.

Jail. The jail can be a roped-off area, an old playpen, or a large cardboard appliance carton, complete with bars on the windows. Make a sign to identify it.

Judge's Bench. A park bench will do, with a box set in front of it for the judge to pound his gavel on.

Wet Sponge Bath. Cut a head hole in a large piece of canvas. Suspend the canvas from two tree limbs. Have a bucket of water and sponges nearby. Those sentenced by the judge stand behind the board and have wet sponges thrown at them.

Midway. Lay out the area using ropes, upright posts, colored streamers, colorful signs for each game. You will also need a loudspeaker, microphone, and tape player for ballyhoo and carnival music. Each game operator needs a supply of individually wrapped candy to give as prizes — perhaps a different kind for each game.

STARTING THE GOLD RUSH

To start the gold rush, line up all players, explain the directions, then fire a starter's gun to begin the rush into the gold field. As soon as a player finds three nuggets (and no more than three) he hurries to the midway to spend them. When they are gone, he returns to the gold field for more nuggets.

The sheriff and deputies keep a lookout for players carrying more than three nuggets (and there will probably be several once the boys get the hang of it). These culprits are "arrested" and taken to the judge for sentencing. They may end up in jail and get the wet-sponge treatment.

Encourage adults to help the small-fry look for their nuggets so that all can enjoy the midway games. Periodically the salter or deputies collect nuggets from midway game operators and inconspicuously replace them in the gold field.

MIDWAY

A prospector must pay one gold nugget to play each game. Players are awarded candy prizes. Some sample midway games are shown below:

Ring the Bottle. Curtain ring attached to fish pole. Get the ring over a pop bottle.

Feed the Snake. Beanbag toss to hit the snake (a board 6 inches wide and 12 feet long).

Feed the Clown. Beanbag toss at a large clown face with cutout mouth.

Balloon Burst. Attach balloons to a 4-by-4-foot board. Throw darts to burst balloons.

Bull Board. Toss jar rings or linoleum discs at numbered squares on a 4-by-6-foot board.

Cover the Spot. Toss 6-inch linoleum discs onto a 2-by-2-foot board with a red 4-inch round spot. The object is to cover the spot with a disc.

Save a Life. Coil and heave a 25-foot line to target — a 4-foot long 2-by-4-inch board with white canvas gloves at ends and tin can head in center.

Sock 'Em. Throw a wet sponge at a person with his head through hole in canvas. (This could be a prisoner from gold rush activity.)

Dutchman's Bowling. Use a tripod which has a string attached with a croquet ball tied to the end. Swing the ball and hit the pins.

Clear the Deck. Throw balls to knock milk cartons or plastic bottles off a platform.

Clothespin Fishery. (See "Fishing Derby.")

Ring a Giraffe. Make neck of wire coils covered with cloth. Toss lightweight, 8-inch rings.

Bowling on the Green. Roll croquet balls into openings in a target backstop.

Flying Saucers. Sail paper plates (two stapled together) through a coat hanger or into the open side of a cardboard box.

Turkey Shoot. Shoot small beanbags or table tennis balls at a target with a large slingshot.

An added attraction in the midway area might be the famous Chokecherry Bar, where for just one gold nugget, prospectors can buy genuine berry juice or sarsaparilla to quench their thirst.

Other contests might be Horseshoes, Quoits, Beanbag Toss, Tin-Can Golf, Indian Poput, and Turtle Race.

CHUCK WAGON

When it's time to eat, the line of prospectors passes along a table where the cooks dish out helpings of such delicacies as hot dogs, baked beans, potato salad, chocolate milk, and ice cream.

Cub Scout Golf Tournament

Either of the two versions of Cub Scout golf shown here can easily be developed into a pack championship tournament complete with hazards and prizes. Or, one of the golf games could be included in the informal games at a pack picnic.

TIN-CAN GOLF

TIN-CAN GOLF

This is a type of golf in which dens compete as teams. It can be played in almost any area. For the holes, fix No. 10 tin cans or gallon ice-cream containers upright on the ground in desired locations. Use natural hazards in setting up the course. Guard against making the course too large so that the game will not be too long. Follow these simple directions:

• A rubber ball or tennis ball is tossed underhand toward the tin can hole.

• Succeeding shots are taken from where the ball stops.

• Overhand toss is permitted on the "green" near the "hole."

• Score is kept as in golf.

PING-PONG GOLF

This is a good parent-son activity for a pack picnic. For the holes, use No. 10 tin cans turned on their sides and fixed to the ground. Use natural hazards in setting up the course.

• Each golfer uses a Venetian blind slat or something similar for a club.

• Each golfer has a colored table tennis ball.

• Each golfer has a card to keep his score.

• Keep score as in golf.

Obstacle Course

Cub Scouts love to climb, crawl, run, and jump, and a good obstacle course includes all of these. An obstacle course is a fine activity for a pack picnic. It could be either an informal event or a race run on a den basis. It should be difficult enough to challenge the imagination of Cub Scouts, but not so difficult that they cannot do it successfully.

PREPARING THE COURSE

A large area is not necessary. This event can be adapted to the facilities available. A park, playground, vacant lot, or a backyard could be used.

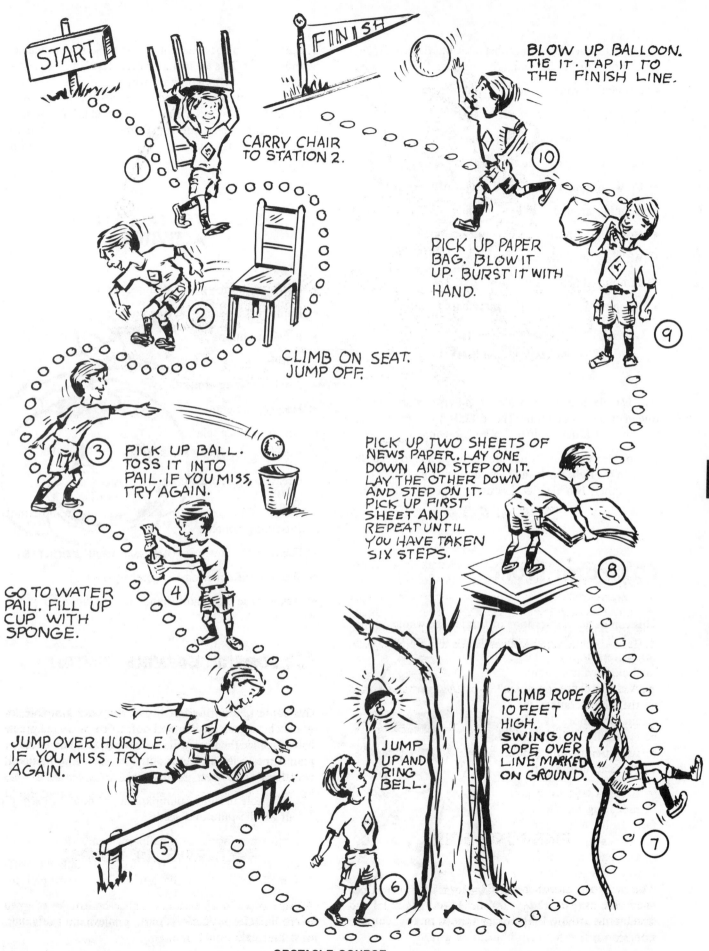

START

CARRY CHAIR TO STATION 2.

CLIMB ON SEAT. JUMP OFF.

PICK UP BALL. TOSS IT INTO PAIL. IF YOU MISS, TRY AGAIN.

GO TO WATER PAIL. FILL UP CUP WITH SPONGE.

JUMP OVER HURDLE. IF YOU MISS, TRY AGAIN.

JUMP UP AND RING BELL.

FINISH

BLOW UP BALLOON. TIE IT. TAP IT TO THE FINISH LINE.

PICK UP PAPER BAG. BLOW IT UP. BURST IT WITH HAND.

PICK UP TWO SHEETS OF NEWS PAPER. LAY ONE DOWN AND STEP ON IT. LAY THE OTHER DOWN AND STEP ON IT. PICK UP FIRST SHEET AND REPEAT UNTIL YOU HAVE TAKEN SIX STEPS.

CLIMB ROPE 10 FEET HIGH. SWING ON ROPE OVER LINE MARKED ON GROUND.

OBSTACLE COURSE

The illustration shows some obstacles, but there are many other possibilities. These might include:

- Crawling through a hoop
- Crawling through a barrel
- Crawling between legs of picnic table
- Crawling under a fence
- Crawling under a rope tied between trees
- Running around a tree three times
- Hopping with a paper cup full of water
- Walking on a low wall or fence
- Jumping through auto tires
- Jumping across a real or imaginary brook

MAKE IT A RACE

An obstacle race can be run on a den basis, starting with one or two boys at a time. The total time is kept for each den so that a den winner can be determined.

Station den chiefs or adults along the course to keep the boys on the right track and prevent them from falling over one another. Two identical layouts can speed up the event.

Fall Farm Frolic

This can be a fall afternoon of fun for the whole family. A real "Heyday"! — an old-fashioned day on the farm, complete with a hayride, corn shelling, haymow jump, greased pig chase, pumpkin carving, handcranked ice cream, and more. It will be especially enjoyable for Cub Scouts and families who are accustomed to city living.

In preparing for the fall farm frolic, follow the guidelines for planning special pack activities. If you know someone who owns an operating farm, you have a head start on this activity. If not, contact the county agricultural extension office for help in locating a farm.

The activities will be determined by the resources available. Several suggestions are included here. The fall frolic committee will probably come up with more ideas. Involve as many parents and other adults as possible in planning and leading the various events. If the group is large, several activities can run at the same time. You may need to arrange for transportation; car pools will cut down on costs.

SUGGESTED FALL FROLIC ACTIVITIES

- Arrive at farm — get acquainted with owner.
- Pumpkin- or apple-carving contest.
- Haymow jump.
- Corn-shelling contest.
- Apple-bobbing contest.
- Hog-calling contest.
- Turkey feather relay.
- Three-legged race.
- Greased-pig chase.
- Tug of war.
- Pie-eating contest.
- Hayride.
- Weiner and corn roast or barbeque.
- Homemade ice cream (hand-cranked freezers).

PUMPKIN-CARVING CONTEST

PUMPKIN CARVING CONTEST

This contest is fun if enough pumpkins are available so that each boy can have one. If not, let them carve apples instead. Since the boys will be working with knives, adequate supervision is important. The following tips will help them carve their pumpkins:

1. Cut a hole in top of pumpkin large enough to scoop out all the pulp and seeds.
2. Draw on a face with a ballpoint pen.
3. Cut out the features. If you accidentally cut off something you need, like a tooth, use a toothpick to stick on the missing part.

Prizes might be given for scariest, funniest, most original, most unusual, etc.

CORN-SHELLING CONTEST

HAYMOW JUMP

Boys climb a ladder to a hayloft where they take turns jumping into a large pile of hay below. Be sure there is plenty of soft hay. Plump the hay pile between jumps. Suggest that the boys jump so they will land seated on the hay with legs in front of them. This should be an optional activity just for fun, not competition. All boys may not wish to jump.

CORN SHELLING CONTEST

Provide each boy with three ears of hard, dried field corn and a bucket or plastic container. Give a preliminary demonstration of how to shell corn (rub two ears together). On signal, they race to see who can finish shelling his ears of corn first.

HOG CALLING CONTEST

This could be a contest for adults only. The boys will enjoy watching. adults try to "call the hogs" with their best "Sou-eee-eeee." Select a winner by applause from the audience.

PIE EATING CONTEST

Have wedges of pie on paper plates set along one edge of a long table. Use a type that is not too rich (such as berry or lemon) so no one will get sick. Have the contestants bend over with hands behind their backs, and on signal, begin eating. The one who cleans his plate first, with no hands, wins a prize.

Variation: A watermelon-eating contest, if watermelons are available.

GREASED PIG CONTEST

How this contest is run will depend on the farmer. If he has two or three small pigs that he doesn't mind being involved, grease them with petroleum jelly or shaving cream and put them in a small penned area. Boys can wear plastic garbage bags with holes cut for head and arms, to protect their clothing. On signal, all race to catch a pig. A boy must hold the pig for at least 5 seconds to win.

If real pigs aren't available, use a large gourd painted to look like a pig and tied to a bamboo pole or hung from a tree limb. Grease the gourd with salad oil or petroleum jelly. Have boys wear plastic gloves which have also been greased. Blindfold each player in turn and have him try to catch the pig as it is raised and lowered.

GREASED PIG CONTEST

TURKEY FEATHER RELAY

Divide group into teams, relay style. First player in each team holds a long turkey feather. On signal, each throws his feather, javelin style, toward a finish line. As soon as it lands, he picks it up and throws it again. When it crosses the finish line, he picks it up, runs back, and hands it to his next teammate, who repeats the action. Each team could use different colored feathers. First team with all players to cross finish line and return to starting position flaps arms and gobbles like triumphant turkeys.

Western Festival

The Wild West still holds a fascination for many people. Playing cowboy can be just as appealing to today's Cub Scouts as it was to their fathers. A pack western festival will give Cub Scouts and their families a taste of the Wild West.

The festival committee must select a suitable location. It can be indoors or outdoors. Follow the guidelines for planning special events. You may want to ask everyone to come dressed in western costume to add to the excitement.

If a meal is served, it could include western chow such as beans and cornbread, chili, or barbeque. It could be served from a chuck wagon (a table decorated to look like a chuck wagon).

GATHERING-TIME ACTIVITIES

Branding. As people arrive, "brand" each with a rubber eraser branding iron. There could a special brand for each den. Use water-soluble ink pad so that brands can be washed off.

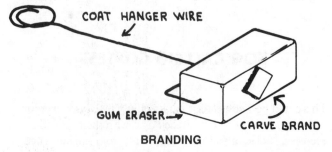

COAT HANGER WIRE

GUM ERASER

CARVE BRAND

BRANDING

Roping Post. Cut a slot in a 3-foot post. Insert a wood cutout of a horse's head. Horse's ears can be made from scrap vinyl and mane from fringed burlap or yarn. Players are given a 25-foot length of rope which has a loop in one end and try to lasso the horse's head from a distance away.

ROPING POST

Buffalo Wheel. Fasten an old bicycle wheel to a post so that it will spin. Remove half of the spokes and mark scores on remaining ones. Make the buffalo from two socks filled with nuts or small pieces of wood, as shown in illustration. To score, throw buffalo into spinning wheel.

Bronco Riding. The body of the bronco can be a heavy fiber drum or large metal oil drum. Wooden legs and rockers are bolted to drum. See illustration for directions.

Steer Lassoing. Cut a steer's head from plywood and paint on features. Hang it from a tree branch so it can be swung. Boys try to lasso it while it's swinging.

Santa Fe Trail is similar to an obstacle course. Some suggested activities are described below:

Broken Wheel. Roll auto tire around a tree.

Wagon in Mud. Wait for next two players before proceeding.

Dust Storm. Follow a string while blindfolded.

Trap Beaver. Using a rod and reel, cast small cardboard cutout of a beaver at a mousetrap until your beaver is "trapped".

Wagon Upset. Play buffalo wheel.

Narrow Pass. Crawl through a barrel.

River Crossing. Wade barefoot through six pans of water.

Repair Harness. Join two ropes using a square knot.

BUFFALO WHEEL

BRONCO RIDING

THE BODY OF THIS BRONCO CAN BE A HEAVY FIBRE DRUM OR A LARGE METAL OIL DRUM. THE HEAD AND ROCKERS CAN BE CUT OUT OF SCRAP LUMBER.

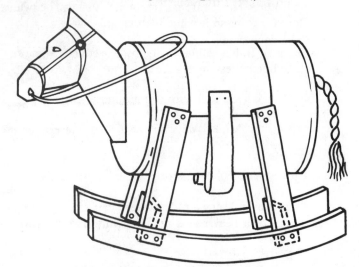

SCREWS

WASHERS

USE BOLTS TO FASTEN LEGS TO DRUM; SCREWS TO FASTEN LEGS TO ROCKERS; BOLTS TO FASTEN STIRRUPS TO DRUM.

USE BOTTOM OF DRUM FOR FRONT. REAR MAY BE LEFT OPEN, OR CLOSED IF YOU HAVE THE COVER.

BRONCO RIDING

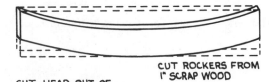

CUT ROCKERS FROM 1" SCRAP WOOD

CUT HEAD OUT OF 1" PLYWOOD OR BOARD. FASTEN TO DRUM WITH SCREWS.

MAKE STIRRUP OUT OF CANVAS STRIP OR PIECE OF OLD LEATHER.

SEW TOGETHER

TAIL: LENGTH OF ROPE, FASTEN TO TOP OF DRUM

FRAY END

LASSOING

HOLE FOR HANGING IN CENTER

CUT A STEER'S HEAD OUT OF PLYWOOD. HANG IT FROM A TREE BRANCH SO IT CAN BE SWUNG. TRY TO LASSO IT WHILE IT'S SWINGING.

STEER LASSOING

SAMPLE WESTERN FESTIVAL PROGRAM

- Gathering-time activities
- Opening ceremony
- Contests and games
- Chuck wagon meal
- Recognition and closing ceremony

GAMES AND CONTESTS

Pony Express Relay. Divide group into equal relay teams. Then divide the teams into two groups stationed 30 to 40 feet apart. First player in each team is given a stick horse and Pony Express bag. On signal, he rides to his teammate in the opposite line, carrying bag over his shoulder. The horse receives a new rider and the bag is transferred. This continues until all players have ridden their section of the Pony Express route.

Bucking Horse Contest. The bucking horses are pogo sticks with horses' heads made of stuffed socks. Riders can be timed or jumps counted.

Hobble Horse Relay. Divide into relay teams. First player on each team slips a band cut from an inner-tube over his ankles, runs up and around a stake at goal line, and back. He removes band and gives it to second player who repeats the action.

Chuck Wagon Contest. Each den team has a chuck wagon. This can be a regular coaster wagon, with a cloth cover attached to a wire frame. Two den members wearing paper-bag horse masks are the horses. Behind each wagon is an equal number of pots and pans (or tin cans). On signal, all den members except the horses load cans into the wagon. When they are finished, they yell, "Wagons, ho!" and the horses dash off, pulling the wagon twice around the track. If any implement falls out, the horses must stop and wait for other den members to put it back. First wagon making the circuit twice wins.

Calf Roping. Each den selects one member to be a Calf and one to be a Roper in this interden contest. The Roper is given 6 feet of ¼-inch rope with a wrist-size loop tied in one end. When the "trail boss" calls out, "Go Den 1," the Calf runs on hands and knees into an open area, and the Roper pursues him, trying to upset him. When he knocks the Calf over, the Roper uses his rope to tie the Calf's hands and feet together. The Calf should cooperate. Each Roper is timed. Continue until each Calf and Roper has competed. Fastest time wins.

Top Spinning Tournament

Top spinning is an old activity with many local variations. It is still a favorite with many boys. A top spinning tournament could be held on either a den or pack basis.

Follow the guidelines for planning special pack activities. Set simple, easy-to-follow rules and make sure everyone understands. Allow a couple of weeks for practice before holding the tournament. Some suggested contests are given here.

BUCKING HORSE CONTEST

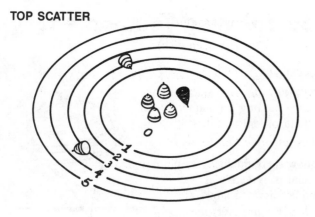

TOP KILLING

Each player gets three tries at spiking a live (spinning) target top that is kept spinning by a waiting contestant. He gets three points if his top strikes a glancing blow, five points for "killing" it, and 10 points for splitting it. The contestant's top must remain spinning after hitting the target.

WHIP FOR DISTANCE

Each contestant throws his top from a starting line. Three tries are allowed. Scoring is determined by the distance from the starting line that the top travels and still spins.

TOP SCATTER

Five concentric circles are drawn, as shown. The bull's-eye is 12 inches in diameter, and each ring is 6 inches wide, making the overall diameter 6 feet. The rings are numbered 0, 1, 2, 3, 4, 5, with 0 in the center. Six "dead" tops (not spinning) are arranged peg-up in the bull's-eye. Each player is given three puts at them, with no rearranging between puts. Score according to the circles into which the dead tops are scattered. The spinner's top must remain spinning after each put. A top resting on a line between circles counts for the higher score ring.

ENDURANCE SPIN

On signal, all Cub Scouts spin their tops. Player whose top spins longest is the winner.

Cub Scout Midway

The midway activities described below can be used for a Cub Scout fair, circus, festival, or any other special event that includes a midway.

- Bounce a rubber ball into a wastebasket.

- Toss beanbags at a target on the floor or through holes in a tossing board.

- Turn a chair upside down. Ring the legs with rings made from old garden hose.

- Mark a target of squares on the floor. Pitch rubber heels at target.

- Mark a shuffleboard target on the floor. Use a broom or mop stick to push pan lids or blocks into the target.

- Shoot checkers with a finger snap into a target of numbered squares on a table. Score is the number. Checkers touching lines don't count.

- Snap tiddlywinks into shallow cups or a muffin pan.

- Bounce balls through an inflated bicycle tube or a ring of garden hose.

- Bounce tennis, sponge, or golf balls into a target made by tying several No. 10 tin cans together.

- Toss or roll balls to knock down Indian clubs or bowling pins set in a straight row or triangle formation.

- Shoot at a target with a suction-cup gun.

- Throw an inflated paper bag for distance.

- Toss cards into a hat.

- Shoot cards into a hat.

- Guess the number of beans in a jar.

- Throw a hat and have it land and stay on a hat rack at least once in five tries.

- Drive a nail into a 2-by-4-inch board in five swings.

OTHER MIDWAY ACTIVITIES

Hat-Making Booth. Have available a good supply of ribbons, pins, needles, feathers, flowers, thread, string, tape, scissors, and some old hats to be remodeled. It's fun for the men to make hats for the women.

Portrait Gallery. Draw comic figures on a piece of 4-by-6-foot wallboard, such as those shown. Cut out two

half circles at the top for the customer's heads. Use an instant-developing camera. Be sure lighting is adequate. Check to see if film can be donated.

Squonk-Um Booth. Toss wet sponges at some agreeable volunteer.

SQUONK-UM BOOTH

Peep Show. Collect several shoe boxes. Cut a peep hole in the front end of each. Make a slot about ½-inch wide across top near other end of box. Paint or decorate boxes with crepe paper, if desired. Put an attraction in each box and arrange them along a table or shelf so peep holes are at eye-level for boys. String Christmas lights over the slots to illuminate the attractions. Add a sign identifying each attraction.

Prehistoric Garden (lump of coal)

Tear Jerker (onion)

Hawaiian Native (coconut)

Ruins of China (broken dish)

Ocean Liner (sand)

Pillars of Greece (candle)

Famous Hole in One (donut)

Rare Invisible Fish (bowl of clear water)

World's Smallest Dog (small hot dog)

Famous Conductor (electric plug)

World's Hardest Head (hammer head)

World's Biggest Foot (a 12-inch ruler)

14-Carat Ring (ring of 14 carrots)

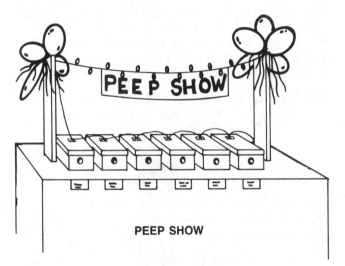

PEEP SHOW

Rainy-Day Field Day

Here's a pack event that can be scheduled ahead of time or used to provide a fun-filled substitute program on a day when the pack has planned an outdoor activity and been rained out. The beauty of the rainy-day field day is that is will take only a short time to gather the materials for it.

You will need such items as feathers, uncooked navy beans, lemons or hard-boiled eggs, paper plates, balloons, string, table tennis balls, paper sacks, marshmallows, and crackers.

The events listed may be run on an individual or den basis, as straight races, or as relays.

EVENTS

Shot-Put. Each boy is given ten navy beans which he

attempts to throw into a quart jar from a chalk line on the floor.

Hammer Throw. An inflated balloon is tied to the end of a string. Each boy throws the "hammer" by the end of the string. The one throwing the farthest wins.

Football Game. One team is on each side of a table. Each team tries to blow a table tennis ball off opponent's side of table.

Standing Broad Grin. The width of grins is measured by judges. The widest wins.

HAMMER THROW

Discus Throw. A paper plate is thrown from a chalk line. Plate must be held flat in hand and not sailed with thumb and fingers.

Sixteen-Pound Put. An inflated bag is put for distance, as though it were shot from the shoulder.

Foot Race. Each boy stands with one foot touching the other, heel to toe. The greatest total length wins.

Running High Whistle. The boy who holds a whistled note the longest with one breath wins.

Feather Blow Relay. Blow a feather 25 feet and return, touching off the next player.

Running High Squeal. Boy who in one breath yells in a high and loud tone of voice the longest wins.

Fifty-Yard Swim. Each boy hops on one foot, carrying a paper cup of water. First one over the finish line with the most water in his cup wins.

Twenty-Foot Relay. Relay teams use a stick to roll lemons or hard-boiled eggs down the course and back.

Bawl Game. Boy who can make a bawling noise with one breath for the longest time wins.

Fluff. Boys carry feathers a certain distance on a paper plate. They must pick up any that drop before continuing the race.

Bean Relay. Boys carry beans, one at a time, between matchsticks or toothpicks, or on a knife.

Water-Drinking Relay. One boy feeds his partner water with a spoon. First team to use all of its water wins.

FOOTBALL GAME

Long Glum. See which boy can stay solemn the longest while everyone else tries to make him laugh.

Balloon Blowing. Give each boy a balloon to blow up. First balloon to break wins.

BALLOON BLOWING

TWENTY-FOOT RELAY

Cubmobile Derby

The Cubmobile derby is a colorful, thrilling pack activity that is fun for the whole family.

Planning for the derby should begin several months before the race date, so that Cub Scouts and adults from each den will have time to build a racer. That's right! Each den builds its own Cubmobile, with dads or other adults helping to supervise the construction. There is no engine; the Cubmobile works by gravity.

Follow the guidelines for planning special pack activities. Each pack family should be furnished with an information sheet listing the rules, awards, procedures, building specifications, date, time, and place. This will help prevent any misunderstandings.

PERSONNEL NEEDED

Program Committee

- Plan a snappy opening ceremony, such as a ribbon-cutting.
- Handle all aspects of awards (platform, signs, tables, trophies, ribbons, etc.)
- Plan for crowd control.
- String pennants for decorations.
- Secure public-address system or bullhorns.
- Have rescue squad or first aiders on hand for emergencies.

INSPECTION TEAM

- Make a jig of cardboard or wood to check overall dimensions of Cubmobiles.
- Check for correct attachments and safety requirements (especially brake system and seat belt).
- Number each car.
- Act as judges for craftsmanship award. Report winner to program committee.

CUBMOBILE DERBY

REGISTRATION TEAM

- Register each boy and give him a number.

- Enter car numbers and names of drivers for each run on tally sheet, to keep track of who drives in each heat.

- Get times from timekeepers at finish line and record.

- Determine final standing of each den car and report results to program committee for presentation of awards.

TRACK OPERATIONS TEAM

- Assign two gatekeepers to line up cars.

- Have three starters with green flags to operate starting ramp.

- Have Official timers with stop watches at finish line (one for each lane).

- Have two judges with checkered flags.

- Mark lanes in street with chalk. Rope off racing area where necessary.

- Provide bales of hay for end of track to make sure Cubmobiles stop.

- Report official times to registration team.

THE TRACK

The track should be a smooth-surfaced street with a gradual slope that is neither too long nor too steep. The suggested track length is about 150 feet, plus additional stopping space. Secure approval from the appropriate city, county, or park authority to close off the street to traffic during the derby.

The lanes should be marked with chalk. Crossing over from one lane to another will happen, especially with inexperienced drivers, but boys should be instructed to stay within their own lanes. Judges should observe the race for any fouls. If a driver is fouled, he should be given another run.

Usually a ramp is set up to start the cars. Cubmobiles start from a standstill, running down the ramp and the slope to the finish line. No pushing or pumping with the feet is allowed.

THE RAMP

This may be as simple or elaborate as the derby committee wishes. Sheets of heavy plywood are effective and usually can be rented. These can be elevated at the back side with cement blocks. Another type of starting ramp is illustrated here. Consider safety factors when determining the angle of the starting ramp. The ramp should allow ample room for the number of cars starting at one time.

CUBMOBILE SPECS AND PARTS

See the illustration for description of building materials and hardware.

- Wheels must not exceed 12 inches in diameter.

- All wheels must be equipped with solid rubber tires.

- Car frame is made from 2-by-4-inch construction lumber.

- The overall length of the car is a maximum of 5 feet; the wheel base a maximum of 4 feet. The outside circumference of the wheel may vary from 30 to 36 inches.

- Use roundhead ¼-inch bolts to hold frame. Screws are a second choice. Nails are not suitable, because they may work loose.

- All cars must have a seat with braced backrest, so the boy can comfortably steer with his feet.

- Steering is done with the feet, which are placed on the front axle, and by the hands holding a rope fastened to the front axle.

- If threaded axles are used, the nuts must be secured with cotter pins or wire.

- Cars must be equipped with an adequate safety belt securely fastened to the main frame of the car.

- Cars must be equipped with a handbrake with its rubbing surface faced with a rubber material such as a strip of an old tire. This will stop the car when dragged on the ground.

- During a race, the two 2-by-4-inch blocks fastened ½-inch from the centerboard will limit the turning radius.

RACING PROCEDURE

1. The derby is run in heats. Each den has one Cubmobile, and each boy in the den races the car one time. The den with the lowest average racing time wins.

2. Cub Scouts bring Cubmobile to inspection station where it is checked and numbered.

3. Cars and drivers go to the registration table where the names and car are checked on the heat schedule.

4. As his name is called by announcer, each boy reports to starting gate and is helped into his car. Seat belt is fastened.

5. All drivers must wear protective head gear, such as

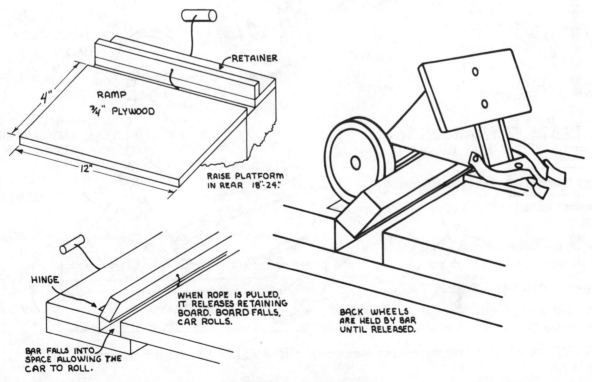

RAMP ¾" PLYWOOD

RETAINER

4"

12"

RAISE PLATFORM IN REAR 18"-24"

HINGE

WHEN ROPE IS PULLED, IT RELEASES RETAINING BOARD. BOARD FALLS, CAR ROLLS.

BAR FALLS INTO SPACE ALLOWING THE CAR TO ROLL.

BACK WHEELS ARE HELD BY BAR UNTIL RELEASED.

CUBMOBILE DERBY RAMP

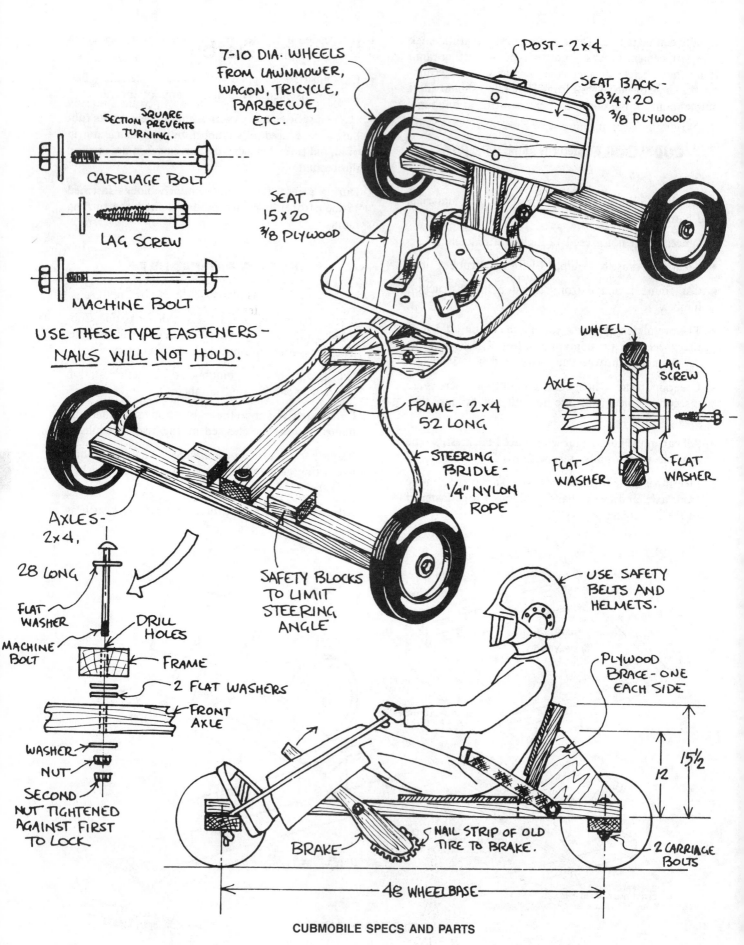

SQUARE SECTION PREVENTS TURNING.

CARRIAGE BOLT

LAG SCREW

MACHINE BOLT

USE THESE TYPE FASTENERS — NAILS WILL NOT HOLD.

7-10 DIA. WHEELS FROM LAWNMOWER, WAGON, TRICYCLE, BARBECUE, ETC.

POST- 2×4

SEAT BACK- 8¾×20 ⅜ PLYWOOD

SEAT 15×20 ⅜ PLYWOOD

WHEEL

AXLE

LAG SCREW

FLAT WASHER

FLAT WASHER

FRAME- 2×4 52 LONG

STEERING BRIDLE- ¼" NYLON ROPE

AXLES- 2×4, 28 LONG

FLAT WASHER

MACHINE BOLT

DRILL HOLES

FRAME

2 FLAT WASHERS

FRONT AXLE

WASHER

NUT

SECOND NUT TIGHTENED AGAINST FIRST TO LOCK

SAFETY BLOCKS TO LIMIT STEERING ANGLE

USE SAFETY BELTS AND HELMETS.

PLYWOOD BRACE- ONE EACH SIDE

15½

12

BRAKE

NAIL STRIP OF OLD TIRE TO BRAKE.

2 CARRIAGE BOLTS

48 WHEELBASE

CUBMOBILE SPECS AND PARTS

football helmet, racing helmet, or construction "hard hat."

6. When cars are released by starter, drivers should stay in their own lanes.

7. No pumping or pushing with the feet is permitted.

8. After driving, the boy returns to the spectator section.

PRIZES

Each boy should receive an award or other memento of his participation in the derby. Winners could be presented with medals or trophies. Multipurpose award ribbons, trophies, and numerous Cub Scout gift items are available at your local Scout distributor.

See "Prizes and Awards" section for additional ideas for prizes.

PUBLICITY

The Cubmobile derby will have considerable appeal to the general public. Invite photographers to take pictures for the local newspaper. See that boys are properly uniformed—they could wear Cub Scout T-shirts and shorts.

Pinewood Derby

The pinewood derby is one of the most popular and successful special events in Cub Scouting. Like all successful activities, it requires planning and preparation, but its value in fun and strengthening family relationships has been proven over the years.

Pinewood derby cars are simply small models of specified dimensions, created, carved, and assembled by the boys, under the guidance of their parents or other family members. The cars are gravity powered and run down a regulation track. The race can be run indoors or outdoors.

The pinewood derby committee sets simple, uncomplicated rules and informs each pack family before the cars are built. The committee should follow the guidelines for planning special pack activities so that nothing important will be overlooked.

Pinewood derby kits with building instructions can be brought individually or in packs of eight at your local Scout distributor. It is best for the derby committee to buy them in quantity and distribute them to pack families. Extra wheels, axles, and pinewood derby trophies, plaster casting molds, medals, and ribbons are also available.

PINEWOOD DERBY TEST TRACK

PERSONNEL NEEDED

Program Committee

- Plan a snappy opening ceremony, such as a ribbon-cutting.

- Handle all aspects of awards (decorated platform, signs, tables, trophies, ribbons, medals, etc.).

- Plan for crowd control.

- String pennants for decorations.

- Secure public-address system or bullhorns, if needed.

Inspection Team

- Weight cars, using a small scale.

- Use a jig made of cardboard or wood to check overall dimensions. (A simple method is to construct a box measuring 2¾-by-7⅜-by-1½ inches. If the car fits in this box, it passes that part of the inspection.)

- Mark numbers on bottom of cars. Use a separate series of numbers at each table.

- Act as judges for craftsmanship award or other special awards. Report winners to program committee.

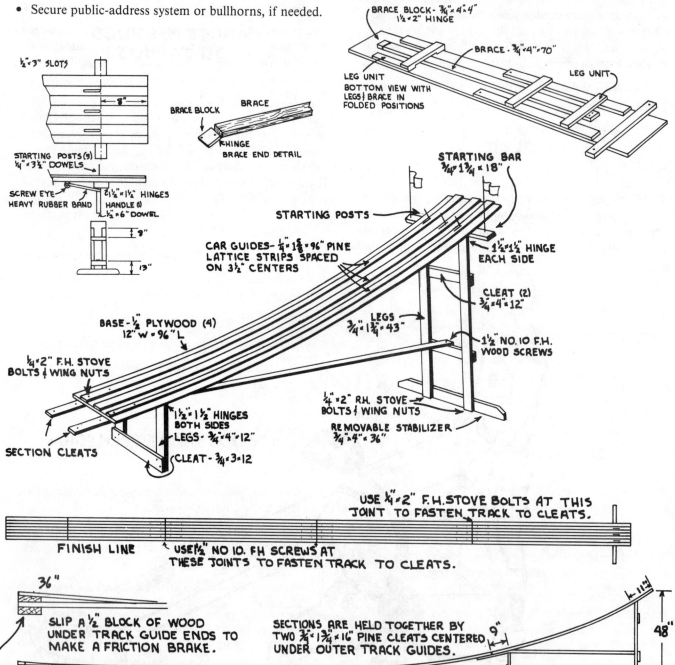

PINEWOOD DERBY TRACK

Registration Team

- Enter car numbers and names of entries on a preliminary heat sheet.
- Enter names of heat winners on semifinal sheets.
- Determine final standing of each car and report results to program committee for presentation of awards.

Track Operations Team

- Have two starters with green flags.
- Have two judges with checkered flags.
- Have two gatekeepers to line up boys.
- Set up derby track.
- Report preliminary winners and final winners to registration team.

SAMPLE PINEWOOD DERBY PROGRAM

Previous day — Begin car inspections, if feasible. This will permit boys and parents to fix problems before derby time.

2:00   Registration of cars; final car inspections.

2:30   Opening ceremony.

Cut ribbon and start heats. Award ribbons and other prizes to heat winners during the running of the derby.

4:00   Recognition ceremony; recognize champions. Then make advancement awards.

Closing ceremony.

THE TRACK

Some packs borrow pinewood derby tracks; others build their own and use it year after year.

The track illustrated will allow three cars to race at one time. It can be built with ordinary workshop tools. The use of loose pin hinges makes it easy to take apart for storage.

The curved sweep of the ramp bends naturally, but if the short legs do not touch the floor when the track is

assembled, weigh them down with a bag of sand across the cleat of the short legs.

Block-sand all track surfaces, particularly where sections are joined. For extra strength, use white glue on all joints before fastening with screws. Finally, a good grade of hard enamel paint is recommended for finishing the track.

The lane strips should be ¼-inch high. The bottom of the Grand Prix derby car is designed to be just ⅛-inch above the lane strip. If the lane strip is too high or the car too low, the racer will drag.

SAMPLE PINEWOOD DERBY RULES

All cars must pass the following inspection to qualify for the race:

1. Width shall not exceed 2¾ inches.
2. Length shall not exceed 7⅜ inches.
3. Weight shall not exceed 5 ounces.
4. Axles, wheels, and body shall be from the materials provided in the kit.
5. Wheel bearings, washers, and bushings are prohibited.
6. No lubricating oil may be used. Axles may be lubricated with powdered graphite or silicone.
7. The car shall not ride on any kind of spring.
8. The car must be free-wheeling, with no starting devices.
9. No loose materials of any kind are allowed in the car.

PINEWOOD DERBY PROCEDURE

1. Each boy brings his car to the inspection table to have it inspected and numbered.
2. After inspection, the boy goes to the registration table where his name and car are entered on the heat schedule.
3. After registration and inspection, cars are brought to the starter's table by dens.
4. As each heat is announced, drivers place their own cars at starting gate. Starter releases the gate.
5. Judges at the finish line will determine results of the race. The car whose nose is first over the finish line

is the winner. Judges will pick first, second, and third places.

6. Winner of heat takes his car to the awards platform. After receiving his ribbon, he goes to the spectator area to await his next heat.

7. Losers of each heat take their cars to the starter for the second running, which will determine the second-place car for the heat.

8. If a car leaves the trace, runs out of its lane, interferes with another car, or loses an axle or other part, let it run in the next heat if it can be repaired quickly. In the first heat of a den race, if a car jumps the track, it is judged as finishing last.

9. After first, second, and third place winners have been selected in each preliminary heat, run as many quarter-final and semifinal heats as necessary to determine contestants for the final heat.

10. Den winners are determined first. The first three places from each den will advance to the championship heats. The remaining drivers participate in consolation heats.

TIPS FOR CONSTRUCTION

The Cub Scout should build his own racer with guidance and minimal assistance from a parent. To prevent parents from giving too much help, some packs have a separate competition for cars built by dads or mothers.

- If your design calls for cutting away much of the block, use a saw first, then a jackknife.

- Paint body parts before assembling them to avoid getting paint on axles.

- Remove burrs on the nail axles before adding wheels, using sandpaper or emery paper.

- If there is a mold seam on the wheels, sand them very lightly. The wheels are hollow and can break if too heavily sanded.

- Use white glue or model airplane cement to hold pin axle in body. Measure center distance between axles before attaching.

- Lubricate axles with powdered graphite or silicone. No oil, grease, or silicone spray should be used. Lubricating oil will slow wheel spin and dripping oil can foul the racetrack.

- Fishing sinkers or other weights may be inserted in the body to add weight, but the total weight of the car may not exceed 5 ounces.

TIPS ON PLANNING AND CONDUCTING DERBY

- Have a pre-race inspection of cars about a week before the derby to catch all possible problems before race time. This minimizes disqualifications and disappointments.

- Have a meeting prior to the derby to orient officials with their jobs.

- Use some type of board to post the derby's progress, such as with tags on hooks.

- Some packs use an instant-developing camera to photograph the finish. This simplifies picking the winners in a close race, and the photo can be given to the winner.

- Consider using judges from outside the pack to prevent parent problems when a boy doesn't win.

- Have some activity planned for about 15 minutes after completion of registration, to allow time to organize den heats.

- Have some activity planned between den finals and pack heats to allow time for organizing the next heats.

- Have enough ribbons and awards so that every Cub Scout can take home an award.

—— DERBY CAR VARIATIONS——

Some packs use special types of pinewood derby racers, such as those shown here.

CONESTOGA PINEWOOD DERBY

Turn the regular pinewood derby kit into a covered wagon. The only additional materials needed are a piece of heavy white fabric, approximately 6½-by-10 inches and two 10-inch pieces of coat hanger or other wire. See illustration for outline of wood block. When it is finished, make holes in wood and glue in wire. Cover wire frame with fabric, turning back edges and gluing fabric securely to wagon frame. Attach the wheels and you're ready to race. (Be sure to taken into consideration the extra weight of the wire and fabric. Standard derby weight still applies.)

FIRE TRUCK DERBY

Cut standard derby block as shown. Glue cardboard

BILL OF MATERIAL			
ITEM	NO. REQ'D.	DESCRIPTION	
1	1	BASIC PINEWOOD DERBY RACER KIT *	
2	2	PIECES WIRE (COAT HANGER) 10" LONG	
3	1	PIECE UNBLEACHED MUSLIN 10" SQUARE	
4	2	PIECES OF STRING, EACH 14" LONG	
* NOTE		SAVE THE CUTTINGS FROM THE WAGON BLOCK TO MAKE SIDEBOARDS & CARGO FOR THE WAGON	

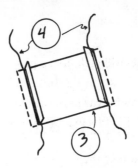

DETAIL OF COVER:
FOLD OVER ½" AT EACH END.
POSITION STRING IN FOLD.
GLUE OR STITCH HEM OVER STRING.
(DON'T GLUE THE STRING)
USE THE DRAWSTRINGS TO
PULL COVER TIGHT OVER BOWS.

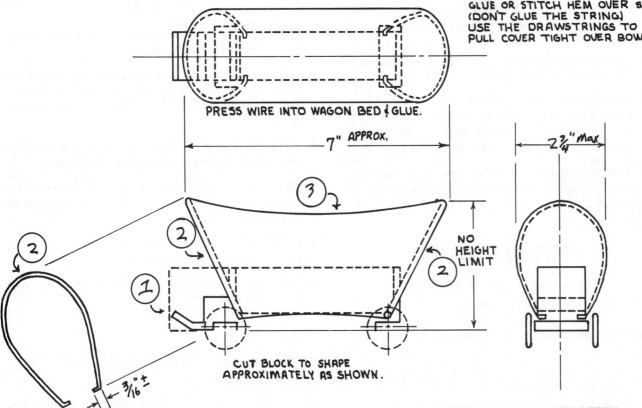

PRESS WIRE INTO WAGON BED & GLUE.

7" APPROX.

2¾" MAX

NO HEIGHT LIMIT

CUT BLOCK TO SHAPE APPROXIMATELY AS SHOWN.

3/16" +
DETAIL OF BOW—
BEND AS SHOWN.

CONESTOGA PINEWOOD DERBY

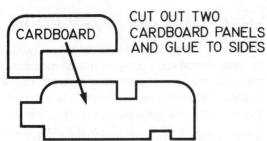

CARDBOARD

CUT OUT TWO CARDBOARD PANELS AND GLUE TO SIDES

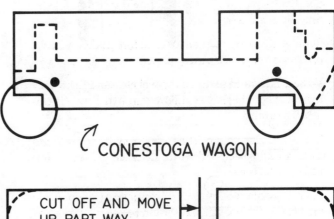

CONESTOGA WAGON

MAKE LADDER FROM BALSA AND TOOTHPICK PIECES.

PAINT RED. GLUE ON LADDERS.

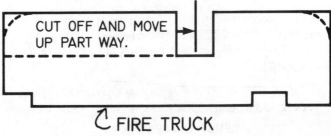

CUT OFF AND MOVE UP PART WAY.

FIRE TRUCK

panels to side. Paint red. Make ladder from toothpick pieces. Add wheels and race to the fire.

HUMPTY DUMPTY DERBY

Here's a new twist that will emphasize the importance of safety belts. Adapt the basic pinewood derby car with a driver's seat (such as soft plastic foam), a safety belt (such as a rubber band) and a plastic or hard-boiled egg "driver." Run the derby in the usual way.

As an added feature, set up a crash test to demonstrate safety belt effectiveness. Use a raw egg with a face painted on it and place it in the car, unrestrained by a safety belt. The car races down the track and hits a wall placed across the end. The egg driver will sail out of his car and smash—a visible lesson of what might happen to a real driver in the event of an accident. (Use aluminum foil to catch the egg splatterings.) Then repeat the demonstration with a safety-belted egg to show how seat belts save eggs—and people.

DERBY CAR SPECIAL

This is an easy-to-make pinewood derby car that can be made by any Cub Scouts or Webelos Scouts who may be unable to handle knives and other tools.

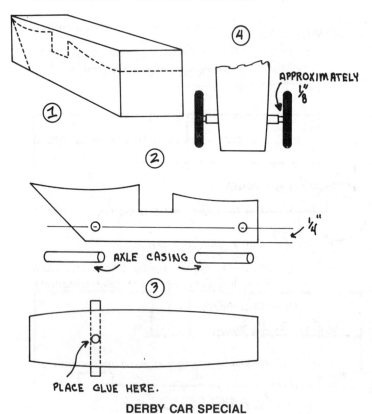

DERBY CAR SPECIAL

Styrofoam block 2-by-2-by-7 inches (car body)
Styrofoam block 2-by-2-by-2 inches (shaping block)
Two thin dowels about 2½ inches long (to fit inside plastic straw axle casings)
Two plastic straws about 2¼ inches long (axle casings)
Four pinewood derby regulation wheels
Sandpaper

1. Use a soft pencil to draw the outline of car on the sides of the body block.

2. With shaping blocks, sand away unwanted parts of the styrofoam until the shape of the car is achieved. Do not sand the bottom of the car at all.

3. Paint and decorate the car and let it dry.

4. Insert plastic axle casings 1¼ inches above the bottom of the car and about 1 inch from each end, being careful to keep casing straight so the wheels will be in line when added. *Tip:* When inserting the axle casing, use the wooden axle to make the opening and then insert the plastic casing. This will help to insure a straighter opening for the casing, as the wood will not bend like the plastic.

5. Once the axle casings are in place, turn the car upside down and use the axle to make a small hole directly over the plastic casing in the center of the car body. Fill the hole with glue and stuff with a small wedge of scrap styrofoam. Repeat for the other axle and set aside to dry.

6. Using sandpaper, sand the ridges off of the wheels so they are smooth. This will give the wheel better balance and more traction. If the axle casings are not even, insert the wood axle and gently pull until the casings are straight.

7. Place the wood axle into the hole in wheel, being careful to keep the axle straight.

8. Before you insert the axle into the casing, place a little graphite in the plastic casing. Graphite will lubricate the wood axle and make it run more smoothly. DO NOT use oil or any liquid of any kind as this will cause the wood to swell and bind.

9. After the axle is inserted, spin it a few times to make sure the graphite coats it well. Add a little glue to the bare end of the axle and insert it into the other wheel, tapping gently into place. *Tip:* When adding the second wheel to the axle, be sure to leave a small space between the inside of the wheel and the plastic casing so that the wheel will not rub against the plastic and bind. Let dry.

10. When competing with pinewood derby cars, the styrofoam cars will need added weight. This is done by cutting a hole in the center of the car bottom and

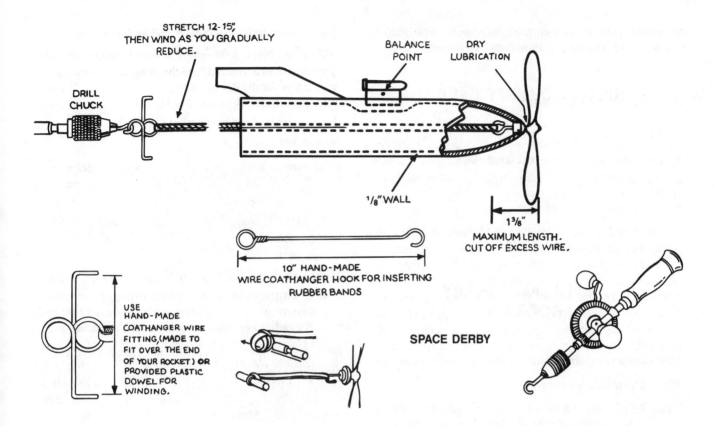

STRETCH 12-15", THEN WIND AS YOU GRADUALLY REDUCE.

DRILL CHUCK

BALANCE POINT

DRY LUBRICATION

1/8" WALL

1 3/8"

MAXIMUM LENGTH. CUT OFF EXCESS WIRE.

10" HAND-MADE WIRE COATHANGER HOOK FOR INSERTING RUBBER BANDS

USE HAND-MADE COATHANGER WIRE FITTING, (MADE TO FIT OVER THE END OF YOUR ROCKET) OR PROVIDED PLASTIC DOWEL FOR WINDING.

SPACE DERBY

inserting a fishing sinker. Fill the hole with glue and pack with scrap styrofoam. Be sure that no more weight than is allowed in the rules is added.

Space Derby

The space derby is similar to the pinewood derby except that the models are miniature "rockets"—propeller-driven and powered by three rubber bands—that travel along a heavy monofilament fishing line. The rockets are carved by the boys, with the guidance of their parents or other family members.

The space derby committee sets simple, uncomplicated rules and informs each pack family before the rockets are built. The races can be run indoors or outdoors. In planning the derby, the committee should follow the guidelines for special pack activities.

Space derby kits with building instructions can be bought individually or in packs of eight at your local Scout distributor. It is more economical for the derby committee to buy them in quantity and distribute them to pack families. Also available are space derby carriers, an accessory kit, extra rubber bands, propeller assembly kit, and space derby medals, ribbons, trophies, and plaster casting molds.

PERSONNEL NEEDED

Program Committee

- Plan an opening ceremony, such as a ribbon-cutting.
- Handle all aspects of awards (decorated platform, signs, tables, trophies, ribbons, medals, etc.)
- Plan for crowd control.
- String pennants for decoration.
- Secure public-address system or bull horns, if needed.

Inspection Team

- Check entries for use of official materials.
- Mark a number on each rocket.
- Act as judges for craftsmanship award and other special awards. Report winners to program committee.

Registration Team

- Enter rocket numbers and boys' name on a preliminary heat sheet.
- List heat winners on semifinal sheets.

- Determine final standing of each rocket and report results to program committee for presentation of awards.

Flight Operations Team

- Have two starters with green flags.
- Have two judges with checkered flags.
- Have two gatekeepers to line up boys.
- Set up space derby raceway.
- Report preliminary winners and final winners to registration team.

SAMPLE SPACE DERBY PROGRAM

7:00 Inspection and registration of rockets.

7:30 Opening ceremony.

7:45 Cut ribbon and start heats. Award ribbons and other prizes to heat winners during running of derby.

8:30 Recognition ceremony. Recognize champions; then make advancement awards.

8:45 Closing ceremony.

CONSTRUCTING AND OPERATING ROCKET

The official space derby kit includes all necessary materials and instructions for building. Decorate the rocket with bright colors. Apply decals furnished in the kit.

Tips for rocket builders:

- Reduce air friction or "drag" by making all surfaces as smooth as possible. A blunt, rounded nose causes less drag than a sharp nose. A good design has all leading edges rounded and trailing edges tapered to reduce drag.
- Rubber bands should be lubricated before the race. They are the "motor" and must be strong and flexible.
- Use a sharp knife for cutting the grooves for the hanger fitting and fins. A dull knife will crush and splinter the balsa wood.
- When you start to carve, remember that the end with the small hole is the rocket nose.

- A potato peeler is good for carving the shape.
- To help increase the rocket's speed, reduce the wall thickness to a minimum of ⅛-inch. Do not weaken the area around the hanger (carrier) or carve away the nose button circle.
- Do not apply too much paint to the outside unless you sand between each coat.
- Be careful not to get glue on the plastic carrier, especially in the holes through which the monofilament line runs. Glue can interfere with smooth operation.
- Make the propeller shaft as short as possible by bending it close to the prop. Cut off the excess wire with wire cutters.
- Test the rocket's balance by hanging it from a string through the hole of the hanger fitting. If the rocket is nose-heavy, carve or sand a little wood off that end. If it's tail-heavy, remove wood from tail area.

Dens may wish to secure a 100-foot length of 50-pound monofilament fishing line for test runs in the backyard before the derby. Tie the line to a tree or post and string the rocket carrier on it. Tie the other end to a tree about 100 feet away. Make the line as tight as possible.

THE ROCKET LAUNCHER

Some packs borrow rocket launchers; other build their own and use it year after year. A materials list and instructions for building and setting up a rocket launcher are found in the space derby kit.

Use 50-pound test monofilament fishing line. It is tough and won't break.

SAMPLE SPACE DERBY RULES

All rockets must pass the following inspection to qualify for the race:

- Only basic materials supplied in kit may be used.
- Rocket body may be no longer than 7 inches, not including propeller and fins.
- There are no restrictions on weight or design of rocket.

SPACE DERBY PROCEDURE

1. Every boy brings his rocket to the inspection table to have his entry checked and numbered.

2. Then he goes to the registration table where his name and rocket's number are entered on a heat sheet.

3. Contestants report to gatekeepers, who line them up in the order in which they will compete. At this point, each boy starts to wind the rubber-band motor of his ship.

4. As his name is called, the boy hooks his rocket on the guideline assigned to him, centering the rocket between the vertical dowels and locking the propeller behind the horizontal dowel on the starting gate.

5. The gatekeeper starts the countdown and fires at zero by lifting the rear of the starting gate frame, which releases the rockets.

6. The race is run in heats, up to four contestants at a time. Each boy gets to try at least twice instead of being eliminated from competition after the first race. For example, in a six-boy den, try heats of three boys each. The winner of each heat goes into the den finals. Then race the other four again with the winner competing with other heat winners for the den championship and entry into the pack finals.

7. The winner takes his rocket to the registration table for recording, then to the awards platform for recognition. He then returns to the spectator area to wait until his name is called again.

8. Run as many quarter-final and semifinal heats as necessary to determine the contestants for the final.

9. As ships are eliminated, make sure the contestants are applauded for their efforts.

TIPS FOR PREPARING FOR FLIGHT

- Lubricate rubber bands before the derby. This prolongs the bands' life and power and will help reduce the possibility of their breaking during the competition. They can be soaked overnight in castor oil. Or mix two parts green soap, one part glycerine, and one part water and rub the mixture on the rubber band about an hour before racing.

- Have extra boxes of rubber bands on hand. Remember, it takes three rubber bands to fly each ship properly.

- Experienced rocket racers "warm up" their space ships by gradually winding the rubber band motor to its full capacity—first 50 turns, then 100, then 200, etc. Release the propeller between each winding.

- A small hand drill is excellent for winding rubber bands. It also helps speed up the event. Check the ratio of the drill by making one revolution of the crank handle and count the number of times the chuck turns. Most drills average a one-to-four ratio, thus it would take 40 turns of the crank to give 160 winds on the rubber-band motor. When using the hand drill winder, it's best for one person to hold the rocket and propeller while another stretches the bands about 12 to 15 inches beyond the rocket tail and turns the rubber bands with the drill. As the winder twists the rubber bands, he gradually shortens the distance between him and the rocket.

- For a more evenly matched race, wind all rocket motors the same number of turns. For 100-foot launch lines, 150 to 170 winds should be sufficient.

SPECIAL SPACE DERBY EVENTS

Speed. First rocket to reach finish line.

Endurance. Last rocket to reach the finish line.

Relay. Use two or more guidelines. Boys form teams of twos. The first boy releases his rocket, and as soon as it reaches the other end of the line, his teammate removes it, rewinds it, puts it back on the guideline, and releases it. The first rocket to return wins.

Altitude. String a guideline which is about 12 inches from the ground at the starting line and 5 feet at the finish line. Gradually, raise the high end of the line until all rockets have been eliminated. The one which climbed the highest wins.

Just For Fun. Have rockets break balloons at the finish line. Do this by inserting several straight pins through a piece of cardboard. Suspend the cardboard from the finish line and place a balloon in front of the pins. The rocket will drive the balloon into the pins.

Raingutter Regatta

Ahoy, mates! This could be the sailing regatta of the century! Although the seas are only 10-foot lengths of raingutter filled with water, and the ships are a mere 6 inches long, the race is an exciting event. Each boy builds his own boat, with supervision and help from parents or other family members. He also provides the wind for the sail with his own lung power.

The regatta committee sets simple rules and informs each pack family before the boats are built. The race can be run indoors or outdoors, but water is sure to splash, so

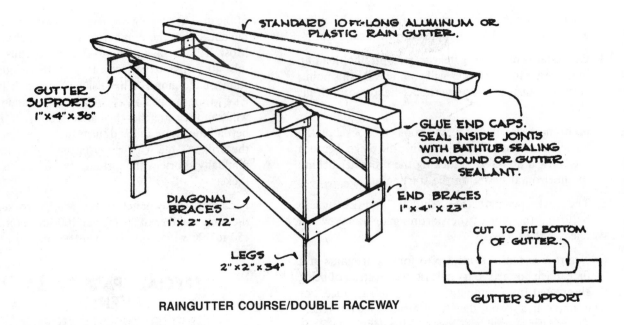

STANDARD 10 FT-LONG ALUMINUM OR PLASTIC RAIN GUTTER.

GUTTER SUPPORTS 1"×4"×36"

GLUE END CAPS. SEAL INSIDE JOINTS WITH BATHTUB SEALING COMPOUND OR GUTTER SEALANT.

DIAGONAL BRACES 1"×2"×72"

END BRACES 1"×4"×23"

CUT TO FIT BOTTOM OF GUTTER.

LEGS 2"×2"×34"

GUTTER SUPPORT

RAINGUTTER COURSE/DOUBLE RACEWAY

take that into consideration. In planning the derby, the committee should follow the guidelines for planning special pack activities to be certain nothing important is overlooked.

The regatta boat kit, available from your Scout distributor, has a pre-shaped balsa hull, metal keel, and plastic sail. Races can also be run with rubber-band powered boats or boats such as those found in the Model Boats elective in the *Wolf Cub Scout Book*. Several classes could be raced, so long as they fit in the raceway.

Regatta boat kits can be purchased individually or in packs of eight. It is more economical for the committee to buy them in quantity and distribute them to pack families along with rules, tips on construction, and any other helpful information. Also available are regatta trophies, medals, ribbons, and plaster casting molds.

RAINGUTTER COURSE

The most popular course is simply a standard raingutter 10 feet long set in grooves on two sawhorses.

A double raceway can be built as shown. It is a simple wood frame that supports two 10-feet lengths of raingutter filled with 8 gallons of water. The frame is designed so it can be easily assembled and dismantled for storage.

With the gutters and sawhorses in place, put a small amount of water into each gutter to make sure it is level. Even on the most level floors or ground, some adjustments may be necessary. Once the gutters are full, it is difficult to move them without causing a minor flood. After making any needed adjustments, fill the gutter to about ½ inch from the top.

Regattas may also be held at a swimming pool or lake.

REGATTA PROCEDURE

1. Boys take regatta boats to inspection table to be checked and numbered.

2. They take their boats to the registration table where the name and boat number of each contestant are entered on the heat sheet.

3. The race is run in heats. The boats are propelled by boys blowing into the sails. Start with the boat's stern touching the end of the gutter. The starter stands at the opposite end with his hands raised. When he drops his hand, the boys begin to blow. With a double raceway, two boys compete at the same time and the first boat to reach the end of the gutter wins. Once the race has started, the boys may not touch the boats with their hands.

4. Winners of the first heats compete against each other in second heat, and third, etc., until a final winner is determined.

5. On courses other than the raingutter, boats must be held by the pilots at the starting line and released at a signal. No pushing is allowed. The first boat to cross the finish line is winner of that heat. If two or more boats run afoul, there is no contest and the heat is re-run.

SAMPLE REGATTA RULES

- Hull may be no longer than 7 inches nor shorter than 6½ inches.

- Mast should measure 6½ inches from deck to top.

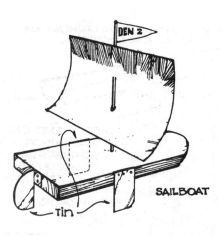

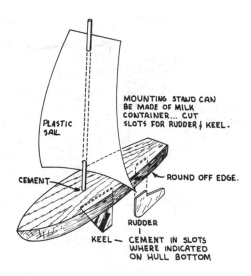

REGATTA BOAT

- The keel and rudder supplied in the kit must be used with no alterations.

- The sail should be no larger than the material supplied in the kit.

- There are no restrictions on color or design.

CONSTRUCTION TIPS

- Sandpaper the balsa hull to the desired shape, adhering to the specifications required. First use a medium-grade sandpaper, then finish with a very fine grade sandpaper.

- Give model two coats of sanding sealer.

- Mast can be tapered with either a hand or electric drill. While you carefully turn the dowel, work a piece of sandpaper back and forth until desired shape is achieved.

- Give entire model two coats of colored lacquer.

Anniversary Week Activities

The anniversary of the Boy Scouts of America is celebrated each February by packs all around the country. The annual blue and gold banquet is usually the highlight of the month. In addition, there are a number of other activities which can be used to mark Scouting's birthday and help make your pack visible in the community.

RELIGIOUS SERVICES

Many packs attend church or synagogue in uniform on Scout Sunday or Scout Sabbath. In some churches and synagogues, Cub Scouts take part in the services.

OPEN HOUSE

Have a pack open house for non-member friends and their families. Hand out copies of the "Join Us" or "Cub Scouting and a Boy" flyer. Display items the boys have made during the year, den doodles, den and pack awards, ceremony boards, etc. Play games, sing songs, serve refreshments.

WEAR THE UNIFORM

Cub Scouts are encouraged to wear their uniforms to school one day during Scouting Anniversary Week. This might be on their regular den meeting day, or on the BSA's birthday, February 8, if it is a school day.

DEMONSTRATIONS

One of the best ways to mark anniversary week is with a live demonstration. This could be held after school or all day Saturday wherever there is plenty of pedestrian traffic, such as a shopping center, vacant lot, centrally-located park, or even a large store display window. Show Cub Scouting in action — boys racing pinewood derby cars

DISPLAY

Store window displays will attract attention to your pack. Make arrangements early with the management to use a store window. A window display might be tied to a particular Cub Scouting theme, or it could cover the pack's activities for a whole year. Decorate with banners, flags, streamers, etc. so the display will be colorful and attractive. Be sure to have a sign identifying the pack and its chartered organization, with the name and phone number of a leader who can be contacted for information. Put your display up on time and remove it on time. Then be sure to send the store owner a letter of thanks.

or space derby rockets, playing games, staging skits or puppet shows. Webelos Scouts could have displays and give demonstrations of various activity badge projects. Be sure to have a big sign identifying your pack, its chartered organization, and the name and phone number of a leader who can be contacted for information about joining. For more ideas on booths and demonstrations, see the section on "Scout Show/Scout-O-Rama Booths" in the chapter, "Communicating Your Pack's Story."

FLAG CEREMONIES

Dens in uniform might raise and lower school flags each day during anniversary week.

GOOD TURNS

Do a Good Turn for the pack's chartered organization or school, a worthwhile project that involves parents and other family members as well as Cub Scouts.

COMBINED PACK/TROOP OPEN HOUSE

Involve as much of the community as possible: clergy, officers of chartered organization; neighbors; and pack families and friends. Plan a 45-minute program of audience participation stunts, songs, mixer games, etc. Follow with refreshments and perhaps a slide show of recent pack or troop activities. Let patrol leaders and den chiefs plan the activities and run the program.

World Friendship Fund. Plan and get approval for a pack money-earning project to raise funds which will be donated to the World Friendship Fund. This is a fund administered by the Boy Scouts of America to help less fortunate Scouts and Scouters around the world.

HELP HANDICAPPED SCOUTS

This could be a long-term project, begun during Anniversary Week. Collect and save postage stamps. Send them to the World Scout Bureau, Box 4204, Station B., Ottawa, Canada K1S 5B2. The stamps will be sold and proceeds donated to the World Handicapped Scout Fund.

WRITE A PEN PAL

This is another long-term project which can be started during Anniversary Week. Den leaders may write to "Dear Pen Pal," Dept. WS, Big Blue Marble, P. O. Box 4054, Santa Barbara, CA 93103. Explain that you are a den leader and would like to establish a pen pal link with an equal group in another country. The boys can exchange letters, photographs, badges, postcards, maps, etc. This will help broaden their horizons and establish an international friendship.

FELLERS CAKE BAKE

Fellers Cake Bake

This is a popular and exciting activity for boy-adult teams, but "fellers" only, please. It can be used any time of year, but is particularly good for February, since the cakes can be used for blue and gold banquet desserts. Families are furnished with the rules below. Before the banquet, cakes are judged and prizes awarded.

RULES

1. Cakes should be delivered to (location) by (time) on (date).

2. Cakes must be baked by a Cub Scout or Webelos Scout and older male. (If there is no father in the family, it can be an uncle, grandfather, older brother, or neighbor.)

3. Cake mixes and icing mixes may be used.

4. No female assistance is allowed.

5. Entire creation must be edible, including all decorations.

6. All cakes should have a title or name, to be shown as part of the cake decoration or on a card attached to the cake. Cakes will be numbered for judging purposes.

7. Cakes should be on a disposable plate or tray.

8. All cakes will be judged and prizes awarded in the following categories:

   - Judges' Choice (Grand Prize Winner)
   - Most Original Creation (1st, 2nd, 3rd)
   - Most Suitably Named (1st, 2nd, 3rd)
   - Biggest Cake
   - Tallest Cake
   - Flattest Cake
   - Best Cub Scout Theme
   - Yummiest Looking

9. Cakes not used for the banquet will be auctioned at the meeting, with proceeds going to the World Friendship Fund.

Note. A "fellers" cake bake is a good pack fund-raising project. Cakes can be auctioned to the highest bidder and proceeds donated to the World Friendship Fund or used to purchase a piece of equipment for the chartered organization. (Be sure to get council approval for all money-earning projects.)

Blue and Gold Banquet

In nearly all packs, the blue and gold banquet is one of the highlights of the program year. It brings together all pack families for a dinner and an evening of fun.

The dinner may be held in a restaurant, catered, potluck, an indoor picnic, or buffet style. The meal is important, but even more important is the warm, congenial atmosphere created as families enjoy each other's company.

For the banquet to be successful, planning must begin early—at least two or three months in advance. Most packs must find a different meeting place because of the size of the crowd. The banquet committee reserves the location, arranges for the meal, sends out invitations, develops the program, and takes care of other responsibilities. Follow the guidelines for planning special pack activities and study the tips included in this section. They should make planning easier.

Involve as many people as possible on the various committees. Take care not to overload the den leaders, who will be busy working with their dens.

BANQUET COMMITTEE

The banquet committee makes the following important decisions, then works in teams on individual responsibilities.

Set Date and Time. Many packs hold the banquet on the regular pack meeting night.

Meal Serving Plan. Decide how dinner will be served. Possibilities are:

- Potluck. Each family brings a dish to share either with the whole pack or with the den group. Families furnish their own plates, utensils, serving dishes. Food is pooled and served buffet style. The pack might furnish the drinks.

- Food Committee. Some packs buy the meat, bread, beverage, plates, utensils, cups, napkins. Pack families are asked to bring salads, vegetables, and desserts. In some packs, the food committee buys all the food and cooks the entire meal. The cost can be prorated among those attending.

- Catered. A caterer can bring in prepared food, or the pack can go to a restaurant or cafeteria for dinner.

Facility. Secure a suitable facility at least six weeks in advance. The space needed will be determined by the number of people attending and the serving arrangement. This could be a school cafeteria, church meeting room, civic center, town hall, restaurant, or cafeteria. Consider these things:

- Rental fee, if any.

- Seating capacity and number of tables available.

- Kitchen availability, if needed.

- Adequate parking space.

- Convenient rest rooms.

- Secure permission to use special equipment—PA system, speaker's stand, etc.

- Confirm reservations at least a month in advance.

PHYSICAL ARRANGEMENTS TEAM

Develop a seating plan. Den families should sit together. The arrangement will be determined by the size and shape of room. Where will head table be located? Will tables be arranged in U-shape, square, parallel, fan-shape Will everyone be able to see and hear?

- Plan for exhibit space.

- Work with dinner committee on serving plan and allow plenty of room for serving lines.

- Make arrangements to get into the building early on the day of the banquet to set up.

- Inform dens what time they may arrive to decorate their tables. Allow time for people to go home to dress for banquet.

- Check restroom and coatroom facilities.

- Recruit an adult clean-up committee. Have trash bags available.

- Plan to arrive early to set up tables, chairs, and exhibit areas. Have signs showing location of restrooms and coatroom.

PROGRAM TEAM

- The Cubmaster and den leader coach should be members of this team.

- Select a theme for the banquet.

- Select a master of ceremonies.

- Working with Cubmaster, plan program and recruit a person to handle each item on the agenda.

- Plan general room decoration and head table decoration.

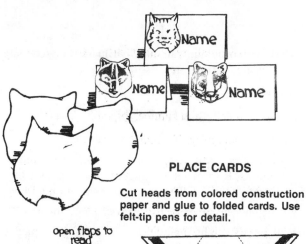

PLACE CARDS

Cut heads from colored construction paper and glue to folded cards. Use felt-tip pens for detail.

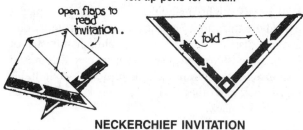

open flaps to read invitation.

fold →

NECKERCHIEF INVITATION

Cut triangle from yellow construction paper. Outline with blue marking pen and write date, time, and place of banquet. Fold as shown.

- Consider having a souvenir program printed.

- Send written invitations to special guests. Ask for RSVP.

- Be sure that Tiger Cubs and their families are invited, either in writing by phone.

- Appoint a welcoming committee to greet people as they arrive. This could be a group of uniformed Cub Scouts.

- Plan to arrive early to decorate.

- Send thank-you notes afterwards to all who helped.

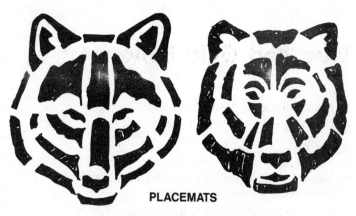

PLACEMATS

Cut stencils from cardboard and have Cub Scouts color them in on blue or gold construction paper with felt pens or crayons.

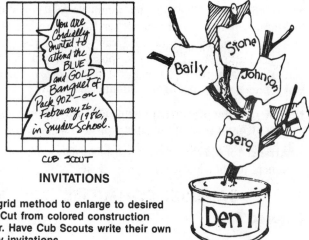

CUB SCOUT

INVITATIONS

Use grid method to enlarge to desired size. Cut from colored construction paper. Have Cub Scouts write their own family invitations.

DEN FAMILY TREE CENTERPIECE

Fill coffee can with plaster of paris and insert branch. Tape on animal heads silhouettes with family names.

BLUE AND GOLD SOUVENIR PROGRAM

DINNER TEAM

Keep the meal cost as low as possible. If the dinner is catered or in a restaurant, select a menu that is acceptable to all pack families. Make sure the food is served hot.

Potluck Plan

- Decide if dens will plan their own menu or if each family will bring food for an overall pack menu.

- Let each family know how much and what type of food to bring.

- Ask each family to bring their own plates and utensils.

- Decide if pack will furnish salt, pepper, sugar, napkins, etc. If so, make arrangements to buy them or have them donated.

- Determine serving arrangement.

Food Committee Plan

- Decide what the pack will furnish (all or part of the food, paper products, etc.)

- Purchase food and other dinner items.

- See that each den receives its share of leftover purchased goods.

- Recruit enough helpers to prepare meal. Follow health rules.

- Accept reservations and estimate attendance. Be sure there is enough food.

- Prorate cost of meal among families attending.

- Determine serving arrangement. Plan for two serving lines if more than 100 people will attend.

- Arrange for kitchen utensils, serving dishes, large containers for hot and cold drinks, if needed.

Catered Plan

- Get estimates and decide on caterer.

- Agree on menu and cost in writing.

- Find out if caterer provides plates, utensils, drinks, dessert.

- Check time of delivery. Be sure someone is there.

- Accept reservations and estimate attendance. The caterer will need to know how many to expect.

- Collect money from families in advance.

Restaurant Plan

- Decide on restaurant or cafeteria. Agree on menu and cost in writing.

- Reserve a private meeting room where program can be conducted.

- Accept reservations and estimate attendance. Let restaurant know how many to prepare for.

- Collect money prior to banquet. (If meal is to be at a cafeteria, you may wish to have pack families go through line and pay for their own meals then.)

- Plan to have birthday cakes or cupcakes. This is a birthday party. Consider having a "fellers" cake bake.

- Work with program team in adhering to time schedule for serving, eating, etc.

INVITATIONS

Invitations are usually sent to every pack family and to special guests. Boys can make invitations in den meetings for their own families. The program team can mail invitations to special guests and their spouses.

Special guests might include: the head of your pack's chartered organization; Scouting coordinator; unit commissioner; district Scout executive; church minister or rabbi; Scoutmaster of nearby troop; former Cubmaster and spouse; pack alumni; school principal; roundtable commissioner; and other district personnel who have been helpful to the pack.

If your pack has an affiliated Tiger Cub group, invite them and their parents also.

If there is no head table, or if there are too many special guests to be seated at a head table, seat them with various dens. Let the den leaders know in advance how many guests to expect.

MEAL PLANNING

The menu selected will be determined by current food prices. However, a well-balanced meal should include meat, vegetables, salads, bread, dessert, and beverages. The following information will help the dinner team in planning.

Potluck Meal. For a den of eight families, two families bring meat dishes, two bring vegetables, two bring salads, one brings dessert, one brings bread and beverages.

Food Committee. The quantity buying table shown here will serve as a guide for the committee in buying food for the banquet.

Quantity Buying Table

Amounts to serve 25 people:

Baked beans—4-quart bowl

String beans—three No. 2 cans

Peas—five No. 2 cans

Mashed potatoes—4-quart bowl

Potato salad—1-quart bowl

Gelatin salad—9-by-13-inch dish

Lettuce—three heads

Salad dressing—1 pint or ½-pound

Catsup—Three 14-ounce bottles

Baked ham (boneless)—8 pounds

Swiss steak—10 pounds

Meat loaf—1½-pounds pork, 3½-pounds beef

Frankfurters—7 pounds (2 each)

Frying chicken—40 pieces

Turkey—18 to 20 pounds

Stuffing for poultry—5 quarts

Rolls—3 to 4 dozen

Jelly—1½ pints

Butter—½ pound (32 servings)

Potato chips—2 pounds

Coffee (regular)—1 pound (40–50 cups)

Coffee (instant)—2-oz. jar (40 cups)

Sugar (tea or coffee)—¾-pound

Punch or Iced Tea—2 gallons (50 5-ounce servings)

Ice Cream—1 gallon

Note. If the banquet is potluck or prepared by a food committee, it is usually best to use paper plates and cups and plastic utensils to avoid dishwashing.

SOUVENIR PROGRAM

A souvenir program is a token of remembrance of this pleasant evening. The cover can be a simple decoration related to the banquet theme. Inside, list the program, menu, and names of pack leaders and special guests. A few facts about pack accomplishments or activities during the past year can be included.

BANQUET PROGRAM

Include in the banquet program all of the regular pack meeting activities, such as songs, skits, stunts, awards, and ceremonies. Something different and special can be added. Most packs prefer to use entertainment from within their own group. The entertainment may include den skits and stunts, a short slide presentation of pack activities during the past year, or den chiefs and leaders performing songs, skits or stunts, as a change from the usual. Avoid long speeches.

Some packs have visiting entertainers—magicians, clowns, puppet shows, or singing groups are frequently used.

Following is a suggested agenda for the banquet program. It can be adjusted to fit your pack's needs. Try to limit the total program time to a maximum of 1½ hours (not including meal). Keep the program moving and interesting.

Gathering Period. Have a welcoming committee to greet people as they arrive, give them nametags, and direct them to their tables. Have displays and exhibits. Also have games or some activity to keep the younger children occupied until the meal is served.

Opening Ceremony. This should be short and simple. A flag ceremony is always good. If the flags are not brought in during an opening ceremony, be sure they are posted in the room.

Invocation. This may be given by a pack leader or clergyman and should be non-sectarian.

Dinner.

Welcome and Introductions. Recognize pack leaders and special guests. Be sure to recognize the Tiger Cub group if they are in attendance. Keep the comments short, with plenty of applause.

Greeting from Head of Chartered Organization. Use song sheets or have songs printed in souvenir program so everyone will join in. Include "Happy Birthday to Cub Scouting."

Skits, Stunts, Entertainment.

Webelos Demonstration.

Advancement Awards Ceremony.

Recognition of Leaders. Present certificates of appreciation to leaders, den chiefs, and parents who have helped during the past year.

Webelos Graduation Ceremony. Involve the Scoutmaster and boy leaders of the troop or troops into which the Webelos Scouts are graduating.

Announcements and Thanks.

Closing Ceremony. At this point in the program, the "tone" should be more serious. Close with something inspirational or patriotic.

RESOURCES FOR BANQUET PROGRAM IDEAS

Program ideas suitable for the blue and gold banquet can be found in *Cub Scout Program Helps, Group Meeting Sparklers, Cub Scout Songbook,* and *Staging Den and Pack Ceremonies,* as well as at Cub Scout leaders' roundtable and the pow wow.

BLUE AND GOLD OPENING CEREMONY

See the "Skits and Costumes," "Songs, Stunts, and Stories," and "Games" section of this book for more ideas.

BLUE AND GOLD CEREMONIES FOR GOD AND COUNTRY
(Opening Ceremony)

Arrangement. Den chief and Cub Scouts, in uniform, carry small U.S. flags and line up on stage. Each speaks his part.

DEN CHIEF. Two hundred years ago, God gave us a nation; a land of wealth and bounty, choice among His creations. We must protect its freedom and defend its worthy cause, and support our Constitution, which is based upon God's laws. We must pledge to be loyal throughout each coming year, and with God's help, we will know no doubt nor fear. When we keep our promise to do our best each day, God will bless our country and us in every way. Please stand and join us in singing, "God Bless America." (After audience is seated, Cub Scouts continue.)

FIRST CUB SCOUT: We're glad you came to our banquet! We have many things to say about our love for America as we celebrate today.

SECOND CUB SCOUT: Independence is a big word, and hard for me to say. But I know it means a lot to all Americans today.

THIRD CUB SCOUT: Our national bird is the eagle. Have you ever wondered why? It may be because it soars above all birds to reach the sky.

FOURTH CUB SCOUT: The Liberty Bell is ringing, though its sound we do not hear. Freedom of speech and worship, freedom from want and fear.

FIFTH CUB SCOUT: Without our flag of red, white and blue, things would be different for me and you. It's a symbol of pride in the American way, so we should be loyal and true each day.

SIXTH CUB SCOUT: Please stand and join us in the Pledge of Allegiance to our flag.

STORY OF CUB SCOUT COLORS
(Opening Ceremony)

Arrangement. As curtain opens, three boys dressed in Indian costume are seated around artificial campfire. One wears a chief's headdress; the other two are braves. Hanging on a tripod over the fire is a kettle which has a small can of dry ice and a Cub Scout neckerchief concealed in it.

NARRATOR (Cub Scout or den chief): Many, many moons ago, the great chief Akela called a council to see what could be done to make his tribe the best of all tribes.

He told the first Indian brave to climb the mountain and tell the eagle to fly high into the sky and bring back part of the beauty of the sun. (*One brave exits.*)

He told the second brave to go into the forest and tell the sparrow to fly high into the sky and bring back part of the beauty of the sky. (*Second brave exits.*)

After a while, both braves returned. (*Both braves enter. One carries a bottle of blue water; the other a bottle of gold water. They hold up bottles to show everyone.*)

NARRATOR: Akela told one brave to pour some of the beauty of the sun into the council mixing pot. (*The brave pours some of the gold water into the can in the pot, causing smoke.*)

NARRATOR: Then he told the other brave to pour some of the beauty of the sky into the council mixing pot. (*The brave pours blue water into the can, causing smoke. Akela, the chief, raises hands toward the sky.*)

NARRATOR: Akela says that from this day forward, blue will stand for truth and loyalty and the sky above. Gold will stand for warm sunlight, happiness, and good cheer. (*Akela reaches into pot and pulls out Cub Scout neckerchief.*)

NARRATOR: And that's why the Cub Scouts colors are blue and gold.

SCOUTING AROUND THE WORLD (Opening Ceremony)

Arrangement. A world globe sets on the head table.

NARRATOR: (*Pointing to United States on globe*): This evening we are holding our blue and gold banquet here. But did you know that all over this world (*spins globe*) Cub Scouts just like us are taking part in Scouting activities too? Well, it's true. The Scouting movement exists in 115 countries—almost every nation of the noncommunist world. Those Cub Scouts are much like us. They have similar ideals, a similar promise, and the same brotherhood of service. So let's think of our brother Cub Scouts around the world as we join in the Cub Scout Promise. (*Leads Promise with everyone standing.*)

CUB SCOUT SPIRIT (Closing Ceremony)

Arrangement. Head table holds candelabra with three candles and one larger candle in separate holder.

BLUE AND GOLD CLOSING CEREMONY

NARRATOR: Tonight we have had a lot of fun at the (number) birthday party of Cub Scouting and the (number) birthday of our own pack. As Cub Scouts and leaders, we are following the trail left by millions of other boys and leaders who have been involved in Cub Scouting since it began in 1930.

All of those boys and leaders have had the Cub Scout spirit, which we symbolize with the flame of this one candle. (*Light large candle. Dim room lights.*) What is Cub Scout spirit? That's easy. It's the three things we promise to do in the Cub Scout Promise. In the Promise, we say, "I promise to do my best to do my duty to God and my country". That's the first part. (*Light first candle on candelabra.*)

The second part is: "To help other people." (*Light second candle*). And the third part is "to obey the Law of the Pack." (*Light third candle.*)

Now while these three candles burn as a reminder to us, I will ask all Cub Scouts and all former Cub Scouts to stand, make the Cub Scout sign, and repeat the Promise with me. (*Lead Promise.*)

THE BLUE AND GOLD (Closing Ceremony)

Arrangement. Eight Cub Scouts speak their lines and place the following cards on a large blue flannelboard—

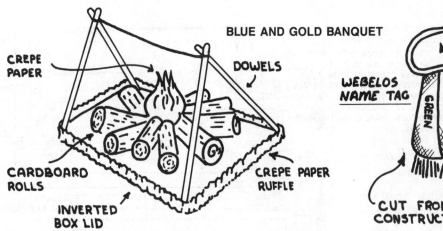

CREPE PAPER

BLUE AND GOLD BANQUET

DOWELS

CARDBOARD ROLLS

CREPE PAPER RUFFLE

INVERTED BOX LID

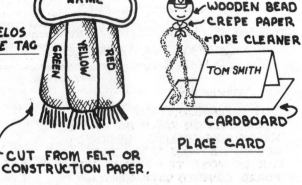

NAME

WEBELOS NAME TAG

GREEN YELLOW RED

CUT FROM FELT OR CONSTRUCTION PAPER.

PAINT ON HAT.
WOODEN BEAD
CREPE PAPER
PIPE CLEANER

TOM SMITH

CARDBOARD PLACE CARD

Truth, Faith, Loyalty, Sunlight, Good Cheer, Happiness, and a cutout golden sun.

FIRST CUB SCOUT: Back in the good old days, school colors gave people a feeling of school pride and loyalty. Today, the blue and gold of Cub Scouting helps to build this spirit among Cub Scouts.

SECOND CUB SCOUT (*points to blue flannel*): The blue reminds us of the sky above. It stands for truth, spirituality, and steadfast loyalty.

THIRD CUB SCOUT (*places "truth" card in upper left corner of board*): Truth means we must always be honest.

FOURTH CUB SCOUT (*places "faith" card in upper right corner*): Faith means a belief in God.

FIFTH CUB SCOUT (*places "loyalty" card across bottom*): Loyalty means being faithful and loyal to God, country, and our fellow man.

SIXTH CUB SCOUT: The gold stands for the warm sunlight (*He places the sun in center of board and the "sunlight" card across top of the sun*).

SEVENTH CUB SCOUT: Gold also stands for good cheer and happiness. We always feel better when the sun is shining and so will those to whom we give good will. (*He places "good cheer" and "happiness" cards on each side of sun cutout.*)

EIGHTH CUB SCOUT: As we wear our Cub Scout uniforms, may the meaning of the blue and gold colors make us remember our Cub Scout ideals, the Cub Scout Promise, and the Law of the Pack.

CLOSING THOUGHT

NARRATOR: Lord Baden-Powell, the founder of Scouting, said: "I often think that when the sun goes down, the world is hidden by a big blanket from the light of heaven, but the stars are little holes pierced in that blanket by those who have done good deeds in this world. The stars are not all the same size; some are big, some

are little, and some men have done small deeds, but they have made their hole in the blanket by doing good before they went to heaven. Try and make your hole in the blanket by good work while you are on earth. It is something to be good, but it is far better to do good." Think of Baden-Powell's words when you promise to help other people.

A Cub Scout Parent's Prayer

Look down upon my son, Dear Lord,

This smiling Cub of mine.

Please take his hand along the way

So he may never stray.

Bless my son tonight, Dear Lord,

And help him walk with Thee.

Give him comfort, warmth, and love;

He's all the world to me.

Bless his daily efforts,

And make him strong and true;

For life's a heavy burden,

And we're all in need of You.

IDEAS FOR BANQUET ADVANCEMENT CEREMONIES

- Make a large "birthday book," using an old wallpaper sample book. Cover the book with blue and gold paper. Fasten awards on the left-hand pages, and opposite each award, write the statement to be read as award is presented.

- Have a den chief, dressed as a delivery boy, deliver to the Cubmaster or awards chairman a package wrapped

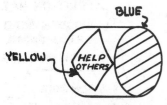

BLUE

YELLOW

HELP OTHERS

NAPKIN RING
CUT A DIAMOND FROM YELLOW
CONSTRUCTION PAPER AND PRINT
"HELP OTHERS" ACROSS THE CENTER.
ADD GUEST'S NAME, IF YOU LIKE.
GLUE DIAMOND TO A RING OF CARD-
BOARD COVERED WITH BLUE.

WEBELOS PLACE MAT
1. GLUE 11"×17" PIECE OF DARK BLUE CON-
STRUCTION PAPER ON TOP OF A 12"×18" PIECE
OF LIGHT BLUE CONSTRUCTION PAPER.
2. CUT ACTIVITY BADGES FROM GREY
CONSTRUCTION PAPER, AND GLUE TO PLACE MAT.
3. CUT ARROW OF LIGHT FROM YELLOW
CONSTRUCTION PAPER, AND GLUE TO
PLACE MAT.

DARK BLUE

LIGHT BLUE

CUT ACTIVITY BADGES
FROM GREY CONSTRUCTION
PAPER, AND GLUE ON.

in blue and gold wrapping paper, containing all awards. After awards are presented, have the same type of package delivered to the Scouting coordinator, containing certificates of appreciation for leaders and den chiefs.

- Make a large papier mâché birthday cake. (See "Crafts" section.) Use whipped soapsuds to ice the cake. Before soapsuds harden, insert candles (one for each year). Candles can be lighted before awards presentation and blown out after ceremony.

- Individual awards can be packaged in small boxes, wrapped in blue paper and tied with gold ribbons. Ask boys to wait until all awards are presented before opening packages. Then, while everyone opens their package, the rest of the pack could sing "Happy Birthday". (For more ceremony ideas, see *Staging Den and Pack Ceremonies*.)

——BLUE AND GOLD SKITS——

SPIRIT OF BADEN-POWELL (A Skit)

Characters: Seven uniformed Cub Scouts, carrying props described below. The narrator is in Scout uniform and wears a campaign hat.

Setting: Narrator stands in front of stage. Cub Scouts enter one at a time and speak their lines.

NARRATOR: I represent the spirit of Lord Baden-Powell, the founder of Scouting. I am also the spirit of Scouting past and present. Here is our future . . . the Cub Scouts of today who will be the men of tomorrow.

FIRST CUB SCOUT (*Enters carrying a replica of a church or carrying a Bible*): I like to wear my uniform to church on Scout Sunday or Sabbath in February. Many Cub

Scout packs in the United States are chartered to religious organizations.

SECOND CUB SCOUT (*Enters*): The two colors of the Cub Scout uniform have special meaning. The blue stands for truth and loyalty; the gold represents good cheer and happiness.

THIRD CUB SCOUT (*Enters carrying* Wolf Cub Scout Book *and Kipling's* Jungle Book): When Cub Scouting began in England, it was based on Kipling's jungle tales. When Cub Scouting began in the United States in 1930, Indian themes were used.

FOURTH CUB SCOUT (*Enters carrying woodcraft project*): Cub Scouting means fun, and we have lots of fun. I like making things that are useful or that fit our monthly theme.

FIFTH CUB SCOUT (*Enters carrying nature collection*): I like to go on hikes and collect things for my nature collection. Cub Scout outdoor activities are fun. We learn about the things that live and grow in our area.

SIXTH CUB SCOUT (*Enters carrying tin can stove*): I like to cook outdoors. All Cub Scouts like to eat! This is a cook stove we made as a den project.

SEVENTH CUB SCOUT: (*Enters carrying U.S. flag*): I am proud to be an American and I'm proud of our flag. I also like our pack flag because it reminds me that I'm part of (number) years of Cub Scouting.

NARRATOR: Yes, I represent the past and the present, but these boys—the future of our country—prove that things will be in good hands.

HISTORY OF SCOUTING

NARRATOR: It's a foggy night in London. The year is 1910. Mr. William D. Boyce, an American publisher and businessman, is lost. (*As curtain opens, Boyce is on stage, dressed in top coat, carrying briefcase and umbrella. He*

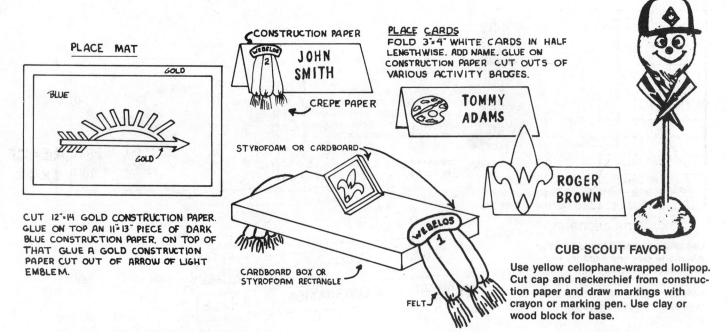

PLACE MAT

BLUE GOLD

GOLD

CUT 12"-14 GOLD CONSTRUCTION PAPER. GLUE ON TOP AN 11"-13" PIECE OF DARK BLUE CONSTRUCTION PAPER. ON TOP OF THAT GLUE A GOLD CONSTRUCTION PAPER CUT OUT OF ARROW OF LIGHT EMBLEM.

CONSTRUCTION PAPER

JOHN SMITH

CREPE PAPER

PLACE CARDS
FOLD 3"×4" WHITE CARDS IN HALF LENGTHWISE. ADD NAME. GLUE ON CONSTRUCTION PAPER CUT OUTS OF VARIOUS ACTIVITY BADGES.

TOMMY ADAMS

ROGER BROWN

STYROFOAM OR CARDBOARD

CARDBOARD BOX OR STYROFOAM RECTANGLE

WEBELOS 1

FELT

CUB SCOUT FAVOR
Use yellow cellophane-wrapped lollipop. Cut cap and neckerchief from construction paper and draw markings with crayon or marking pen. Use clay or wood block for base.

wanders around stage as if looking for a house number. He comes to a street light and peers at the slip of paper in his hand.)

BOYCE: I don't think I can find my way in this fog! (*A Scout comes on stage, dressed in old-style uniform.*)

SCOUT: May I help you, sir?

BOYCE: I'm looking for this address. Can you tell me where to find it? (*Shows him the slip of paper.*)

SCOUT: Yes, I can. I'll take you there. (*They walk to other side of stage*)

SCOUT (*pointing*): There you are, sir.

BOYCE: Thank you very much! And here you are (*pretends to offer him money*) for helping me.

SCOUT: Thank you, sir. But I can't accept money. I am a Scout, and this is my good turn. (*Scout waves, walks across stage, and exits. Boyce exits on other side.*)

NARRATOR: Mr. Boyce was so impressed with this Scout that he found out more about the Scouting movement in England. He brought back to America a suitcase full of ideas and information. He incorporated the Boy Scouts of America on February 8, 1910. The Boy Scouts of America grew by leaps and bounds. A Federal Charter was granted by Congress in 1916, an honor given to only a few organizations. Today, Scouting is a world brotherhood, bound together by common ideals and a common oath or promise. Would you please stand and repeat with me the Cub Scout Promise?

CUB SCOUT STEW

Characters: Boy in chef's hat, any number of uniformed Cub Scouts, den leader.

Setting: On stage is a large kettle made from a cardboard carton. There is a short stepladder at each side for the boys to climb up to get into the kettle. Put an air mattress or other pad in the bottom of the kettle for boys to land on. As curtain opens, a boy wearing a chef's hat is standing on one of the stepladders, stirring in pot with a broomstick. He holds a large piece of paper on which is the word "Recipe" is written in large letters.

DEN LEADER (*entering*): What are you making?

CHEF: This is a Cub Scout stew. Would you like to watch?

DEN LEADER: Yes, I would. What goes in it?

CHEF (*pretends to read recipe*): First, add any number of Cub Scouts who do their best. (*Uniformed Cub Scouts come on stage and climb into kettle.*) Then add a sense of humor. (*Grinning Cub Scout wearing sign, "Humor," climbs into kettle.*) Next, add a pinch of service to others. (*Cub Scout wearing "Service" sign climbs into kettle.*) Then add a dash of mischief. (*Cub Scout wearing "Mischief" sign climbs into kettle.*) And a big helping of sunshine. (*Cub Scout wearing "Sunshine" sign climbs into kettle.*) And last, add a ton of energy! (*Cub Scout wearing "Energy" sign climbs into kettle.*)

CHEF (*pretends to stir*): Stir well, and you have a Cub Scout stew. (*Pretends to take a taste and offers a taste to den leader.*)

DEN LEADER: That's delicious! I'd like your recipe.

See the "Skits and Costumes" and the "Songs, Stunts, and Stories" sections of this book for more ideas.

BANQUET GAMES

Banquet Quiz. Make copies for each boy and adult to complete during banquet.

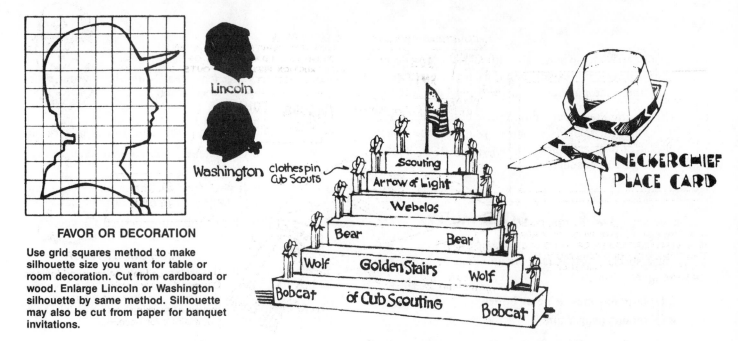

FAVOR OR DECORATION

Use grid squares method to make silhouette size you want for table or room decoration. Cut from cardboard or wood. Enlarge Lincoln or Washington silhouette by same method. Silhouette may also be cut from paper for banquet invitations.

How much do you know about Cub Scouting? Can you answer the following questions?

1. How old is Cub Scouting this year?

2. How old is the Boy Scouts of America this year?

3. Who was the founder of Scouting?

4. Who started the Boy Scouts of America?

5. What is the first rank in Cub Scouting?

6. How many achievements are required to earn the Wolf badge?

7. How many electives are required to earn an arrow point?

8. How many Webelos activity badges may be earned?

9. What is your den number?

10. What is our pack number?

11. What chartered organization sponsors our pack?

12. What district are we a part of?

13. What council are we a part of?

14. What is the Cub Scout motto?

Over and Under Relay. Each team is given a Cub Scout hat. The teams form rows with players one behind the other. The team leaders stand at the front of the line and hold the hats above their heads with both hands. On signal, each leader passes the hat between his or her legs. The second player passes it over his head. The third, between the legs again, and so on, over and under. The last player in line runs to the front and starts again. The first side to have the original leader run to the front wins.

Clip It. Each table has a small dish filled with paper clips. On signal, the first person joins two paper clips together and passes the bowl and beginning of the chain to the next person. That player adds another clip to the chain and passes it on. After a set time (5–8 minutes), the paper clip chains are held high in the air to see which group has the longest.

Match Box Relay. Form relay lines. First person in each line sticks a penny match box cover over his nose. He transfers it to the nose of the next player without using his hands, and so on down the line. First team to finish is the winner.

Orange Passing Relay. Divide into relay teams. On signal, first player in each team puts an orange beneath his chin. Without using his hands, the player next to him must get the orange from him between his own chin and neck, and so on down the line. If the orange drops to the floor, the player must pick it up and replace it under his chin before resuming play.

Stringer. People at each table form a team. Give each team a chenille stem and several buttons or wooden beads. On signal, the first person strings a button on the stem and passes it to the next player, who does the same. Continue until all buttons are on the stem. First team to finish holds its stem in the air and yells, "We did our best!"

See "Games" section of this book for more games suitable for the banquet.

BANQUET DECORATIONS

Dens usually provide their own table decorations. They might include a centerpiece, place mats, napkins, place cards, napkin rings, nut cups. Your local Scout distributor has many of these items, or they can be made in den meetings from scrap materials. Although den table decorations will vary, it is usually best if each den makes essentially the same number, so there are no hard feelings.

The program team can add a festive note by decorating the room with balloons, streamers, pennants, and a photo display of pack activities. Lively recorded music will add to the gala atmosphere.

BLUE AND GOLD MINTS

For a special treat, make blue and gold mints for your banquet. You need:

6 tablespoons margarine or butter

2 teaspoons peppermint

3 pounds powdered sugar

7 tablespoons water (color half with blue and the other half with yellow food coloring)

Dash of salt

1. Cream margarine or butter. Add flavoring and salt.

2. Divide into two batches. Add colored water to each batch.

3. Add 1 pound powdered sugar to each batch. Blend with mixer, then knead in another ½-pound of sugar.

4. Press into molds or roll out to desired thickness and cut or shape mints. Let dry on cookie sheet in refrigerator.

5. When mints are dry, store in covered tin or airtight box to prevent hardening.

See "Crafts" section of this book for Blue and Gold Magic Candles.

WOVEN PLACE MATS

Weave from strips of blue and gold construction paper.

CEILING TRIM

Twist lengths of dark blue and gold crepe paper. Attach to the ceiling and walls. Add a cluster of balloons.

NUT CUP

Use a long section of paper towel core for Indian totem.

STAR NUTCUPS

CUT BOTTOM STAR FROM BLUE CONSTUCTION PAPER. CUT TOP STAR FROM GOLD CONSTUCTION PAPER. GLUE TOGETHER. FOLD UP ON DOTTED LINES.

DARK BLUE

YELLOW FOR WOLF
LIGHT BLUE FOR BEAR
PLAID FOR WEBELOS

YELLOW FOR CUB SCOUTS
LIGHT BLUE FOR WEBELOS SCOUTS

FOLD ON DOTTED LINES

CUB SCOUT NUTCUP

USING PATTERN SHOWN, TRACE ONTO CONSTRUCTION PAPER AND CUT OUT. FOLD LOWER TABS UNDER AND FOLD ON UPRIGHT DOTTED LINES TO FORM A THREE-SIDED NUTCUP. GLUE ALL EDGES TOGETHER.

Mr. & Mrs. Johnson — you are invited

CUT TWO (BLUE).

1½"

6½"

CUT ONE (GOLD).

CUT ONE (GOLD).

4"

PUNCH HOLES.

1"

CUT ONE (SECOND COLOR).

CUT TWO (SECOND COLOR).

PAPER KNIFE INVITATIONS

YELLOW

BROWN

CUT FROM CONSTRUCTION PAPER.

ANIMAL NUTCUPS

MAKE FEATURES WITH MARKING PEN.

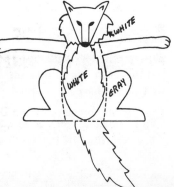

WHITE

WHITE

GRAY

The Value of Special Awards

Many den and pack activities call for some type of prize or special award. In a pack competitive event, there might be a simple reward for the winner; special pack activities such as derbies call for numerous prizes and awards.

Often a leader or other adult in the pack performs some special service which calls for a special type of "thank-you." Verbal recognition at pack meeting is always good, but sometimes the pack committee wants to do a little more.

Awards and prizes for special events or to say "thank-you" for a job well done can be obtained in several different ways.

Resources for Prizes and Gifts

The Supply Division of the Boy Scouts of America has an extensive line of trophies, medals, and ribbons for win-

ners of pack competitions, as well as gifts for leaders. Your local Scout distributor carries or can order them for you. Some are designed for special events. Others can be suited to the occasion and the individual.

The available Supply Division items are listed at the end of this section.

Direct Order. The same items can be ordered direct by phone or mail from the Supply Division distribution centers. Shipments are usually delivered within two to four weeks after the order is received. Catalogs are available from your local council service center and Scout distributor.

COMMUNITY RESOURCES

Restaurants, theaters, and other businesses will sometimes donate tickets, coupons, or other items which can be used as prizes or awards. Check with your district Scout executive or unit commissioner to see if these are available in your area.

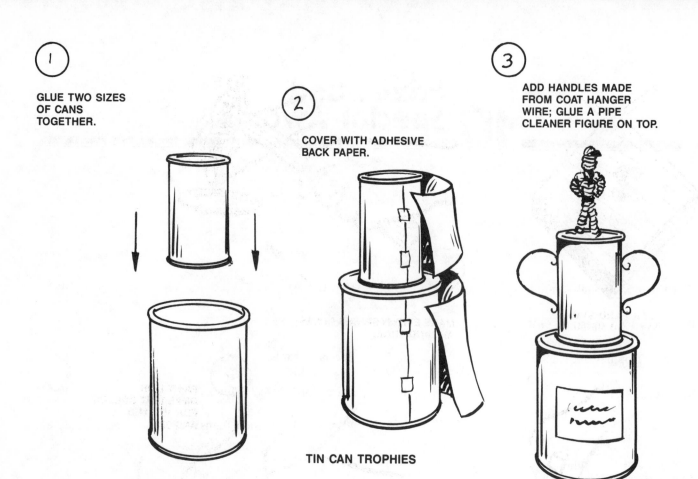

① GLUE TWO SIZES
OF CANS
TOGETHER.

② COVER WITH ADHESIVE
BACK PAPER.

③ ADD HANDLES MADE
FROM COAT HANGER
WIRE; GLUE A PIPE
CLEANER FIGURE ON TOP.

TIN CAN TROPHIES

HANDMADE PRIZES AND AWARDS

Many packs like to make their own awards and prizes for special events or occasions. Not only does this add a personal touch, it also cuts down on expense. Some pack parents may be crafts hobbyists who could make awards and prizes. Use your Parent-Talent Survey sheet to identify them.

Several examples are included here to start your imagination working. You will be able to come up with some good ideas of your own.

Tin-Can Trophies

Attractive trophies can be made from tin cans, a piece of wood, glue, and spray paint or adhesive-back paper. Glue two sizes of clean tin cans together, upside down, with the smaller can on top. When glue has dried, spray paint with gold, silver, or bronze metallic paint, or cover with adhesive-back paper. (Gold for first place, silver for second, and bronze for third.) Glue to a small wood base which has been stained or coated with varnish. Lettering can be done with plastic label tape, by writing on a piece of foil wrapping paper, or by using alphabet macaroni. The trophy can be turned into a loving cup by adding

handles made from coat-hanger wire. If you wish, glue a pipe cleaner figure or small plaster figure on top.

Medals

Make first-, second-, and third-place medals for competitive events by covering two ½-inch cardboard circles with appropriate color foil wrapping paper. Write on the paper with a permanent felt marking pen or use plastic label tape. Punch a hole in the top of the medal and suspend from a ribbon to be worn around the neck. Or, tape a large safety pin on the back so medal can be worn on lapel.

Wood circles or squares may also be used. Sand and stain. Drill hole in top for ribbon. Use permanent fine-line marking pen or wood-burning for inscription.

Canning jar lids make good medals. Begin by making evenly-spaced holes around the edge. Then weave yarn in and out of the holes. Make the yarn long enough to hang around the neck. The lids may be painted different colors for first, second, or third place, or for different events. Ribbons can also be glued on.

Wide red, white, and blue striped ribbon would be nice for Cub Scout Olympics medals.

SAND AND STAIN
A WOOD MEDAL.

① MAKE EVENLY-SPACED HOLES
AROUND EDGE.

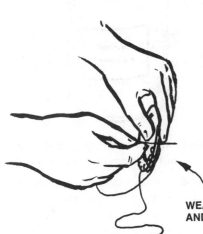

② WEAVE YARN IN
AND OUT OF HOLES.

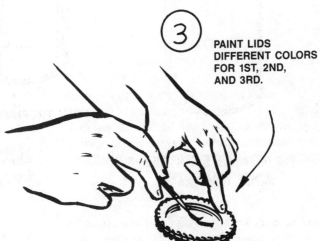

③ PAINT LIDS
DIFFERENT COLORS
FOR 1ST, 2ND,
AND 3RD.

CUT 2½" CARDBOARD CIRCLE.
COVER WITH COLORED FOIL
WRAPPING PAPER.

PUNCH A HOLD IN TOP
FOR RIBBON.

MEDALS

Plaques

PLASTER

Commercial molds are available in all shapes and sizes. A plaster plaque can be made from such a mold, with a ring for hanging inserted before the plaster dries. (See "Crafts" section for on working with plaster.) Casting molds for the pinewood derby, bicycle rodeo, raingutter regatta, space derby, and Cub Scout ranks are available from the Supply Division through your local Scout distributor.

WOOD

Wood, cut to desired shape and size, can be used for many types of plaques. Sand and stain or paint wood. A small plaster figure, picture, or object can be molded, painted, and glued to a wood background. Inscribe wood plaques with alphabet macaroni letters, permanent ink, stick-on plastic letters, or wood-burning.

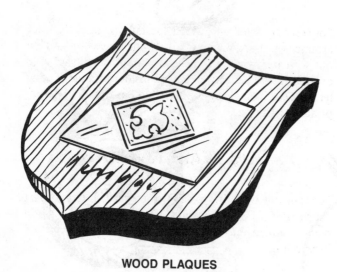

WOOD PLAQUES

LEATHER

Scrap leather can be used to make plaques. Use a type that is fairly stiff. Cut in desired shape and size. Tool a design on the leather, burn with a wood-burning pen, or

LEATHER PLAQUES

use a fine-line permanent marking pen. Leather can also be laced, painted, or stained. A hole can be punched in the top for hanging, or a leather thong attached. (See "Crafts" section for working with leather.)

Ribbons and Pennants

Inexpensive, colorful, and unique awards can be made from craft felt. They can be in the form of pennants, ribbons, or streamers. Cut felt in desired shape. See illustration for ideas. Use liquid embroidery pens (for fabric) to write message. Glue felt pieces together with white glue. For ribbons, fold back top, add a metal eyelet and a loop of colored string at the top.

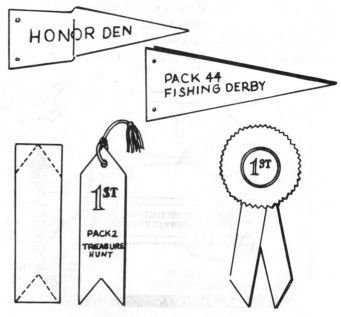

RIBBONS AND PENNANTS

Certificates

Appreciation certificates are available from your local Scout distributor. You can also design your own certificate, using rub-off letters and clip-art pictures, and take it to a quick-copy company for reproduction. Most variety stores carry certificate frames.

For most competitive events, it's a good idea to present every boy with a participation certificate as recognition for doing his best. Those who don't win other prizes won't feel left out.

Neckerchief Slides

Homemade neckerchief slides make good "thank-you's" and mementos of a pinewood derby, bike rodeo, or other special event. Neckerchief slides also make excellent, inexpensive prizes. Slides can be made by the Cub Scouts as well as adult committee members. See neckerchief slide ideas in the "Crafts" section of this book.

Special Awards

SILVER SPOON AWARD

An appropriate award for those who have helped serve a dinner or banquet. Paint a plastic spoon with silver paint, or use an old spoon found around the house or at a flea market. Glue on a wood plaque which has been stained or varnished. Add appropriate inscription.

SILVER SPOON AWARD

SQUARE KNOT AWARD

Make a square knot with a short piece of lightweight rope. Glue to a wood plaque which has been stained or varnished. Add a wood-burned inscription.

HELPING HAND AWARD

HELPING HAND AWARD

For someone who has given a special type of help. Trace around your hand on a piece of ¼-inch plywood and cut out with jigsaw. Or fill a plastic or rubber glove (oiled or rubbed with petroleum jelly on inside) with plaster and let set. Glue hand upright on a wood base and add appropriate inscription.

BIG HEART AWARD

For someone who always helps when needed. Cut a heart shape from ¼-inch plywood. Paint red. Glue to wood plaque which has been finished. Add appropriate inscription.

BIG HEART AWARD

SPONGE AWARD

This gag gift is suitable for new leaders to encourage them to soak up the ideas and energies of the experienced leaders around them. It's just what it sounds like—a sponge.

DOOR PRIZE

Imagine everyone's surprise when you announce the winner of the door prize and present a real door. Check with lumberyards or construction companies to find a slightly damaged or discarded hollow-core door.

GOOD EGG AWARD

Make an egg from plaster and glue it to a wood plaque. Pour a little plaster on a greased piece of aluminum foil. This is the egg white. Let it set. Then mix a small amount of plaster and pour in center of other circle for the yolk. Let it harden, then paint the yolk yellow. Another type of "Good Egg" award can be made from a blown egg. (Make small pin or nail holes in the top and bottom of a raw egg. Blow contents out.) Glue alphabet macaroni to put "Good Egg Award" or other desired wording on the egg. Glue to a small bone ring and spray the whole thing with gold paint. Also, you can use the L'Eggs "eggs" to make an award by wiring them to wooden plaques.

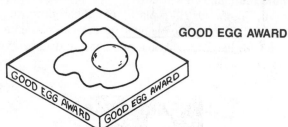

GOOD EGG AWARD

PROSPECTIVE SCOUT AWARD

This award may be presented to Webelos Scouts who sign up to join a troop when they graduate. The base is ¼-inch plywood which has been stained and varnished. Cut Arrow of Light from ¼-inch plywood and paint blue. Drill ¹⁄₁₆-inch holes in top of arc and insert gold-painted toothpicks for sun's rays. Glue to base. Cut Cub Scout emblem from ¼-inch plywood, paint gold, and glue on at left of Arrow of Light. Cut Boy Scout emblem from plywood, paint green, and glue on at right of Arrow of Light. Determine balance point and drill a ¼-inch hole for hanging.

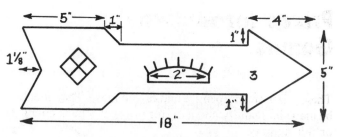

PROSPECTIVE SCOUT AWARD

WEBELOS GRADUATION PLAQUE

This plaque could be presented to boys who have earned the Arrow of Light and graduated into a troop. The base is ½-inch plywood. Touch it lightly with the flame of a propane torch to bring out grain highlights, then use fine steel wool to smooth finish. Spray with clear lacquer or varnish. Cut Cub Scout emblem from ¼-inch plywood with grain opposite to baseboard. Spray with gold paint

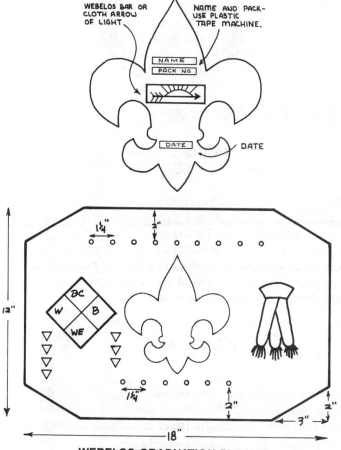

WEBELOS GRADUATION PLAQUE

and tone down with fine steel wool. Drill small holes for each activity badge the boy has earned. Glue on only the badges of rank and arrow points a boy has earned, plus the Webelos colors. Activity badges earned by the boy are glued in the holes. Add name, pack number, and date, using plastic label-tape.

Prizes for Midway Games

These prizes are inexpensive and easy to make. They could be made in quantity and used for prizes at a pack circus or fair midway.

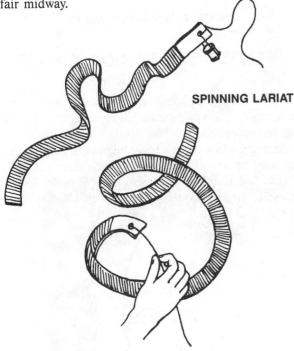

SPINNING LARIAT

SPINNING LARIAT

Cut a 2-inch wide strip from the end of a package of crepe paper. Open full length and glue one end to a piece of 2-by-4-inch cardboard. Tie a spool or other small weight to a hole punched in the other end of the cardboard, leaving about 4 feet of string dangling. To manipulate, hold free end of string in one hand and swing lariat in a wide arc, forming circles, sideways figure **8**s, etc.

PIGGY BANK

Cut a cardboard pig to fit on top of a metal or plastic spray can top. Cut a slot in the cardboard and glue to can top. Add construction paper or felt pig's ears, eyes, nose, etc.

CLOWN SUCKER

Glue a paper triangle hat, a ruffled paper collar, and facial features to a cellophane-wrapped sucker.

PENNANT PENCIL

Cut a pennant from construction paper and print the pack number on it with a marking pen. Glue the pennant near the eraser end of a pencil.

COMICAL PENCIL

Glue a soda bottle cap on the end of a spool. Paint as desired and draw a funny face on the spool with permanent fine-line marking pen. Push eraser end of pencil into spool.

PINWHEEL

On a 5-inch square of heavy paper, draw diagonals from corner to corner. Cut on lines within ¾-inch of center. Pin corners to center, as shown in illustration, with small square of heavy paper on top. Push pin into dowel piece or pencil, using ¼-inch piece of soda straw as a washer.

PINWHEEL

BSA Supply
Division Items

The following is a list of trophies, medals, ribbons, and gifts for boys and leaders that are available from the Supply Division of the Boy Scouts of America. They may be ordered through your Scout distributor or your local Scout service center.

PINEWOOD DERBY

Individual Cub Scout winners, dens, and packs may require awards for their part in the Pinewood Derby. They include:

Grand Prix Pinewood
Derby Trophies

For the top winners, these official trophies have 2- by 3-inch marble bases with a plate for engraving winner's name. First Place, No. 5710; Second Place, No. 5711; Third Place, No. 5712. Grand Prix Pinewood Derby Ribbon, No. 7708, is available for participation awards and to honor officials.

Pinewood Derby Medals

These colorful medals may be given to the first, second, and third place winners individually. Gold Medal, No. 5112; Silver Medal, No. 5113; or Bronze Medal, No. 5114.

Do It Yourself

You may make and decorate your own recognition plaque and two 2½-inch miniature race cars as awards. Use Derby Casting Mold kit, No. 1624.

Raceway Flag

Start your Pinewood Derbys with your own official Derby Flag, No. 1108. It also can be used as a table decoration.

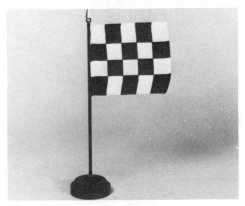

RAINGUTTER REGATTA

Winners of this splashing event can be recognized several ways. Try the following:

Regatta Trophies and Ribbons

These 2- by 3-inch marble-based trophies have a special engraved plate for winner's name, pack, and date. First Place, No. 5780; Second Place, No. 5781; Third Place, No. 5782. Regatta Ribbon, No. 7711, will identify officials and participants.

Regatta Medals

These attractive medals can be used to identify your top winners. They include: Gold Medal, No. 5121; Silver Medal, No. 5122; and Bronze Medal, No. 5123.

Cast Your Own

Make your own 5-inch "Regatta Champion" plaque out of clear plastic, using Regatta Casting Mold, No. 1626. Two lapel pins or special awards can also be made. Use the mold over and over.

SPACE DERBY

Make your space derby into a real "outer space" show by recognizing your winner with colorful awards. Try these:

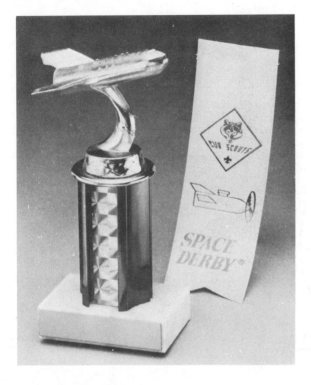

Space Derby Trophies

These impressive rocket-topped awards will really make a hit with your Cub Scout astronauts. Mounted on 2-by-3-inch marble bases, they each have a name plate for engraving the winner's name. First Place, No. 5730; Second Place, No. 5731; Third Place, No. 5732. Use Space Derby Ribbons, No. 7714, to recognize officials and participants.

Space Derby Medals

Use these distinctive medals to recognize heat winners or for special categories. They include Gold Medal, No. 5115; Silver, No. 5116, and Bronze, No. 5117.

Space Derby Mold

Cast your own "Space Derby Champion" plaque using the special mold and kit, No. 1688. You may also use the kit to make two 2½-inch model rockets as prizes.

GENERAL AWARDS FOR EVENTS

Ribbons and trophy cups are available to recognize individuals and dens. Blue, red, and yellow ribbons will mark the first, second, and third place winners of your events. Use Award Ribbons, No. 7709.

The Plastic Trophy Award Cup, No. 5077, can also be used to recognize winners. Print name and and winning place and event on the pre-glued label.

11 Communicating Your Pack's Story

Your Pack's Public Relations

A strong, active Cub Scout pack has a story to tell, both within the pack family and to the larger community it serves. And if it hopes to remain strong and active, it's important that the story be told.

Good communication with the pack's parents is obviously essential because without their help the pack is bound to flounder. And telling the pack's story to the community—thus keeping it in the public eye—is an excellent method of attracting recruits.

This section covers several ways of communicating to your internal audience—the pack's families—and to the community. It also includes such useful things as ceremonial boards and artificial council fires that help to tell the Cub Scouting story by serving as symbols of our ideals and methods.

Pack Newsletter

Ideally all the pack's parents will attend every pack meeting and keep abreast of what's going on and what's planned. But that isn't always the case. So a pack newsletter, issued about once a month, is a good communications

device to keep all pack families informed about activities and plans. It is also an opportunity to give Cub Scouts who have advanced or done special Good Turns an extra measure of recognition by listing their names in the newsletter.

A pack newsletter doesn't have to be an elaborate, printed production. It may be nothing more than a single typewritten sheet, duplicated by photocopying, mimeograph, or hectograph (see "Crafts" section). Every issue should include short articles covering coming events and the names of boys who have advanced.

Each den may contribute a short article on its activities for the month. A different den member can be assigned the job of reporting each month.

Select a pack committee member or parent as newsletter editor, another as typist, and a third as production person. The newsletter can be mailed home or distributed to families at pack meetings. It is not recommended that copies be given to the boys to take home because those copies may be lost, misplaced, or forgotten.

Individual dens may want to have their own occasional newsletter, with all articles and production in the hands of the boys.

News Releases

Pack activities are news. Newspaper editors and news directors of radio and television stations are interested in stories about unusual pack activities. Most newspapers don't have the resources to cover every event in every community, but they do appreciate getting factual information about unusual or interesting events. Neighborhood and small-town newspapers are more likely to print a story of this type than large city newspapers. A news release, typewritten in the proper form, stands a better chance of being used than if you merely call the paper or turn in some penciled notes.

Community access cable TV offers another place to get your pack's story before the public. Some cable TV stations will also schedule dens or packs to produce their own TV show.

WRITING THE RELEASE

Your pack event must compete with all the other activities that are going on in the community at the time. If you have something unique, it's more likely that your news release will be used.

Consider writing releases on such things as an unusual pack activity, a special service project, a special anniversary, visits by well-known individuals, or unusual outdoor activities. But many newspapers will also use stories about recruiting drives and monthly pack meetings with lists of boys who received awards.

First check with the editor or broadcast news director to see if they have a special format which should be followed. If not, the sample shown here should be adequate. Follow these guidelines in writing the release:

- Timing is essential. Be sure to deliver the news release well before the deadline. If the story is about an event already held, it's no longer news after a day or two.

- The first paragraph of a news release should catch the reader's attention. It should tell who, what, when, and where. Succeeding paragraphs should give further details. The least important information should be at the end of the story, so it may be cut if necessary for space.

- Terminology. Use correct titles (with capital letters as indicated): Cub Scout, Webelos Scout, den chief, Cubmaster, assistant Cubmaster, den leader, Webelos den leader, pack, den. The word "Scouting" is always capitalized.

- When mentioning the pack for the first time in the story, identify it as Cub Scout pack with your number, followed by the name of your chartered organization. In other paragraphs, refer to "pack," or "Pack 10."

- Always use the full names of any individuals the first time they are mentioned in the news release. When only one or two Cub Scouts are mentioned (as for important awards), add his parent's or guardian's name. It is usually best not to add addresses, but if more than one town is involved, the names of towns may be used. Adult names should include Scouting titles.

Photographs. Check with the editor to find out if photographs can be used, and if so, what size and type are needed. If you furnish photos, try to get "action" shots. They are more interesting than "mug" shots or handshaking photos. Identify the people in the photo (left to right), giving their full names.

Scout Shows

Your pack will want to be part of your council's (or district's) Scout Show, Scoutorama, or Exposition. It will help pack families understand that they are part of the whole Scout family, which includes Tiger Cubs, Boy Scouting, Varsity Scouting, and Exploring.

Your Cub Scouts will have a wonderful time participating. The Scout Show shows the public how the Scouting program serves youth and the community.

In some local councils, Scout shows are held each year; in others, every other year. Your pack will be informed in plenty of time and will probably be asked to provide a demonstration or exhibit. Probably you will be assigned a booth or asked to make one.

The council will provide guidelines and suggestions. Here are some tips as you prepare for the Scout show.

- Boys should be well-trained and thoroughly familiar with the booth subject.

- They should be able to explain what they are doing, how, and why. Courtesy and good behavior are important.

- The boys should be in proper uniform (except where the booth subject calls for costumes of some type).

- One of the boys can act as a barker to attract attention to your booth and help tell the story.

- Colorful, eye-catching backgrounds and decorations will draw people to your booth.

- Boy-made displays on the booth subject add to its appeal and are sometimes an important factor in judging.

- Give-aways attract interest and attention. Inexpensive prizes can be given for participating in booth activities or games. The boys might make craft items to give away.

- Nothing should be sold. The pack will earn profits from ticket sales.

- Action in the booth is important. If the boys are making a craft item, it should be simple and quickly made while the spectator looks on. Some subjects might involve the spectators in games and other activities.

- Each den is usually assigned a time to be in the booth. Be sure to let them know when, and what they are supposed to do.

- The den chief can help the Cub Scouts in the booth while the den leader or other adults are nearby.

TYPES OF BOOTH ACTIVITIES

The type of activity will depend on the theme of the Scout Show, the criteria for judging, and the resources you have. A continuous demonstration, manned by the boys and with plenty of action, is better than a static display.

Some examples for booth demonstrations and activities are:

Pinewood derby	Beanbag toss
Puppet show	Turtle race
Space derby	Woodworking
Kites	Bird feeders
Bicycle safety	Indian craft
Skits	Neckerchief slides
Costumes	Model building
Paper airplanes	Block printing
Obstacle course	Masks
Physical fitness	Leatherwork
Cub Scout Sports	Tossing games
Musical instruments	Wolf, Bear, and Webelos advancement projects
Soap carving	

DECORATING THE BOOTH

Crepe paper is one of the best materials for booth decoration. It comes in many colors and can be stretched, twisted, fringed, crushed, scalloped, fluted, or ruffled.

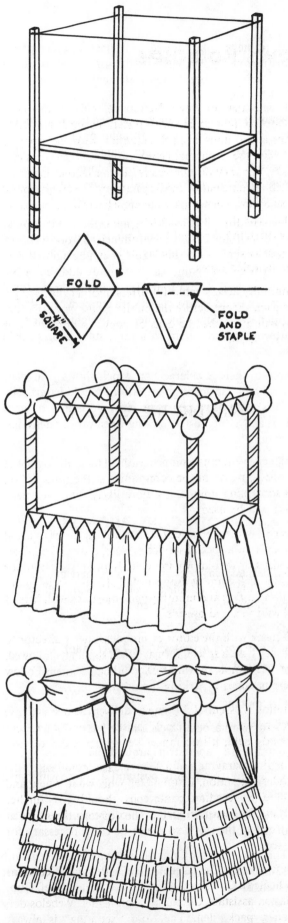

CONSTRUCTING AND DECORATING THE BOOTH

Booth frames can be covered with sheets of crepe paper. Colorful crepe paper twists, ruffles, or streamers can be used to trim the booth. Only flameproof crepe paper should be used.

Brown wrapping paper can also be used to cover a booth frame. It can be decorated with paint or crayons before it is tacked or stapled to a wood frame. Burlap or other inexpensive fabric is another type of covering for booth frames. Lightweight posters and displays can be pinned to the fabric.

If sheet cardboard is available, it can be used to make sturdy booth sides. It is easily fastened to wooden booth frames with tacks or a staple gun. It can be painted with left-over latex wall paint which not only adds color but strength as well. Use a roller for painting large pieces. Details can be added over latex with tempera or wide-line felt-tip markers. Signs and other lightweight displays can be attached to cardboard with tape, staples, or straight pins.

Be sure to include a large sign which shows your pack numeral and chartered organization in bold letters. You may wish to post a chart showing the names of pack leaders, and a duty roster showing when various dens man the booth.

BOOTH CONSTRUCTION

The quick and easy designs described here can be used for a pack circus or fair as well as a Scout show. The following materials are needed:

Table
Four stout posts or poles (6 to 7 feet long)
Wire or cord
Crepe paper
Stapler or tape

1. Tie or wire a pole to each table leg.

2. Wind crepe paper strips around the poles.

3. Tie a cord from post to post and decorate with paper flags or drapes.

4. Balloons add color and can be tied together at the top of the poles.

5. The lower part of the booth can be covered with 12-inch wide crepe-paper fringes or gathered fabric (such as an old sheet).

Pack Equipment

The equipment shown here will help to tell Cub Scouting's story to your pack's families. This equipment will be used time and again to display photos and other materials, recognize den families for their participation, and symbolize our program's ideals in ceremonies.

Portable Exhibit Panels

Pegboard, hook board, and hanger board are some of names manufacturers use to describe these 2-by-4-foot sections or panels. Two of these panels laced together with shoelaces can stand upright by opening the panels to a 60 degree angle. With it you can call attention to timely articles in books and magazines by displaying the publication opened to the pages you wish to emphasize.

EXHIBIT PANEL

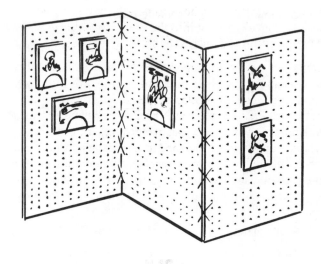

Bookholders for the exhibit panel can be made from coat hanger wire. Using pliers, cut a coat hanger in two. Straighten each piece, then bend into a U-shape. Turn upside down, put a sharp angle into each arm, then bend the arms back to parallel the sides of the U. Bend back and up to form the pegboard anchor for each arm. (See illustration.)

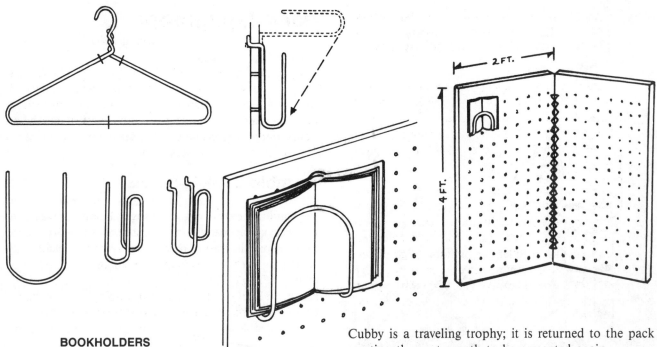

BOOKHOLDERS

Another way to hold material in place on the exhibit panel is with stretched rubber bands held in place on the panels by two coat-hanger rods. Put three large rubber bands around a rod. Use a small hook made from a paper clip to pull each rubber band through a panel hole. Stretch the band down to the series of holes opposite the bottom rod. Use the paper-clip hook to pull the band through the hole, then slide the rod into the band to keep it in place. Magazines can be displayed by slipping the issues in place.

Dens may use the portable exhibit panel idea on a smaller scale. Cut the panels in half and join two or more sections together with shoelaces. (See illustration.) A three-panel section is more versatile because it can be arranged in a number of ways—zigzag, wings forward, wings back, upright, and triangle. Fastened in the triangle form, it can be placed on its side for an easel, lectern, or support for a flip chart. In the wing-forward position, the panels provide background for a den's exhibit, display, or advancement chart.

CUBBY

Cubby is a pack trophy, designed like the Tin Man in the "Wizard of Oz." It can be awarded to the den with the largest percentage of parents at pack meetings. Some packs also award Cubby for "best uniformed den" or "best behaved den." The category is determined by the pack committee and may be kept secret until the pack meeting.

Cubby is a traveling trophy; it is returned to the pack meeting the next month to be presented again.

Cubby is approximately 27 inches in height. His size depends on the tin cans used. See "Crafts" section of this book for suggestions for working with tin. The following materials are suggested:

$5\frac{9}{16}$-inch funnel (hat)
$4\,\frac{11}{16}$-inch tall can (head)
$2\frac{3}{8}$-inch tall can (neck)
Two $2\frac{1}{8}$-inch pieces cut from can (ears)
12-inch tall can (body)
Four $3\frac{3}{4}$-inch tall cans (upper and lower arms)
Two $2\frac{7}{8}$-inch tall cans (hands)
Two $4\frac{15}{16}$-inch tall cans (thighs)
Two $3\frac{3}{4}$-inch tall cans (lower legs)
Two $3\frac{3}{4}$-inch tall cans (feet)
Fabric for neckerchief

To assemble Cubby:

1. Cut hole in bottom of head for neck can. Cut hole in top of body can for neck. Flange both ends of neck can. Insert neck in head and body—solder in place.

2. Assemble the leg parts. Flange top ends of thigh cans. Solder closed ends of thigh and lower leg cans together. Trim to fit foot cans. Remove both ends from foot cans and flatten to about 2 inches. Solder to lower leg.

3. Cut holes in bottom of body can close to outer rim to hold thighs. Insert thigh flanges in body and solder in place.

4. Cut ears from can tops so the ridges form the edges of the ears. Cut flanges and spread them to fit the head. Solder in place.

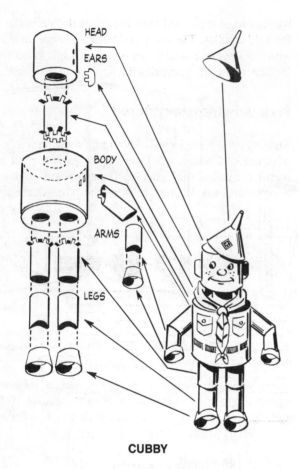

CUBBY

5. To make the arms, remove rims from cans. Cut upper arm cans to fit body, flatten slightly, and solder to body. Remove both ends from lower arm cans. Cut off lower rim, flatten slightly, and solder to hand. Then push lower arms over upper arms and solder.

6. Tilt funnel and solder to head.

7. Sand rough spots and sharp edges.

8. Paint Cubby to resemble a Cub Scout.

9. Add a neckerchief made of fabric.

ELECTRIC COUNCIL FIRE

Cub Scout ceremonies are more dramatic when centered around an illuminated council fire in a darkened room. This electric council fire can also be used in den skits. The effect is so realistic you can almost smell the smoke.

Materials needed:

Birch logs

8-inch diameter cardboard carton (such as a 3-gallon ice cream carton)

Lamp base, extension cord, and plug

Screws

Two ½-inch and 3-inch finishing nails

2-by-16-inch shingle pieces

Aluminum foil

Wood base

Log lengths and diameters are not critical, but the pile should taper in thickness and length. The smaller logs may be dismantled for easy storage.

To assemble:

1. The four bottom layers of logs are screwed together and fastened to a wood base. The three top layers are nailed together with finishing nails. These two sections can be separated for easy access to the inside.

2. The shingles used for the tinder effect are not fastened in place permanently, but placed tepee style around the container.

3. Assemble and wire the lamp base. Insert it in the cardboard container, which has been covered with aluminum foil. Build the log sections as described above.

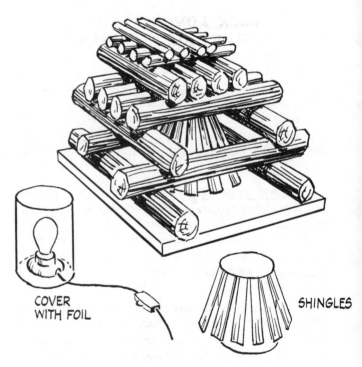

ELECTRIC COUNCIL FIRE

4. Use a 60- or 100-watt red or orange bulb for illumination. (A white bulb can be painted red or orange.) The light will filter through the slots in the shingles. Add a few short lengths of ¼-inch wide red and white crinkled ribbon to top of pile to create a flame-leaping effect. An alternative is to use a set of seven colored Christmas-tree lights. Blinking bulbs would make the fire more animated.

TOP SECTION

NAIL TOGETHER

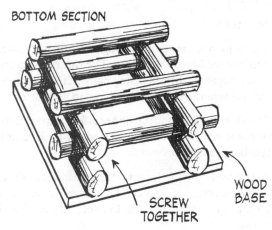

BOTTOM SECTION

SCREW TOGETHER

WOOD BASE

PACK ADVANCEMENT BOARDS AND LADDERS

Pack advancement boards and ladders can be used to stimulate advancement and help make advancement ceremonies more colorful and interesting. The examples shown here can become a permanent part of the pack's equipment. See *Staging Den and Pack Ceremonies* for more ideas.

Den doodles are also a good way to stimulate advancement in the den. See "Crafts" section of this book for examples.

Ceremony Ladder

A pack ceremony ladder like the one shown here can be used over and over. The ladder folds for easy storage. This ladder is made from pine and finished with varnish or shellac. Badge shapes are cut from wood and fastened to rungs. The badge designs can be wood-burned or large Cub Scout insignia stickers can be used. Candleholders are fastened to each rung and candles lighted as that particular badge is presented in the ceremony.

Two-Way Ceremony Board

This board is easy to make and can be used in many ceremonies. The board is a 1-by-2-inch frame covered with hardboard. It is painted blue. Holes are drilled in the top for gold candles. The front and back sides are identical, with storage space inside. The Arrow of Light is cut from ¼-inch plywood, painted gold, and glued to board.

Pack Advancement Board

The boys will look forward to adding their names to an advancement board. As Cub Scouts earn a rank and receive the badge, they hang small name boards under the appropriate rank as a part of the advancement ceremony.

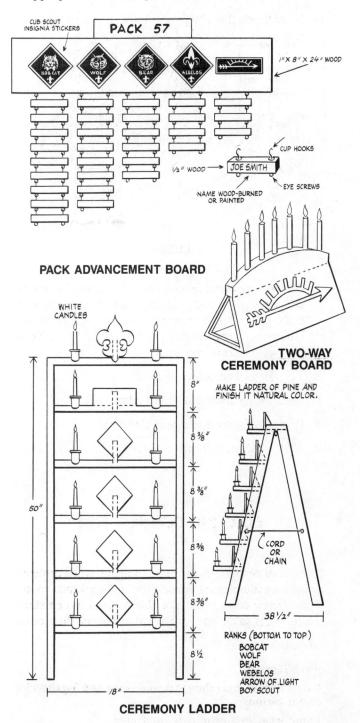

PACK ADVANCEMENT BOARD

TWO-WAY CEREMONY BOARD

MAKE LADDER OF PINE AND FINISH IT NATURAL COLOR.

RANKS (BOTTOM TO TOP)
BOBCAT
WOLF
BEAR
WEBELOS
ARROW OF LIGHT
BOY SCOUT

CEREMONY LADDER

Pack History

If your pack does not have a pack history, it isn't too late to start now. You will probably need to do some searching to find the information you need. Clues may be found in your chartered organization's records, council office records, copies of old district or council newsletters, old charter papers, local newspaper files, and libraries. Talk to senior citizens and former members of the pack to get additional information.

These are some things you will want to find out:

• When was pack originally chartered?

• Who was the chartered organization?

• Who were the first leaders registered?

• Who were the first Cub Scouts registered?

• Has the pack been continuously chartered since that time?

List in chronological order all chartered organizations, leaders, former Cub Scouts, activities and events, with pictures if available.

Keep a list of former Cub Scouts living in your area, whether they were members of your pack or not. You might try newspaper want ads to locate former Cub Scouts.

Ask pack families and neighborhood friends to look for books, uniforms, pictures, and articles from earlier days when they are cleaning out the attic.

Develop a pack scrapbook including information on past special activities, traditions, special recognitions. Include photos, sketches, ribbons, certificates, etc. It makes an excellent display for a blue and gold banquet.

Once the history is developed, make sure it is passed down as the pack leadership changes. This could be done as part of a leader induction ceremony.

12 Resources

BOY SCOUTS OF AMERICA PUBLICATIONS

Big Bear Cub Scout Book, No. 3228

Boy Scout Songbook, No. 3224

Camping Skill Award, No. 6580

Citizenship Through Service, No. 3707

Cooking Skill Award, No. 6585

Cub Scout Fun Book, No. 3215

Cub Scout Leader Book, No. 3220

Cub Scout Magic, No. 3219

Cub Scout Songbook, No. 3222

Cub Scout and Webelos Scout Program Helps, No. 7359—(year)

Cub Scout Sports

Leader Guide, No. 2152

Archery, No. 2153

Baseball, No. 2156

Basketball, No. 2155

Bowling, No. 2154

Golf, No. 2157

Marbles, No. 2158

Physical Fitness, No. 2161

Skiing, No. 2159

Soccer, No. 2162

Softball, No. 2160

Swimming, No. 2163

Table Tennis, No. 2164

Tennis, No. 2166

Volleyball, No. 2165

Den Chief Handbook, No. 3211

Group Meeting Sparklers, No. 3122

Hiking Skill Award, No. 6589

Introduction to Cub Scout Camping, No. 13-545

Introduction to Family Camping, No. 3820

Knots and How to Tie Them, No. 3170

Official Boy Scout Handbook, No. 3227

Swimming Skill Award, No. 6591

Webelos Scout Book, No. 3232

Wolf Cub Scout Book, No. 3230

Your Flag, No. 3188

OTHER PUBLICATIONS AVAILABLE FROM BSA

Golden Nature Guide—Insects, by Clarence Cottam and Herbert Zim, No. 3544

Golden Nature Guide—Rocks & Minerals, by Paul Shaffer and Herbert Zim, No. 3545

Golden Nature Guide—Sky Observers Guide, by R. Newton Mayall, No. 3525

Golden Nature Guide—Stars, by Herbert Zim and Robert H. Baker, No. 3527

Golden Nature Guide—Trees, by Alexander Martin and Herbert Zim, No. 3541

Golden Nature Guide—Weather, by Herbert Zim, No. 3528

Gospel of the Redman, by Earnest Thompson Seton and Julia M. Seton, No. 3547A

OBIS for Cub Scouts, Delta Education, No. 3575

Sharing Nature with Children, by Joseph B. Cornell, No. 3530

Trail and Campfire Stories, by Julia M. Seton, No. 3529

OTHER BOOKS

American Sports Heroes of Today, by Frederic Katz, Random House, 1970

Backyard Roughing It Easy, by Diane Thomas, Fawcett 1980

Be a Magician, by Jay Boyar, Julian Messner, 1981

Bet You Can!, by Vicki Cable and Kathy Darling, Avon 1983

Bet You Can't!, by Vicki Cable and Kathy Darling, Lothrop 1980

Carpentry for Children, by Lester Walker, Overlook Press, 1982

Collecting for the City Naturalist, by Lois Hussey and Catherine Pressino, Harper and Row, 1975

Easy Puppets, by Gertrude J. Pels, Harper and Row, 1951

Easy to Make Contraptions, by Roland Berry, Harvey, 1978

Experiments with Everyday Objects, by Kevin Goldstein-Jackson, Prentice-Hall, 1978

A Field Guide to the Birds East of the Rockies, by Roger Tory Peterson, Houghton Mifflin, 1980

A Field Guide to the Birds of Texas and Adjacent States, by Roger Tory Peterson, Houghton Mifflin, 1979

A Field Guide to the Western Birds, by Roger Tory Peterson, Houghton Mifflin, 1972

Fishing Basics, by John Randolph, Prentice-Hall, 1981

Football Basics, by Larry Fox, Prentice-Hall, 1981

Fun with Skits, Stunts and Stories, by Larry and Helen Eisenberg, Baker Books, 1975

Golden Nature Guide—Birds, by Ira Gabrielson and Herbert Zim, Western Publishing Co., 1956

Grandfather Tales, by Richard Chase, Houghton Mifflin, 1948

Growing Up Green, by Alice Skelsey and Gloria Huckaby, Workman Publishing Co., 1973

Handbook for Storytellers, by C. F. Bauer, American Library Assoc., 1977

How to Know the Birds, by Roger Tory Peterson, New American Library, 1982

Indian Crafts and Lore, by Ben Hunt, Western Publishing Co., 1976

Just So Stories, by Rudyard Kipling, Doubleday, 1956

Kids' Outdoor Gardening, by Aileen Paul, Doubleday, 1978

The Kids' Garden Book, by Patricia Petrich and Rosemary Dalton, Nitty Gritty, 1974

Making Puppets Come Alive, by Larry Engler, Taplinger Publishing Co., 1980

Modern Olympic Superstars, by George Sullivan, Dodd, Mead, 1979

More New Games, Andrew Fluegelman, ed., Doubleday, 1981

The New Games Book, Andrew Fluegelman, ed., Doubleday, 1976

Outdoor Games, by David Buskin, Lion Books, 1966

Paper Bag Puppets, by Deatna M. Williams, Pitman Learning, 1966

Perplexing Puzzles and Tantalizing Teasers, by Martin Gardner, Archway Paperbacks, 1971

Physical Fitness for Young Champions, by Robert J. Antonacci, McGraw-Hill, 1975

Puddles and Wings and Grapevine Swings, by Imogene Forte and Margorie Frank, Incentive Publications, 1982

Puppets for Beginners, by Moritz Jagendorf, Plays, Inc., 1952

Puppets for Dreaming and Scheming, by Judy Sims, Early Stages Press, 1978

Recipes for Science Fun, by Susan S. Moad, Watts, Franklin, 1979

Science in a Vacant Lot, by Seymour Simon, Viking Press, 1970

Snips and Snails and Walnut Whales, by Phyllis Fiarotta, Workman Publishing, 1975

Story Telling: What to Tell and How to Tell It, by Edna Lyman, Gale Research Co., 1971

Super Colossal Book of Puzzles, Tricks and Games, by Sheila A. Barry, Sterling Publishing, 1981

Swimming Basics, by C. Robert Orr and James B. Tyler, Prentice-Hall, 1980

Swimming and Diving, by Tony Duffy, Silver Burdett, n.d.

The Tree Identification Book, by George Symonds, William Morrow, 1973

What Does a Geologist Do?, by R. V. Fodor, Dodd, Mead, 1977

Wonders of the Forest, by Francene Sabin, Troll Association, 1981

OUT OF PRINT BOOKS

These books are no longer being printed but may be found in a local library, school library, or church library. Used book stores and garage sales also may yield "oldies but goodies."

Act It Out, by Bernice Carlson

Beginner's Puppet Book, by Alice M. Hobon

Campfire Adventure Stories, by Alan MacFarlan

Campfire Programs, by Jack Pearse

Campfire Tonight!, by Richard J. Hurley

Cokesbury Stunt Book, by A. M. Depew

Collecting Small Fossils, by Lois Hussey and Catherine Pressino

Complete Book of Campfire Programs, by LaRue D. Thurston

Creating With Puppets, by Lothar Kampmann

Creative Dramatics, by Winifred Ward

The Everything Book, by Eleanor Vance

Exploring as You Walk in the City, by Phyllis Busch

Exploring as You Walk in the Meadow, by Phyllis Busch

The Forest Rangers, by Montgomery M. Atwater

Foxtails, Ferns and Fish Scales, by Ada Graham

From Petals to Pinecones, by Katherine N. Cutler

The Fun Encyclopedia, by E. O. Harbin

Fun in the Backyard, by Arthur Lawson

Fun Time Puppets, by Carrie Rassmussen

Fun With Brand New Games, by A. MacFarlan

Fun With Puppets, by Sylvia Cassell

Golden Book of Camping and Campcrafts, by Lynn Gordon

Golden Book of Crafts and Hobbies, by Ben Hunt

Golden Book of Nature Crafts, by John R. Saunders

Growing Strong, by R. V. Fodor

Great Fables of All Nations, by Manuel Komroff

Handbook of Skits and Stunts, by Larry and Helen Eisenberg

Home Made Games, by Arthur Lawson

The Incredible Year-Round Play Book, by Elin McCoy

Indian Why Stories, by Frank B. Linderman

Insect Friends, by Edwin W. Teale

The Insect Guide, by Ralph Swain

Instant Fun for All Kinds of Groups, by Lorell Burns

Invite a Bird to Dinner, by Beverly C. Crook

Nature Activities and Hobbies, by William Hillcourt

Phunology, by E. O. Harbin

Puppet Plays for Children, by Antonia Ridge

The Right Play for You, by Bernice Carlson

Simple Puppetry, by Sheila Jackson

Stories and Storytelling, by Angela Keyes

The Story of Rocks and Minerals, by David Seaman

Stunt Night Tonight, by Catherine Miller

Tales for Telling, by Katherine Watson

Why Glass Breaks, Rubber Bends, and Glue Sticks, by Malcolm Weiss

The Wonderful World of Engineering, by David Jackson

Woodland Tales, by Ernest Thompson Seton

The Young Rockhound's Handbook, by W. R. C. Shedenhelm

Your Own Book of Campcraft, by Catherine Hammett

101 Costumes for All Ages, by Richard Cummings

101 Hand Puppets, by Richard Cummings

101 Masks, False Faces and Make-Up for All Ages, by Richard M. Gardner

MAGAZINES

Boys' Life

Scouting